Pu
Housing
Law

AUSTRALIA AND NEW ZEALAND
The Law Book Company Ltd.
Sydney : Melbourne : Perth

CANADA AND U.S.A.
The Carswell Company Ltd.
Agincourt, Ontario

INDIA
N. M. Tripathi Private Ltd.
Bombay
and
Eastern Law House Private Ltd.
Calcutta and Delhi
M.P.P. House
Bangalore

ISRAEL
Steimatzky's Agency Ltd.
Jerusalem : Tel Aviv : Haifa

PAKISTAN
Pakistan Law House
Karachi

Public Housing Law

By

DAVID C. HOATH LL.B.

Solicitor
Reader in Law,
University of Sheffield

London
Sweet & Maxwell
1989

Published in 1989 by
Sweet & Maxwell Limited
183 Marsh Wall, London E14
Computerset by Promenade Graphics Limited, Cheltenham
Printed in Scotland

British Library Cataloguing in Publication Data

Hoath, David C. (David Charles), *1944–*
Public housing law.
1. England. Public housing. Law
I. Title
344.204'636358

ISBN 0–421–38710–6

Preface

This book attempts to cover the law and practice relating to public sector housing, as interpreted in a somewhat wide sense; it thus includes detailed consideration not merely of the allocation, management and disposal of council housing, but also of the responsibilities of local authorities towards the homeless (even though, as will be seen, where a housing duty is owed to a homeless person, the duty does not necessarily have to be discharged by the allocation of *council* housing as such).

The publishers' Modern Legal Studies series already includes my books on *Council Housing* (2nd ed., 1982), and *Homelessness* (1983). However, due to the complexity of the recent legislation concerning public sector housing and the extent of the recent case law (particularly as regards homelessness), a more detailed and less discursive approach now appears to be justified than that attempted in those earlier works.

I hope that this book will prove useful to students on a variety of courses concerning law, social work or housing. The book is also designed for a variety of practitioners (in particular lawyers, local authority housing officers and social workers, and advisers in Citizens' Advice Bureaux and cognate agencies).

I have not attempted to deal in detail with the financial regime governing council housing. Nor have I sought to cover the law relating to housing associations (which in some respects may still be regarded as part of the "public" sector); such coverage would have led to a considerable increase in the length of the book, and in any event the complexities of housing associations are now such as to deserve separate treatment (see, for example, J. Alder and C. Handy, *Housing Association Law* (1987)).

Housing law has never been an area for the narrow specialist; it embraces aspects of many other more "traditional" subjects, such as public law, local government law, family law, conveyancing and land law, welfare law, and, of course, landlord and tenant law. I have therefore been very fortunate in the help which I received from my colleagues at the University of Sheffield, particularly Professor Graham Battersby, Vaughan Bevan, Mary Hayes, John Mesher, and Cathy Williams. However, the customary statement that "the author alone takes responsibility for the remaining errors" needs even greater emphasis than normal on this occasion, in view of the need to incorporate at a very late stage of preparation of the manuscript the relevant provisions of the Housing Act 1988 (a good example of blockbusting modern legislation at its least user-friendly).

The staff at Sweet and Maxwell were, as always, most supportive throughout the production process. I would also like to record particular debts of gratitude to Jean Hopewell, who cheerfully produced an immaculate typescript notwithstanding the volatility of the subject-matter, and to my wife and children, who accepted with good humour my almost monastic seclusion during the final stages of the preparation of the manuscript.

The law is in general stated as at December 31, 1988, although some later changes have been incorporated.

The University of Sheffield David Hoath

Contents

Table of Cases

[All references are to paragraph numbers]

Table of Statutes

[All references are to paragraph numbers]

Table of Bills

Table of Statutory Instruments

[All references are to paragraph numbers]

Abbreviations

A.A.	Adoption Act
A.D.C.	Association of District Councils
A.M.A.	Association of Metropolitan Authorities
C.C.A.	County Courts Act
C.C.R.	County Court Rules
C.H.A.C.	Central Housing Advisory Committee
C.H.A.R.	Campaign for the Homeless and Rootless
C.I.P.F.A.	Chartered Institute of Public Finance and Accountancy
Cm., Cmnd.	Command Paper
C.R.E.	Commission for Racial Equality
D.H.S.S.	Department of Health and Social Security
D.O.E.	Department of the Environment
D.P.M.C.A.	Domestic Proceedings and Magistrates' Courts Act
D.S.S.	Department of Social Security
D.V.M.P.A.	Domestic Violence and Matrimonial Proceedings Act
F.A.	Finance Act
H.A.	Housing Act
H.A.A.	Housing Associations Act
H.C. Deb	House of Commons Debate
H.C.P.	House of Commons Paper
H.D.D.	Housing Development Directorate
H.E.O.	Housing Emergency Office
H.F.A.	Housing Finance Act
H.L. Deb.	House of Lords Debate
H.S.A.G.	Housing Services Advisory Group
J.S.W.L.	Journal of Social Welfare Law
L.A.M.S.A.C.	Local Authority Management Services and Computer Committee
Law Comm.	Law Commission
L.C.A.	Land Compensation Act
L.G.A.	Local Government Act
L.G.F.A.	Local Government Finance Act

L.G. & H.B.	Local Government and Housing Bill
L.P.A.	Law of Property Act
L.R.A.	Land Registration Act
L. & T.A.	Landlord and Tenant Act
M.C.A.	Matrimonial Causes Act
M.H.A.	Matrimonial Homes Act
M.H.L.G.	Ministry of Housing and Local Government
M.O.H.	Ministry of Health
N.A.A.	National Assistance Act
O.L.A.	Occupier's Liability Act
P.f.E.A.	Protection from Eviction Act
P.H.A.	Public Health Act
R.A.	Rent Act
R.I.C.S.	Royal Institute of Chartered Surveyors
R.S.C.	Rules of the Supreme Court
S.C.A.	Supreme Court Act
S.C.O.L.A.G.	Journal of the Scottish Legal Action Group
S.H.A.C.	Shelter Housing Aid Centre
S.I.	Statutory Instrument

1 Introduction

1. *The Current Housing Scene*

It is impossible to attempt to understand the current state of the law relating to public sector housing without some awareness of the broader housing scene within which it operates. Few people can feel complacent about the housing difficulties currently facing this country. Homelessness applications are escalating,[1] and hard-pressed councils have increasingly been forced to accommodate the homeless in unsatisfactory (but very expensive) bed-and-breakfast type accommodation[2]; council house waiting lists are growing[3]; council tenants are becoming relatively poorer[4]; council housebuilding rates have dramatically declined[5]; there are serious disrepair problems affecting all the housing sectors[6]; and the private rented **1.01**

[1] The number of *applications* to English councils for help under the homelessness legislation reached a record figure of 250,000 in 1986, and the number of homeless households actually *accepted* for rehousing in that year was 103,000 (whereas in 1978 the number of acceptances had only been 53,100): H.C. Debs., February 4, 1987, col. 985; May 6, 1987, col. 721.

[2] See, *e.g.* P. Q. Watchman, [1988] J.S.W.L. 147–150; J. Conway (ed.), *Prescription for Poor Health: the Crisis for Homeless Families* (1988); H.C. Deb., January 21, 1988, col. 826; C.I.P.F.A., *Homelessness Statistics* (1988).

[3] In 1987 a record number of around 1,350,000 households were registered on housing waiting lists in England, and the average waiting time was then nine years: *Shelter Campaign News*, Issue 3, Autumn 1987.

[4] More than 50 per cent. of households headed by council tenants now fall within the poorest third of all households, compared with just over 30 per cent. in 1968: P. Willmott and A. Murie, *Polarisation and social housing* (Policy Studies Institute, 1988).

[5] Council housebuilding in Great Britain fell from an average of 109,000 dwellings a year between 1974 and 1979 to an average of 26,000 a year between 1983 and 1987: H.L. Deb., July 20, 1988, col. 1303.

[6] According to the R.I.C.S., in 1988 there were more homes in serious disrepair than in 1981, one home in 10 required more than £2,500 spending on it for essential repairs, and one in 20 needed more than £4,000 spending on it for such repairs: see C. McGhie, *The Sunday Times*, January 15, 1989.

sector currently caters for only a very small section of the population,[7] thus placing increasing pressure on the public rented sector.

1.02 Despite the ravages of the "right to buy" and reductions in public sector housebuilding, councils still retain large amounts of rented housing.[8] Indeed, it appears that this country has a greater proportion of its housing stock rented from public authorities than any comparable nation.[9] However, the role of councils in the housing field, as perceived by central government, is currently undergoing a sea-change. The government believes that some councils have proved to be "appallingly bad landlords,"[10] and it has therefore sought severely to restrict the housing role of councils generally. The Housing Act 1980 introduced the "right to buy," giving secure council tenants the right to acquire the freeholds or long leases of their dwellings, often with a substantial discount off the purchase price.[11] The Housing Act 1988, as will be seen, has carried the process of privatisation of council housing much further: it provides for the compulsory disposal into the private sector of entire council estates via the "change of landlord" and "Housing Action Trust" schemes.[12]

1.03 Underlying these new reforms are a belief in the benefits of the "market economy", and an anxiety to attack the "dependency culture" which council housing has been thought to engender. Instead of being the primary providers of rented housing, the role of many councils is now seen to be shifting to that of entrepreneurs: a 1987 consultation paper stated clearly that the government envisaged a "change in emphasis . . . for the housing role of local authorities, from acting as landlords towards acting as enablers and facilitators of housing provision by others."[13] Indeed, it is envisaged that some councils will dispose of their entire housing stock.[14]

[7] See below, para. 1.10.
[8] *Ibid.*
[9] See, *e.g.* J. S. Fuerst (ed.), *Public Housing in Europe and America* (1974); *Housing Policy* (1977), Cmnd. 6851, Technical Vol., Pt. III, Chap. 11.
[10] H.L. Deb., July 30, 1986, col. 851 (Lord Elton).
[11] The details of the "right to buy" are discussed in Chap. 14.
[12] For the details of these privatisation schemes, see Chap. 15.
[13] D.O.E., *Housing Action Trusts: A Consultation Document*, para. 24; see also *Housing: The Government's Proposals* (1987), Cm. 214, para. 5.1; in March 1987 the Housing Minister, when addressing the Conservative Local Government Conference, had urged councils to think of themselves as "catalysts for diverse forms of 'social housing,' " built and managed by private bodies: *The Times*, March 7, 1987.
[14] D.O.E., *Large Scale Voluntary Transfers of Local Authority Housing to Private Bodies* (1988), para. 1.

The legislative means for changing the housing role of councils are to be found not only in the Housing Acts of 1985 and 1988, but also in such "peripheral" legislation as the Local Government Act 1988, which contains wide powers[15] for housing authorities to give (normally with the consent of the Minister) financial assistance to private landlords and housing associations for the provision of rented housing. **1.04**

The practical effects of this intended change of emphasis in the functions of housing authorities (allied to the partial deregulation of the private rented sector achieved by Part I of the Housing Act 1988) remain to be seen. As regards the public rented sector, if a council does dispose of all its housing, it will nevertheless retain statutory responsibilities towards the homeless,[16] who may well find themselves increasingly consigned to poor quality private accommodation; and many council tenants who have hitherto resisted the blandishments of the "right to buy" may feel compelled to exercise that right if they consider that there is a real danger that the council may choose (or be forced) to sell the freeholds to a "predatory" private landlord. However, some council tenants have already detected a welcome change of attitude on the part of their landlords (concerning, for example, responses to requests for repairs); this change has been directly attributed to a desire by such councils to appear "good" landlords, so that the tenants as a body will resist any privatisation moves[17]! **1.05**

The separate private rented sector decontrol provisions in Part I of the Housing Act 1988 may not prove very effective in wooing back private landlords on a long-term basis; paradoxically, this may partly be because of the public sector privatisation provisions in Parts III and IV of the 1988 Act: potential private landlords may fear that a future Labour government could take a leaf out of the present government's book and indiscriminately force *private* landlords to sell their properties, either to the short-term sitting tenants or to "social" landlords. **1.06**

Further important changes are being planned in relation to the financial regime affecting council housing,[18] which will have the **1.07**

[15] L.G.A. 1988, ss.24–26.

[16] In the case of Housing Action Trusts, the government considered that "[to] place a duty on a HAT with regard to homeless people would distract it from its regeneration function": *Housing Action Trusts: A Consultation Document, op. cit.* para. 26.

[17] See *Shelter Campaign News*, Winter 1988.

[18] D.O.E., *Local Government in England and Wales: Capital Expenditure and Finance: A Consultation Paper* (1988); D.O.E., *New Financial Regime for Local Authority Housing in England and Wales: A Consultation Paper* (1988); see now the Local Government and Housing Bill 1989, the relevant provisions of which are discussed in outline in Chap. 10.

effect of forcing up council rents in many areas; and rumours abound that new legislation may relax the homelessness duties of councils.[19] Moreover, the "simple" solution of turning all remaining council tenants into owner-occupiers, and transforming their rent payments into mortgage payments, is being periodically resurrected.[20]

2. *The Growth of Council Housing*[21]

1.08 Bearing in mind the current housing scene described in outline above, it may be useful to sketch in a little of the history of the system of council housing in this country, which has no precise equivalent in other developed countries.

1.09 Council housing began in earnest immediately after the First World War, primarily because the introduction of rent control in 1915 had meant that private enterprise could no longer be relied on to provide working-class housing. Although council housing did not grow at a uniform rate over the next 60 years, it eventually far outstripped the private rented sector. Section 1 of the Housing Act 1949 significantly removed the previous limitation whereby councils could only provide housing "for the working classes," so that henceforth account could be taken of "the housing conditions and housing needs of all members of the community"; and it is important to recall that under post-Second World War Conservative governments both Winston Churchill and Harold Macmillan showed great enthusiasm for the expansion of council housing.

1.10 By 1977, the D.O.E. was able to record[22] that although in 1975 the total number of rented dwellings in England and Wales was similar to that of 30 years previously, the balance between the two rented sectors had completely changed: in 1945 there had been about 8.5 million rented dwellings, of which 7.1 million were privately owned and 1.3 million were council owned, while by 1975 there were 8.1 million rented dwellings, of which 2.9 million were privately owned and 5.2 million were council owned. By 1988,

[19] See, *e.g.* J. Stearn, [1989] January Legal Action 10.

[20] Notably by Mr. Peter Walker M.P.: see, *e.g. The Sunday Times*, May 29, 1988; *The Times*, January 25, 1989.

[21] For more detailed accounts of the development of council housing, see, *e.g.* A. Murie, P. Niner and C. Watson, *Housing Policy and the Housing System* (1976), pp. 92–101; *Whatever Happened to Council Housing?* (National Community Development Project, 1976), pp. 9–32; *Housing Policy, op. cit.*, Technical Vol., Pt. I, Chap. 1; S. Merrett, *State Housing in Britain* (1979), Chaps. 1–2.

[22] *The Review of the Rent Acts: A Consultation Paper*, p. 3.

although owner-occupation in Britain had increased to cover around 70 per cent. of the housing stock, 24 per cent. of homes were still rented from councils, while only six per cent. were rented from non-council landlords.[23]

3. *The Centralisation of Control Over Council Housing*

The relationship between a council and its tenants involves not merely that of landlord and tenant, but also the more nebulous connection between local authority and citizen. This connection between local authority and citizen also governs the relationship between a council and an applicant for housing (whether or not the applicant is homeless). Thus, as will be seen, matters such as the proper application by housing authorities of the "administrative law principles," and the role of the local government "ombudsmen," are of considerable importance in policing the obligations of housing authorities. **1.11**

However, there is another relationship affecting housing authorities which (although it has long been significant) has grown dramatically in importance over recent years: this is the relationship between the council and central government.[24] The local government—central government relationship operates at various levels: at the most benign level, councils are offered guidance by the D.O.E. in the shape of various departmental circulars, letters and reports; while at the most acute level, councils may be forced to take unpalatable decisions (concerning, for example, rent levels, housebuilding rates, and the maintenance of the existing stock), because of the great financial control exercised by central government[25]: thus the government can directly control such matters as the extent to which councils can borrow money, and the extent to which councils can use their own capital receipts (arising, for example, from council house sales) for particular housing purposes. Councils are now very **1.12**

[23] See, *e.g.* R. Oakley, *The Times*, October 11, 1988.

[24] See, *e.g.* M. Loughlin, *Local Government in the Modern State* (1986). One reason why the Housing (Homeless Persons) Act 1977 (currently the Housing Act 1985, Pt. III) was resented by many councils was because the government of the day refused to allow any additional money to housing authorities in order to fund their new responsibilities.

[25] See, *e.g.* Forbes J. in *R.* v. *Secretary of State for Health and Social Security, ex p. City of Sheffield* (1985) 18 H.L.R. 6, 12 (D.C.): " . . . we have a central government of one political persuasion determined to seek to curb local authority spending, and we have local authorities of an opposite political persuasion equally determined to resist that endeavour by central government."

much seen as participators (willing or unwilling) in the "market economy," but their freedom of action can be severely curtailed by a straitjacket imposed by central government.

1.13 It has been argued that the imposition of statutory duties on local authorities to house the homeless (originating in the Housing (Homeless Persons) Act 1977 but now contained in Part III of the Housing Act 1985), and the introduction of the statutory package of "secure" council tenants' rights (originating in the Housing Act 1980, but now contained in Parts IV and V of the Housing Act 1985), may both have had "as much to do with [the] struggles between central and local government as with concern for the creation of [individual] rights."[26] Viewed in this somewhat cynical way, the reason for the paucity of exemptions from the legal definition of the "secure tenancy" could be because the categories of tenants enabled to exercise the "right to buy" were thereby extended as widely as possible,[27] thus denuding councils of much of their better housing; this by-product of the "central-local" power struggle has since been carried further by the Housing Act 1988.

4. *Is Council Housing Doomed?*

1.14 In the light of the somewhat pessimistic remarks made above, it may perhaps be questioned whether this is the right time to be producing a book dealing with the details of public sector housing law. However, the law discussed in the following pages still affects around one in four of the population (including not only those who are housed, but also those who are homeless). Approximately eight out of ten dwellings originally owned by councils are still rented from them. It is by no means clear that the privatisation provisions in Parts III and IV of the Housing Act 1988 will actually achieve the dramatic effects which the government originally intended,[28] nor is it certain that the decontrol provisions in Part I of the 1988 Act will achieve

[26] M. Partington, *Landlord and Tenant* (2nd ed., 1980), p. 468.

[27] Shelter, *The Tenants' Charter* (1981), p. 7.

[28] The opposition of the sitting tenants may have been underestimated: see, *e.g.* D. Walker, *The Times*, January 17, 1989; it has been calculated that after the 1988 Act around 50,000 council dwellings might be taken over by co-operatives, 500,000 might pass to housing associations, and around 100,000 to Housing Action Trusts, thus still leaving 3.5 million council tenants (a higher figure than all the tenants of "social" housing in France, and twice as high as all the public sector tenants in the U.S.A.): A. Power, speaking at the 1988 Shelter Conference, as reported in *Roof*, July 1988, p. 6.

the planned shift in emphasis from the public rented sector to the private rented sector.[29]

It is significant that the then Housing Minister predicted in 1987 that "the vast bulk" of council housing would still be in council ownership by the year 2000[30]; moreover, the Secretary of State for the Environment asserted in 1987 that it was "nonsense" to suggest that the government wanted to end the role of local authorities in housing: he observed that "with some 4.5 million homes on their books, it is inconceivable that they will not remain major providers of rented housing for the foreseeable future."[31] It is also not unknown for an unexpected change of government to produce sudden and dramatic alterations in housing policy. **1.15**

As noted in the Preface, public sector housing law embraces many different "traditional" legal areas; it seems far too soon to consign the whole of the subject to a further "traditional" pigeonhole labelled "Legal History." **1.16**

[29] Partial decontrol of the private rented sector was attempted in the Rent Act 1957, but far from reviving private renting, the 1957 Act hastened its decline: see, *e.g.* P. Spicker, *Roof*, January 1988, p. 42.

[30] *Roof*, January 1987, p. 23.

[31] H.C. Deb., November 30, 1987, col. 621 (Mr. N. Ridley).

Part I: The General Rehousing Obligations of Local Authorities

2 The Statutory Rehousing Duties

1. *General*

2.01 The importance of the allocation and transfer policies of housing authorities has been enhanced by the decline in council housebuilding rates, the high capital cost of some council housing and the introduction of a generous "right to buy" for public sector tenants.[1] However, in allocating their housing, authorities have long had to face a difficult situation involving "[f]ewer houses to rent, an increasing dependence upon council housing, more single-person and elderly households, [and] a decreasing supply of large family type houses."[2]

2.02 We shall see that authorities have primary statutory responsibilities to house those displaced from their accommodation by some form of public action (such as clearance or redevelopment), and certain other categories of people such as the homeless and those in special need of care and attention. In some areas, as the result of the discharge of these primary responsibilities, there has been little or no council accommodation left over even for those who have reached the top of the general waiting list.

2. *The Statutory Requirements*

2.03 Authorities still enjoy a wide discretion in the allocation of their housing. Although much of the law relating to council housing was fundamentally reformed by the Housing Act 1980, the Act intro-

[1] See Chap. 14.

[2] Central Housing Advisory Committee, *Council Housing Purposes, Procedures and Priorities* (1969), para. 26 (this Report is hereafter referred to as the "Cullingworth Report": the chairman of the sub-committee which produced it was Professor J. B. Cullingworth).

duced only minor changes concerning allocation schemes, which were mainly concerned to secure wider publicity for such schemes rather than to "police" them as such.

2.04 Although the general discretion of authorities in this area has not been seriously eroded by Parliament, there are various statutory provisions which do affect allocation and transfer policies. Some of these provisions are directly relevant (concerning, for example, rehousing obligations following slum clearance or redevelopment), while others are indirectly relevant (concerning, for example, the prohibition of discrimination on the grounds of race or sex). Several of these provisions have been the subject of litigation, and the courts have recently shown some willingness to regulate the discretion of authorities in allocation matters where the circumstances are appropriate.

(a) *National Assistance Act 1948: persons "in need of care and attention"*

2.05 Section 21(1)(*a*) of the National Assistance Act 1948 states in effect that social services authorities[3] are under a duty to provide "residential accommodation for persons who by reason of age, infirmity or any other circumstance are in need of care and attention which is not otherwise available to them." Although this subsection was amended by the Local Government Act 1972,[4] to the effect that the duty to provide the accommodation could only be imposed on the direction of the Secretary of State (for Social Services), the duty has since been duly re-imposed by Ministerial Circular.[5]

2.06 Section 21(1)(*a*) of the 1948 Act is not exclusively concerned with the relief of homelessness, since the specified need is "need of care and attention," not need for shelter as such. The need can arise "by reason of age, infirmity or any other circumstance," so it extends beyond the aged and infirm to cover (for example) the socially inadequate. According to a 1948 Circular, although the provision does not cover "sick persons needing treatment in hospital,"[6] it is

[3] See Local Authority Social Services Act 1970, ss.2(1), 3 and Sched. 1.

[4] L.G.A. 1972, Sched. 23.

[5] D.H.S.S. Circ. 13/74, para. 4.

[6] M.O.H. Circ. 87/48, para. 14; such persons may fall within other social services responsibilities: see, *e.g.* National Health Service Act 1977, s.21 (1) and Sched. 8, para. 2 (residential accommodation for the physically or mentally ill).

intended to include "a wide range of elderly, infirm, disabled or subnormal people who are unable to look after themselves in their own homes and cannot obtain from relatives, friends or others the care and attention they require."[7]

There is an overlap between the responsibilities of *social services* authorities under section 21(1)(*a*) of the 1948 Act and the responsibilities of *housing* authorities towards the homeless under Part III of the Housing Act 1985.[8] The Ministerial Code of Guidance to Part III of the 1985 Act[9] (to which housing authorities must have regard[10] in exercising their responsibilities towards the homeless) recognises the continuing relevance of section 21(1)(*a*) of the 1948 Act by suggesting[11] that the securing of accommodation under this section from a social services authority is one method whereby (in appropriate circumstances) a *housing* authority can discharge the duty to accommodate imposed by Part III of the 1985 Act. **2.07**

The relevant social services authority to which application should be made under the 1948 Act is normally the one in whose area the applicant ordinarily resides, but if he has no settled residence, or is in urgent need and ordinarily resident elsewhere, then responsibility lies with the authority in whose area he is found.[12] **2.08**

The accommodation is intended to be "a substitute for a normal home, and must meet all reasonable needs of the residents."[13] However, concern has sometimes been expressed at the conditions in accommodation provided by certain social services authorities, particularly in hostels for single men.[14] The accommodation is by definition *residential*, and therefore will not necessarily be temporary. It must presumably be provided until (in accordance with the wording of section 21(1)(*a*)) the relevant "need" ends, or the relevant "care and attention" becomes "otherwise available." **2.09**

It would appear that the duty in section 21(1)(*a*) cannot be enforced by a disappointed applicant against the authority through **2.10**

[7] M.O.H. Circ., *ibid.*

[8] See Chaps. 4 to 6.

[9] D.O.E., *Housing (Homeless Persons) Act 1977 Code of Guidance (England and Wales)* (2nd ed., 1983).

[10] See H.A. 1985, s.71(1); for a discussion of the legal status of the Code see below, para. 4.03, n. 5.

[11] *Op. cit.* para. 4.4; see below, para. 5.64.

[12] National Assistance Act 1948, s.24(1), (3); D.H.S.S. Circ. 13/74, para. 3(a).

[13] M.O.H. Circ. 87/48, para. 16.

[14] See, *e.g.* R. Middleton, *Roof*, November 1980, p. 161; C.H.A.R., *Parker Street Hostel.*

court action, since the 1948 Act provides expressly[15] for complaint to be made to the Secretary of State (for Social Services), following which he may order the authority to discharge its functions as he directs; and it is a well-established principle of administrative law that where an Act creates an obligation and provides a specific remedy for the enforcement of that obligation, recourse to the courts will not normally be allowed as an alternative remedy.[16]

2.11 Where accommodation is provided under the 1948 Act, it "is to be available to those in need of it irrespective of their means."[17] However, the residents are normally required to pay sums towards the costs of their accommodation in accordance with a "standard rate" fixed by the authority, which may be reduced in cases of hardship, though not below the minimum charge fixed by regulations.[18] If the resident is receiving income support, and is a single person, he will currently receive £32.90 per week, plus £8.25 per week for personal expenditure.[19]

(b) *Housing Act 1985: the obligations in relation to the provision of council housing*

2.12 Allocation and transfer policies are obviously affected by the amount of housing which individual authorities have available to them, so that it is important initially to consider the obligations governing the provision of council housing. Councils are not under any *general* duty to provide council housing,[19a] although they may be

[15] N.A.A. 1948, s.36; however, the Secretary of State cannot act as a tribunal of fact under s.36, and can only intervene if satisfied that the council has misdirected itself in law or formed an irrational view of the facts: *R.* v. *Kent C.C. and Others, ex p. Bruce, The Times*, February 8, 1986 (D.C.).

[16] *Doe d. Bishop of Rochester* v. *Bridges* (1831) 1 B. & Ad. 847, 859; this principle was applied to s.36 of the 1948 Act in *Southwark L.B.C.* v. *Williams* [1971] Ch. 734 (C.A.); *Roberts* v. *Dorset C.C.* (1976) 75 L.G.R. 462; *Wyatt* v. *Hillingdon L.B.C.* (1978) 122 S.J. 349 (C.A.).

[17] M.O.H. Circ. 87/48, para. 19.

[18] N.A.A. 1948, s.22; National Assistance (Charges for Accommodation) Regulations 1989 (S.I. 1989 No. 307).

[19] Income Support (General) Regulations 1987 (S.I. 1987 No. 1967), Sched. 7, para. 13.

[19a] This is made clear by the introduction of a new s.9(5) of H.A. 1985 by cl. 128(1) of the Local Government and Housing Bill 1989, providing that "[n]othing in [H.A. 1985] shall be taken to require (or to have at any time required) a local housing authority itself to acquire or hold any houses or other land" for the purposes of H.A. 1985, Pt. II; this clarifying amendment is particularly significant in view of the "privatisation" provisions in H.A. 1988, discussed in Chap. 15 below.

obliged to provide it, or to consider providing it, in certain specific circumstances.

2.13 Thus there is a duty imposed on housing authorities[20] by section 8 of the Housing Act 1985 to *consider* housing conditions in their districts and the *need* for the provision of further housing accommodation[21]; in carrying out this duty, authorities must have regard to the special needs of the chronically sick and disabled.[22] Authorities are permitted to provide accommodation by way of erection, conversion, acquisition, alteration, enlargement, repair or improvement.[23] However, an authority cannot provide "council housing" by compelling a private developer to provide equivalent housing through the device of attaching conditions which have this effect to his planning permission.[24]

2.14 These general provisions in the 1985 Act, in effect, leave to the discretion of the individual authority the decision as to the amount and type of council housing (if any) which it will actually provide; however, they do go some way towards ensuring that it will at least be aware of the *need* for council housing in its area. It is increasingly common, however, for authorities to find themselves unable to provide the housing which they perceive to be necessary, due to financial restraints imposed by central government.[25]

2.15 There are separate and more specific obligations in the Housing Act 1985 concerning the provision of council housing in certain cases where there is unfitness or overcrowding. By section 289, where an authority proposes to declare an area of unfit houses to be a "clearance area" (*i.e.* in order to purchase the area and demolish the houses), it must first be satisfied (*inter alia*) that it can provide or secure the provision of "suitable accommodation" for those who will be displaced by the clearance, in so far as such accommodation does not already exist.[26] However, the court will be slow to quash a compulsory purchase order, following the declaration of a clearance area, on the ground that the accommodation provided for rehousing is not "suitable": it has been held that "suitable accommodation" for these purposes does not mean ideal or identical accommodation,

[20] "Local housing authorities" for these purposes are primarily district councils and London borough councils: H.A. 1985, ss.1, 2(2).

[21] See Housing Services Advisory Group, *The Assessment of Housing Requirements* (1977).

[22] Chronically Sick and Disabled Persons Act 1970, s.3(1).

[23] H.A. 1985, s.9.

[24] *R.* v. *Hillingdon L.B.C., ex p. Royco Homes* [1974] 2 W.L.R. 805 (D.C.).

[25] See above, paras. 1.11–1.13.

[26] H.A. 1985, s.289(4)(*a*).

and that the court will not interfere unless the council has acted arbitrarily, or otherwise irregularly or improperly.[27] As regards overcrowding, section 334 provides that if it appears to an authority that it should make a report on overcrowding in its district, or if the Minister so directs, then it must make an inspection and submit a report to the Minister showing the number of new houses required to abate the overcrowding, together with proposals for providing them.

(c) *Housing Act 1985: the general powers and duties relating to allocation*

2.16 **(i) The general discretion conferred by section 21.** With regard to the allocation of such accommodation as has been provided by housing authorities, section 21(1) provides that the "general management, regulation and control of a local housing authority's houses is vested in and shall be exercised by the authority".

2.17 **(ii) The "reasonable preference" duties in section 22.** The wide discretion in section 21(1) is however qualified by section 22, which provides that the authority must ensure that in selecting its tenants it gives a "reasonable preference" to those who occupy "insanitary or overcrowded houses," have "large families," or live under "unsatisfactory housing conditions," and to those towards whom the authority is "subject to a duty under section 65 or 68 (persons found to be homeless)." It has been suggested that this obligation should be extended to require that preference must also be given to persons at risk of violence, for example by virtue of racial harassment.[28]

2.18 We shall see later that where an insanitary house is unfit, and action is taken by the authority pursuant to Part VI or Part IX of the 1985 Act, special rehousing obligations are imposed by the Land Compensation Act 1973; while overcrowding, family size and unsatisfactory housing conditions are all factors which (as will be seen) should in practice normally be catered for by the authority's individual selection scheme relating to those on the general waiting list.

[27] *Savoury* v. *Secretary of State for Wales* (1974) 119 S.J. 167.
[28] D. Forbes, *Action on Racial Harassment: Legal Remedies and Local Authorities* (1988), p. 87.

The duties to house the homeless pursuant to Part III of the 1985 Act are considered in detail in Chapters 4 to 6. Section 22 (which is contained in Part II of the Act) requires that a "reasonable preference" in the allocation of council housing is given to all those who are found to be *homeless:* this does not cover those found to be *threatened* with homelessness,[29] but it does cover homeless people whether or not they are in "priority need,"[30] so that (for example) all single homeless people are entitled to receive such a "reasonable preference" although they will often not be in priority need. In any event, however, even where an authority owes a specific duty to *house* a homeless person under Part III of the Act, it does not have to provide its own housing held under Part II of the Act, but can secure instead that "some other person" provides the accommodation.[31] **2.19**

It was originally thought that the "reasonable preference" obligation imposed by section 22 was so widely and vaguely couched that it would not be capable of enforcement in court, with the result that councils could "pick and choose their tenants at their will."[32] However, it is now clear from *R.* v. *Canterbury C.C., ex p. Gillespie*[33] that the applicant can successfully challenge a council's allocation policy by seeking judicial review where he falls within one or more of the categories to which "reasonable preference" has to be given and the council has failed to afford him such preference. **2.20**

In *Gillespie* the applicant, having left the council house of which she was joint secure tenant, was living in accommodation which was both "overcrowded" and gave rise to "unsatisfactory housing conditions" within the terms of section 22, but the authority initially refused to allow her to join the housing waiting list on the grounds that she held a secure tenancy elsewhere and she did not fall within either of the only two expressed exemptions to this stated policy. Subsequently, the council allowed her to join the housing waiting list but refused to consider her for the allocation of accommodation, again because of their stated policy debarring those holding secure tenancies elsewhere. Simon Brown J. quashed the council's decision because it: **2.21**

[29] The concept of threatened homelessness is discussed below, paras. 4.93–4.95.

[30] See below, paras. 4.96–4.113.

[31] H.A. 1985, s.69(1), see below, paras. 5.53, 5.59–5.60.

[32] *Per* Lord Porter in *Shelley* v. *L.C.C.* [1948] 2 All E.R. 898, 900 (H.L.); see also J. B. Cullingworth, *Housing and Local Government* (1966), p. 121.

[33] (1987) 19 H.L.R. 7 (D.C.).

> "constitutes a rule which requires to be followed slavishly rather than merely a stated general approach which is always subject to an exceptional case and which permits each application to be individually considered."[34]

He acknowledged that the council is perfectly entitled to adopt a general allocation policy (as is recognised by the publication duties in section 106[35]), but he emphasised that it is not allowed, in applying that policy, to close its mind to the individual circumstances of the applicant's case.

2.22 The *Gillespie* case clearly shows that the "reasonable preference" obligation in section 22 applies as much to admission to the general housing waiting list as to the allocation of housing to those already on that list.[36] Similar principles to those laid down in *Gillespie* have been applied by local ombudsmen[37] in finding maladministration where councils have improperly fettered themselves in the operation of their allocation schemes.[38] Allocation schemes which impose requirements relating to past residence in the area[39] or the age of the applicant, or which operate on a date-order basis,[40] are particularly vulnerable to attack (either in court, after *Gillespie*, or through reference to the ombudsmen) unless the council has made provision for the due consideration of the circumstances of each individual case.

[34] (1987) 19 H.L.R. 7, 15 (D.C.); for another example of the application of this rule in a different context, see *Tilley* v. *Wandsworth L.B.C.* [1981] 1 All E.R. 1162 (C.A.), discussed below, para. 4.163.

[35] See below, para. 2.24.

[36] Note also, regarding discrimination against certain applicants who are already on the list, *R.* v. *Blackpool B.C., ex p. Smith,* July 29, 1987 (D.C., unreported); here leave to apply for judicial review was granted to challenge (as an arguable breach of s.22) the council's policy of automatically moving someone already on the housing list to a lower place on the list if he was declared homeless.

[37] For a discussion of the ombudsman's role in allocation matters, see below, paras. 2.44–2.45.

[38] See, *e.g.* Complaint No. 1088/C/84 (maladministration found where the council's officers applied an initially unpublished "house rule" that no allocation would be made to an applicant with an interest in a former matrimonial home; thus the effects of *Gillespie* cannot be sidestepped by the council's adoption of secret "policy guidance": see N. Madge and J. Luba, [1986] Legal Action 163, 165).

[39] See also Ombudsman Complaint No. 18/B/86 (rule that applicants with less than three years' residence would not be considered under the allocation scheme held to amount to maladministration, being inconsistent with the responsibilities in s.22 of the 1985 Act).

[40] The various types of allocation scheme in common use are discussed below, at paras. 3.13–3.17.

(iii) Housing obligations in cases of designated defective dwellings. A quite separate allocation duty may arise under the 1985 Act where a former council dwelling has been bought (for example, under the "right to buy"[41]) and is later found to suffer from certain designated defects, and the council re-purchases the defective dwelling under the scheme laid down in Part XVI of the 1985 Act[42]: in this situation the council must normally grant the occupier, at his request, a secure tenancy of the dwelling in question or of another suitable dwelling.[43] 2.23

(d) *Housing Act 1985: publicity duties in relation to allocation, transfer and exchange schemes*

(i) Publication of rules. Under section 106 of the 1985 Act, councils must publish a *summary* of their rules relating to allocations, transfers and exchanges,[44] and must have a *complete set* of these rules readily available for inspection.[45] A copy of the summary must be supplied on request free of charge, while a copy of each set of rules must be supplied on request, on payment of a reasonable fee.[46] 2.24

Compliance with these publication requirements will not necessarily provide all the information which applicants or potential applicants may wish to know: authorities can comply with section 106 merely by publishing their eligibility requirements and basic schemes (section 106 refers to "rules . . . for determining priority as between applicants" and "rules . . . governing the procedure to be followed in allocating [the authority's] housing accommodation"), without revealing the crucial aspects of how long applicants have to wait and what sort of property (and area) they are likely to be offered.[47] However, it is the practice of some authorities regularly to publish in the local press comprehensive information as to how long applicants will have to wait for properties in each particular area. 2.25

There have been reports which indicate that some authorities have not even complied with the minimum publication requirements of section 106, and that even where schemes have been published, in some cases the restrictions which have been revealed 2.26

[41] See below, Chap. 14.
[42] See below, paras. 14.151–14.154.
[43] H.A. 1985, ss.554, 556–557.
[44] Transfer and exchange schemes are discussed below, paras. 3.38–3.46.
[45] H.A. 1985, s.106(1)–(2).
[46] *Ibid.* s.106(4).
[47] V. Karn, *Roof*, January 1981, p. 15.

appear to contravene the "reasonable preference" obligations in section 22.[48]

2.27 **(ii) Disclosure to the applicant of personal information.** There is a separate provision in section 106(5) whereby, at the request of an applicant for housing, the authority must furnish him free of charge with details of the particulars given by him to the authority, and recorded by it as relevant to his application. Again, however, this right may be of limited practical use to the applicant, since he has no right to see the whole file relating to his application, nor has he the right to be given the reasons behind the authority's ultimate assessment of his particulars for the purpose of its allocation scheme.

2.28 More comprehensive rights of inspection are conferred on the applicant by the Data Protection Act 1984 and the Access to Personal Files Act 1987. The Data Protection Act enables him to inspect "personal data" which is held by the authority on computer or is processed automatically,[49] but the Act does not cover manual filing systems. The Access to Personal Files Act requires authorities to afford access to "accessible personal information"[50] in accordance with the relevant regulations.[51]

(e) *Land Compensation Act 1973: rehousing duties owed to those displaced by public action*

2.29 It is necessary to deal with the position of those eligible for rehousing by the local authority under the Land Compensation Act 1973 separately from the position of those on the general housing waiting list, since the 1973 Act imposes special duties on authorities regarding those displaced by (for example) clearance or redevelopment, and in practice many authorities treat those covered by the 1973 Act as a quite distinct group from those on the waiting list (though some authorities operating "points" allocation schemes[52] still award

[48] Shelter (Scotland), *Council House Allocation in Scotland* (1982); Welsh Consumer Council, *Who Gets Council Homes in Wales?* (1985); see also Ombudsman Complaints No. 397/C/84, 1082/C/84 and 903/C/84, discussed by J. Luba and N. Madge, [1985] Legal Action 170.

[49] See D.P.A. 1984, ss.1(2)–(3), 2, 21, and Sched. 1.

[50] A.T.P.F.A. 1987, ss.1–3 and Sched. 1; note that H.A. 1985, s.106(5) (above) does not apply to any information recorded by an authority in respect of which the authority is obliged to give access under the 1987 Act: A.T.P.F.A. 1987, s.1(3).

[51] Access to Personal Files (Housing) Regulations 1989 (S.I. 1989 No. 503).

[52] See below, paras. 3.13, 3.15.

households displaced by clearance or redevelopment a large number of "points", thus technically bringing them within such schemes).[53]

Under section 39(1) of the Land Compensation Act, where a person is displaced[54] from residential accommodation in consequence of certain types of public action, and "suitable alternative residential accommodation on reasonable terms is not otherwise available" to him, then the relevant local authority must secure that such accommodation will be provided. **2.30**

The public action covered by section 39 is: the acquisition of land by an authority possessing compulsory purchase powers[55] (for example, where a "clearance area" has been declared relating to unfit property[56]); the improvement or redevelopment of land previously acquired by such an authority[57]; the making or acceptance of a housing order or undertaking (including[58] a demolition or closing order relating to unfit property under Part IX of the Housing Act 1985[59]); and the service of an improvement notice under Part VII of the Housing Act 1985. **2.31**

Section 39 does not define which classes of residents it intends to cover. The section would appear to extend beyond tenants and subtenants to include any residents who are displaced, "whether families (with or without children) or lodgers or single residents,"[60] with the exception[61] of trespassers and those permitted to reside in the property pending its demolition or improvement. Certain caravan dwellers are included by section 40. **2.32**

However, in order to qualify for rehousing, the displaced resident must have been in occupation at a particular time, which is defined **2.33**

[53] See the Cullingworth Report, *op. cit.* para. 135, and Housing Services Advisory Group, *Allocation of Council Housing* (1978), para. 2.25 (this latter report is hereafter referred to as the "H.S.A.G. Report").

[54] Where there is a compulsory purchase, an applicant who leaves the property before service of the notice to treat can still be regarded as "displaced . . . in consequence of . . . the acquisition of the land by an authority possessing compulsory purchase powers" for the purposes of the Land Compensation Act: *Prasad* v. *Wolverhampton B.C.* [1983] Ch. 333 (C.A.).

[55] See above, n. 54.

[56] H.A. 1985, s.289, see above, para. 2.15.

[57] *Cf. R.* v. *Corby D.C., ex p. McLean* [1975] 1 W.L.R. 735 (D.C.), *Armstrong* v. *G.L.C.* [1980] L.A.G. Bull. 269 (Cty. Ct.).

[58] L.C.A. 1973, s.29(7).

[59] These unfitness procedures do *not* apply to *council* houses as such: see *R.* v. *Cardiff C.C., ex p. Cross* (1982) 6 H.L.R. 1 (C.A.), discussed below, para. 12.55.

[60] D.O.E. Circ. 18/74, App., para. 7.

[61] L.C.A. 1973, s.39(3).

in detail by section 39(6) and depends on the type of public action involved.

2.34 A major difficulty with section 39 lies in deciding whether "suitable alternative residential accommodation on reasonable terms" is "otherwise available" (for if it is so available, the duty disappears). This will be a matter of fact. Some authorities have argued that they have no duty to rehouse single residents, since they should be able to find suitable accommodation in the privately rented sector; however, we have seen that a Ministerial Circular envisaged that single residents will prima facie be eligible,[62] and evidence from accommodation agencies, etc. may well indicate that in many parts of the country opportunities in the privately rented sector have become severely diminished.

2.35 Assuming that an authority accepts that it has an obligation to rehouse a displaced resident, section 39(1) requires that the accommodation shall be offered on "reasonable" terms; the accommodation offered need not be on identical, or even similar, terms to those governing the applicant's previous accommodation. It appears, indeed, that the accommodation offered may legally be subject to far worse terms (for example, regarding security) than those governing the previous accommodation.[63]

2.36 There is no easy answer to the question of the priority to be given for council housing as between "1973 Act" claimants and those on the general waiting list. Clearly a "1973 Act" claimant is not entitled to automatic priority for council housing.[64] However, in many areas the quality of accommodation offered pursuant to the 1973 Act tends to be markedly superior to that offered to the *homeless* under Part III of the Housing Act 1985, so that in practice it may be very important for an applicant to show that he falls within the 1973 Act. The Commission for Racial Equality has pointed out[65] that a typical allocation scheme in order of the *quality* of the properties

[62] See n. 60.

[63] *R.* v. *Bristol Corpn., ex p. Hendy* [1974] 1 W.L.R. 498 (C.A.), where the authority's decision to offer a former Rent Act tenant temporary accommodation, to be followed when practicable by the allocation of a council house on the normal terms, was upheld; this decision is still significant even after the introduction of statutory security for council tenants, since certain tenancies of "short-life" property and other short-term arrangements do not attract security: see below, paras. 7.32, 7.43–7.44.

[64] *R.* v. *Bristol Corpn., ex p. Hendy, ibid.*

[65] *Local Authorities and the Housing Implications of Section 71 of the Race Relations Act 1976* (1980), p. 12; see also H.S.A.G. Report, *op. cit.* para. 2.26.

offered is: first, "decants" (*i.e.* Land Compensation Act cases[66]); secondly, transfers[67]; thirdly, waiting list cases; and finally, the homeless.

(f) *Rent (Agriculture) Act 1976: displaced agricultural employees*

Under section 28(7) of the Rent (Agriculture) Act 1976, an authority is under a duty to use its best endeavours to provide suitable alternative accommodation for certain agricultural employees, whose employers require their houses for other employees and cannot themselves provide the required alternative accommodation. **2.37**

(g) *Race Relations Act 1976: racial discrimination*

It is unlawful under the Race Relations Act 1976 for an authority to discriminate against a person on racial grounds (*i.e.* grounds of colour, race, nationality or ethnic or national origins), in the terms on which the premises are offered, or on which his application for the premises is refused, or in his treatment in relation to any list of applicants.[68] Furthermore, section 71 of the 1976 Act imposes a duty on every local authority to endeavour to eliminate racial discrimination and promote racial harmony in the carrying out of its various functions.[69] If the Act is broken, remedies are available to the person discriminated against and to the Commission for Racial Equality.[70] **2.38**

The practical implications of the race relations legislation for authorities and their prospective tenants are considered later.[71] **2.39**

(h) *Sex Discrimination Act 1975: sexual discrimination*

It is similarly unlawful under the Sex Discrimination Act 1975 for an authority to discriminate against a woman (or man) on the ground of her (or his) sex or marital status, in the terms on which the premises are offered, or by refusing the application, or in its treatment of her (or him) in relation to any list of applicants.[72] If the **2.40**

[66] Notwithstanding the effect of the decision in *Hendy's* case, above.

[67] See below, para. 3.39.

[68] 1976 Act, ss.1, 3, and 21(1).

[69] The general scope of s.71 was discussed in *Wheeler* v. *Leicester C.C.* [1985] A.C. 1094 (H.L.).

[70] R.R.A. 1976, ss.57–62; see, *e.g. Commission for Racial Equality* v. *Griffiths* [1985] Legal Action 170 (Cty. Ct.): action against 53 white signatories to a petition asking the G.L.C. not to house an Asian family on a particular estate.

[71] Paras. 3.26–3.28.

[72] 1975 Act, ss.1, 2 and 30(1).

Act is broken, remedies are available to the person discriminated against and to the Equal Opportunities Commission.[73] The impact of the 1975 Act on local government services, including housing, was discussed in a 1978 Circular.[74]

3. *Challenges to the Authority's Decision*

2.41 An applicant who seeks council housing under the authority's general allocation scheme[75] has no right to be given the reasons for the authority's refusal to grant him the priority which he anticipated. Nevertheless, the authority's decision may be challenged in various ways.

(a) *Internal review*

2.42 It may be possible informally to persuade the authority to review its own decision, for example by having it looked at by a more senior officer; the intervention of an interested local councillor or M.P. may help to secure such a review. Some authorities have introduced formal internal appeal mechanisms (notwithstanding the absence of any legal obligation to do so), and the Housing Services Advisory Group has recommended the general introduction of internal appeal procedures, which it saw as providing "an important role for councillors."[76] Where the authority operates such a procedure, then the applicant is entitled to receive reasonable notice of the time and place of any hearing and of the matters which the authority is minded to use against him[77]; there is however no right to demand an oral hearing as such, if the review procedure does not specifically provide for it, so that the authority may determine the appeal purely in the light of written submissions.[78]

2.43 It has been suggested that dissatisfaction regarding allocation processes could be reduced by the introduction of a statutory requirement for all authorities to produce "grievance procedures,"

[73] 1975 Act, ss.66–71.
[74] D.O.E. Circ. 1/78.
[75] *Cf.* the position of applicants under the homelessness provisions in Pt. III of the H.A. 1985, who have the right to be notified of the authority's reasons where it decides that it owes less than the full rehousing duty: H.A. 1985, s.64(4), see below, para. 4.165.
[76] H.S.A.G. Report, *op. cit.* paras. 2.59, 13.9.
[77] *Kanda* v. *Government of the Federation of Malaya* [1962] A.C. 322 (P.C.).
[78] See *R.* v. *Housing Appeal Tribunal* [1920] 3 K.B. 334.

giving rights of appeal within the particular authority in the light of Ministerial Circulars.[79]

(b) *Local ombudsmen*

If it appears that "maladministration" has taken place as regards an allocation decision, the matter can be referred (either by the complainant personally or via a local councillor[80]) to a Local Commissioner (popularly called an "ombudsman") under Part III of the Local Government Act 1974.[81] Although there is no statutory definition of "maladministration," this concept relates to the manner in which the decision was reached rather than the decision itself,[82] and the Local Commissioners interpret it as including "neglect and unjustified delay," "failure to follow the Council's agreed policies, rules or procedures," "bias or unfair discrimination," "failure to have proper procedures," and "failure to take into account matters which should have been taken into account."[83] There have been several instances where complaints about individual allocations and transfers have been upheld by ombudsmen[84]; in particular, if an authority in deciding an application has ignored its own allocation rules (as published pursuant to section 106), then this will prima facie amount to maladministration.[85] **2.44**

The reference to the ombudsman need not specify an act of "maladministration" as such, provided it contains an allegation that the **2.45**

[79] See Report of the Committee on *Conduct in Local Government*, Cmnd. 5636 (1974), Vol. 1, pp. 34–35; N. Lewis and P. Birkinshaw, *Welfare Law and Policy* (ed. M. Partington and J. Jowell, 1979), p. 130; Commission for Local Administration, *Code of Practice on Complaints Procedures* (1978).

[80] Local Government Act 1974, s.26(2) (as amended by L.G.A. 1988, Sched. 3, para. 5(2)).

[81] For a general account of the role of the local ombudsman concerning housing matters, see D. J. Hughes, *Public Sector Housing Law* (2nd ed., 1987), pp. 147–157; amendments to Pt. III of the 1974 Act are contained in Pt. II of the Local Government and Housing Bill 1989, whereby (*inter alia*) if the ombudsman has found that injustice has been caused in consequence of maladministration, and he is not satisfied with the authority's response to his report, then he may require the authority to publish details of his recommendations in a newspaper circulating in the authority's area, and if it fails to do so he can himself arrange for such publication.

[82] *R.* v. *Commissioner for Local Administration, ex p. Croydon L.B.C., The Times,* June 9, 1988 (D.C.).

[83] Commission for Local Administration in England, leaflet, *Your Local Ombudsman*, p. 1.

[84] See generally D. J. Hughes and S. R. Jones, [1979] J.S.W.L. 273.

[85] See Complaint No. 850/C/83.

complainant has suffered injustice arising from a specified act or omission of the authority.[86] However, the procedure is not designed to afford speedy relief, and a "guilty" authority is under no legal duty to comply with the ombudsman's recommendations.[87] The High Court has jurisdiction to entertain judicial review proceedings in relation to an ombudsman's report.[88]

(c) *Court action*

2.46 We have seen that in *R.* v. *Canterbury C.C., ex p. Gillespie*[89] the court accepted that the decisions of authorities regarding the general allocation of council housing could be challenged by way of judicial review in accordance with the general administrative law principles. The *Gillespie* case involved the imposition by an authority of fetters which prevented it from properly discharging its statutory allocation duties in section 22. Other examples of situations where actions for judicial review would be likely to succeed in the context of allocations are where an authority fails to publish properly its allocation scheme in accordance with section 106,[90] or acts in clear contravention of its published allocation rules,[91] or bases its decision on irrelevant considerations,[92] or allows the decision to be taken by a person not properly authorised to make it.[93]

86 *R.* v. *Local Commissioner for Administration, ex p. Bradford M.C.C.* [1979] Q.B. 287 (C.A.).

87 It has often been proposed that a local ombudsman's determination which is adverse to the council should enable the complainant to pursue a remedy in the courts: see, *e.g. Administrative Justice: Some Necessary Reforms: Report of the Committee of the JUSTICE—All Souls Review of Administrative Law in the United Kingdom* (1988), p. 128.

88 *R.* v. *Commissioner for Local Administration, ex p. Eastleigh B.C.* [1988] 3 W.L.R. 113 (C.A.); *R.* v. *Commissioner for Local Administration, ex p. Croydon L.B.C., The Times*, June 9, 1988 (D.C.).

89 (1987) 19 H.L.R. 7 (D.C.), see above, paras. 2.20–2.22.

90 See D. Yates, [1981] J.S.W.L. 129, 132.

91 A. Arden, [1981] L.A.G. Bull. 38, 39; *R.* v. *Port Talbot B.C., ex p. Jones* [1988] 2 All E.R. 207 (D.C.): allocation in clear contravention of council's stated policy.

92 *R.* v. *Port Talbot B.C., ex p. Jones, ibid.* (allocation of house to councillor to assist her in fighting a local election: the decision to grant the tenancy was quashed by the court).

93 *R.* v. *Port Talbot B.C., ex p. Jones, ibid.* (where the dominant role in deciding to make the allocation was taken by the chairman of the council's housing tenancy committee, whereas the council's standing orders delegated the decision to the borough housing officer).

A detailed discussion of proceedings for judicial review (and of the relevant administrative law principles) is contained in Chapter 6, since particularly frequent use has been made of this procedure in order to challenge the homelessness decisions of authorities. **2.47**

3 The Mechanics of Selection

1. *General*

3.01 We saw in the previous chapter that the law still allows authorities considerable discretion in the allocation of their housing. This chapter examines in outline the practices of authorities concerning allocations (to those who are not existing council tenants), and transfers and exchanges (which involve existing council tenants changing their accommodation).

3.02 The allocation process involves two separate procedures, namely deciding who should receive council housing, and deciding which particular property each successful applicant should receive. It has become increasingly necessary in recent years for authorities to ensure that their allocation schemes give proper consideration to the claims of "non-traditional" applicants, such as couples without children, single working people and students, and mobile households[1]; surveys have shown that in some inner-city areas families with children no longer constitute the principal claimants for council housing.[2]

3.03 Since allocation problems are subject to considerable regional variations, it has never been possible for central government to prescribe any single method of selection for general use. An influential 1969 report considered that more central intervention could prove less effective than the existing system, and that the need was for a "clearer lead from central government, not greater control."[3] A subsequent report on allocation processes in 1978[4] made several useful

[1] See Green Paper on *Housing Policy*, Cmnd. 6851 (1977), p. 79.

[2] See, *e.g.* J. Conway, *Roof*, May 1982, p. 14.

[3] Central Housing Advisory Committee, *Council Housing Purposes, Procedures and Priorities* (1969), para. 64 (hereafter referred to as the "Cullingworth Report").

[4] Housing Services Advisory Group, *The Allocation of Council Housing* (1978), hereafter referred to as the "H.S.A.G. Report."

suggestions (some of which are dealt with below), but it also broadly sought to preserve the discretion of councils in allocation matters.[5]

2. *Allocations*

(a) *The housing waiting list*

Authorities which retain a stock of housing[6] will keep "housing waiting lists" on which general applicants for council housing (not being, for example, "clearance or redevelopment" cases or homeless persons[7]) may register, and from which the authorities will make their allocations in accordance with their individual selection schemes. Authorities usually keep not only general lists based on the characteristics of applicants, but also separate lists of applicants for different types of properties (family houses, single persons' accommodation, old people's dwellings, etc.): this reflects the dual nature of the allocation process, noted above. Shelter has estimated that in 1987 there was a record number of 1,350,000 households registered on housing waiting lists kept by English authorities, and that the average waiting time was nine years.[8] **3.04**

It is an offence under section 1(1) of the Accommodation Agencies Act 1953 for anyone to demand or accept payment for registering or agreeing to register details of any person seeking the tenancy of a house or flat: although this provision was designed to cure abuses in the private sector, it would seem to extend to authorities' housing lists as well. **3.05**

Registration on a housing list is not always allowed automatically[9]: sometimes the applicant must first satisfy a condition. The most common condition is one requiring residence in the authority's area for a designated minimum period. The imposition of such mini- **3.06**

[5] H.S.A.G. Report, paras. 7.2–7.3.

[6] Where an authority has disposed of its entire stock under one of the privatisation schemes discussed in Chap. 15, then there will be no need for the authority to maintain a waiting list (although the new landlord(s) could do so); in such a case, the authority will remain subject to the statutory rehousing duties referred to in Chap. 2, but it may be able to enter into arrangements with the new landlord(s) for the provision of the necessary housing: D.O.E., *Large Scale Voluntary Transfers of Local Authority Housing to Private Bodies* (1988), para. 12; D.O.E., *Housing Action Trusts: A Consultation Document* (1987), para. 26.

[7] See above, paras. 2.17, 2.29–2.31.

[8] *Shelter Campaign News*, Issue 3, Autumn 1987.

[9] See Shelter, *Restrictive Practices*.

mum residential qualifications for acceptance on a housing list has been repeatedly criticised.[10]

3.07 Residential qualifications for housing lists were at one time illegal for the London boroughs, which had to register every application which was made to them by residents in their areas under the London Government Act 1963.[11] However, many London boroughs have imposed requirements of between one and five years' residence (depending on the particular borough) anywhere in the Greater London area before the applicant is eligible for *consideration* (as opposed to acceptance on the list).

3.08 Residential qualifications have still not been generally prohibited by statute for England and Wales.[12] One reason often advanced for their abolition is that it is only possible for the authority to assess housing needs if it admits all applicants to its list.[13] However, even the most comprehensive of housing lists may be poor indicators of need, since they may well be out of date, or contain the names of people who are registered on the lists of other authorities also or who have registered merely as a precautionary measure.[14]

3.09 Although residential qualifications have not been outlawed by Parliament (save for the London boroughs), the impact of the important decision in *R.* v. *Canterbury C.C., ex p. Gillespie*,[15] discussed in Chapter 2,[16] must not be forgotten. Thus, as regards both admission to the general housing waiting list and the actual allocation of properties to those on the list, the authority must ensure that it gives a "reasonable preference" to the groups set out in section 22 of the Housing Act 1985.[17] If members of these groups are totally excluded from consideration (for example, through rigid residential requirements), they will not receive a "reasonable prefer-

[10] See, *e.g.* Cullingworth Report, *op. cit.* para. 169; Report of the Committee on *One-Parent Families*, Cmnd. 5629 (1974), p. 384; Green Paper on *Housing Policy*, *op. cit.* pp. 79–80; H.S.A.G. Report, *op. cit.* para. 6.10.

[11] London Government Act 1963, s.22(3); this provision was repealed by the Local Government Act 1985, Sched. 17.

[12] *Cf.* Housing (Scotland) Act 1987, s.19(2); the Labour Party announced in 1982 that, if returned to office, it would prohibit all qualifications preventing adults from registering on housing waiting lists or from being considered for the allocation of council housing: *The Times*, June 16, 1982.

[13] See, *e.g.* Cullingworth Report, *op. cit.* para. 169.

[14] See H.S.A.G., *The Assessment of Housing Requirements* (1977), paras. 5.18–5.19; 1978 H.S.A.G. Report, *op. cit.* paras. 13.11–13.12; I. Sier, *Roof*, March 1981, p. 3; *The Times*, March 25, 1988.

[15] (1987) 19 H.L.R. 7 (D.C.).

[16] See above, paras. 2.20–2.22.

[17] See above, para. 2.17.

ence" and the courts will be likely to strike down the authority's scheme. Although it is still lawful for an authority to have general guidelines, relating for example to past residence, it is necessary for the scheme to be devised in such a way that consideration can be given, where necessary, to the individual circumstances of applicants who do not conform to the guidelines.

(b) *Who should do the selecting?*

Before the various types of allocation schemes are discussed, it is relevant to consider who should operate them: for even the very best of schemes depends ultimately for its effectiveness on the ability of those applying it. **3.10**

Most commentators consider that the individual decisions on allocations, unless particularly difficult, should be left to the officers of the housing department rather than to the members of the housing committee, since the matter is not (or should not be) a political one, and councillors might be subject to undesirable pressures.[18] **3.11**

Whether the final decision is to be taken by housing officers or councillors, the applicant will previously have been seen, often at home, in order to check the facts on his application form, and to make a preliminary assessment regarding his claim to council housing and the sort of property which he ought to be offered. Much disquiet has been voiced at the way in which this vitally important "visiting" stage is sometimes conducted, which can involve applicants being "graded" in accordance with arbitrary criteria.[19] **3.12**

(c) *Types of schemes*

Allocation schemes differ greatly in matters of detail, and some exhibit a high level of eccentricity.[20] However, schemes tend to fall into four main types: **3.13**

—"date order" schemes (where allocation is generally on the basis of "first come, first served");

—"points" schemes (where allocation is generally made to those amassing sufficient "points," for example for overcrowding);

[18] See, *e.g.* Cullingworth Report, *op. cit.* paras. 119–123; H.S.A.G. Report, *op. cit.* para. 13.2; see also *R.* v. *Preseli D.C., ex p. Fisher* (1984) 17 H.L.R. 147, 159 (D.C.); *R.* v. *Port Talbot B.C., ex p. Jones* [1988] 2 All E.R. 207 (D.C.).

[19] See Cullingworth Report, *op. cit.* para. 84; H.S.A.G. Report, *op. cit.* para. 7.17; Shelter, *Homes Fit For Heroes* (1975), p. 19.

[20] See P. Spicker, *The Allocation of Council Housing* (Shelter, 1983).

—"merit" schemes (where each application is treated on its merits); and

—"combined" schemes (involving, for example, a "points" scheme for families, a "date order" scheme for single applicants, and a "merit" scheme for "special cases").

3.14 Every scheme must conform to the principles in *Gillespie* (considered above) by affording a "reasonable preference" to the groups designated in section 22 of the 1985 Act. We have noted[21] that schemes which place emphasis on past residence or age, or which are based on date order, are now particularly vulnerable to attack in the light of *Gillespie* unless they make adequate provision for the due consideration of the circumstances of individual cases falling outside the standard framework.[22]

3.15 The Cullingworth Report examined a sample of some 30 selection schemes. It considered that "date order" schemes were only acceptable in areas with no real housing problem, and then only if "individual hardship cases and key workers" were treated separately.[23] The report judged "points" schemes to be "excellent in concept but exceedingly difficult to devise in detail with fairness," and emphasised that they should be kept up to date[24]; it also stressed that points merely for length of residence (rather than for length of housing need) were undesirable except for the purpose of deciding between cases of equal housing need.[25] The H.S.A.G. Report approved of points schemes as being "particularly suitable where there is still considerable housing stress," but warned authorities against making such schemes too complicated.[26]

3.16 "Merit" schemes were disapproved of by the Cullingworth Report for being "unworkable,"[27] and the H.S.A.G. Report, after noting that very few merit schemes still remained, recommended their total discontinuance[28]; while on "combined" schemes, the Cullingworth Report noted that every authority which it examined

[21] See above, para. 2.22.

[22] For particular examples of schemes which would not appear to pass the *Gillespie* test without significant modification, see *Roof*, September 1983, pp. 10, 32.

[23] *Op. cit.* para. 128; there are recorded cases of applicants only receiving council housing many decades after their initial entry on the waiting list: see, e.g. *Roof*, May 1982, p. 6 (31 years), January 1986, p. 32 (50 years).

[24] *Op. cit.* para. 130.

[25] *Op. cit.* para. 170.

[26] H.S.A.G. Report, *op. cit.* para. 7.9.

[27] Cullingworth Report, *op. cit.* para. 133.

[28] H.S.A.G. Report, *op. cit.* paras. 2.31, 7.5.

operated in effect a sort of "combined" scheme, since cases of "exceptional hardship" were always dealt with separately, although the definition of "exceptional" varied.[29]

The Cullingworth Report was unable to recommend an ideal all-purpose selection scheme, since each scheme had to be devised in the light of local conditions,[30] a conclusion endorsed by the H.S.A.G. Report.[31] However, the Cullingworth Report did make some general observations: for example, authorities were urged to stop adopting "moralistic" attitudes towards "unmarried mothers, cohabitees, 'dirty' families, and, 'transients,' "[32] and to give more weight to "social need" as a separate priority, *i.e.* by taking into account both the housing conditions of an individual household and its ability to cope with those conditions, with the highest priority going to those unable to cope with bad conditions.[33] The report also stressed that cases of severe ill-health should similarly be dealt with as having priority outside the general selection schemes.[34] The H.S.A.G. Report re-emphasised that housing need should be the main criterion for deciding priorities.[35] **3.17**

(d) *Special cases*

Certain types of applicant raise particular difficulties, and some of these merit separate consideration here. **3.18**

(i) The homeless. We have seen[36] that under section 22 of the Housing Act 1985 authorities have to give a "reasonable preference," in allocating their housing, to people found to be homeless under Part III of the 1985 Act. **3.19**

It appears that due to recent cutbacks in council housebuilding, many people who a few years ago would have been rehoused from the general waiting list without becoming homeless at all, are now no longer being helped through the "normal" waiting list system at this earlier stage; thus those in the greatest housing need tend nowadays to surface as homelessness cases, whereas previously they **3.20**

[29] Cullingworth Report, *op. cit.* para. 135.
[30] *Op. cit.* para. 125.
[31] H.S.A.G. Report, *op. cit.* para. 7.4.
[32] Cullingworth Report, *op. cit.* para. 96; for an example of such a "moralistic" policy directed against cohabitees, see L. Moroney, *Roof*, July 1982, p. 3.
[33] *Op. cit.* paras. 117–118.
[34] *Op. cit.* para. 136.
[35] H.S.A.G. Report, *op. cit.* para. 4.2.
[36] See above, para. 2.17.

would have been likely to secure rehousing through the general waiting list without the "homelessness" stigma.[37] However, there has long been a tendency for some authorities to regard homeless families as potential "queue jumpers" for council housing, especially if they have been evicted from their previous accommodation for rent arrears[38]; and some judges have expressed similar sentiments.[39] The H.S.A.G. Report reluctantly acknowledged that in practice a number of authorities "allocate only the least desirable vacancies to homeless households and/or permit them only a limited choice, or no choice."[40]

3.21 The "considered view" of the H.S.A.G. on this issue was clear and uncompromising: although many authorities "see a dilemma in the selection process between . . . the relative claims of the homeless and those who have been on the housing list for some years,"[41] nevertheless:

> ". . . it is essential that people should not be penalised in terms of quality by the urgency of their need: every applicant, from whatever allocation group, should be offered the best available property consistent with his degree of priority, and not the poorest that he is likely to accept because of his desperation."[42]

3.22 **(ii) Single applicants and one-parent families.** Many allocation schemes, particularly those based on "points" and residential qualifications, tend to place the single applicant and the one-parent family at a disadvantage, when compared with married couples with children, and the elderly.[43] The H.S.A.G. Report urged that the needs of single people should be carefully considered, that they

37 See N. Magee and S. Beardon, *Roof*, September 1981, p. 3 (discussing research by Brent Housing Aid Centre).

38 See, *e.g.* J. Forsyth, *Roof*, March 1979, p. 36; S. Billcliffe, *Roof*, July 1979, p. 118; see also above, para. 2.36.

39 See, *e.g. Chef & Brewer Ltd.* v. *Clarke, Roof*, May 1977, p. 92; *R.* v. *Hillingdon L.B.C., ex p. Islam* [1981] 2 All E.R. 1089, 1093 (C.A.); *Puhlhofer* v. *Hillingdon L.B.C.* [1986] 1 All E.R. 467, 473 (H.L.); *R.* v. *L.B. of Tower Hamlets, ex p. Monaf* (1988) 20 H.L.R. 529, 550 (C.A.).

40 *Op. cit.* para. 2.26.

41 *Op. cit.* para. 4.22.

42 *Ibid.*

43 Report of the Committee on *One-Parent Families, op. cit.* pp. 382–384; H.S.A.G., *The Housing of One-Parent Families* (1978), paras. 3.6–3.8; S. Venn, *Singled Out: local authority housing policies for single people*, C.H.A.R., 1985.

should be accepted onto housing lists, and that specific assessment and allocation policies should be introduced for them.[44]

3.23 With regard to the type of housing which should be offered to one-parent families in particular, a 1977 Ministerial Circular advised authorities to integrate them with other families amongst the housing stock, in order to avoid any stigma which might arise from segregation[45]; while the H.S.A.G. Report emphasised the need for battered women to be allocated "ordinary family accommodation," in order to ensure that "places in emergency refuges are freed to meet short term needs."[46]

3.24 **(iii) Applicants with rent arrears.** Some authorities will not consider allocating their normal housing stock to tenants with rent arrears. Both the Cullingworth Report[47] and the H.S.A.G. Report[48] recommended that rent arrears should not automatically preclude a family from obtaining a council house. Indeed, the Cullingworth Report emphasised that authorities should in fact take increased responsibility for families with arrears, since they are "the most vulnerable."[49]

3.25 At least one authority has made offers subject to the applicants paying one month's rent in advance[50]; while not illegal, such offers will compound the problems of those already carrying an arrears debt from their previous property, and they can have serious implications where the applicant is claiming income support.[51]

3.26 **(iv) Black applicants.** The problems experienced by black applicants are largely the result of the adverse effects on them of indirect discrimination on account of general rules adopted by authorities (regarding, for example, residential qualifications), rather than of any direct discrimination.[52] Nevertheless, there is clear evidence of

[44] *Allocation of Council Housing, op. cit.* paras. 10.13–10.16.
[45] D.O.E. Circ. 78/77, Annex B, para. 4.
[46] *Op. cit.* para. 10.8.
[47] *Op. cit.* para. 350.
[48] *Op. cit.* para. 6.21.
[49] *Ibid.*
[50] I. Sier, *Roof*, November 1981, p. 6.
[51] See Direction 12(o) (ii) of the *Social Fund Directions* (issued by the Minister pursuant to the Social Security Act 1986), under which a "budgeting loan" *cannot* be awarded in respect of rent in advance where the landlord is a local authority.
[52] See, *e.g.* W.W. Daniel, *Racial Discrimination in England* (1968), pp. 178–182; Cullingworth Report, *op. cit.* paras. 366–376; Green Paper on *Housing Policy, op. cit.* p. 118; H.S.A.G. Report, *op. cit.* paras. 11.2–11.3; G. Bindman, (1979) 129 New L.J. 408, 411; P. Healy, *The Times*, July 8, 1985.

considerable racial discrimination in the allocation process, proceeding from a variety of motives[53]; there is also evidence of racial harassment being experienced by black families from other tenants on the estates to which they have been allocated.[54]

3.27 Particular concern has arisen regarding the danger of creating "ghettos" of black people: the Cullingworth Report suggested that *voluntary* dispersal should be "an aim, but not the overriding preoccupation of policy,"[55] and the 1975 White Paper on *Race Relations and Housing* considered that obstacles to dispersal should be removed if possible, but that people "must be free to make up their own minds whether or not to move from established communities."[56] The 1976 Report from the Community Relations Commission on *Housing in Multi-Racial Areas* pointed out[57] that there is nothing wrong with all-black estates in the abstract, but that in practice they are likely to form on poor-quality estates and to become targets for political criticism. Under the Race Relations Act 1976[58] the *compulsory* dispersal of households on racial grounds is clearly unlawful, as is a quota system such as allocating only one house in five to a black family.[59]

3.28 The keeping of specific records of coloured people in connection with allocations has frequently been sanctioned as an aid to avoiding discrimination.[60]

[53] See, *e.g. Colour and the Allocation of G.L.C. Housing* (1976); H.S.A.G. Report, *op. cit.* paras. 11.1–11.2; C.R.E., *Housing in the London Borough of Hackney: Report of a formal investigation* (1984); A. Grosskurth, *Roof*, March 1984, p. 8; A.M.A., *Housing and Race: policy and practice in local authorities* (1985); J. Barelli, *Roof*, July 1985, p. 3.

[54] See: C.R.E., *Racial Harassment on Local Authority Housing Estates* (1981); *The Times*, March 12, 1982; P. Healy, *loc. cit.*; C.R.E., *Living in Terror* (1987); see also *Commission for Racial Equality* v. *Griffiths* [1985] Legal Action 170 (Cty. Ct.), discussed above, para. 2.38, n.70; the bringing of possession proceedings against tenants guilty of racial harassment is discussed below, para. 8.37.

[55] *Op. cit.* para. 406.

[56] Cmnd. 6232, p. 9.

[57] At pp. 33–34.

[58] See above, para. 2.38.

[59] C.R.E., *Local Authorities and the Housing Implications of Section 71 of the Race Relations Act 1976* (1980), p. 13.

[60] See, *e.g.* Cullingworth Report, *op. cit.* paras. 414–427; White Paper on *Race Relations and Housing, op. cit.* pp. 6–8; Report on *Housing in Multi-Racial Areas, op. cit.* p. 36; H.S.A.G. Report, *op. cit.* para. 11.8; Report on *Local Authorities and the Housing Implications of Section 71 of the Race Relations Act 1976, op. cit.* pp. 10–11; *Housing in the London Borough of Hackney: Report of a formal investigation, op. cit.*; Reply to First Report from the Home Affairs Committee, Session 1986–87, Cm. 193.

(v) Infants. It appears that until recently many authorities refused to accept infants (*i.e.* persons under 18) on their waiting lists,[61] though several of these authorities have doubtless reviewed their policies regarding infants in the light of the *Gillespie* decision.[62] **3.29**

Where an authority decides to allocate one of its properties to an infant, then it must bear in mind that an infant cannot hold a legal estate in land,[63] but only an equitable interest,[64] although a purported grant of a legal lease operates to give the infant the equitable interest in the lease.[65] This restriction should not however deter authorities from allocating properties for the benefit of infants, since there are three principal ways in which it can be successfully overcome.[66] First, in the case of spouses or cohabitees of whom one has attained the age of majority and the other is an infant, the lease can simply be granted to the adult partner alone.[67] Secondly, in those circumstances where the authority can effectively grant a licence,[68] then the infancy of the licensee is irrelevant to the grant of the licence: the law prevents an infant from holding a legal estate, but does not prevent him from holding a licence, which does not rank as a legal estate. Thirdly, where a legal lease is to be granted, the legal estate can be vested in an adult or body corporate on trust for the infant[69]; where there is no suitable adult to act as trustee, then several housing authorities have adopted the practice of granting the lease to the social services authority for the benefit of the infant. **3.30**

Where the infant holds the property on licence or as the beneficiary of a lease under a trust (for example, by virtue of a purported grant of a legal lease), he is liable to observe the relevant clauses and conditions of the licence or lease (including in particular those relating to the payment of rent): in the case of a licence, the liability arises under the hallowed principle that infants can bind themselves **3.31**

[61] See M. Goodman, *Roof*, November 1984, p. 18.
[62] See above, paras. 2.20–2.22.
[63] Law of Property Act 1925, s.1(6).
[64] Settled Land Act 1925, s.27(2).
[65] L.P.A. 1925, s.19; S.L.A. 1925, s.27.
[66] See M. Goodman, *loc. cit.*
[67] For the position where the legal estate is purportedly vested in the adult and the infant jointly, see L.P.A. 1925, s.19(2).
[68] See below, paras. 7.15–7.24.
[69] S.L.A. 1925, s.27(2).

contractually for "necessaries," which include housing[70]; and in the case of a beneficial interest under a lease, liability arises under the general law of trusts.[71] Where the infant is in a direct contractual relationship with the landlord, the contract is voidable at the infant's option during his infancy or within a reasonable time thereafter; but he is subject to the obligations of the contract while it remains on foot.[72]

(e) *Voluntary "mobility" schemes*

3.32 The need for prospective (and actual) council tenants to be able to move across local authority boundaries has often been emphasised.[73]

3.33 A National Mobility Scheme was set up in 1981,[74] and is co-ordinated through a National Mobility Office. The cost of setting up the scheme was met by the Department of the Environment pursuant to special powers in what is now section 107 of the Housing Act 1985. The scheme is voluntary, but the vast majority of the housing authorities in England and Wales (together with some other landlords, such as new town development corporations and housing associations)[75] are participating in it. The scheme is designed to allow participating authorities to assist people who are high on waiting lists, other people with "pressing needs," and existing public sector tenants. Such persons are eligible for help where they want to move to a different region either because they have secured permanent employment there which is beyond reasonable travelling distance of their current accommodation, or because they have strong social reasons for moving there (as in the case of an elderly applicant who needs to move nearer to relatives or friends).

3.34 There are two parts to the scheme. First, a "knock-for-knock" arrangement for mobility within county areas, whereby each participating authority offers an appropriate number of lettings each year

[70] See *Cheshire, Fifoot and Furmston's Law of Contract* (11th ed., 1986), pp. 411–415; *Law Commission's Report on Law of Contract: Minors' Contracts* (Law Comm: No. 134, 1984), p. 2; *Portman Registrars and Nominees* v. *Mohammed Latif* [1987] 6 C.L. 217 (Cty. Ct.); contracts for "necessaries" are not affected by the Minors' Contracts Act 1987.

[71] *Law of Contract: Minors' Contracts, op. cit.* pp. 21–22.

[72] *Ibid.*; this principle also is not affected by the Minors' Contracts Act 1987.

[73] See, *e.g.* H.S.A.G. Report, *op. cit.* Chap. 9; D.O.E. Circ. 71/77, paras. 25–26.

[74] For a general account, see J. Shears, *Roof*, July 1981, p. 29.

[75] Where the authority disposes of housing under one of the privatisation schemes discussed in Chap. 15, the D.O.E. "strongly encourage(s)" participation by the new landlord(s) in the National Mobility Scheme: *Large Scale Voluntary Transfers of Local Authority Housing to Private Bodies, op. cit.* para. 20.

for people who need to move to its area from other areas within that same county (the number of relevant lettings depending on the number of households which have left the authority in question and have been accommodated by other housing authorities within the same county). Secondly, there is a separate arrangement for mobility between county areas, under which each participating authority makes available at least one per cent. of its annual lettings (a rather low minimum figure, given the likely demand), for people who need to move into its area from outside the county boundaries, together with additional lettings representing the number of households from its own area who move out and are accommodated by authorities outside its own county boundaries.

Applications under the scheme must initially be made to each applicant's own local authority. Applications do not have to be accepted: the normal allocations criteria of the recipient authorities are used to decide these cases, save that any residential qualifications are waived. **3.35**

The National Mobility Scheme has been criticised regarding, for example, its frequent failure to meet the needs of the elderly,[76] the over-emphasis given in practice by many authorities to job-related moves at the expense of moves for "social reasons,"[77] the excessive time which can elapse before completion of the necessary formalities to enable a move to take place,[78] and the exclusion of applicants who wish to move in order to look for work in their preferred area but who have not actually secured employment there.[79] **3.36**

There is a separate voluntary mobility scheme operated within the areas of the London boroughs, called the London Area Mobility Scheme.[80] **3.37**

3. *Transfers and Exchanges*

(a) *General*[81]

Moves by council tenants are normally for the principal benefit of the tenants themselves (as for example under the National Mobility Scheme which has just been described). However, moves in the pub- **3.38**

[76] J. Minter, *Roof*, September 1981, p. 8.
[77] C. Schofield, *Roof*, March 1982, p. 5.
[78] E. Ramsay, *Roof*, November 1983, p. 4; but *cf.* B. Affleck, *Roof*, January 1984, p. 10.
[79] E. Ramsay, *loc. cit.*
[80] The operation of this scheme now falls within L.G.A. 1985, s.89.
[81] For general discussions of transfer, exchange and mobility schemes see S.H.A.C., *The Right Move: A Guide to Mobility and Housing* (1983); National Consumer Council, *Moving Home: Why is it difficult for Council Tenants?* (1984).

lic sector may sometimes be for the primary benefit of the authority, as for example where it persuades a tenant to move because of under-occupation. Prior to the introduction of statutory security of tenure for council tenants, authorities had frequently been urged to minimise under-occupation, in particular by encouraging tenants to move from under-occupied family houses to smaller units.[82] Since the introduction of statutory security for most council tenants,[83] such moves can in general only be achieved on a purely voluntary basis, since "under-occupation" is only a statutory ground for possession against a secure tenant in extremely limited circumstances.[84]

(b) *The difference between a "transfer" and an "exchange"*

3.39 There is a technical but significant difference between a "transfer" and an "exchange": a "transfer" takes place where an existing council tenant moves to vacant accommodation also owned by the local authority, thus leaving his previous property available for re-allocation; whereas an "exchange" involves an interchange of properties between a council tenant and another council tenant (perhaps in a different area), or a private sector tenant, and does not depend on a vacancy.[85]

3.40 There is also the quite distinct concept of the "assignment" of a council tenancy, whereby the tenant himself assigns his tenancy to a third party, not necessarily by way of "exchange": while the usual result of an "assignment" is the automatic cessation of the *secure* tenancy,[86] we shall see[87] that this principle is subject to exceptions, particularly in the case of certain assignments by way of exchange between secure tenants. The devolution of council tenancies on death, and the destination of council tenancies following marriage breakdown, do not have direct relevance to the concepts of "transfers" and "exchanges" as here defined; these aspects also, therefore, are separately discussed later.[88]

[82] See, *e.g.* D.O.E. Circ. 18/74, App., para. 9(v); C.H.A.C., *Transfers, Exchanges and Rents* (1953), pp. 2–4; *cf.* V. Karn, *Roof*, September 1979, p. 139.
[83] See Chap. 8.
[84] See H.A. 1985, Sched. 2, gd. 16, discussed below, para. 8.63.
[85] See *Transfers, Exchanges and Rents, op. cit.* pp. 3–5; H.S.A.G. Report, *op. cit.* p. 1, n.1.
[86] See below, paras. 9.15, 9.18.
[87] See below, paras. 3.45, 9.16, 9.19.
[88] See below, paras. 9.27–9.42, 11.28–11.41.

(c) *Transfers*

Where a tenant requests a transfer, the authority often has to make a difficult decision between his claim and the claims of applicants at the head of the general waiting list. The H.S.A.G. Report found that few authorities had any formal scheme for deciding priorities either as between general waiting list applicants and transfer applicants, or as between transfer applicants *per se*.[89] However, the publication requirements in section 106 of the Housing Act 1985[90] extend to transfer schemes, so that some authorities have felt the need to introduce formal transfer arrangements for the first time. Some authorities use the same system of "points" for transfer cases as for general waiting list cases, but others adopt a lower standard of need for transfer cases, since a transferring tenant will vacate a property which the authority can use. It is also quite common, however, for authorities to insist upon strict conditions being satisfied before entertaining a transfer application, such as a satisfactory record of rent payments.[91] **3.41**

An authority which lacks a proper policy on transfers can find that an unfortunate "bottleneck" effect has been produced on its general waiting list, since "[a] family offered a poor house in an unattractive area may . . . refuse it, no matter how desperate they are, because they will not easily be able to get a transfer."[92] **3.42**

(d) *Exchanges*

Authorities normally adopt a more liberal attitude towards exchanges than they do regarding transfers, since, unlike transfers, exchanges do not involve any vacant accommodation and will help at least two households. It is possible for exchanges to be arranged between council tenants and tenants in the private sector, but these have not proved popular, *inter alia* because of the suspicions of private landlords that unsatisfactory council tenants might be "dumped" on them.[93] **3.43**

[89] *Op. cit.* paras. 2.46, 2.48.
[90] See above, para. 2.24.
[91] See, *e.g.* Welsh Consumer Council, *Council Housing* (1976), p. 27.
[92] V. Karn, *Roof*, January 1981, p. 15.
[93] See *Transfers, Exchanges and Rents, op. cit.* pp. 6–7.

3.44 Exchange schemes are subject to the general publication requirements imposed on authorities by section 106 of the 1985 Act. Tenants desiring exchanges may nevertheless have difficulty in publishing their needs to other tenants who might be interested in exchanges. Some tenants advertise in the local press, or make use of the various commercial concerns which disseminate exchange information nationally. However, a computer-based Tenants Exchange Scheme was introduced by central government on a nationwide basis in 1982,[94] in order to help in matching up tenants of local authorities, new towns and housing associations who want to exchange their properties with tenants in other areas; tenants wishing to exchange can register with the computer bureau running the scheme, which regularly circulates to individual local authorities, new towns and housing associations lists of potential "exchangers" desiring to move into their areas. Individual tenants can themselves consult these lists. No charge is made to tenants using the Scheme.

3.45 The technical machinery whereby an "exchange" is to be effected needs careful consideration. One method is for the respective tenants to surrender the tenancies of their former dwellings to the council(s), following which new (secure) tenancies can be granted by the council(s) to them as "incoming" tenants. The other method is assignment; we shall see that, although the normal rule is that secure council tenancies are not capable of assignment, one of the exceptions to this rule permits assignments between secure tenants by way of exchange, provided the written consent of each council is obtained.[95] Whichever method of exchange is adopted, it is essential that each tenant gets the consent of his authority to the arrangement[96]; an informal "swapping" exercise between the tenants themselves, without the involvement of their landlords, will not be effective and will normally result in both tenants losing their security.[97]

[94] See D.O.E. leaflet, *Do you want to move to another area? Tenants Exchange Scheme* (1984); where the authority disposes of housing under a privatisation scheme (see Chap. 15), the D.O.E. has encouraged participation by the new landlord(s) in the Tenants Exchange Scheme: *Large Scale Voluntary Transfers of Local Authority Housing to Private Bodies, loc. cit.*

[95] H.A. 1985, ss.91–92, see below, paras. 9.13–9.24.

[96] The D.O.E. leaflet (n. 94, above) makes it clear that tenants must always seek written permission from the respective landlords before the exchange can go ahead.

[97] See *Warwick D.C.* v. *Smith and Benton, Roof*, March 1982, p. 5 (Cty. Ct.), discussed below, para. 9.20.

(e) *Removal expenses*

Under section 26 of the Housing Act 1985 an authority may pay the removal expenses of a tenant moving from a council house, whether into another council house or into a private dwelling. However, the provision contained in section 107 for central government funding of mobility schemes[98] only covers general administrative costs, and not the removal costs incurred by individual tenants. **3.46**

[98] See above, para. 3.33.

Part II: The Obligations of Local Authorities Regarding Homeless Persons

4 The Three Key Concepts: "Homelessness," "Priority Need" and "Intentional" Homelessness

1. *Outline of the General Duties owed by the Authority*

The precise responsibilities owed by a housing authority[1] to an individual applicant under Part III of the Housing Act 1985 depend upon the results of the authority's inquiries[2] concerning the three key concepts of "homelessness," "priority need," and "intentional" homelessness (the definitions of which will be examined later in this chapter, together with the separate concept of "threatened" homelessness). **4.01**

A preliminary duty to secure accommodation for the applicant is imposed by section 63(1) of the 1985 Act, where, as a result of the initial interview, the authority has "reason to believe" that the applicant may be "homeless" and may have a "priority need": in such a case, the authority must secure that accommodation is temporarily made available for him (and for his family unit[3]) while it reaches a final decision on the application. **4.02**

This preliminary duty arises "irrespective of any local connection which the applicant may have with the district of another local hous- **4.03**

[1] As defined in H.A. 1985, ss.1 and 2(2): see below, para. 4.16.

[2] The details of the inquiry process are discussed below, paras. 4.19–4.29.

[3] See H.A. 1985, s.75, discussed below, paras. 5.65–5.67.

ing authority,"[4] and section 63 makes no reference to "intentional" homelessness, so that temporary accommodation must be provided even if the authority suspects that the homelessness may be intentional, and is pursuing further inquiries in order to "satisfy" itself on this point. Nevertheless, as the Ministerial Code of Guidance[5] to Part III of the 1985 Act points out, in clear cases it may be "possible for all the issues to be covered to be taken together in the course of a single interview,"[6] so that a decision can sometimes be reached swiftly and without the need for any further inquiries.

4.04 All applicants who are considered by the authority to be "homeless" or "threatened with homelessness" are entitled to some help, under sections 65(1) and 66(1). The precise nature of the authority's duties[7] depends on the following criteria:

(a) *Where the authority is satisfied that the applicant is homeless or threatened with homelessness, but does not have a priority need*

4.05 Here the authority must furnish the applicant with "advice and such assistance as [it] consider[s] appropriate in the circumstances" in any attempts he may make to find accommodation (if he is homeless) or to secure that he does not lose his existing accommodation (if he is threatened with homelessness).[8] The Code asks authorities "to respond as helpfully and constructively as they are able in giving advice and other forms of assistance," and suggests that the advice given could cover, *inter alia*, "action to avert homelessness, financial

[4] H.A. 1985, s.63(2); see, *e.g. R.* v. *Tower Hamlets L.B.C., ex p. Camden L.B.C., The Times*, December 12, 1988 (D.C.); for the "local connection" provisions, see below, paras. 5.14–5.52.

[5] D.O.E., *Housing (Homeless Persons) Act 1977 Code of Guidance (England and Wales)*, (2nd ed., 1983), hereafter referred to as "the Code of Guidance" or "the Code." This document (which continues in force under the Housing (Consequential Provisions) Act 1985, s.2) is evidently intended to have a more exalted status than a traditional Ministerial Circular, since authorities "shall have regard" to it (H.A. 1985, s.71(1)). An authority is not necessarily bound to follow the Code in an individual case (see, *e.g. De Falco* v. *Crawley B.C.* [1980] 1 All E.R. 913, at 921, 925 (C.A.); *Mazzaccherini* v. *Argyll & Bute D.C.* [1987] 9 C.L. 679 (Ct. of Session: O.H.)). However, it would seem that an authority has the onus of justifying a refusal to follow clear guidance in the Code (see below, para. 6.12), and it would certainly be unlawful for an authority to have a practice of systematically disregarding such guidance (see *R.* v. *Police Complaints Board, ex p. Madden* [1983] 2 All E.R. 353, 370 (D.C.)).

[6] *Op. cit.* para. 2.3.

[7] The various duties may operate cumulatively where appropriate: see, *e.g. Dyson* v. *Kerrier D.C.* [1980] 3 All E.R. 313, 320 (C.A.).

[8] H.A. 1985, ss.65(4), 66(3).

aspects of accommodation, rent rebates and allowances, and mortgages."[9] Legal advice and assistance may be offered to the applicant, where appropriate.[10]

Concern has been expressed at the inadequacy of some of the advice and assistance which has been given to applicants who are not in priority need[11]; and the Under-Secretary of State at the Department of the Environment has emphasised that the mere offer to a young single homeless person of a list of bed and breakfast establishments whose charges are above the relevant D.S.S. ceilings for board and lodging payments "would not count as appropriate advice or assistance."[12] **4.06**

(b) *Where the authority is satisfied that the applicant is homeless or threatened with homelessness, and has a priority need, but the authority is also satisfied that he became homeless, or threatened with homelessness, intentionally*

Here again, the authority must furnish the applicant with "advice and such assistance as [it] consider[s] appropriate in the circumstances" in any attempts he may make to find accommodation (if he is homeless) or to secure that he does not lose his existing accommodation (if he is threatened with homelessness).[13] The advice and assistance offered to those found intentionally homeless has also been criticised.[14] **4.07**

(c) *Where the authority is satisfied that the applicant is homeless, has a priority need, but became homeless intentionally*

Here, in addition to the "advice and assistance" duty just considered, the authority must secure that accommodation is made available for the applicant's occupation for such period as it considers will give him a reasonable opportunity of himself securing accommodation for his occupation.[15] In such "priority need plus intentionality" cases the authority can therefore largely transfer responsibility for securing accommodation back to the applicant, although in order to give him an opportunity to make his own **4.08**

[9] *Op. cit.* para. 6.2.
[10] See L.G.A. 1972, ss.111, 137, and 222.
[11] Shelter, *Submission to the Review of the Code of Guidance* (1978), p. 37.
[12] H.C. Deb., May 24, 1985, col. 1308 (Sir George Young).
[13] H.A. 1985, ss.65(3)(*b*), 66(3).
[14] Shelter, *op. cit.* p. 27.
[15] H.A. 1985, s.65(3)(*a*).

arrangements the authority must normally provide him with what is in effect "temporary bridging accommodation."[16]

4.09 If the authority has previously housed the applicant temporarily under this provision as an intentionally homeless person in priority need, and he later re-applies to the *same* authority after being forced to leave the accommodation temporarily provided for him, then if there are no material changes in his circumstances[17] he cannot demand that the authority rehouse him temporarily yet again: for the Act does not permit an intentionally homeless applicant to gain indefinite accommodation by the simple expedient of making repeated applications for temporary accommodation, and the fact that the authority has temporarily rehoused him already does not of itself give rise to a change of circumstances.[18] However, if an intentionally homeless applicant who is in priority need is ingenious enough to move successively to the areas of several *different* authorities, it would seem that each authority will owe him the limited rehousing duty, and he can thereby in effect gain indefinite accommodation through a series of "short stays."

4.10 An applicant who is intentionally homeless and in priority need is entitled to temporary rehousing for a reasonable time after he becomes homeless, even though he may have already been assisted by the authority at a time when he was threatened with homelessness intentionally; however, in determining the reasonableness of the rehousing period to be allowed, it seems that account can be taken of warnings given before the homelessness arose.[19] Authorities cannot operate the concept of a "deemed" application with a view to avoiding their housing responsibilities towards those who eventually become intentionally homeless.[20]

4.11 The matters to be taken into account by an authority in deciding how long the temporary rehousing period must be, in order to give the applicant a "reasonable opportunity" of securing his own accommodation, are discussed in the following chapter.[21]

[16] *Per* Lord Fraser in *Din* v. *Wandsworth L.B.C.* [1981] 3 All E.R. 881, 997 (H.L.).

[17] For a discussion of reapplications on the ground of material changes of circumstances, see below, paras. 4.32–4.34.

[18] *Delahaye* v. *Oswestry B.C., The Times,* July 29, 1980.

[19] See *Smith* v. *Bristol C.C.* [1981] L.A.G. Bull. 287 (Cty. Ct.); for the current relationship between the concepts of homelessness and threatened homelessness, see below, paras. 4.42–4.48.

[20] *R.* v. *East Northamptonshire D.C., ex p. Spruce* (1988) 20 H.L.R. 508 (D.C.); see also [1985] Legal Action 123.

[21] See below, paras. 5.02–5.06.

(d) *Where the authority is satisfied that the applicant is threatened with homelessness and has a priority need, and the authority is not*[22] *satisfied that he became threatened with homelessness intentionally*

Here the authority must take "reasonable steps to secure that accommodation does not cease to be available for [the applicant's] occupation."[23] In effect, this obligation is two-fold: first, the authority should try (where appropriate) to preserve the applicant's current accommodation; but secondly, where loss of his existing accommodation cannot be prevented, then the authority must make other accommodation available for him. These twin aspects are discussed further in the following chapter.[24] **4.12**

This duty "does not affect any right of the local housing authority, whether by virtue of a contract, enactment or rule of law, to secure vacant possession of accommodation."[25] Thus the authority's duty to secure that accommodation does not cease to be available for the applicant cannot hamper any claim to possession[26] which the authority may have against him in respect of one of its own council houses. **4.13**

(e) *Where the authority is satisfied that the applicant is homeless and has a priority need, and the authority is not satisfied that he became homeless intentionally*

Here the applicant has cleared all the hurdles presented by the Act, and the authority is normally under the full duty to secure that accommodation becomes available (on a permanent basis[27]) for his occupation.[28] **4.14**

Where the authority decides that the full duty is owed to the applicant, but it also decides that there is no "local connection" with its own area, and that there is a "local connection" with another authority's area, then we shall see that it may implement the special "transfer" provisions in order to compel the latter authority to **4.15**

[22] In cases of *intentionally* threatened homelessness plus priority need, the authority is only subject to the "advice and appropriate assistance" duty in H.A. 1985, s.66(3), above.

[23] H.A. 1985, s.66(2).

[24] See below, paras. 5.08–5.10.

[25] H.A. 1985, s.66(4).

[26] See Chap. 8.

[27] See below, para. 5.07.

[28] H.A. 1985, s.65(2).

accept responsibility for the applicant.[29] There is however no obligation to use these transfer provisions, even where the necessary conditions are satisfied; and in any event, even where the provisions are being implemented, the authority to which the initial application was made must secure accommodation for the applicant pending acceptance of responsibility by the authority to which the matter has been referred.[30]

2. *The Inquiry Process*

(a) *The relevant local housing authority*

4.16 Applicants falling within Part III of the Housing Act 1985[31] are the responsibility of "local housing authorities," *i.e.* primarily district councils and London borough councils.[32] In practice, the applicant will usually apply to the housing authority in whose area he finds himself "homeless" or "threatened with homelessness."

4.17 Homelessness problems do not always keep to regular hours, and the Code therefore urges authorities to produce "clearly worked out and widely known procedures for emergency situations when people become homeless out of office hours."[33] The Code further points out[34] that although the responsibility will lie with the housing authority to which the application is made, the social services authority may be able to co-operate in organising a 24-hour service. It is particularly important for authorities to furnish local police stations with the relevant emergency telephone numbers.

4.18 It will be recalled that there is a preliminary duty imposed on the authority to accommodate the applicant, while a final decision is reached, if the authority has reason to believe that he may be "homeless" and in "priority need."[35] Even if the authority to which the applicant initially applies wishes ultimately to transfer responsibility for him to another authority under the "local connection" pro-

[29] H.A. 1985, s.67: see below, paras. 5.14–5.52.

[30] *Ibid.* s.68(1).

[31] There are separate, and much more limited, obligations towards the homeless which still fall on social services authorities: see above, paras. 2.05–2.11.

[32] H.A. 1985, ss.1, 2(2).

[33] *Op. cit.* para. 7.5(c); see also *R.* v. *Camden L.B.C., ex p. Gillan, The Times,* October 17, 1988 (D.C.), suggesting that 24–hour cover might be required in heavily-populated areas.

[34] *Op. cit.* para. 7.5(c).

[35] H.A. 1985, s.63(1); see above, para. 4.02.

visions,[36] it must still provide temporary accommodation for him pending such transfer of responsibility, provided he appears to be "homeless" and in "priority need."[37]

(b) *The making of "necessary inquiries"*

Once an application is made to a local housing authority for accommodation or assistance in obtaining accommodation (whether or not the applicant specifically refers to Part III of the 1985 Act), then if the authority has reason to believe that the applicant may be "homeless" or "threatened with homelessness," it must make such inquiries as are necessary to satisfy itself as to whether he is "homeless" or "threatened with homelessness," and if so, whether he has a "priority need"[38] and whether he became homeless or threatened with homelessness "intentionally."[39] The complete closure of a council's homeless persons' section for a significant period (for example, because of industrial action), without the provision of proper emergency cover, will be a breach of this duty to make the necessary inquiries.[40] **4.19**

The burden lies on the authority to make the necessary inquiries in order to "satisfy" itself on the relevant issues: thus the authority cannot call on the applicant himself to produce "positive proof" of the issues.[41] **4.20**

The inquiries should be made "with due diligence and speed,"[42] and must take account of any new information arising before the date when the authority actually makes its decision.[43] **4.21**

There is a line of cases establishing that, in making the necessary **4.22**

[36] See above; the details of the "local connection" provisions are discussed below, at paras. 5.14–5.52.

[37] H.A. 1985, ss.63, 68(1).

[38] It is important to inquire into each relevant limb of priority need (discussed below, paras. 4.96–4.113), since this could have important implications regarding the type of accommodation which the authority should provide: *R.* v. *Ryedale D.C., ex p. Smith* (1983) 16 H.L.R. 66 (D.C.).

[39] H.A. 1985, s.62.

[40] *R.* v. *Camden L.B.C., ex p. Gillan,* above, where the court decided that a shortage of money due to "rate-capping" was not an adequate excuse for the closure; see also Ombudsman Complaint No. 1196/A/85.

[41] *R.* v. *Woodspring D.C., ex p. Walters* (1984) 16 H.L.R. 73 (D.C.).

[42] *R.* v. *L.B. of Ealing, ex p. Sidhu* (1982) 2 H.L.R. 45 (D.C., *per* Hodgson J.); see also *R.* v. *Hillingdon Homeless Families Panel, ex p. Islam, The Times,* February 10, 1981 (D.C.); but *cf. Family Housing Association* v. *Miah* (1982) 5 H.L.R. 94, 103 (C.A.).

[43] See, *e.g. Jones* v. *City of Bristol* [1981] L.A.G. Bull. 163, 287 (Cty. Ct.); *R.* v. *Wycombe D.C., ex p. Mahsood* (1988) 20 H.L.R. 683, 690 (D.C.).

inquiries, the authority must give the applicant a fair hearing, in accordance with the general rules of natural justice[44]; for example, in the case of homelessness arising through the applicant's failure to pay rent or mortgage instalments, a finding of intentional homelessness will not be justified until the applicant has been given an opportunity to explain why the arrears have arisen.[45] Moreover, an authority must not merely "rubber-stamp" a decision reached by a previous authority which is adverse to the applicant, without at least affording the applicant an opportunity of commenting on this previous decision and explaining any intervening circumstances.[46]

4.23 Inquiries may need to be made, in an appropriate case, not merely of the applicant but also of relevant third parties, for example in order to decide whether (for the purposes of the definition of "homelessness") accommodation is in fact still available to the applicant in a relative's house,[47] or whether (for the purposes of the definition of "intentional" homelessness) it would have been reasonable for the applicant to have continued to occupy a third party's accommodation which he has vacated.[48]

4.24 In an appropriate case, it may not be enough for the authority merely to accept the applicant's statements at their face value[49]: it may have to take the initiative itself, and pursue its own independent inquiries,[50] since otherwise it may not be in possession of all the facts necessary for it to reach a properly informed decision.

4.25 Nevertheless, the courts have established certain other principles which have considerably lessened the burdens on authorities when conducting the necessary inquiries. For example, there has been judicial approval of a significant departure from the normal rules of

[44] See, *e.g. Afan D.C.* v. *Marchant* [1979] J.S.W.L. 367 (Cty. Ct.); *Stubbs* v. *Slough B.C.* [1980] L.A.G. Bull. 16 (Cty. Ct.); *Barry* v. *Newham L.B.C.* [1980] L.A.G. Bull. 142 (Cty. Ct.); *Brown* v. *Hamilton D.C.* 1983 S.L.T. 397, 418 (H.L.); Code, para. 2.4; see further de Smith's *Judicial Review of Administrative Action* (4th ed., 1980), Chap. 4.

[45] *R.* v. *Wyre B.C., ex p. Joyce* (1983) 11 H.L.R. 73 (D.C.); the question in such cases is whether the arrears accrued due to the applicant's "wilful default": see below, para. 4.122.

[46] *R.* v. *South Herefordshire D.C., ex p. Miles* (1983) 17 H.L.R. 82 (D.C.).

[47] *Tickner* v. *Mole Valley D.C.* [1980] L.A.G. Bull. 187 (C.A.).

[48] *R.* v. *Hambleton D.C., ex p. Geoghan* [1985] J.P.L. 394 (D.C.); *Krishnan* v. *Hillingdon L.B.C.* [1981] L.A.G. Bull. 137; see also *Hammell* v. *R.B. of Kensington and Chelsea* (1988) 20 H.L.R. 666 (C.A.).

[49] *R.* v. *L.B. of Harrow, ex p. Holland* (1982) 4 H.L.R. 111, 116 (C.A., *per* Kerr L.J.); note also *Fezoui* v. *Torbay B.C.*, July 27, 1983 (C.A., unreported).

[50] *e.g.*, where the applicant has language difficulties: *R.* v. *Surrey Heath B.C., ex p. Li* (1984) 16 H.L.R. 79 (D.C.).

evidence by which the courts themselves are governed[51]: in particular, authorities are apparently entitled to rely on hearsay evidence, even where this is provided anonymously, without the need to have it corroborated by direct evidence.[52] In the context of intentional homelessness, the courts have been anxious to emphasise that there is no duty to conduct "detailed CID-type inquiries" before an authority can be "satisfied" that the applicant's homelessness was intentional[53]; and in the case of applicants who have recently arrived from overseas, the courts have upheld somewhat superficial inquiries.[54]

The Code, while recognising that authorities must be "satisfied" regarding intentionality, states that the Act "does not say they must have 'proof' of the issue."[55] However, although irrefragable evidence of intentionality is clearly not necessary, it is important to note that the Code also acknowledges that if there is any doubt remaining in the relevant officer's mind on the intentionality issue, then the applicant is entitled to the benefit of that doubt[56]; and this "benefit of the doubt" rule has frequently been applied by the courts.[57] **4.26**

More generally, the authority's decision cannot be faulted merely because it failed to take account of a relevant factor which the applicant himself omitted to bring to its notice, provided that there was nothing in the information before the authority when it made its decision which suggested the existence of this factor or the need to make further investigations to discover it[58]; in effect, then, there is no obligation on the authority to indulge in "crystal-ball gazing." **4.27**

[51] *R.* v. *Reigate & Banstead B.C., ex p. Henry*, December 16, 1982 (D.C., unreported).

[52] *R.* v. *Southampton C.C., ex p. Ward* (1984) 14 H.L.R. 114 (D.C.); *R.* v. *Surrey Heath B.C., ex p. Li*, see above; *R.* v. *Nottingham C.C., ex p. Costello, The Times*, February 14, 1989 (D.C.).

[53] *Lally* v. *Kensington & Chelsea B.C., The Times,* March 27, 1980; see also *Miller* v. *Wandsworth L.B.C., The Times,* March 19, 1980.

[54] *De Falco* v. *Crawley B.C.* [1980] Q.B. 460 (C.A.); *R.* v. *R.B. of Kensington and Chelsea, ex p. Cunha* (1988) 21 H.L.R. 16 (D.C.).

[55] *Op. cit.* para. 2.19.

[56] *Op. cit.* para. 2.20.

[57] *R.* v. *Thurrock B.C., ex p. Williams* (1982) 1 H.L.R. 128 (D.C.); *R.* v. *Preseli D.C., ex p. Fisher* (1984) 17 H.L.R. 147 (D.C.); *R.* v. *West Dorset D.C., ex p. Phillips* (1984) 17 H.L.R. 336 (D.C.); *R.* v. *Gravesham B.C., ex p. Winchester* (1986) 18 H.L.R. 207 (D.C.); see further below, para. 4.115.

[58] See, *e.g. Miller* v. *Wandsworth L.B.C.,* above; *R.* v. *L.B. of Harrow, ex p. Holland* (1982) 4 H.L.R. 111 (C.A.); *Brown* v. *Hamilton D.C.* 1983 S.L.T. 397, 417 (H.L.); *R.* v. *L.B. of Wandsworth, ex p. Henderson* (1986) 18 H.L.R. 522, 530 (D.C.); *R.* v. *Wycombe D.C., ex p. Mahsood* (1988) 20 H.L.R. 683 (D.C.); *R.* v. *R.B. of Kensington and Chelsea, ex p. Cunha* (1988) 21 H.L.R. 16 (D.C.).

4.28 The authority itself can normally cure defects in its original inquiry process in an individual case by subsequently carrying out the proper inquiries.[59]

4.29 Considerable criticism has been expressed at the way in which some authorities approach the making of inquiries.[60]

(c) *The making of additional inquiries*

4.30 In addition to the "necessary inquiries" which have just been discussed, which the authority *must* make, it *may* also make inquiries as to whether the applicant (or a member of his family unit) has a "local connection" with another authority's area,[61] as a result of which the authority may be able to transfer responsibility to some other authority.[62]

4.31 Furthermore, the authority may make inquiries regarding the applicant's financial situation, even though this is not expressly referred to in the relevant section.[63] The purpose of such an inquiry should not be to show that the applicant could find and pay for his own accommodation in the private sector (since, even if this is established, it would not absolve the authority from responsibility towards him under Part III of the 1985 Act, although it might mean that by giving him advice and assistance enabling him to obtain such private sector accommodation the authority will discharge its statutory duties[64]); this inquiry would in fact be designed to elicit information as a result of which the authority could subsequently decide on the "reasonable charges" which it can require the applicant to pay in respect of such accommodation as it secures for him.[65]

(d) *Re-application by the same applicant*

4.32 After an application has been fully dealt with, the authority is under no duty to make further inquiries on a subsequent application being made to it by the same applicant, if the fresh application is based entirely on the same matters which were relied on for the orig-

[59] See *R.* v. *Hambleton D.C., ex p. Geoghan* [1985] J.P.L. 394 (D.C.); *R.* v. *Gravesham B.C., ex p. Winchester,* above.

[60] See, *e.g.* S. Billcliffe, *Roof,* July 1979, p. 118.

[61] H.A. 1985, s.62(2); there is a *duty* to make the "necessary inquiries" (above) regardless of whether the applicant has a "local connection" with the area of the inquiring authority: see, *e.g. R.* v. *Tower Hamlets L.B.C., ex p. Camden L.B.C., The Times,* December 12, 1988 (D.C.).

[62] H.A. 1985, ss.67–68, see below, paras. 5.14–5.52.

[63] See Code, *op. cit.* para. 2.2A.

[64] H.A. 1985, s.69(1)(*c*), see below, paras. 5.53, 5.59.

[65] *Ibid.* s.69(2), see below, paras. 5.82–5.85.

inal application; thus it has been held that the mere fact that an authority has temporarily accommodated an intentionally homeless family[66] does not give rise to a change of material circumstances allowing a further application to be made once the family is forced to leave the temporary accommodation.[67]

However, the applicant does have the right to re-apply to the same authority at a later date if there has been a change of material circumstances, whereupon, pursuant to the Interpretation Act 1978,[68] the authority must consider his case afresh.[69] **4.33**

Even if there have been no changes in the applicant's material circumstances since the original application, he may apply at any time to a *different* authority, which must then make its own necessary inquiries, and cannot merely rubber-stamp the previous authority's decision[70]; such an authority may eventually be able to transfer responsibility for the applicant back to the original authority under the "local connection" provisions,[71] so that an applicant who has been found intentionally homeless by one authority has an incentive to "shop around" various other authorities in an effort to try and secure a decision that his homelessness was in fact not intentional.[72] **4.34**

(e) *Offences which the applicant may commit in connection with the inquiry process*

Criminal offences are created by section 74 of the 1985 Act, which may be committed by an applicant where his acts or omissions have resulted in the authority pursuing erroneous or insufficient inquiries. **4.35**

66 H.A. 1985, s.65(3)(*a*), see above, para. 4.08.

67 *Delahaye* v. *Oswestry B.C., The Times,* July 29, 1980.

68 See s.12(1), which states that where an Act confers a power or imposes a duty then it is implied, unless the contrary intention appears, that the power may be exercised, or the duty is to be performed, from time to time as occasion requires; this provision was applied in the present context in *Wyness* v. *Poole B.C.* [1979] J.S.W.L. 368 (Cty. Ct.), and *R.* v. *Ealing L.B.C., ex p. McBain* [1986] 1 W.L.R. 1351 (C.A.).

69 See *R.* v. *South Herefordshire D.C., ex p. Miles* (1983) 17 H.L.R. 82 (D.C.): here, subsequent to the original finding of intentionality, the applicants had voluntarily separated and moved into individual units of settled accommodation; following a reconciliation, they were held to be entitled to a reconsideration by the authority of the original decision, because it was arguable that the "chain of intentionality" had been broken: see below, paras. 4.135–4.143; *R.* v. *Ealing L.B.C., ex p. McBain,* above: here the accommodation which the applicant had originally and unreasonably refused was no longer suitable for her following the birth of her second child.

70 *R.* v. *South Herefordshire D.C., ex p. Miles,* see above.

71 See below, paras. 5.14–5.52.

72 See *R.* v. *Slough B.C., ex p. Ealing L.B.C.* [1981] Q.B. 801 (C.A.), discussed below, para. 5.45.

4.36 The first two offences are knowingly or recklessly making false statements, and knowingly withholding information which the applicant has been reasonably required by the authority to give[73]; the applicant is not however bound to give any information unless specifically asked to do so, or unless the situation falls within the third offence, discussed below. These first two offences also require an:

> "intent to induce a local housing authority to believe . . . that he or another person . . . is homeless or threatened with homelessness, or . . . has a priority need, or . . . did not become homeless or threatened with homelessness intentionally."[74]

Thus false statements or omissions relating to, for example, "local connections" would not fall within these provisions. It is also significant that these first two offences can be committed by "a person" in connection with his own "or another person['s]" application,[75] and are therefore wide enough to catch the applicant's adviser (solicitor, Citizen's Advice Bureau worker, social worker, etc.) if that adviser has the requisite *mens rea* (*i.e.* "knowingly or recklessly" making false statements, or "knowingly" withholding the required information).

4.37 The third offence is failing to notify the authority of changes in material facts occurring after the initial application and before receipt by the applicant of the authority's final decision.[76] This offence is an example of a statutory departure from the old common law principle that a bare omission to act customarily did not give rise to criminal liability.[77] A warning relating to this offence must be given by the authority to all applicants "in ordinary language,"[78] and it has been suggested that such warnings have sometimes been given right at the start of the interview in less than compassionate terms,[79] despite the Code's emphasis on "the importance of doing this clearly and sensibly in the context of the interview or the inquiries as a whole."[80] An applicant charged with this third offence has a defence if he can show that he was not given the required explana-

[73] H.A. 1985, s.74(1).
[74] *Ibid.*
[75] *Ibid.*
[76] H.A. 1985, s.74(2).
[77] See, *e.g.* J. C. Smith and B. Hogan, *Criminal Law* (6th ed., 1988), p. 48.
[78] H.A. 1985, s.74(2).
[79] B. Widdowson, *Roof*, January 1978, p. 3; R. Franey, *Roof*, November 1980, p. 173.
[80] *Op. cit.* para. 2.7.

tion, or that although he was given that explanation he nevertheless had a "reasonable excuse for non-compliance."[81]

Each of the three offences in section 74 carries a maximum fine of **4.38**
£1,000.[82] Although the government's original policy appeared to be to discourage prosecutions for these offences,[83] the current version of the Code states that if it is evident that an offence has been committed, the authority should be "ready to consider the case for prosecution."[84]

3. *"Homelessness" and "Threatened Homelessness"*

Having looked in outline at the general duties owed by the auth- **4.39**
ority, and at the inquiry process, it is now necessary to consider in detail the key concepts which govern the exact nature of the authority's duties. The most significant concepts are those of "homelessness" and "threatened homelessness," since no duties at all can arise under Part III of the 1985 Act unless the authority either has "reason to believe," or is "satisfied" as a result of its inquiries, that the applicant is "homeless" or "threatened with homelessness."[85]

(a) *The definition of "homelessness" in section 58(2)*

For the purposes of Part III of the 1985 Act, "homelessness" is **4.40**
not synonymous with "rooflessness": it has a technical meaning, extending far beyond those who literally have no roof over their heads. A person is "homeless" if he has "no accommodation in England, Wales or Scotland"[86]; thus, where the applicant arrives in this country from abroad, the authority cannot have regard to the existence of any housing abroad with a view to treating him as not being "homeless" in this country[87] (although in an appropriate case an authority may be able to treat the homelessness in this country of a

[81] H.A. 1985, s.74(3).
[82] *Ibid.* s.74(4).
[83] See H.L. Deb., July 27, 1977, col. 997 (Baroness Birk).
[84] *Op. cit.* para. 2.7.
[85] H.A. 1985, ss.62–63, 65–66; see, *e.g. R.* v. *Hillingdon L.B.C., ex p. Tinn* (1988) 20 H.L.R. 305, 310 (D.C.); *R.* v. *East Northamptonshire D.C., ex p. Spruce* (1988) 20 H.L.R. 508, 517 (D.C.).
[86] H.A. 1985, s.58(1).
[87] Even prior to the law being clarified on this point by H.A. 1985, s.58(1), the same result had in effect been arrived at by the case law (see, *e.g. R.* v. *Hillingdon L.B.C., ex p. Streeting* [1980] 1 W.L.R. 1530 (C.A.); *R.* v. *Hillingdon L.B.C., ex p. Islam* [1981] 2 All E.R. 1089, 1095 (C.A.)); however, the point appeared to have been overlooked in *R.* v. *Woodspring D.C., ex p. Walters* (1984) 16 H.L.R. 73 (D.C.).

foreigner who has left available accommodation in his home country as "intentional"[88]). It is clear that Part III of the 1985 Act applies to all homeless people who are lawfully in this country, whether or not E.E.C. nationals, and is not limited to those with a present or past local connection with the area of a British local authority[89]; illegal immigrants, however, are completely outside the Act's protection.[90]

4.41 A person is treated as having no accommodation if there is no accommodation "which he, together with any other person who normally resides with him as a member of his family or in circumstances in which it is reasonable for that person to reside with him," occupies or is entitled to occupy in one of the following ways:

— entitlement to occupy by virtue of an interest or a court order;
— possession of an express or implied licence to occupy;
— occupation by virtue of any enactment or rule of law giving him the right to remain or restricting the right of another person to recover possession.[91]

(b) *The meaning of "accommodation" in section 58*

4.42 **(i) The introduction of the "reasonableness" criterion.** "Accommodation" means, for the purposes of this definition, "accommodation which it would be reasonable for [the applicant] to continue to occupy," and in determining this question regard may be had to "the general circumstances prevailing in relation to housing" in the district of the authority to which the application has been made.[92]

4.43 Prior to the introduction[93] of this "reasonableness" criterion into the definition of homelessness, there had been much confusion as to whether an applicant could nevertheless rank as "homeless" if he had accommodation but that accommodation was in a very bad state or there were some other circumstances in the light of which it would not be reasonable for him to continue to occupy it. Originally,

[88] See below, para. 4.147.
[89] *R.* v. *Hillingdon L.B.C., ex p. Streeting,* above; *De Falco* v. *Crawley B.C.* [1980] Q.B. 460 (C.A); *Islam* v. *Hillingdon L.B.C.* [1981] 3 All E.R. 901, 911 (H.L.); the "local connection" provisions are discussed below, paras. 5.14–5.52.
[90] *R.* v. *Hillingdon L.B.C., ex p. Streeting,* above; *R.* v. *Crawley B.C., ex p. L.B. of Brent,* March 24, 1983 (D.C., unreported); see C. Wolmar, *Roof,* May 1980, p. 67.
[91] H.A. 1985, s.58(2).
[92] *Ibid.* s.58(2A)–(2B).
[93] By Housing and Planning Act 1986, s.14(2).

a distinction had been drawn between the definition of homelessness in what is now section 58, and the definition of intentional homelessness in what is now section 60: it was thought that there were important differences of degree between the two sections, in that accommodation might be of a sufficiently poor standard to entitle the applicant to leave it, thereby clearly becoming homeless, but unintentionally so, because it would not have been reasonable for him to stay[94]; and yet such accommodation might not be bad enough to render the applicant homeless while he was actually living in it.[95] Nevertheless, there were some decisions which actually recognised that accommodation could sometimes be of such poor quality that it would not even rank as accommodation for section 58 purposes, so that the applicant was homeless even while living in it.[96]

Particular difficulties were caused, however, by the decision of the House of Lords in 1986 in *Puhlhofer* v. *Hillingdon L.B.C.*[97] Here a husband and wife and their two children were living in a single bedroom at a guest house; the room contained a double bed and a single bed; there were no cooking or washing facilities in the room. The House of Lords upheld the council's decision that the family was not homeless: issues of the appropriateness or reasonableness of the applicant's current accommodation were said to be irrelevant for section 58 purposes, and it was normally irrelevant that the accommodation might be statutorily unfit for habitation or overcrowded. The test was simply whether the accommodation could properly be described as accommodation "within the ordinary meaning of that word,"[98] and section 60 (intentionality) was irrelevant to this issue. Although the question was said to be one of fact for the local authority, and there were "no rules,"[99] the House of Lords did impose the qualification that "accommodation must by definition, be capable of accommodating"[1]; and it was acknowledged that some places where **4.44**

[94] See H.A. 1985, s.60(1) (discussed below, paras. 4.154–4.159).

[95] See, *e.g. R.* v. *South Herefordshire D.C., ex p. Miles* (1984) 17 H.L.R. 82 (D.C.); *R.* v. *Hillingdon L.B.C., ex p. Puhlhofer* [1985] 3 All E.R. 734 (C.A.).

[96] *R.* v. *South Herefordshire D.C., ex p. Miles,* above (hop-picking hut with rats and without mains services); *R.* v. *Gloucester C.C., ex p. Miles* (1984) 17 H.L.R. 292 (C.A.) (flat so badly vandalised as to be uninhabitable); see also *R.* v. *Preseli D.C., ex p. Fisher* (1984) 17 H.L.R. 147 (D.C.); *R.* v. *Borough of Dinefwr, ex p. Marshall* (1984) 17 H.L.R. 310 (D.C.).

[97] [1986] 1 All E.R. 467; see also, *e.g.* D. Hoath, [1986] J.S.W.L. 305.

[98] [1986] 1 All E.R. 467, 474 (*per* Lord Brightman).

[99] *Ibid.*

[1] *Ibid.*

a person lives could not properly be regarded as accommodation at all, so that, for example, Diogenes would rank as a homeless person.[2]

4.45 The introduction, following the *Puhlhofer* case, of the "reasonableness" criterion (set out above) has gone some way towards diminishing the unfortunate effects of this decision. Clearly the case law which had been previously decided on the "reasonableness" criterion in section 60 (intentionality) is now directly relevant to the question of homelessness itself within section 58; and this reform partly avoids the previous dilemma[3] whereby if the applicant left unsatisfactory accommodation he would undoubtedly have rendered himself homeless, but having left without compulsion from any other person, he ran the risk of being found intentionally homeless.

4.46 Nevertheless, it is wrong to imagine that the new "reasonableness" criterion has had the effect of reversing the *Puhlhofer* decision. It may be very difficult for the applicant to prove a relevant "administrative law breach" by the authority.[4] Furthermore, the express inclusion of the "general circumstances prevailing in relation to housing" as a relevant issue in determining whether it would be reasonable for the applicant to stay[5] means that the question of whether an applicant living in poor conditions is "homeless" will often receive different answers in different parts of the country, depending on local housing pressures; and it is significant that although Ackner L.J. in the Court of Appeal in *Puhlhofer's* case differed in his reasoning from that of the other Lords Justices, taking the view that (for the purposes of the definition of "homelessness") "the accommodation must be such that it is reasonable for the applicant and his family to continue to occupy it, having regard to the general circumstances prevailing in relation to housing in the area of the housing authority to whom he has applied"[6] (which was in effect the same test as that now imposed by the reformed section 58), he nevertheless concurred in the result, holding that the council "were

[2] [1986] 1 All E.R. 467, 474 (*per* Lord Brightman).

[3] Referred to by Glidewell L.J. in *R.* v. *Hillingdon L.B.C., ex p. Puhlhofer* [1985] 3 All E.R. 734, 744 (C.A.).

[4] See Chap. 6; in *R.* v. *Blackpool B.C., ex p. Smith*, July 29, 1987 (D.C., unreported), the court made it clear that, even in the light of the new s.58(2A)–(2B), the mere fact that a dwelling is unfit, or constitutes a fire risk, does not automatically oblige an authority to decide that the dwelling does not constitute "accommodation": each case depends on its facts.

[5] H.A. 1985, s.58(2B), see above.

[6] [1985] 3 All E.R. 734, 739.

entitled to conclude, having regard to housing in their area, that it was reasonable for the Puhlhofers to continue to live in the accommodation,"[7] so that they were not homeless.

Another difficulty with the new "reasonableness" criterion is that in *Puhlhofer's* case the House of Lords made it plain that the almost identical reasonableness criterion in section 60 (intentionality) had "nothing whatever to do with the inherent quality of the accommodation"[8]; these observations were purely *obiter dicta*, since the case was not concerned with intentional homelessness, and, although it is perhaps unfortunate that the reforms to section 58 used the same "reasonableness" criterion as that in section 60, it seems clear that the poor quality of accommodation must now be taken into account for section 58 purposes, regardless of the former position concerning section 60. **4.47**

The "reasonableness" criterion in section 58 is drafted in general terms, and, as stated above, in interpreting this criterion the previous case law on the "reasonableness" criterion in section 60 is clearly relevant. The principles emerging from this case law will therefore now be discussed. **4.48**

(ii) The question is whether it would be unreasonable to stay, not whether it would be reasonable to go. Where the applicant still retains his accommodation, then a finding of "homelessness" cannot be supported merely because it is *reasonable* for him to *leave*; it must rather be *un*reasonable for him to *continue to occupy*, so that if on the facts it would be reasonable for him either to leave or to remain, it cannot properly be concluded that he is homeless under the "reasonableness" criterion.[9] **4.49**

(iii) Poor quality accommodation: the significance of local housing conditions. In deciding whether it would be reasonable for the applicant to continue to occupy his accommodation, regard may be had to the general housing circumstances in the authority's area.[10] This consideration was expressly included in the Act, **4.50**

[7] [1985] 3 All E.R. 734, 740.
[8] [1986] 1 All E.R. 467, 473 (*per* Lord Brightman).
[9] *R.* v. *Gravesham B.C., ex p. Winchester* (1986) 18 H.L.R. 207 (D.C.); *R.* v. *L.B. of Croydon, ex p. Toth* (1986) 18 H.L.R. 493 (D.C.).
[10] H.A. 1985, s.58(2B), see above.

because it would otherwise not have been regarded as relevant.[11] It will often be difficult to balance the applicant's personal difficulties against the objective matter of the local housing circumstances.[12] Thus the Code, although recognising that in general it is not reasonable for applicants to continue to occupy accommodation where the conditions have "degenerated to a point when they could not in all the circumstances reasonably be expected to remain—perhaps because of overcrowding or lack of basic amenities or severe emotional stress,"[13] also points out that the authority may "have regard to the general housing conditions of [its] area; *e.g.* whether there are many people in the area living in worse conditions than the applicants."[14] There have indeed been several cases where, despite the poor condition of the accommodation, the courts have decided that it was reasonable for the applicant to stay put, and consideration of the general housing circumstances in the area has often been a major feature of these decisions.[15]

4.51 However, where the accommodation seriously infringes the statutory standards relating to unfitness or overcrowding, it seems rather less likely that the general housing circumstances in the area will be allowed to predominate in the assessment of the reasonableness issue, so that the applicant may rank as "homeless" while living in his unsatisfactory accommodation even though general conditions in the locality are undoubtedly poor.[16] By way of example, in *R.* v.

[11] *R.* v. *L.B. of Tower Hamlets, ex p. Monaf* (1987) 19 H.L.R. 577, 585–586 (D.C.): in the context of s.60(4) (intentionality).

[12] See, as to this balancing exercise, *R.* v. *L.B. of Tower Hamlets, ex p. Monaf* (1988) 20 H.L.R. 529 (C.A.): here the council's stated reasons were held to be defective because they did not indicate that the council had properly balanced the general housing conditions in Tower Hamlets against the applicants' own "pattern of life" and connections with the U.K.

[13] *Op. cit.* para. 2.16.

[14] *Ibid.*

[15] See particularly *Tickner* v. *Mole Valley D.C.* [1980] L.A.G. Bull. 187 (C.A.); *Goddard* v. *Torridge D.C.* [1982] L.A.G. Bull. 9; *R.* v. *Eastleigh B.C., ex p. Beattie* (*No.* 2) (1984) 17 H.L.R. 168 (D.C.); see also *Din* v. *Wandsworth L.B.C.* [1981] 3 All E.R. 881, 889 (H.L.); *R.* v. *L.B. of Wandsworth, ex p. Wells,* November 23, 1983 (D.C., unreported); *R.* v. *L.B. of Wandsworth ex p. Henderson* (1986) 18 H.L.R. 522, 527 (D.C.).

[16] See, *e.g. Krishnan* v. *Hillingdon L.B.C.* [1981] L.A.G. Bull. 137; *Galbraith* v. *Midlothian D.C.* [1979] S.C.O.L.A.G. 122; even where these statutory standards are not infringed, the conditions may still make it unreasonable for the applicant to continue to occupy: *R.* v. *Westminster C.C., ex p. Alouat* [1989] March Legal Action 21 (D.C.): family in occupation of cramped, but not statutorily overcrowded, two-bedroomed maisonette.

Westminster C.C., ex p. Ali[17] McCullough J. fou
that "anyone should regard it as reasonable tha
of the applicant, his wife and five children] sh
10 feet by 12 feet in size,"[18] and, as regards th
to the general housing circumstances in the area, he co
"[n]o evidence has been placed before me that accommodation
the area of the Westminster City Council is so desperately short that it is reasonable to accept overcrowding of this degree."[19]

(iv) Reasonableness issues unconnected with the condition of the accommodation. It is clear that in deciding whether it is reasonable for the applicant to continue to occupy his accommodation the authority must have regard, where appropriate, to matters other than merely those relating to the condition of the accommodation; in such cases the "general circumstances prevailing in relation to housing in the district" may well have to be a less relevant factor in the authority's decision.[20] 4.52

Violent domestic disputes. In the context of domestic disputes,[21] the Code suggests that it should never be regarded as reasonable for a battered woman to remain in the marital home.[22] The courts appear to have drawn a clear, if unrealistic, distinction between violent and non-violent domestic disputes. 4.53

Where the relationship has been or is likely to be violent, then it will normally be considered unreasonable for the victim to remain in the home with the other spouse or cohabitee, and the authority should not automatically find that it is reasonable for the victim to continue to occupy merely because he or she can seek a court order 4.54

[17] (1983) 11 H.L.R. 83 (D.C.).

[18] *Ibid.* at 93.

[19] *Ibid.*

[20] But *cf. R.* v. *Peterborough C.C., ex p. McKernan,* July 17, 1987 (D.C., unreported), where the general housing circumstances in Peterborough were given prominence in upholding a decision that it would have been reasonable for British families to remain in Northern Ireland, despite being subjected to persecution from the local community; see also *R.* v. *L.B. of Tower Hamlets, ex p. Monaf,* above, n. 12.

[21] For a general account of the homelessness implications of domestic violence, see, *e.g.* Womens Aid Federation, *Leaving Violent Men* (1981), Chap. 8; M. Bryan, [1984] J.S.W.L. 195; F. Logan, *Homelessness and Relationship Breakdown,* Brunel Socio–Legal Working Paper (1987), Chap. 5.

[22] *Op. cit.* para. 2.16.

against the other partner.[23] Even if a court order has been obtained against the other partner to restrain or exclude him, it may still not be reasonable to remain, since such orders are not necessarily obeyed: a representative of the National Women's Aid Federation has written that "a court order cannot prevent a man from battering the woman he lives with. Many men will defy a court order and repeatedly harass, attack or threaten to kill the woman."[24]

4.55 In cases of violence or threatened violence, section 58 of the 1985 Act contains a separate "deeming" provision whereby a person is "also homeless" even if he or she has accommodation, if "it is probable that occupation of it will lead to violence from some other person residing in it or to threats of violence from some other person residing in it and likely to carry out the threats"[25]; but in view of the general "reasonableness" criterion in section 58, this separate "deeming" provision should have little scope, since an applicant in fear of violence will not "ha[ve] accommodation" within the terms of the "deeming" provision at all, as it would not be reasonable to continue to occupy it.

4.56 In either case, however, the courts appear to require very clear evidence of violence or threats of violence,[26] in marked contrast both to the more flexible approach indicated by the Code (which asks authorities to "respond sympathetically to applications from women who are in fear of violence," pointing out that "the fact that violence has not yet occurred does not, on its own, suggest that it is not likely to occur"[27]), and to the more specific advice given in the Scottish Code of Guidance, which states:

[23] See, *e.g. R.* v. *L.B. of Ealing, ex p. Sidhu* (1982) 2 H.L.R. 45 (D.C.); *Charles* v. *Charles* [1984] Legal Action 81 (C.A.): here the court refused to give a battered wife an ouster injunction against her husband, because on the facts the injunction would expose her to further risk, and in a significant passage Dunn L.J. stated. " . . . it was reasonable . . . for this lady to leave . . . because of the husband's violence . . . it appears that this lady . . . is homeless . . . and could not be held to be intentionally homeless" (taken from LEXIS transcript); *Hammell* v. *R.B. of Kensington and Chelsea* (1988) 20 H.L.R. 666, 677 (C.A.); *R.* v. *Broxbourne B.C., ex p. Willmouth* [1988] December Legal Action 19 (D.C.).

[24] H. Watson, *Roof,* January 1981, p.4; see also *Leaving Violent Men, op. cit.* p. 86; *Charles* v. *Charles*, see above.

[25] H.A. 1985, s.58(3)(*b*), see below, paras. 4.89–4.91; see above, *e.g. Charles* v. *Charles*.

[26] See, *e.g. R.* v. *Purbeck D.C., ex p. Cadney* (1985) 17 H.L.R. 534 (D.C.), where the woman was held not to be homeless because her assertion of violence "was made late in her application to the [authority], and [was] not corroborated" (*per* Nolan J. at p. 538).

[27] *Op. cit.* para. 2.10b.

"It may . . . be impossible to obtain evidence in the usual forms and in such cases the woman's fears may be considered as sufficient evidence. If evidence of violence is available, perhaps from police sources, it would of course be relevant but its absence should not by itself result in the application being refused. In no circumstances should an applicant be required to provide evidence from her husband or any other person who may be the source of violence."[28]

Non-violent domestic disputes. Where there has been neither violence nor any threat of violence, then however unpleasant the relationship may be, it appears to be generally regarded as reasonable for the applicant to continue to occupy.[29] **4.57**

Pressures originating from outside the domestic sphere. With regard to difficulties outside the domestic sphere, it appears that, although authorities are not entitled completely to disregard harassment simply because it is "not domestic,"[30] the applicant can nevertheless be expected to put up even with situations where violence is threatened or actually used by third parties: it may be regarded as reasonable for the applicant to continue to occupy because the problems can be reported to the police,[31] or because the applicant is a council tenant who can seek relief by way of relocation with the authority's assistance.[32] **4.58**

[28] Para. 2.22(b).

[29] *R.* v. *Reigate & Banstead B.C., ex p. Henry,* December 16, 1982 (D.C., unreported): husband a heavy drinker, but no violence; *R.* v. *Wandsworth L.B.C., ex p. Nimako-Boateng* (1984) 14 Fam. Law 117 (D.C.): husband stayed away from home, sometimes for several days at a time, without giving wife any explanation, but again there was no violence; *R.* v. *Eastleigh B.C., ex p. Evans* (1986) 2 F.L.R. 195 (D.C.): general matrimonial difficulties, but no violence.

[30] *R.* v. *L.B. of Hillingdon, ex p. H* (1988) 20 H.L.R. 554 (D.C.) (threats by I.R.A.); *Hammell* v. *R.B. of Kensington and Chelsea* (1988) 20 H.L.R. 666 (C.A.) (violence from applicant's former husband, who lived nearby, held relevant to the s.58(2A) issue even though the violence emanated from outside applicant's home).

[31] *R.* v. *L.B. of Croydon, ex p. Toth* (1987) 20 H.L.R. 576 (C.A.): applicant threatened with violence by criminal associates of her husband; *R.* v. *Warwick D.C., ex p. Wood,* August 15, 1983 (D.C., unreported): applicants threatened with violence by gang armed with weapons; see also *Fezoui* v. *Torbay B.C.,* July 27, 1983 (C.A., unreported): threats from local children; *R.* v. *Peterborough C.C., ex p. McKernan,* July 17, 1987 (D.C., unreported): threats coupled with actual violence suffered by British families in Northern Ireland.

[32] *R.* v. *L.B. of Hillingdon, ex p. H,* see above.

4.59 *Possession claims by landlords and mortgagees.* A frequently litigated issue is whether it is reasonable for a tenant to continue to occupy accommodation after his landlord has sought possession.

4.60 If the landlord has actually obtained an unconditional possession order, then it is not normally regarded as reasonable for the tenant to stay any longer[33]: he does not have to await actual eviction by the bailiffs before it can be said that it is unreasonable for him to remain, so that he ranks as "homeless" even before his actual departure.

4.61 If the landlord has made clear to his tenant that he intends to seek possession, but the landlord has not yet obtained a possession order, then it seems that it will still not be reasonable for the tenant to continue to occupy if it is clear that there is no defence to the landlord's claim[34]; and a similar principle applies to an owner-occupying mortgagor who is inescapably faced with possession by his mortgagee because he has no chance of maintaining his mortgage instalments and discharging the arrears.[35] The mere fact that the occupier may have protection under the Protection from Eviction Act 1977[36] against eviction without a court order does not of itself make it reasonable for him to stay.[37]

4.62 Where, however, there is a viable defence to the threatened possession proceedings, then it will normally be reasonable for the occupier to continue in occupation and fight the possession claim[38]; he will not therefore rank as "homeless." Recent decisions[39] which have rendered it less easy for landowners to ensure that the occupiers of their properties do not enjoy statutory security of tenure by creating licences rather than tenancies, have increased the likelihood of an occupier having a viable defence, in which case he will not rank as homeless while he remains in occupation following the land-

[33] *R.* v. *Mole Valley D.C., ex p. Minnett* (1983) 12 H.L.R. 48 (D.C.).

[34] See, *e.g. Din* v. *Wandsworth L.B.C.* [1981] 3 All E.R. 881, 887 (H.L.); *R.* v. *Portsmouth C.C., ex p. Knight* (1983) 12 H.L.R. 60 (D.C.); *R.* v. *Surrey Heath B.C.,ex p. Li* (1984) 16 H.L.R. 79 (D.C.); *R.* v. *Exeter C.C., ex p. Gliddon and Draper* [1985] 1 All E.R. 493 (D.C.); Code, para. A.1.3.

[35] See Code, para. 2.15; *R.* v. *L.B. of Hillingdon, ex p. Tinn* (1988) 20 H.L.R. 305, 308 (D.C.) (in this case the mortgagor was held not to be homeless because she had not left the house; however, at that time the new s.58(2A) could not apply; had s.58(2A) applied, a decision of unintentional homelessness would surely have been reached).

[36] See below, paras. 4.84–4.85.

[37] *R.* v. *Portsmouth C.C., ex p. Knight*, see above.

[38] *Din* v. *Wandsworth L.B.C.* [1983] 1 A.C. 657 (H.L.); *R.* v. *Penwith D.C., ex p. Hughes* [1980] L.A.G. Bull. 188 (D.C.).

[39] Such as *Street* v. *Mountford* [1985] A.C. 809 (H.L.): see below, paras. 7.15–7.19.

owner's claim to possession (and the occupier may be regarded as intentionally homeless if he departs prior to a court order being obtained against him).

Other relevant "reasonableness" issues. Other matters which (on the particular facts) have been treated as indicating that it would be unreasonable for the applicant to continue to occupy his accommodation include the "custom and lifestyle" of his own community,[40] his "pattern of life,"[41] loss of entitlement to social security benefits,[42] imminent contravention of immigration rules,[43] and pressures relating to employment.[44] Where an immigrant has received refugee status from the Home Office, it cannot be regarded as reasonable for him to have continued to live in the country from which he has fled,[45] so that he was "homeless" even before he left (and no question of "intentional" homelessness can therefore arise). **4.63**

(v) Disregard of "crisis-type" accommodation. Quite apart from the statutory "reasonableness" criterion, there is a distinct set of cases deciding that temporary "crisis-type" accommodation does not rank as "accommodation" for the purposes of section 58, so that the applicant is "homeless" even while he has the right to occupy the accommodation and even though it may in a sense be reasonable for him to continue to occupy it; crisis-type accommodation has been held to include refuges for battered women,[46] and night shelters.[47] **4.64**

(c) *"Homelessness" and the family unit*

(i) The relevance of the family unit. It will be recalled that for the purposes of the definition of homelessness, a person is treated as having no accommodation if there is no accommodation which he, **4.65**

[40] *R.* v. *L.B. of Tower Hamlets, ex p. Monaf* (1987) 19 H.L.R. 577 (D.C.).
[41] *R.* v. *L.B. of Tower Hamlets, ex p. Monaf* (1988) 20 H.L.R. 529 (C.A.).
[42] *R.* v. *L.B. of Hammersmith & Fulham, ex p. Duro Rama* (1983) 81 L.G.R. 702 (D.C.); but *cf. R.* v. *L.B. of Tower Hamlets, ex p. Monaf* (1987) 19 H.L.R. 577, 586 (D.C.).
[43] *R.* v. *L.B. of Hillingdon, ex p. Wilson* (1983) 12 H.L.R. 61 (D.C.).
[44] See, *e.g. R.* v. *L.B. of Hammersmith & Fulham, ex p. Duro Rama,* above; *R.* v. *R.B. of Kensington and Chelsea, ex p. Cunha* (1988) 21 H.L.R. 16 (D.C.); problems concerning departure from accommodation for reasons of employment are discussed in more detail below, paras. 4.126–4.128, 4.160–4.162.
[45] *R.* v. *Crawley B.C., ex p. L.B. of Brent,* March 24, 1983 (D.C., unreported).
[46] *Williams* v. *Cynon Valley B.C.* [1980] L.A.G. Bull. 16 (Cty. Ct.); *R.* v. *L.B. of Ealing, ex p. Sidhu* (1982) 80 L.G.R. 534 (D.C.).
[47] *R.* v. *Waveney D.C., ex p. Bowers* [1983] Q.B. 238 (D.C.).

"together with any other person who normally resides with him as a member of his family or in circumstances in which it is reasonable for that person to reside with him," occupies or is entitled to occupy in one of the prescribed ways.[48] Thus, even though the applicant himself has accommodation which he occupies or is entitled to occupy, and which it is reasonable for him to continue to occupy, he may nevertheless be "homeless" for the purposes of this definition if he cannot reside there together with his family unit.

4.66 **(ii) Members of the family.** In order for a "member of [the applicant's] family" to be taken into account for the purposes of the first limb of this definition of the family unit, it is clear that there must have been some previous period of "normal residence" with the applicant. There is no relevant definition[49] of "member of [the applicant's] family" in the Act, although according to the Code the expression covers "not only established households where there is a blood or marriage relationship but also other circumstances where people are living together as if they were members of a family—*e.g.* cohabiting couples, or adults with foster-children."[50] The word "family" has been judicially described as "a popular and not a technical expression" which "may mean several different things."[51] The expression "member of the . . . family" is, nevertheless, used, and is similarly left undefined, in the Rent Act 1977,[52] and the considerable case law which has accrued regarding family membership in the Rent Act context may be helpful by analogy.

4.67 The Rent Act cases emphasise that the expression must be given its popular meaning, and so extends beyond strict blood and marriage relationships. It appears to have been established that:

> "children, including adopted, illegitimate and step-children qualify, as do brothers and sisters, including in-laws of a deceased tenant . . . nephews and nieces by blood or marriage, grandchildren, and persons to whom the deceased tenant was *in loco parentis*."[53]

With regard to heterosexual "cohabitees," some of the Rent Act

[48] H.A. 1985, s.58(2).
[49] The definition in *ibid.* s.113 is restricted to Pt. IV of the Act.
[50] *Op. cit.* para. 2.8.
[51] *Per* Wickens V.-C. in *Burt* v. *Hellyar* (1872) L.R. 14 Eq. 160, 164.
[52] Sched. 1 (dealing with statutory succession to protected or statutory tenancies on the death of the current tenant).
[53] D. Yates and A. J. Hawkins, *Landlord and Tenant Law* (2nd ed., 1986), pp. 440–441 (footnotes omitted).

cases are difficult to reconcile,[54] but the following propositions seem now to be established (for Rent Act purposes): a cohabitee of long standing qualifies, provided there has been a sexual relationship[55]; but a short-term cohabitee does not qualify, even though there has been a sexual relationship,[56] nor does a purely platonic cohabitee of however long standing[57]; yet cohabitees who would otherwise qualify can still be members of each other's family even though one or both of them is married to someone else, since a person can have two "families."[58]

It appears that homosexual cohabitees may not be covered, although the case which suggests this conclusion[59] was concerned with a specific statutory definition referring to persons who "live together as husband and wife."[60] **4.68**

(iii) Persons who may reasonably be expected to reside with the applicant. The second limb of the definition of family unit refers to "any other person . . . in circumstances in which it is reasonable for that person to reside with [the applicant]." If a person is a "member of [the applicant's] family" who "normally resides with him" then the first limb of the definition is satisfied and the question of whether it was reasonable for that person to have so resided with the applicant in the past, or whether it will be reasonable for him so to reside in the future, does not arise.[61] But even if the first limb is not satisfied, the second may be, for example in the case of people who do not rank as members of the family but whose residence with the applicant is considered reasonable, such as where "elderly or disabled people are accompanied by housekeepers or other companions."[62] **4.69**

[54] See, *e.g.* B. Berkovits, [1981] J.S.W.L. 83, who argues *inter alia* that as regards cohabitees the courts in Rent Act cases have over-emphasised the need for sexual union as a condition precedent for "family membership."

[55] *Dyson Holdings Ltd.* v. *Fox* [1975] 3 All E.R. 1030 (C.A.).

[56] *Helby* v. *Rafferty* [1979] 1 W.L.R. 13 (C.A.).

[57] *Carega Properties S.A.* v. *Sharratt* [1979] 1 W.L.R. 928 (H.L.).

[58] *Watson* v. *Lucas* [1980] 3 All E.R. 647 (C.A.).

[59] *Harrogate B.C.* v. *Simpson* [1986] 2 F.L.R. 91 (C.A.).

[60] H.A. 1985, s.113 (secure tenancies: see below, para. 9.31).

[61] See *R.* v. *Hillingdon Homeless Families Panel, ex p. Islam, The Times,* February 10, 1981 (D.C.).

[62] Code, *op. cit.* para. 2.8; *cf. Carega Properties S.A.* v. *Sharratt,* above (a Rent Act decision establishing that two adult former strangers living together platonically could never artificially establish a "familial nexus").

4.70 **(iv) Split families.** The second limb of the definition of family unit seems wide enough to cover those who have never resided with the applicant (even on a "non-normal" basis), but whose immediate residence with him is considered to be reasonable, since it appears that the "normal residence" requirement is only attached to the first limb of the definition, and not to the second.[63] There is some support for this interpretation in the case law,[64] and in the Code[65]; if correct, it would mean, for example, that a man and woman (married or unmarried[66]) who have dependent children, but who have no accommodation in which they can live together as a family unit, can apply as being "homeless" even though the respective parties are separately accommodated with each set of parents (neither set being able or willing to accommodate the whole family unit), and even though they have never yet been able to reside together in the same accommodation.

4.71 Even if "split families," whose individual members are separately housed, are not "homeless" (because the "normal residence" requirement is interpreted as attaching to both limbs of the definition), the applicant member can, of course, undoubtedly render himself statutorily "homeless" by throwing up his existing accommodation; this homelessness will not be intentional, because he will not have left accommodation which was "available for his occupation,"[67] since the accommodation was not "available for occupation both by him and by any other person who might reasonably be expected to reside with him."[68] However, this approach is undesirable in practice, because it requires the applicant to "burn his boats" by throwing up his individual unit of accommodation, a course which will frequently give rise to uncertainty and stress; there is also the problem that some authorities take a tough line in deciding issues of intentional homelessness.[69]

63 See D.C. Hoath, [1987] J.S.W.L. 15; *cf.* however Andrew Arden, *Homeless Persons—The Housing Act 1985, Part III* (2nd ed., 1986), paras. 4.23–4.24, 4.27, 6.92–6.93.
64 *R.* v. *Westminster C.C., ex p. Chambers* (1982) 6 H.L.R. 24, 30 (D.C.); *R.* v. *Preseli D.C., ex p. Fisher* (1984) 17 H.L.R. 147, 157 (D.C.).
65 *Op. cit.* para. 2.8.
66 See *R.* v. *Wimbourne D.C., ex p. Curtis* (1985) 18 L.G.R. 401 (D.C.).
67 H.A. 1985, s.60(1); see below, paras. 4.148–4.153.
68 *Ibid.* s.75; see above, *R.* v. *Wimbourne D.C., ex p. Curtis*; *Islam* v. *L.B. of Hillingdon* [1981] 1 A.C. 688 (H.L.); see below, paras. 4.149–4.151.
69 See below, para. 4.115.

(d) *Legal rights of occupation within section 58(2)*

As noted earlier,[70] the definition of homelessness in section 58 states, in effect, that a person is treated as having no accommodation if there is no accommodation which he (together with his family unit) occupies or is entitled to occupy in one of the following ways: **4.72**

- — entitlement to occupy by virtue of an interest or a court order;
- — possession of an express or implied licence to occupy;
- — occupation by virtue of any enactment or rule of law giving him the right to remain or restricting the right of another person to recover possession.

Thus the mere fact that the applicant has a roof over his head, affording shelter to himself and his family unit, does not prevent him from being "homeless" if he does not occupy and is not entitled to occupy in one of these ways. For example, a pure squatter who is occupying a house with his family unit would rank as "homeless," even if it could be said to be reasonable[71] for him to continue to occupy the house (because, say, the owner has made no demand for possession[72]); for the squatter's occupation does not fall within any of the prescribed categories.[73] **4.73**

It is necessary to examine each of these categories of occupation with some care. **4.74**

(i) Entitlement to occupy "by virtue of an interest . . . or by virtue of an order of a court." Owner-occupiers and contractual tenants will obviously have an "interest" for these purposes; moreover, the Housing Acts of 1985 and 1988 provide for the artificial continuation of the contractual tenancy of a "secure" public sector tenant and of an "assured" private sector tenant right up until the date on which he is due to give up possession in pursuance of a court possession order.[74] **4.75**

An entitlement to occupy by virtue of a court order, although there is no "interest" in the property, would arise for example in the **4.76**

[70] See above, para. 4.41.

[71] So that he is not treated as having no accommodation under the separate provision in H.A. 1985, s.58(2A), see above.

[72] See above, paras. 4.59–4.62.

[73] See *Hemmings* v. *Stoke Poges Golf Club Ltd.* [1920] 1 K.B. 720 (C.A.); *McPhail* v. *Persons Unknown* [1973] Ch. 447 (C.A.); *R.* v. *Phekoo* [1981] 1 W.L.R. 1117 (C.A.); Criminal Law Act 1977, s.6(3).

[74] H.A. 1985, ss.82, 86 (see below, paras. 8.12, 8.14); H.A. 1988, ss.5(1), 7(7).

following cases: under the Matrimonial Homes Act 1983,[75] where the High Court or a county court makes an order authorising a non-occupying and non-owning spouse to enter and occupy the matrimonial home; under the Domestic Violence and Matrimonial Proceedings Act 1976,[76] where a county court makes an order authorising a non-occupying and non-owning spouse or cohabitee to enter and remain in the family home; and under the Domestic Proceedings and Magistrates' Courts Act 1978,[77] where a magistrates' court makes an order authorising a non-occupying and non-owning spouse to enter and remain in the matrimonial home.

4.77 **(ii) Possession[78] of an "express or implied licence to occupy."** A licence is a right to use land in circumstances which would otherwise constitute a trespass, but it normally does not confer any proprietary interest, and is therefore distinguishable from a lease,[79] although it is not always easy to decide whether a particular relationship is a licence or a lease.[80] Although certain licensees of public bodies are to be treated[81] as secure tenants for the purposes of Part IV of the Housing Act 1985, this does not affect the construction of Part III of the Act, so that such an occupier must be treated, while his licence lasts, as a licensee without an interest in the property for the purposes of the definition of "homelessness."

4.78 The most common example of a licence in the present context is where a person shares accommodation with relatives or friends on an informal basis. Such licences are normally revocable by notice, and the notice will normally become operative upon the expiry of a reasonable "packing-up period" following service of the notice.[82] After the licence has been duly ended, then assuming the licensee held an "excluded licence" there will normally be no statutory right

[75] M.H.A. 1983 s.1(1)(*b*); see below, paras. 11.12–11.16.
[76] D.V.M.P.A. 1976, s.1(1)(*d*), (2); see below, paras. 11.17–11.19, 11.21.
[77] D.P.M.C.A. 1978, s.16(4); see below, para. 11.20.
[78] H.A. 1985, s.58(2)(*b*) uses the words "*has* an express or implied licence to occupy," thus the mere fact that the applicant has been *offered* a licence to occupy, which he *refuses to accept,* will not cause his "homelessness" to cease: *R.* v. *Kensington & Chelsea L.B.C., ex p. Minton* (1988) 20 H.L.R. 648 (D.C.).
[79] See, *e.g.* A. Arden and M. Partington, *Housing Law* (1983), pp. 48–62.
[80] See below, paras. 7.15–7.24.
[81] Under H.A. 1985, s.79(3); see below, para. 7.15.
[82] *Minister of Health* v. *Bellotti* [1944] K.B. 298 (C.A.); but see P.f.E.A. 1977, s.5(1)–(1A): below, para. 8.81, nn. 6 and 7.

for him to remain,[83] nor any right to remain pursuant to a court order,[84] so that the former licensee will then be "homeless" even though he may not be "roofless"; indeed, he may now rank as "homeless" immediately after receiving a notice to quit, and before the notice expires, since it may no longer be reasonable for him to continue to occupy the accommodation.[85] The unwillingness or inability of relatives or friends to continue to accommodate applicants is a very common cause of homelessness.

However, certain types of *contractual* licence are not revocable at the whim of the licensor[86]; in such cases, attempts at premature revocation by the licensor will be ineffective, and the licensee will not be "homeless." Moreover, certain "licences" may in fact give rise to proprietary interests under the aegis of a proprietary estoppel, or a resulting or constructive trust[87]; where such proprietary interests arise, the occupier may properly be said to be "entitled to occupy by virtue of an *interest*" within the first category (above), and will not therefore rank as "homeless." **4.79**

Where the licence relates to purely "crisis-type" housing, this will not rank as "accommodation" for the purposes of section 58, so that the applicant is "homeless" even while the licence is on foot[88]; however, the mere fact that a licence is of a temporary nature will not of itself prevent the applicant having "accommodation" for these purposes.[89] **4.80**

[83] P.f.E.A. 1977, ss.3(2B), 3A; former *non*-excluded licensees have statutory protection against eviction without a court order, as do certain former "restricted contract licensees" and former "service occupiers" (*ibid.* ss.3(2A)–(2B), 3A, 8(2)); see below, paras. 4.81, 4.84–4.85.

[84] *Cf.* R.A. 1977, ss.19, 106A, whereby the court may give certain former "restricted contract licensees" up to three months' security of tenure; however, it is not generally possible to create new "restricted contracts" after January 15, 1989: H.A. 1988, s.36.

[85] H.A. 1985, s.58(2A), see above.

[86] See, *e.g. Tanner* v. *Tanner* [1975] 1 W.L.R. 1346 (C.A.); *Hardwick* v. *Johnson* [1978] 1 W.L.R. 683 (C.A.).

[87] See, *e.g. Eves* v. *Eves* [1975] 3 All E.R. 768 (C.A.); *Re Sharpe* [1980] 1 W.L.R. 219; *Midland Bank Ltd.* v. *Farmpride Hatcheries Ltd.* (1980) 260 E.G. 493 (C.A.); *Grant* v. *Edwards* [1986] Ch. 638 (C.A.); *Re Basham* (*deceased*) [1987] 1 W.L.R. 1498. For a full discussion of the many difficulties arising out of the relationship between licences and trusts, see, *e.g. Hanbury and Maudsley's Modern Equity* (12th ed., 1985), Chap. 27.

[88] *R.* v. *Waveney D.C., ex p. Bowers,* [1983] Q.B. 238 (D.C.); see above, para. 4.64.

[89] See *Din* v. *Wandsworth L.B.C.* [1981] 3 All E.R. 881, 899 (H.L.), where Lord Bridge thought that the applicants, while living as licensees in temporary accommodation with a relative, "had at least an express or implied licence to occupy the accommodation . . . and therefore were not 'homeless' within the definition"; but *cf.* Lord Lowry at p. 894.

4.81 **(iii) Occupation "by virtue of any enactment or rule of law giving . . . the right to remain in occupation or restricting the right of another person to recover possession."** This category is concerned with actual *occupation,* rather than with rights to occupy. Thus an applicant who does not fall within one of the other categories, and who is merely *entitled* to occupy the accommodation by virtue of a relevant enactment or rule of law, but who does not actually occupy the accommodation, will rank as "homeless" despite the entitlement to occupy.

4.82 A basic knowledge of landlord and tenant law is helpful here. An example of an "enactment" which both confers a right to remain in occupation and restricts the right of some other person to recover possession for these purposes would be the provisions in the Rent Act 1977 dealing with *statutory* tenants: a statutory tenancy can only arise after the termination of a protected, (*i.e.* contractual) tenancy,[90] and it does not confer a proprietary interest but rather a "status of irremovability"[91] entitling the tenant to remain in occupation unless the court orders him to leave on one or more of certain specified grounds.[92] Thus a statutory tenant does not fall within the category of entitlement to occupy by virtue of an interest or court order (above), unless an order for possession has been made but he remains in occupation, for example because the date for giving up possession has been postponed, or execution of the order has been stayed or suspended.[93]

4.83 Another example of an "enactment" which both confers a right to remain in occupation and restricts the right of some other person to recover possession for these purposes is the Matrimonial Homes Act

[90] R.A. 1977, ss.1–3; it is not normally possible to create new protected tenancies after January 15, 1989: H.A. 1988, s.34.

[91] See, *e.g. Keeves* v. *Dean* [1924] 1 K.B. 685, 686 (C.A.).

[92] R.A. 1977, s.98; *cf.* however *Dyson* v. *Kerrier D.C.* [1980] 3 All E.R. 313, 317 (C.A.), where the implications of H.A. 1985, s.58(2) for statutory tenants appear to have been overlooked.

[93] R.A. 1977, s.100 (2); it appears that a statutory tenant can remain such even after the issue of a warrant of possession by the court, and that only an eviction under the warrant by the appropriate court officers can determine the statutory tenancy where the tenant remains in occupation: *Kyriacou* v. *Pandeli* [1980] C.L.Y. 1648 (Cty. Ct.); thus after the court makes the possession order and before such lawful eviction, the occupier is entitled to occupy by virtue of a court order, and also occupies by virtue of an enactment, and is clearly not "homeless" within H.A. 1985, s.58(2) (but see the discussion of H.A. 1985, s.58(2A) at paras. 4.59–4.60 above).

1983, which gives a spouse who has no beneficial interest[94] in the matrimonial home, but who is currently in occupation of it, the right "not to be evicted or excluded from the dwelling house or any part thereof by the other spouse except with the leave of the court,"[95] which is expressly described as a "right of occupation."[96] We have seen that if the spouse without any beneficial interest is not in occupation of the matrimonial home, he or she only has the right to enter and occupy it under the Matrimonial Homes Act with the leave of the court, in which case he or she will fall within the first category of section 58(2) of the 1985 Act as being entitled to occupy by virtue of "an order of a court," and will not be "homeless" for that quite separate reason.[97]

An example[98] of an "enactment" which simply "restrict[s] the right of another person to recover possession" of accommodation for these purposes, without actually conferring any entitlement to occupy, is section 3(1) of the Protection from Eviction Act 1977: this provides that where premises have been let under a tenancy which was neither a "statutorily protected tenancy,"[99] nor an "excluded tenancy,"[1] and the tenancy has ended, but the occupier continues to reside in the premises, then "it shall not be lawful for the owner to enforce against the occupier, otherwise than by proceedings in the court, his right to recover possession of the premises." Thus former tenants who are "holding over" (otherwise than as statutory tenants under the Rent Act 1977 or as former assured tenants under the Housing Act 1988) are nevertheless normally protected against eviction without a court order, and are therefore not "homeless" within section 58(2) of the Housing Act 1985 even though they no longer have a proprietary interest in the property. They may now, however, be "homeless" under the separate provision in section 58(2A), since it may not be considered that they have accommodation "which it would be reasonable for [them] to continue to occupy."[2] **4.84**

[94] Statutory "rights of occupation" are in fact conferred by the 1983 Act on spouses even though they have beneficial interests (s.1(11)), but for the purposes of the definition of homelessness in Pt. III of the Housing Act such a spouse would fall within the first category (above), being entitled to occupy by virtue of that interest.

[95] M.H.A. 1983, s.1(1)(*a*); see below, paras. 11.12–11.16.

[96] *Ibid.* s.1(1).

[97] See above, para. 4.76.

[98] See *R.* v. *Portsmouth C.C., ex p. Knight* (1983) 10 H.L.R. 115, 119 (D.C.).

[99] This expression covers *inter alia* protected tenancies under R.A. 1977 and assured tenancies under H.A. 1988 (see P.f.E.A. 1977, s.8(1)).

[1] As defined in P.f.E.A. 1977, s.3A.

[2] See above, paras. 4.59–4.62.

4.85 Similar protection against eviction without a court order is extended by the Protection from Eviction Act 1977 to certain former licensees[3]; again, however, such occupiers may now be "homeless" under section 58(2A) of the 1985 Act.[4] Former licensees who remain in occupation and who do not fall within these special provisions in the Protection from Eviction Act will not be occupying by virtue of "any enactment" for these purposes,[5] and will therefore be "homeless" under the terms of section 58(2) of the 1985 Act.

4.86 Examples of "rules of law" (as opposed to "enactments") which confer the right to remain in occupation and/or restrict the right of some other person to recover possession, within the terms of section 58(2), are rather more difficult to find. It has been held[6] that an infant child, however young, has no entitlement by virtue of any "rule of law" to occupy its parents' house, but merely has a revocable licence (together, of course, with rights to be financially maintained). However, a wife has a common law right to be provided with a roof over her head by her husband[7]; this is a personal right, which is not referable to any implied licence,[8] and can properly be considered to arise under a "rule of law" for present purposes, although in practice, of course, this common law right has been largely eclipsed by the statutory rights of occupation conferred by the Matrimonial Homes Act 1983, which ranks as an "enactment" for the purposes of section 58(2) of the 1985 Act.

(e) *"Deemed homelessness" under section 58(3)*

4.87 A further special meaning of the word "homeless" as used in Part III of the 1985 Act is provided by section 58(3), under which an applicant in the circumstances specified is regarded as "homeless" even though he has "accommodation" for the purposes of section 58(1)–(2B), discussed above.

[3] See above, para. 4.78 and n. 83.
[4] See above, paras. 4.59–4.62; *R.* v. *Portsmouth C.C., ex p. Knight,* above.
[5] See *R.* v. *Blankley* [1979] Crim.L.R. 166; it is not thought that the limited protection against violent entry afforded by Criminal Law Act 1977, s.6(1), suffices as a relevant "enactment": see *R.* v. *Phekoo* [1981] 1 W.L.R. 1117 (C.A.).
[6] *Metropolitan Properties Co.* v. *Cronan* (1982) 126 S.J. 229 (C.A.) (child aged seven); see also *Egan* v. *Egan* [1975] Ch. 218.
[7] *Gurasz* v. *Gurasz* [1969] 3 All E.R. 822, 823 (C.A.).
[8] *National Provincial Bank Ltd.* v. *Ainsworth* [1965] 2 All E.R. 472, 485 (H.L.); *Hall* v. *King* (1987) 19 H.L.R. 440, 443 (C.A.).

(i) Inability to secure entry. Under section 58(3)(*a*), a person is "also homeless" if he "cannot secure entry" to his accommodation, even though he may still have the legal right to occupy it under section 58(2) and even though it is reasonable for him to continue to occupy it under section 58(2A)–(2B). This would clearly cover an illegally evicted tenant,[9] or an owner-occupier who is excluded from his accommodation by squatters.[10] **4.88**

(ii) Probability of occupation leading to violence or threats of violence from some other resident. Under section 58(3)(*b*), a person is "also homeless," even though he has accommodation to which he can gain entry, if: **4.89**

> "it is probable that occupation of it will lead to violence from some other person residing in it or to threats of violence from some other person residing in it and likely to carry out the threats."

Originally, this provision was seen to be particularly appropriate for "battered women,"[11] who may well have a legal right to occupy the family home,[12] but who may be frightened to exercise that right. However, the introduction of the "reasonableness" criterion into the definition of homelessness through section 58(2A)–(2B)[13] means that battered women, and those clearly at risk of violence, should now be treated as "not having accommodation" since it would not be reasonable for them to continue to occupy; it follows that section 58(3)(*b*) cannot apply, since they will not " have accommodation" for the purposes of section 58. The relationship between domestic violence and the definition of homelessness has therefore already been discussed in the particular context of the "reasonableness" criterion.[14] **4.90**

As regards section 58(3)(*b*), it appears that the person likely to cause the violence or to make the threats of violence must actually be residing in the applicant's accommodation, since the repeated use of the word "it" seemingly refers exclusively to such accommodation. For example, a tenant who is frightened to return to his accommo- **4.91**

[9] See *Islam* v. *Hillingdon L.B.C.* [1981] 1 A.C. 688 (H.L.).

[10] In this situation both the owner-occupier and the squatters would rank as "homeless": see above, para. 4.73.

[11] See Code, para. 2.12ciii.

[12] See above, paras. 4.75–4.76, 4.83.

[13] See above, paras. 4.42–4.48.

[14] See above, paras. 4.53–4.56.

dation because of violence or threats of violence from his landlord would not be "homeless" under section 58(3)(*b*), because the landlord, even if resident in the same building, would not be residing in the separate accommodation let to the tenant (exclusive possession being essential for a tenancy); in such a situation, however, it may not be reasonable for the tenant to continue in occupation, so that he may be treated as "homeless" under the separate definition in section 58(2A). It thus appears that the relevant violence or threats of violence for the purposes of section 58(3)(*b*) must be likely to emanate either directly from some other resident, or from another person (even though not himself a resident) who is acting on that resident's behalf.[15]

4.92 **(iii) Inability to find suitable location for movable structure, vehicle or vessel.** Section 58(3)(*c*) provides that a person is "also homeless" if he has accommodation consisting of a "movable structure, vehicle or vessel designed or adapted for human habitation," but there is "no place where he is entitled or permitted both to place it and to reside in it."

(f) *"Threatened" homelessness under section 58(4)*

4.93 Quite separately from the definition of "homelessness" in section 58(1)–(3), section 58(4) introduces the concept of "threatened" homelessness. A person is "threatened with homelessness" if it is "likely that he will become homeless within 28 days." This definition originally covered, for example, applicants who had been asked to leave by friends or relatives with whom they had been staying; and in such cases, the Code stated that authorities should not require possession orders to be obtained against the applicants.[16] Similarly, the Code advised that an applicant whose landlord was seeking possession should be treated as threatened with homelessness if it was clear that there was no defence to the landlord's claim, and, again, the authority should not insist on a possession order in such a situation.[17]

4.94 However, since the introduction of the reasonableness criterion into the definition of homelessness, it will frequently be unreason-

[15] In accordance with the principle, *qui facit per alium, facit per se.*

[16] *Op. cit.* para. A1.10.

[17] *Op. cit.* para. A1.3; see further *Goddard* v. *Torridge D.C.* [1982] L.A.G. Bull. 9; *Din* v. *Wandsworth L.B.C.* [1981] 3 All E.R. 881, at 895, 900 (H.L.); *Dyson* v. *Kerrier D.C.* [1980] 3 All E.R. 313, 317 (C.A.).

able for someone to continue to occupy his accommodation if he is likely to lose it within 28 days[18]; in such a situation (for example, that of an applicant who is a tenant holding over after expiry of a notice to quit and facing a clear demand for possession from his landlord, to which there is no defence), the applicant will already be "homeless" (even while remaining in occupation) since he is not to be treated as having "accommodation," and therefore, on this analysis, there is no question of it being "likely that he *will* become homeless" within the terms of section 58(4). The concept of "homelessness" is distinct from that of "threatened homelessness," and, as we have seen, the two concepts frequently attract differing duties on the part of authorities[19]; yet the distinction between the two concepts has undoubtedly become somewhat blurred following the introduction of the "reasonableness" criterion into the definition of homelessness.

Where the applicant is neither homeless nor threatened with homelessness, but "the possibility of [him] becoming homeless is known . . . more than 28 days in advance," then the Code asks the authority to be "ready to advise and assist," since "[t]he earlier action can be taken, the greater is the likelihood that measures to avert homelessness can be effective," and "[a]uthorities will wish to avoid adding the stress of uncertainty to existing stress."[20] Specific guidance is also contained in the Code relating to the advance action which should be taken by authorities in order to help ex-service personnel and their dependants where it is known that they will be leaving service quarters within the next six months.[21] **4.95**

4. *"Priority Need"*

We have seen[22] that the major duties towards homeless applicants can only arise where they have a "priority need." Many authorities are reluctant to accept responsibility for applicants falling outside the priority need categories. **4.96**

Priority need is defined by section 59(1), which covers (broadly speaking) cases of pregnancy, dependent children, vulnerability, and emergency. These four categories will now be considered in more detail. **4.97**

18 See discussion of H.A. 1985, s.58(2A); above, paras. 4.59–4.62.
19 See above, paras. 4.07–4.15.
20 *Op. cit.* para. 2.11.
21 *Op. cit.* paras. A1.17–A1.19.
22 See above, paras. 4.05–4.15.

(a) *Pregnancy*

4.98 The applicant has a priority need if she is pregnant, or he or she is a person with whom a pregnant woman resides or might reasonably be expected to reside.[23] It follows that a single man who has made a girl pregnant can himself apply to the authority as a person with a priority need if he intends to live with the girl, even if he has never lived with her before (unless, presumably, she is under 16, in which case he might not "reasonably be expected" to reside with her, in view of the fact that intercourse with a girl under 16 is normally a criminal offence[24]). Of course, if in this situation the pregnant girl is the applicant, she has a priority need in her own right, and accommodation must normally be offered in which she can reside with the father of the child also, under section 75[25] (unless, once again, she is under 16, when the father might not "reasonably be expected to reside" with her according to the terms of section 75).

4.99 The Code makes it clear that pregnant women are in priority need "irrespective of the length of time they have been pregnant."[26] The question of priority need has to be determined at the date when the authority makes its decision.[27] Thus if a pregnant woman loses the child she is carrying after making her application but before the authority's decision, the authority can treat her as not being in priority need at the relevant time (provided of course that she does not fall within one of the other categories, such as "vulnerability"); and if she were to fail to inform the authority of the termination of her pregnancy before receipt of the notification of its decision, she may be guilty of the offence of failing to notify the authority of any change in the material facts.[28]

(b) *Dependent children*

4.100 Priority need also arises where dependent children reside with the applicant, or might reasonably be expected to do so.[29] This seems to be the most common category of priority need. The Code states that

[23] H.A. 1985, s.59(1)(*a*).
[24] Sexual Offences Act 1956, s.6.
[25] See below, paras. 5.65–5.67, and *R.* v. *Wimbourne D.C., ex p. Curtis* (1985) 18 H.L.R. 79 (D.C.).
[26] *Op. cit.* para. 2.12.d.
[27] *R.* v. *Hillingdon Homeless Families Panel, ex p. Islam, The Times,* February 10, 1981 (D.C.).
[28] H.A. 1985, s.74(2)–(3), see above, para. 4.37.
[29] *Ibid.* s.59(1)(*b*).

this category extends to one-parent families, including battered women with their children, and that child custody orders should not be required.[30] Although the Act contains no definition of "dependent" children, the Code advises authorities to treat as dependants *all* children under 16, and others under 19 who are receiving full-time education or training or are otherwise unable to support themselves[31]; the Code further points out that the children need not be those of the applicant, but may for example be his grandchildren, adopted children or foster-children.[32]

With regard to the requirement that the dependent children must be those who *either* "reside" with the applicant *or* who "might reasonably be expected to reside" with him, it is clear that the applicant can establish a priority need even though the children are not actually living with him at the time, as in the case of a "split" family whose children are temporarily staying with other relatives.[33] Furthermore, if the applicant's children are already residing with him, the authority cannot decide that it is not reasonable for them to reside with him: the word "or"[34] is not to be interpreted as meaning "and."[35] As already mentioned, the question of priority need has to be decided in the light of the facts current at the date when the council makes its decision, rather than by reference to past history[36]; and if there are dependent children who live with the applicant (or who might reasonably be expected to reside with him) at the date of the decision, then there is no additional requirement that the authority must be satisfied that this situation will continue: the authority cannot therefore delay its inquiries simply in order to ensure that the situation does not subsequently change.[37] Thus the issue of dependent children is normally crystallised at the moment when the decision of the authority falls to be made. **4.101**

[30] *Op.cit.* para. 2.12; see also *R.* v. *L.B. of Ealing, ex p. Sidhu* (1983) 80 L.G.R. 534 (D.C.), confirming that it is "wholly inappropriate" for an authority to require custody orders in these cases.

[31] *Loc. cit.;* children aged 16 or 17 will not normally receive income support, but are generally required to attend full–time training schemes, for which they are paid; if they do *not* attend such schemes, then, because they will not in general be receiving income support either, they should be treated as "unable to support themselves" for priority need purposes.

[32] *Loc. cit.*

[33] See Code, *loc. cit.*

[34] In H.A. 1985, s.59(1)(*b*).

[35] *R.* v. *Hillingdon Homeless Families Panel, ex p. Islam* (D.C.), see above.

[36] *Ibid.*

[37] *R.* v. *L.B. of Ealing, ex p. Sidhu,* see above.

(c) *Vulnerability*

4.102 The third category of priority need is concerned with vulnerability: an applicant is in priority need if he is "vulnerable as a result of old age, mental illness or handicap or physical disability or other special reason," or such a person resides or might reasonably be expected to reside with him.[38]

4.103 This category clearly extends beyond families. "Vulnerability" is to be assessed in the context of housing,[39] and has been judicially defined as meaning "less able to fend for oneself [when homeless or in finding and keeping accommodation] so that injury or detriment will result when a less vulnerable man will be able to cope without harmful effects."[40]

4.104 As regards "old age," the Code asks authorities to treat as vulnerable those above the normal retiring age (65 for a man, 60 for a woman), and also any others approaching normal retiring age who are "particularly frail or in poor health" or are otherwise vulnerable.[41]

4.105 Turning to the words "mental illness or handicap," the Act is here drawing a distinction between mental illness which is psychotic, and mental handicap which can exist without the presence of illness and is concerned with subnormality.[42]

4.106 The Code seeks to define the statutory reference to "disability" as meaning "substantial disability"[43]; but the courts have refused to accept this "substantiality" qualification, since the section itself expressly omits it.[44] Difficult questions of degree can arise in considering whether someone suffering from AIDS has a priority need.[45]

4.107 With regard to the "other special reason" limb of this "vulnerability" category, the Code states[46] that this should include "battered

[38] H.A. 1985, s.59(1)(*c*).
[39] *R.* v. *Bath C.C., ex p. Sangermano* (1984) 17 H.L.R. 94 (D.C.).
[40] *R.* v. *Waveney D.C., ex p. Bowers* [1982] 3 All E.R. 727, 730 (C.A., *per* Waller L.J.); the words in parentheses were added by Webster J. in *R.* v. *Lambeth L.B.C., ex p. Carroll* (1988) 20 H.L.R. 142, 146 (D.C.).
[41] *Op. cit.* para. 2.12.
[42] *R.* v. *Bath C.C., ex p. Sangermano,* see above.
[43] *Op. cit.* para. 2.12 c ii.
[44] *R.* v. *Lambeth L.B.C., ex p. Carroll, ibid.* at 145.
[45] See R. Jeffery and G. Popplestone, *Roof,* March 1988, pp. 38, 39; M. Barratt, *Roof,* November 1988, p. 38; the "other special reason" category may also be relevant in AIDS cases.
[46] *Op. cit.* para. 2.12.

women without children who are at risk of violent pursuit or, if they return home, at risk of further violence," and also "homeless young people who are at risk of sexual or financial exploitation." The housing problems experienced by homeless young people have been widely documented.[47] It is clear from the case law that in order for such young people to demonstrate vulnerability it suffices for priority need purposes that there is a risk of sexual or financial exploitation of the young person in question[48]; actual exploitation does not need to have taken place, and the views of a social worker may be particularly helpful.[49] However, each case depends on its facts: not all homeless young people are vulnerable, and the locality may be relevant.[50]

Where the circumstances of the particular case are appropriate, there may be an overlap between the specific factors laid down in the Act as giving rise to vulnerability ("old age, mental illness or handicap or physical disability") and the general factor of vulnerability on the ground of "other special reason": thus in one case[51] where the applicant suffered from a long-standing drink problem and from a residual disability following brain surgery after a road accident, the court decided that although the alcoholism would not (on the facts) have sufficed for vulnerability purposes, the brain injury itself did give rise to vulnerability, and it was immaterial whether this was regarded as "mental . . . handicap" or as falling within the "other special reason" category; and in a later decision,[52] where the applicant was of subnormal intelligence (though no treatment was warranted), it was held on the facts that no reasonable authority could have concluded that the applicant was other than vulnerable, either because of "mental . . . handicap" or because of some "other special reason" (being a combination of her mental handicap together with extreme language difficulties, although these language difficulties **4.108**

[47] See, *e.g.* the Report of the Working Group on *Homeless Young People,* D.H.S.S. (1976); in the particular context of those leaving children's homes, it is relevant to note that under the Child Care Act 1980, s.27(1), social services authorities have specific powers to provide financial assistance towards the cost of the accommodation and maintenance of children leaving care.

[48] *Kelly* v. *Monklands D.C.* 1986 S.L.T. 169 (Ct. of Session: O.H.).

[49] *Ibid.*

[50] Thus in *Crichton* v. *Harrogate B.C.* 1980 (Cty. Ct., unreported) the applicant was a 17–year–old girl living in a tent in Harrogate; the authority's decision of no priority need was upheld because the authority had properly addressed itself to the risk of exploitation.

[51] *R.* v. *Waveney D.C., ex p. Bowers* [1983] Q.B. 238 (C.A.).

[52] *R.* v. *Bath C.C., ex p. Sangermano* (1984) 17 H.L.R. 94 (C.A.).

would not have sufficed as "special reasons" on their own). People who are vulnerable may also come within the separate accommodation duties imposed on social services authorities by the National Assistance Act 1948.[53]

4.109 The courts have emphasised the importance of guidance given in the Code (and discussed above) on the question of vulnerability.[54]

4.110 Medical evidence can clearly be of very great assistance in deciding issues of vulnerability. Where such expert evidence is presented on the applicant's behalf, the authority must either accept it or pursue its own specialist inquiries,[55] for example through its own Medical Officer of Health or equivalent officer; in an appropriate case, the council might also need to obtain the opinion of someone with expertise in the field of housing and social welfare.[56] If the authority obtains its own medical report, it may in an appropriate case rely on that report in preference to that produced by the applicant's own medical advisers,[57] but the decision on vulnerability in the context of Part III of the Housing Act must be taken by the council itself and not by its medical adviser as such (in other words, the council's expert has an advisory role, and the council should not merely "rubber-stamp" his opinion).[58]

(d) *Emergency*

4.111 The final category of priority need arises where a person is "homeless or threatened with homelessness as a result of an emergency such as flood, fire or other disaster."[59] It seems that the contemplated disasters are restricted to the "Act of God" variety.[60] Thus the enforcement by a council of a demolition order on the applicant's property was held not to fall within the category of "disaster" for priority need purposes[61]; furthermore, an eviction through

[53] N.A.A. 1948, s.21(1)(*a*): see above, paras. 2.05–2.11.

[54] See above, *Kelly* v. *Monklands D.C.; R.* v. *Waveney D.C., ex p. Bowers.*

[55] *R.* v. *Bath C.C., ex p. Sangermano,* see above.

[56] *R.* v. *Lambeth L.B.C., ex p. Carroll,* see above.

[57] *R.* v. *Tandridge D.C., ex p. Hayman,* September 29, 1983 (D.C., unreported); *R.* v. *Reigate and Banstead B.C., ex p. Di Dominico* (1988) 20 H.L.R. 153 (D.C.).

[58] *R.* v. *Tandridge D.C., ex p. Hayman,* see above; *R.* v. *Wandsworth L.B.C., ex. p. Banbury* (1987) 19 H.L.R. 76 (D.C.); *R.* v. *Lambeth L.B.C., ex p. Carroll,* see above.

[59] H.A. 1985, s.59(1)(*d*).

[60] See, *e.g. R.* v. *L.B. of Camden, ex p. Wait* (1986) 18 H.L.R. 434 (D.C.): fire.

[61] *Noble* v. *South Herefordshire D.C.* (1984) 17 H.L.R. 80 (C.A.): here the applicants had moved into the property after the demolition order had been made, and were therefore ineligible for rehousing under the Land Compensation Act 1973, see s.39(6), discussed above, para. 2.33.

the courts pursuant to a possession order will clearly not count as a disaster,[62] although an illegal eviction may suffice for priority need.[63]

The Code points out[64] that in "larger scale emergencies" the housing authority may discharge its obligations by providing special forms of temporary accommodation in church halls, schools, etc. pursuant to separate powers in the Local Government Act 1972[65] (covering "an emergency or disaster involving destruction of or danger to life or property"). **4.112**

(e) *Changes to the categories of priority need*

Changes to the priority need categories can be achieved relatively swiftly: the Minister may by order specify further categories of priority need, or alter or remove any of the existing categories.[66] At present, the main omission from the categories of priority need is the non-vulnerable single homeless person.[67] **4.113**

5. *"Intentional" Homelessness*

(a) *The definition of "intentional" homelessness*

Under section 60, a person becomes homeless intentionally if he "deliberately does or fails to do anything in consequence of which he ceases to occupy accommodation which is available for his occupation and which it would have been reasonable for him to continue to occupy"[68]; and a person becomes threatened with homelessness intentionally if he "deliberately does or fails to do anything the likely result of which is that he will be forced to leave accommodation which is available for his occupation and which it would have been reasonable for him to continue to occupy."[69] The concept of "inten- **4.114**

[62] *Cf.* M.O.H. Circ. 87/48, issued in relation to the former duty towards the homeless imposed by N.A.A. 1948; para. 15 of this Circ. referred to "such circumstances as fire, flood or eviction."

[63] See Andrew Arden, *op. cit.* para. 5.20.

[64] *Op. cit.* para. 2.12.b.

[65] L.G.A. 1972, s.138.

[66] H A. 1985, s.59(2)–(4).

[67] Surveys have shown that the single homeless come from every walk of life, and are not predominantly rootless or feckless: see, *e.g.* M. Drake, M. O'Brien and T. Biebuyck, *Single and Homeless* (D.O.E., 1981), especially at pp. 98–99.

[68] H A. 1985, s.60(1).

[69] *Ibid.* s.60(2).

tionality" has attracted a phenomenal amount of case law, and it is necessary carefully to analyse each part of the definition.

(b) *The burden of proof*

4.115 We have already noted that the burden clearly lies on the authority to "satisfy" itself on intentionality, and that if there is any doubt on the issue then the applicant is entitled to the benefit of that doubt so that his homelessness or threatened homelessness must be found to be unintentional.[70] Nevertheless, in the case of several authorities the percentage of applicants found intentionally homeless has been rising significantly over recent years, and it is perhaps significant that the passage in the first edition of the Code which predicted that "[t]he numbers of those to be regarded as having become homeless intentionally are expected to be small"[71] was omitted from the second edition.

(c) *"A person"*

4.116 **(i) The need to concentrate on the conduct of the applicant.** It is clear from the wording of sections 65 and 66 that the "person" referred to in the definition of intentionality in section 60 is the applicant, and not any other person who resides or might reasonably be expected to reside with him[72]; thus section 60 is not concerned, as such, with the wider question of whether the "family unit" as a whole is intentionally homeless.[73] The result may be that an intentionally homeless person has to be accommodated by or on behalf of the authority as part of the non-intentionally homeless applicant's family unit,[74] so that it may be crucial for the family to pick a "blameless" member as the applicant. Thus where a husband spent

[70] *R.* v. *Thurrock B.C., ex p. Williams* (1982) 1 H.L.R. 128 (D.C.); *R.* v. *Preseli D.C., ex p. Fisher* (1984) 17 H.L.R. 147 (D.C.); *R.* v. *West Dorset D.C., ex p. Phillips* (1984) 17 H.L.R. 336 (D.C.); see above, para. 4.26.

[71] (1st ed., 1977), para. 2.19.

[72] See, *e.g. Lewis* v. *North Devon D.C.* [1981] 1 W.L.R. 328; *R.* v. *L.B. of Hillingdon, ex p. Puhlhofer* (1985) 17 H.L.R. 278 (D.C.); *cf.* the provisions relating to "homelessness" (s.58(2)), "priority need" (s.59(1)), transfer of responsibility under the "local connection" provisions (s.67(2)), and "available" accommodation (s.75), in each of which the position of the "family unit" as a whole can be relevant.

[73] *Cf.* the *dicta* of Lord Denning M.R. in *R.* v. *Hillingdon L.B.C., ex p. Islam* [1981] 2 All E.R. 1089, 1093 (C.A.).

[74] See H.A. 1985, s.75 (below, paras. 5.65–5.67).

the rent money on drink, resulting in the family's eviction, and the wife applied to the authority for accommodation, she was entitled to be found unintentionally homeless because on the evidence she did not acquiesce in her husband's behaviour[75]; similarly where the family home was lost through the husband's default on the mortgage payments, despite the wife's constant efforts to persuade him to maintain the payments, she was entitled, as applicant, to a finding of unintentional homelessness even though the husband in his own right was intentionally homeless.[76]

A family member has the right, as applicant, to have his conduct separately considered even though he is still living with the "guilty" member[77]; and even where a joint application is made by two or more family members, the position of each applicant must be considered independently, so that one joint applicant may be found unintentionally homeless and the other may be found intentionally homeless.[78] **4.117**

(ii) The concept of "infectious intentionality." Despite emphasising the need to concentrate on the conduct of the applicant, the courts have developed what is, in effect, a limited concept of "infectious intentionality," whereby acquiescence by the applicant in the conduct of other members of his family unit can be found provided there is reasonable evidence of this.[79] Acquiescence has frequently been found where the family has been evicted on the grounds of nuisance or annoyance to neighbours[80]; but if there is any doubt as to whether the applicant has acquiesced in the conduct **4.118**

[75] *R.* v. *West Dorset D.C., ex p. Phillips*, see above.

[76] *R.* v. *Eastleigh B.C., ex p. Beattie* (*No.* 2) (1984) 17 H.L.R. 168 (D.C.).

[77] *R.* v. *Eastleigh B.C., ex p. Beattie* (*No.* 2), *ibid.; R.* v. *Mole Valley D.C., ex p. Burton* (1988) 20 H.L.R. 479 (D.C.).

[78] *R.* v. *Eastleigh B.C., ex p. Beattie* (*No. 2*), *ibid.; R.* v. *Penwith D.C., ex p. Trevena* (1984) 17 H.L.R. 526 (D.C.).

[79] See, *e.g. R.* v. *Swansea C.C., ex p. Thomas, The Times*, April 14, 1983 (D.C.); separate consideration must be given to the position of each relevant family member where the facts raise the possibility of non-acquiescence: *R.* v. *East Northamptonshire D.C., ex p. Spruce* (1988) 20 H.L.R. 508 (D.C.).

[80] *Smith* v. *Bristol C.C.* [1981] L.A.G. Bull. 287 (C.A.); *R.* v. *Swansea C.C., ex p. Thomas*, see above; *R.* v. *Swansea C.C., ex p. John* (1982) 9 H.L.R. 58 (D.C.); *R.* v. *East Herts D.C., ex p. Bannon* (1986) 18 H.L.R. 515 (D.C.); for the "nuisance or annoyance to neighbours" ground for possession against public and private sector tenants, see H.A. 1985, Sched. 2, gd. 2 (below, para. 8.37); R.A. 1977, Sched. 15, Case 2; H.A. 1988, Sched. 2, gd. 14.

of other family members, the applicant must, of course, be given the benefit of that doubt.[81]

4.119 **(iii) Responsibility for rent or mortgage arrears.** In the particular context of the responsibility of family members for rent or mortgage arrears, it is important to remember that an applicant spouse or cohabitee is not legally responsible for arrears built up by the other spouse or cohabitee where the latter is the sole tenant or mortgagor, so that the applicant spouse or cohabitee should not automatically be treated as intentionally homeless merely because he or she refuses to discharge the arrears of the other partner: the Code advises that the authority should try to discover whether responsibility for the arrears was shared in practice, before treating the applicant as intentionally homeless.[82] Even in the case of spouses who are joint tenants, the mere fact that the wife eventually becomes aware of extensive arrears, accrued due to her husband's default, does not of itself mean that she acquiesced in his non-payment.[83]

(d) *"Deliberately does or fails to do anything"*

4.120 **(i) The act or omission must be deliberate, but not the homelessness itself.** In order for the act or omission to be "intentional" for these purposes, it must be "deliberate." It is clear, however, that there is no requirement that the applicant should deliberately become homeless: the applicant's act or omission can properly be treated as "deliberate" even though he did not actually intend to lose his home thereby, since the word "deliberately" qualifies only the act or omission itself rather than its consequences.[84] One useful

[81] In *Lewis* v. *North Devon D.C.*, see above, Woolf J. was apparently prepared to assume, in the absence of evidence to the contrary, that other members of the family were parties to the conduct of the "guilty" member; but in *R.* v. *Swansea C.C., ex p. Thomas*, see above, he emphasised that acquiescence could only be found on the basis of reasonable evidence.

[82] *Op. cit.* para. 2.15; see also *Williams* v. *Cynon Valley B.C., Roof*, November 1979, p. 194 (Cty. Ct.); *cf. R.* v. *L.B. of Croydon, ex p. Webb*, December 14, 1983 (D.C., unreported), where acquiescence was found because the non-tenant husband had the means to discharge the tenant-wife's arrears, even though there was no evidence that he had regularly contributed towards the rent payments.

[83] *R.* v. *East Northamptonshire D.C., ex p. Spruce*, see above.

[84] *Jones* v. *Bristol C.C., Zold* v. *Bristol C.C.* [1981] L.A.G. Bull. 287 (Cty. Ct.); *Robinson* v. *Torbay B.C.* [1982] 1 All E.R. 726; *R.* v. *Salford C.C., ex p. Devenport* (1983) 127 S.J. 306 (C.A.); *Din* v. *Wandsworth L.B.C.* [1981] 3 All E.R. 881, 895 (H.L.); the *dictum* of Lord Denning M.R. in *R.* v. *Slough B.C., ex p. Ealing L.B.C.* [1981] 1 All

judicial test for deciding on the "deliberateness" criterion is to ask whether "the fair-minded bystander could say [of the applicant's predicament] 'He asked for it,' and say that in either sense of those words."[85]

According to the Code, where homelessness is caused by "real personal or financial difficulties," or because the applicant was "incapable of managing his affairs on account of *e.g.* old age or mental illness," then his acts or omissions should not be regarded as having been deliberate[86]; more specifically, the Code states that it would not be appropriate to treat a homeless pregnant woman as intentionally homeless "simply because she is pregnant."[87] **4.121**

(ii) Homelessness due to rent or mortgage arrears. With regard to rent or mortgage arrears, before the failure to pay can properly be regarded as a "deliberate" omission the authority must be satisfied that there has been "wilful default"[88]: according to the Code, a "wilful and persistent" refusal to pay can be "deliberate,"[89] but where the homelessness is the result of "serious financial difficulties arising, for example, from loss of employment or greatly reduced earnings," then the failure to pay the rent or mortgage should not normally be regarded as intentional.[90] Where the rent has been withheld on account of disrepair, the failure to pay may well not be "deliberate" for these purposes.[91] **4.122**

E.R. 601, 612–613 (C.A.), that the word "deliberate" in s.60(1) is used in the sense of acting or failing to act "deliberately so as to get turned out," has not been followed.

[85] *Robinson* v. *Torbay B.C.* [1982] 1 All E.R. 726, 731 (*per* Judge Goodall).

[86] *Op. cit.* para. 2.15.

[87] *Op. cit.* para. 2.16; see also *per* Woolf J. in *R.* v. *Eastleigh B.C., ex p. Beattie* (*No.* 1) (1983) 10 H.L.R. 134, 141 (D.C.): "[I]t cannot be said that a family fall within section [60(1)] because they have chosen to have additional children."

[88] *R.* v. *Wyre B.C., ex p. Joyce* (1983) 11 H.L.R. 73 (D.C.); *Robinson* v. *Torbay B.C.* [1982] 1 All E.R. 726.

[89] *Op. cit.* para. 2.15.

[90] *Ibid.*

[91] *Jones* v. *Bristol C.C.* [1981] L.A.G. Bull. 163, 287 (Cty. Ct.); *cf. Tickner* v. *Mole Valley D.C.* [1980] L.A.G. Bull. 187 (C.A.), and *R.* v. *Wandsworth L.B.C., ex p. Henderson* (1986) 18 H.L.R. 522 (D.C.), where the defects which had given rise to the "rent strike" were being remedied by the landlords, and the council's finding of intentionality was upheld; if a tenant correctly operates his right to "set off" the repair costs against the rent (see below, paras. 12.65–12.68), there will in law be no "arrears" as regards the sums correctly "set off," in which case the withholding of the rent cannot possibly justify a finding of "intentionality" should the tenant nevertheless become homeless (*e.g.* as a result of unlawful eviction).

4.123 In the case of rent arrears accrued in relation to a council dwelling, the Code states that it would be "inappropriate to assume that tenants who are evicted for rent arrears have become homeless intentionally" until the relevant preventative measures have been discussed, such as the tenant's entitlement to welfare benefits.[92]

4.124 **(iii) The limited relevance of possession orders.** It is clear that the mere fact that an order for possession has been granted, whether on account of the applicant's acts or his omissions, does not of itself entitle the authority to find that the homelessness was intentional: in each case the authority must carefully inquire into the circumstances which gave rise to the possession action.[93]

4.125 **(iv) Omission to pursue civil law remedies.** Sometimes it may be appropriate for the authority to find that a failure by the applicant to pursue civil law remedies available to him, as a result of which homelessness arises, can be "deliberate" and therefore give rise to intentionality; examples include the failure of an illegally evicted tenant to take action against his landlord to gain re-entry, and the failure by a spouse or cohabitee to use remedies offered by family law in order to secure peaceful occupation of the home. However, the failure to take such proceedings should not be regarded as "deliberate" if they would have been unlikely to succeed, or to offer suitable protection.[94] This issue is also relevant to the separate limb of section 60 which deals with the question of whether it would have been "reasonable for [the applicant] to continue to occupy."[95]

4.126 **(v) Loss of job-related accommodation.** With regard to the loss of accommodation which was "tied" to the applicant's job, the Code states that "[a] person who loses tied accommodation because the employment has ended through no fault of his own should not be treated as intentionally homeless."[96] The crucial question is

[92] *Op. cit.* para. A1.16; since the introduction of statutory security of tenure for most public sector tenants, the council will normally only be able to gain possession on the ground of rent arrears where this is reasonable: see below, paras. 8.31–8.36.

[93] *R.* v. *Swansea C.C., ex p. John* (1982) 9 H.L.R. 58 (D.C.); *Lazere* v. *Slough D.C., Roof*, January 1981, p. 32 (Cty. Ct.); *Smith* v. *Bristol C.C.* [1981] L.A.G. Bull. 287 (C.A.); *McKenzie* v. *West Lothian D.C.* [1979] S.C.O.L.A.G. 123 (Ct. of Session); *Roughead* v. *Falkirk D.C.* [1979] S.C.O.L.A.G. 188 (Sh. Ct.).

[94] See *Charles* v. *Charles* [1984] L.A.G. Bull. 81 (C.A.); Andrew Arden, *op. cit.* paras. 6.28–6.33.

[95] See above, paras. 4.53–4.56, and below, paras. 4.154–4.159.

[96] *Op. cit.* para. 2.16.

whether the element of fault is present,[97] and there is no distinction when determining the fault issue between an employee who resigns from employment carrying "tied" accommodation and one whose acts result in a termination of such employment.[98]

By way of example, a serving soldier who buys himself out of the Army (thereby losing his married accommodation), because his wife cannot withstand the pressures of Army life, should not normally be regarded as "deliberately" giving up the accommodation, since his actions would be caused by "real personal . . . difficulties."[99] However, an employee who engages in conduct leading to his dismissal and consequent loss of "tied" accommodation can thereby render himself intentionally homeless where the circumstances are appropriate[1]; yet dismissal for incompetence should not of itself give rise to a finding of intentionality if there is no evidence that the employee deliberately adopted a course of conduct in order to provoke the dismissal.[2] **4.127**

Such cases frequently involve the making of difficult inferences from conflicting evidence, and it is necessary to bear in mind the overriding principle that the applicant is entitled to the benefit of any doubt on the intentionality issue.[3] Separate consideration often needs to be given, in these "tied accommodation" cases, to the criterion of whether it would have been reasonable for the applicant to continue to occupy the accommodation.[4] **4.128**

(vi) Acts or omissions in good faith and in ignorance of relevant facts. The word "deliberately" in section 60 is qualified by the proviso that an act or omission in good faith on the part of a person who was unaware of any relevant fact shall *not* be treated as deliberate.[5] Another person's state of mind, even in relation to future events, can constitute a relevant " fact" of which the applicant may be unaware for these purposes.[6] **4.129**

97 *R.* v. *Thurrock B.C., ex p. Williams* (1982) 1 H.L.R. 128 (D.C.).
98 *Lewis* v. *North Devon D.C.* [1981] 1 W.L.R. 328; *R.* v. *Thanet D.C., ex p. Reeve* (1981) 6 H.L.R. 31 (D.C.).
99 Code, para. 2.15; see above, para. 4.121.
1 *R.* v. *Thanet D.C., ex p. Reeve,* see above.
2 *R.* v. *Thurrock B.C., ex p. Williams,* see above.
3 *Ibid.*
4 See below, paras. 4.160–4.162.
5 H.A. 1985, s.60(3).
6 *Wincentzen* v. *Monklands D.C.* 1988 S.L.T. 847 (Ct. of Session: I.H.).

4.130 The mistake must however be one of fact rather than of law[7]; thus an applicant who, pursuant to legal advice, refused to pay his mortgage in an effort to compel rehousing by the local authority was intentionally homeless following eviction on account of the arrears.[8] Furthermore, the relevant "fact" of which the applicant was unaware must be one relating to the permanent cessation of accommodation,[9] and must apparently amount to something "more than a statement of the obvious which must be well known to the general public."[10]

4.131 Situations where the courts have held that ignorance of a relevant "fact" was capable of resulting in a non-deliberate act or omission (and therefore in a finding of unintentional homelessness) have included the following: where a time-limit had been imposed by a landlord within which the tenant had to claim an extension of the lease, but the tenant had misunderstood correspondence relating to the time-limit which she had received from the landlord's solicitors[11]; where the applicant had failed to pay his mortgage interest instalments due to a mistaken belief that they were being paid in full by the D.H.S.S. through direct deduction from his supplementary benefit entitlement[12]; where the applicant left secure accommodation to live with her father, having misunderstood his letters as a result of which she had assumed that he would be able to accommodate her indefinitely, whereas in fact he was only willing to accommodate her on a temporary basis[13]; and where a wife agreed to leave

[7] *R.* v. *Eastleigh B.C., ex p. Beattie* (*No.* 2) (1984) 17 H.L.R. 168 (D.C.); *Brown* v. *Hamilton D.C.* 1983 S.L.T. 397, 418 (H.L.); see also *R.* v. *L.B. of Croydon, ex p. Toth* (1987) 20 H.L.R. 567 (C.A.): mistake as to legal effect on secure tenancy of departure held not to relate to a "relevant fact."

[8] *R.* v. *Eastleigh B.C., ex p. Beattie* (*No.* 2), *ibid.*

[9] *R.* v. *Wandsworth L.B.C., ex p. Henderson* (1986) 18 H.L.R. 522 (D.C.).

[10] *Per* McNeill J. in *R.* v. *Eastleigh B.C., ex p. Evans* (1984) 17 H.L.R. 515, 523 (D.C.): here the applicant wife had left army married quarters because of non-violent matrimonial troubles; the army had not attempted to end the tenancy prior to her departure, and it was held that her ignorance of the fact that occupation in these circumstances for a short period was of assistance to the council was not ignorance of a relevant fact within s.60(3).

[11] *R.* v. *Christchurch B.C., ex p. Conway* (1987) 19 H.L.R. 238 (D.C.).

[12] *White* v. *Exeter C.C.* [1981] L.A.G. Bull. 287 (Cty. Ct.).

[13] *R.* v. *Wandsworth L.B.C., ex p. Rose* (1983) 11 H.L.R. 107 (D.C.); an alternative way of dealing with this situation would be to say that any previous "chain of intentionality" forged through leaving the previous secure accommodation had been broken, because the father's accommodation was not known by the applicant at the outset to be short-term, see below, paras. 4.135–4.141; *cf. R.* v. *Wandsworth L.B.C., ex p. Wells,* November 23, 1983 (D.C., unreported), where a finding of

the tied accommodation which constituted the matrimonial home in the mistaken belief (induced by her husband, who had in turn misunderstood the effect of an agreement between his employers and the council) that they would be entitled to council housing.[14]

(e) *"In consequence": the chain of intentionality*

(i) The deliberate act or omission must be one in consequence of which the applicant ceases to occupy available accommodation. We have seen that, in order for an act or omission to be regarded as "deliberate" for the purposes of section 60, the applicant need not actually have intended to lose his home as a result thereof. However, the "deliberate" act or omission must be one in *consequence* of which the applicant ceases to occupy available accommodation, which can involve difficult questions of "causation."[15] The key principle is that there must be "a continuing causal connection between the deliberate act [or omission] in consequence of which homelessness resulted and the homelessness existing at the date of the inquiry."[16] **4.132**

However, in examining the cause of the homelessness it is necessary to have primary regard to the position at the time when the homelessness arose, and not to the position at the time of the application or inquiry. Thus in *Din* v. *Wandsworth L.B.C.*[17] the applicants were held by the House of Lords to have been properly found intentionally homeless through leaving secure accommodation in August 1979 prematurely and contrary to the authority's advice to stay put (at a time when they had a possible defence to a claim by their landlord for possession[18]), even though by the time they actually applied to the authority as homeless persons in December 1979 they would have become unintentionally homeless if they had followed the authority's advice to stay put in August; the speeches of the majority in the *Din* case were to the effect that at the time of the authority's decision in December 1979 it could still properly be said that the applicants' conduct in August had directly caused their homeless- **4.133**

intentionality was upheld, since the applicant had not inquired as to how long he could stay with his father before leaving his own secure accommodation in order to move in with his father.

[14] *R.* v. *Mole Valley D.C., ex p. Burton* (1988) 20 H.L.R. 479 (D.C.).

[15] See *R.* v. *Thanet D.C., ex p. Reeve* (1981) 6 H.L.R. 31, 35 (D.C.); *Lambert* v. *Ealing L.B.C.* [1982] 2 All E.R. 394, 400 (C.A.).

[16] *Per* Lord Fraser in *Din* v. *Wandsworth L.B.C.* [1981] 3 All E.R. 881, 890 (H.L.).

[17] See above.

[18] See above, paras. 4.59–4.62.

ness, since hypothetical events which might have taken place if they had remained in their original accommodation were immaterial.

4.134 The *Din* principle can work in reverse, so as to ensure that an applicant who is unintentionally homeless at a particular point in time remains unintentionally homeless even though, had he not then become unintentionally homeless, he may well have become intentionally homeless at a subsequent date. Thus in *R.* v. *Gloucester C.C., ex p. Miles,*[19] at a time when the applicant's joint tenancy of her flat was still on foot even though she had left, her husband, unknown to her, vandalised the flat to such an extent that it became uninhabitable; the applicant subsequently decided never to return to the flat; it was held that the applicant became unintentionally homeless on the date when the flat was vandalised (even though the lease was then still on foot),[20] despite the likelihood that, had the vandalism not taken place, she would have eventually become homeless intentionally because the landlord would probably have terminated the tenancy for rent arrears: the authority could not have regard to the hypothetical consideration that the applicant would probably have become homeless through her own acts or omissions if she had not already become homeless through her husband's acts.

(ii) The "chain of intentionality."

4.135 *The concept of "chainbreaking."* A separate issue of causation can arise after a person has made himself intentionally homeless: in what circumstances can he subsequently make application (or further application) to a housing authority on the ground that he is now unintentionally homeless? Obviously it must be possible for the applicant eventually to "purge" himself of his initial intentionality.

4.136 *Looking behind the immediate cause of the homelessness.* The Code points out that in assessing whether someone has become intentionally homeless "it is open to an authority to look beyond the most immediate cause of that homelessness," and that "[i]n particular, where homelessness arises from loss of accommodation of a temporary nature, it may therefore be relevant to consider the circumstances in which previous accommodation was given up"[21]; but the Code also states, by way of example, that it would be inappropriate automatically to treat a person as intentionally homeless where he

[19] (1985) 83 L.G.R. 607 (C.A.).
[20] See above, paras. 4.42, 4.51.
[21] *Op. cit.* para. 2.18; the original wording of this paragraph was amended to take account of the decision in *De Falco* v. *Crawley B.C.* [1980] Q.B. 460 (C.A.).

gives up (permanent) accommodation (thereby doing a deliberate act in consequence of which he loses his accommodation) in order to move in with relatives or friends, "who then decided after a few months that they could no longer continue to accommodate him": each such case must be considered individually.[22]

In these cases the authority may indeed sometimes be obliged to look beyond the immediate circumstances which have now rendered the applicant homeless, and involve itself in a process of "looking back into the past and seeing how it came about that he ceased to occupy available and reasonable accommodation."[23] Although section 60 is drafted in the present tense, it is dealing with "cause and effect," and therefore by inference must be concentrating on past events; thus section 60(1) has been interpreted judicially as meaning: **4.137**

> "a person becomes homeless intentionally if he deliberately *has* done or failed to do anything in consequence of which he *has* ceased to occupy accommodation which *was* available for his occupation and which it would have been reasonable for him to continue to occupy."[24]

There is certainly nothing in section 60 to suggest that the accommodation that a person ceased to occupy so as to become homeless intentionally has to be the same accommodation that gives rise to the current "homelessness" under section 58: it is a question of causation as to whether the act or omission rendering the applicant homeless in relation to his secure accommodation still remains a cause of the homelessness which resulted from him eventually leaving his subsequent accommodation.[25] **4.138**

Obtaining "settled" accommodation. The principal (though not the sole) way in which a "chain of intentionality" can be broken is by the applicant obtaining his own "settled"[26] accommodation; if he **4.139**

[22] Code, *loc. cit.*
[23] *R.* v. *Preseli D.C., ex. p. Fisher* (1984) 17 H.L.R. 147, 158 (D.C., *per* McCullough J.).
[24] *Per* Brightman L.J. in *Dyson* v. *Kerrier D.C.* [1980] 3 All E.R. 313, 319 (C.A., italics in original).
[25] *Lambert* v. *Ealing L.B.C.* [1982] 2 All E.R. 394, 400 (C.A.).
[26] The word "settled" means the same thing, in this context, as "not temporary": *R.* v. *Merton L.B.C., ex p. Ruffle, The Independent,* December 16, 1988 (D.C.).

thereafter leaves that "settled" accommodation, the question of whether his current homelessness is intentional is governed by the circumstances of departure from that accommodation, and not by reference to previous events. The considerable case law on this aspect of "chain-breaking" would appear to support the following propositions: the "chain of intentionality" will be broken where the applicant (having left such accommodation as may already have been temporarily provided for him by an authority[27]) obtains long-term accommodation legally, (*i.e.* otherwise than by squatting); and the accommodation which the applicant obtains will normally rank as "long-term" if it was reasonably[28] thought by the applicant, at the outset, to be available for at least a year.

4.140 Thus in the following cases the "chain of intentionality" (though initially forged or assumed for the purposes of argument to have been forged) was held to have been broken by the obtaining of "settled" accommodation: where the applicant moved to stay with relatives in the reasonable expectation that he could remain for at least a year, although in the event the relatives decided to emigrate and the applicant was therefore asked to leave after only two months[29]; where, following an initial finding of intentionality, the members of the applicants' family unit voluntarily split up due to domestic discord and each part of the family unit found its own respective "settled" accommodation (even though they never found "settled" accommodation in which the whole family unit could live together)[30]; and where the applicant obtained a "shorthold" tenancy under the Housing Act 1980.[31]

4.141 By contrast, in the following cases it was held that the applicant had not obtained "settled" accommodation, so that the "chain of intentionality" had not been broken: where the applicant surrendered her council flat in order to take on what she knew to be an

[27] Under s.63(1) or s.65(3).

[28] The test thus has an objective element: *R.* v. *Purbeck D.C., ex p. Cadney* (1985) 17 H.L.R. 534, 538 (D.C.).

[29] *Krishnan* v. *Hillingdon L.B.C.* [1981] L.A.G. Bull. 137.

[30] *R.* v. *South Herefordshire D.C., ex p. Miles* (1983) 17 H.L.R. 82 (D.C.).

[31] *R.* v. *Christchurch B.C., ex p. Conway* (1987) 19 H.L.R. 238 (D.C.); "shorthold" tenancies, granted pursuant to H.A. 1980, ss.51–55, had by definition to be granted for a fixed term of at least one year. However, the new "assured shorthold tenancies" under H.A. 1988, s.20, can be granted for as short a term as six months, which may not be considered to be long enough to break a "chain of intentionality."

insecure "winter let" of private sector accommodation[32]; where a family moved out of their council flat into a succession of decrepit caravans and, finally, into a car[33]; where a family obtained accommodation by way of two successive "holiday lets," which in aggregate lasted for more than 12 months[34]; and where a family moved into a relative's flat knowing that she was on the verge of moving elsewhere.[35]

Other ways of breaking the chain. The courts have also recognised that the "chain of intentionality" can be broken in other ways besides the acquisition of a "settled residence": thus in *R.* v. *Basingstoke & Deane D.C., ex p. Bassett,*[36] although the applicant had never obtained a "settled residence" following the (assumed) forging of the chain of intentionality, the chain had nevertheless been broken by her marriage breakdown, which, although causing her immediate homelessness, had nothing to do with the fact that her current accommodation had been of a short-term nature[37]; the marriage breakdown ranked as a sufficiently catastrophic event for chain-breaking purposes. **4.142**

Practical difficulties in breaking the chain. Despite the scope for "chain-breaking" indicated by the case law, an applicant may in practice experience considerable difficulty in achieving this; in particular, where he is in an area of acute housing need it may be virtually impossible for him to find accommodation ranking as a "settled residence" for these purposes.[38] In the light of the practical problems **4.143**

[32] *Dyson* v. *Kerrier D.C.* [1980] 1 W.L.R. 1205 (C.A.); a "winter let" is a fixed-term tenancy, not exceeding eight months in duration, of a former holiday home, and it gives the landlord a mandatory ground for possession when the term expires, see H.A. 1988, Sched. 2, Pt. I, gd. 3. The landlord must however give the tenant prior notice in writing that possession might be recovered under this ground, and the relevant notice was duly given in *Dyson* (which involved R.A. 1977, Sched. 15, Pt. II, Case 13).

[33] *Davis* v. *Kingston L.B.C., The Times,* March 28, 1981 (C.A.).

[34] *Lambert* v. *Ealing L.B.C.* [1982] 1 W.L.R. 550 (C.A.); "holiday lets" are outside the private sector statutory security scheme. See now H.A. 1988, s.1 and Sched. 1, Pt. I, para. 9.

[35] *R.* v. *Hambleton D.C., ex p. Geoghan* [1985] J.P.L. 394 (D.C.).

[36] (1983) 10 H.L.R. 125 (D.C.).

[37] *Cf. Lambert* v. *Ealing L.B.C.*, above.

[38] See, *e.g. Din* v. *Wandsworth L.B.C.* [1981] 3 All E.R. 881, 900 (H.L.).

facing applicants, authorities have been urged to apply the chain-breaking principles "benevolently."[39]

(f) *"Ceasing" to occupy accommodation*

4.144 Section 60 refers to the relevant act or omission as being one in consequence of which the applicant *ceases* to occupy accommodation.

4.145 **(i) Refusal of an offer of accommodation.** It is clear that the mere refusal by the applicant of an offer of accommodation elsewhere cannot of itself constitute intentional homelessness, however "deliberate" and unreasonable that refusal might be, since the word "ceases" in section 60 is inapt to describe something which has never begun.[40] Thus it is clearly wrong for authorities to label applicants as intentionally homeless if they turn down the first offer of accommodation made to them.[41]

4.146 However, if an authority, in the proper discharge of its duties, offers suitable[42] accommodation to an applicant which he refuses, then that authority will not be in breach of the Act: it cannot force accommodation upon an applicant who is determined not to accept it[43]; but the refusal of the offer clearly cannot be a relevant "omission" constituting intentional homelessness.

4.147 **(ii) Applicants arriving from overseas.** A separate aspect of the "cessation" requirement can be seen in cases where applicants arrive in this country from overseas: here it will not be enough, in order to establish intentional homelessness, for the authority merely to show that the applicant arrived in England without ensuring that he had permanent accommodation here; rather, the authority must show that the applicant deliberately ceased to occupy accommodation available to him in his home country.[44] Although this principle is clear, the courts have varied in their willingness or otherwise

[39] *R.* v. *Merton L.B.C., ex p. Ruffle, The Times*, November 12, 1988 (D.C.), *per* Simon Brown J.

[40] *R.* v. *Westminster C.C., ex p. Chambers* (1983) 81 L.G.R. 401 (D.C.); *Wyness* v. *Poole B.C.* [1979] J.S.W.L. 368 (Cty. Ct.).

[41] A practice described in *Leaving Violent Men, op. cit.* p. 81.

[42] See H.A. 1985, s.69, discussed below, paras. 5.68–5.71.

[43] *R.* v. *Westminster C.C., ex p. Chambers*, see above.

[44] *De Falco* v. *Crawley B.C.* [1980] Q.B. 460 (C.A.).

to expand the stated reasons of the authority in order to fall within it where the expressed reasons are deficient.[45]

(g) *Departure from "available" accommodation*

The accommodation which the applicant has ceased to occupy must also have been "available for his occupation" before the homelessness can properly be judged to have been intentional under section 60; in order to apply this "availability" criterion it is necessary to ignore (for this specific purpose only) the applicant's acts or omissions and their consequences.[46] **4.148**

In this context it is particularly important to bear in mind that under section 75, accommodation is only "available" for a person's occupation if it is available for occupation "both by him *and* by any other person who might reasonably be expected to reside with him": thus section 60 is in effect providing that a person can only make himself intentionally homeless if he deliberately does or fails to do anything in consequence of which he ceases to occupy accommodation which is available for occupation *both* by him *and* by any other person who might reasonably be expected to reside with him. **4.149**

In deciding for section 75 purposes who might reasonably be expected to reside with the applicant, no account can be taken of his lack of accommodation: such an approach would be "circular," because such lack of accommodation is precisely what section 75 is designed to relieve.[47] Thus if an applicant has thrown up accommodation which was too small for his family unit realistically to occupy with him, he is not intentionally homeless because he has not vacated "available" accommodation; and it is immaterial whether his family unit has ever been able actually to reside there with him.[48] **4.150**

Those who "might reasonably be expected to reside with" applicants can include cohabitees.[49] There is no requirement that the **4.151**

45 *De Falco* v. *Crawley B.C., ibid.; Lambert* v. *Ealing L.B.C.* [1982] 2 All E.R. 394, 396–397 (C.A.); *R.* v. *Gravesham B.C., ex p. Winchester* (1986) 18 H.L.R. 207 (D.C.); *cf.* the stricter approach to the council's stated reasons adopted in *R.* v. *Reigate and Banstead B.C., ex p. Paris* (1984) 15 Fam. Law 28 (D.C.), where it was clear that the council had never addressed itself to the correct issue.

46 *R.* v. *Salford C.C., ex p. Devenport* (1983) 8 H.L.R. 54, 65 (C.A.).

47 *Islam* v. *Hillingdon L.B.C.* [1981] 3 All E.R. 901, 912 (H.L.).

48 *Islam* v. *Hillingdon L.B.C.*, see above; *R.* v. *Westminster C.C., ex p. Ali* (1983) 11 H.L.R. 83 (D.C.); *Krishnan* v. *Hillingdon L.B.C.* [1981] L.A.G. Bull. 137; *cf. R.* v. *L.B. of Tower Hamlets, ex p. Monaf* (1988) 20 H.L.R. 529 (C.A.), where on the facts the applicants' accommodation in Bangladesh had been available to the entire family unit.

49 *R.* v. *Wimbourne D.C., ex p. Curtis* (1985) 1 F.L.R. 486 (D.C.).

other persons must, in order to qualify, have previously resided at some time with the applicant. However, under the current immigration rules, where the spouse or other relative of a person who is present and settled in the U.K. seeks admission in order to join him, entry clearance will be refused unless the entry clearance officer is satisfied (*inter alia*) that there will be adequate accommodation for the person seeking admission without "recourse to public funds," an expression which includes a claim under Part III of the Housing Act 1985.[50] Clearly, in the case of an applicant for housing who is in this country and who hopes to be joined by relatives from overseas, those relatives are not persons who might reasonably be expected to reside with him until entry clearance has been given for them[51]; and since such clearance will not be forthcoming where the applicant seeks accommodation under Part III of the 1985 Act, he is placed in something of a Catch-22 situation.

4.152 Although there were *dicta* in the controversial decision of the House of Lords in *Puhlhofer* v. *Hillingdon L.B.C.*[52] to the effect that section 60 has nothing to do with the inherent quality of the accommodation, these *dicta* were apparently directed to the "reasonableness" criterion in section 60, and had no effect on the relevance of the "availability" criterion in cases of (for example) departure from grossly overcrowded accommodation.[53]

4.153 In deciding whether accommodation is "available" for the applicant's occupation, it is of course immaterial whether the applicant actually owns it.[54]

(h) *Departure from accommodation "which it would have been reasonable . . . to continue to occupy"*

4.154 **(i) General.** As well as requiring a "deliberate" act or omission in consequence of which the applicant ceases to occupy "available" accommodation, section 60(1) also stipulates that it must have been "reasonable for him to continue to occupy" that accommodation before the homelessness can properly be said to have been intentional; and a similar requirement is imposed by section 60(2) for the

[50] Immigration Act 1971, s.1(4); Immigration Act 1988, s.1; *Statement of Changes in Immigration Rules*, H.C.P. 169, paras. 1, 46–48.
[51] *Islam* v. *Hillingdon L.B.C.*, see above, at 911–912.
[52] [1986] 1 All E.R. 467, 473.
[53] The effects of these *dicta* are discussed above, para. 4.47.
[54] *R.* v. *Tower Hamlets L.B.C., ex p. Monaf* (1987) 19 H.L.R. 577, 585 (D.C.): fact that the accommodation in question belonged to applicant's mother held irrelevant.

purpose of deciding whether an applicant becomes intentionally threatened with homelessness. However, amendments to the definition of homelessness in section 58 have caused problems in interpreting this "reasonableness" requirement in section 60.

(ii) The introduction of the "reasonableness" criterion into section 58. Before the amendment of the definition of "homelessness" in section 58 by the addition of a "reasonableness" criterion, in a situation where it would not have been reasonable for the applicant to continue to occupy his accommodation he was nevertheless not normally "homeless" until he left, but on his departure he would then be homeless, and unintentionally so. However, we have seen that the Housing and Planning Act 1986 introduced the "reasonableness" criterion into section 58, to the effect that an applicant is "homeless" even while he retains legal rights of occupation, if it is not reasonable for him to continue to occupy the accommodation (having regard to the general circumstances prevailing in relation to housing in the district of the authority to which he has applied).[55] **4.155**

Thus where the applicant has left his accommodation, and it would not have been reasonable for him to continue to occupy it, his departure is now logically irrelevant: in view of the current definition of "homelessness," there is no question of intentional homelessness because he was statutorily "homeless" *even before he left the accommodation*: in effect, the closing words of section 60(1) ("and which it would have been reasonable . . . to continue to occupy") are now redundant, because the word "accommodation" in section 60(1) must now itself mean (by virtue of section 58(2A)) "accommodation which it would be reasonable for him to continue to occupy." The "reasonableness" criterion in section 58(2A) is not restricted to section 58 itself, but forms part of the "main definition" of "homelessness" throughout Part III of the Act, including section 60. **4.156**

Although the end result of this reasoning is basically the same as under the pre-1986 law, this particular construction is important in distinguishing the *dicta* in *Puhlhofer* v. *Hillingdon L.B.C.*[56] to the effect that section 60 has nothing whatever to do with the inherent quality of the accommodation; "inherent quality" issues are now clearly relevant to the "reasonableness" criterion in section 58, which is now itself separately incorporated into section 60. **4.157**

[55] See above, paras. 4.42–4.48.
[56] See above, para. 4.152.

4.158 The detailed earlier discussion in this chapter of the "reasonableness" criterion in section 58 (including the discussion of the significance of the general housing circumstances in the district) is directly relevant to the "intentionality" issue where there has been a cessation of occupation; and although subsections (1) and (4) of section 60 still refer to the "reasonableness" criterion, it is submitted that this criterion is best viewed in the context of the definition of "homelessness."

4.159 Where, however, the applicant has ceased to occupy accommodation which it would have been reasonable for him to continue to occupy, then he is not to be treated as statutorily "homeless" until he left, and the authority must then decide whether the departure was in fact intentional (for example, even though it was reasonable to continue to occupy, the departure may not have been "deliberate").

4.160 **(iii) Departure for reasons of employment.** One aspect of the "reasonableness" requirement in section 60 which has been frequently discussed by the courts (and which was not considered in detail in the account of the definition of "homelessness" earlier in this chapter), involves "job-related" departures; these can involve intentionality issues either because the applicant has lost his current job (through dismissal or resignation), or because, being already unemployed, he moves to another area in search of work. Although the "reasonableness" question is now linked to the definition of "homelessness," the cases have been largely concerned with section 60 rather than with the amended section 58, and it is convenient to deal with "job-related" departures when discussing intentionality because they frequently also raise the question of "deliberateness."[57]

4.161 Where the applicant has voluntarily resigned from his job, and has in consequence lost his accommodation, then the Code recognises that he should nevertheless not be treated as intentionally homeless "if the circumstances indicate that it would not have been reasonable for him to continue in the employment"[58]; nevertheless, the courts have sometimes adopted a tough approach here, upholding decisions of intentional homelessness on the ground that it would have been reasonable to continue to occupy where applicants have

[57] This is discussed, in the present context, at paras. 4.126–4.128 above.
[58] *Op. cit.* para. 2.16.

lost "tied" accommodation through resigning from their employment, even though continued occupation would have been attended by "difficulties and problems,"[59] and even though the situation was "deserving."[60]

Where the applicant ceases to occupy accommodation in order to look for work, the Code asks authorities to "exercise care."[61] The courts have sometimes recognised that it may not have been reasonable for the applicant to stay in the vacated accommodation because of the interests of "mobility of labour"[62]; however, other cases have adopted a much tougher line,[63] with one judge expressing the very extreme view that "it would require Parliamentary intervention to enable a court to say that the availability of work in one place rather than another bears on reasonableness under section [60]."[64] **4.162**

(i) *"Blanket" resolutions on intentionality*

Despite detailed advice in the Code, and despite the general administrative law requirement that an authority must make an individual decision in each particular case,[65] it seems that some authorities have adopted "blanket resolutions" whereby whole groups such as rent arrears cases are automatically labelled as intentionally homeless without consideration being given to every indi- **4.163**

59 *Goddard* v. *Torridge D.C.* [1982] L.A.G. Bull. 9.

60 *Lewis* v. *North Devon D.C.* [1981] 1 All E.R. 27; see also *Jennings* v. *Northavon D.C.* [1982] L.A.G. Bull 9; but *cf. R.* v. *Thurrock B.C., ex p. Williams* (1982) 1 H.L.R. 128(D.C.).

61 *Op. cit.* para. 2.18.

62 *Islam* v. *Hillingdon L.B.C.* [1981] 3 All E.R. 901, 911 (H.L.); *R.* v. *Hammersmith L.B.C., ex p. DuroRama* (1983) 81 L.G.R. 702 (D.C.); see also *R* v. *R.B. of Kensington & Chelsea, ex p. Cunha* (1988) 21 H.L.R. 16 (D.C.), held, while the applicant's difficulty in obtaining employment in Brazil was a relevant "intentionality" factor, it would have been an "unwarranted burden" for the authority to have to inquire further into local employment conditions there.

63 *De Falco* v. *Crawley B.C.* [1980] Q.B. 460 (C.A.); *R.* v. *L.B. of Wandsworth, ex p. Wells,* November 23, 1983 (D.C., unreported); *R.* v. *South Hams D.C., ex p. Proctor,* September 24, 1985 (D.C., unreported); *Mazzaccherini* v. *Argyll & Bute D.C.* [1987] 9 C.L. 679 (Ct. of Session, O.H.); *R.* v. *L.B. of Tower Hamlets, ex p. Monaf* (1987) 19 H.L.R. 577, 586 (D.C.).

64 *Per* McNeill J. in *R.* v. *South Hams D.C., ex p. Proctor,* see above (LEXIS transcript).

65 See below, para. 6.16; for the application of this principle in the context of council house waiting lists, see *R.* v. *Canterbury C.C., ex p. Gillespie* (1987) 19 H.L.R. 7 (D.C.), discussed above, paras. 2.20–2.22.

vidual application.[66] In the context of intentionality, a "blanket resolution" has been successfully challenged where it resulted in the spouses of tenants being automatically held intentionally homeless by the council on account of the tenants' rent arrears, regardless of whether the spouses were aware of the arrears[67]; and it was held unlawful for a council to seek to fetter its social services department by deciding that the department should never provide assistance under section 1 of the Child Care Act 1980[68] for families found intentionally homeless by the housing department.[69]

6. *Notification of Decisions and Reasons*

4.164 On completion of its inquiries, the housing authority must notify the applicant of its decision[70] on the questions of whether he is homeless or threatened with homelessness, and if so, whether he has a priority need, and if so, whether he became homeless or threatened with homelessness intentionally, and whether the authority is using the "local connection" provisions.[71] The duties owed by the authority under sections 65 and 66 do not of course depend on the authority first notifying its decision to the applicant, but arise as soon as the authority is "satisfied" as to the relevant matters.[72] The decision should not be taken entirely by councillors, but rather (at least initially) by officers familiar with the relevant law.[73]

[66] See, *e.g.* L.A.M.S.A.C., *Report No.1: Homelessness* (1978), p.3; B. Widdowson, *Roof*, July 1978, p. 100; L. Burrows, *Roof*, March 1979, p. 42; B. Martin, *Roof*, July 1979, p. 107.

[67] *Williams* v. *Cynon Valley B.C.* [1980] L.A.G. Bull. 16 (Cty. Ct.).

[68] The Child Care Act, s.1(1), imposes a duty on social services authorities to make available such advice, guidance and assistance as may promote the welfare of children by diminishing the need to receive them into (or keep them in) care. The assistance may be given in kind or (exceptionally) in cash, and can involve the provision of accommodation enabling a child to live with its parents.

[69] *Tilley* v. *Wandsworth L.B.C.* [1981] 1 All E.R. 1162 (C.A.); however, provided that the social services authority does not impose a blanket resolution, it may be very difficult to upset an individual decision not to assist an intentionally homeless family under the Child Care Act: *R.* v. *L.B. of Tower Hamlets, ex p. Monaf* (1988) 20 H.L.R. 529 (C.A.).

[70] Although the decision must be that of the *authority*, the authority may delegate the power to make it to sub-committees or individual officers under L.G.A. 1972, s.101; see further, I. McLeod [1988] L.S.Gaz., October 12, p. 37.

[71] H. A. 1985, s.64(1)–(3); the "local connection" provisions are discussed below, paras. 5.14–5.52.

[72] *R.* v. *Beverley B.C., ex p. McPhee* (1978) 122 S.J. 760 (D.C.).

[73] *R.* v. *Preseli D.C., ex p. Fisher* (1984) 17 H.L.R. 147, 159 (D.C.).

If the authority notifies the applicant that it considers itself under anything less than the full duty to accommodate in section 65(2), or that it wishes to transfer him to another authority under the "local connection" provisions, then it must at the same time additionally notify him of its reasons[74]; the duty to give reasons does not depend on any request therefor having been made by the applicant. **4.165**

If an authority's decision is queried by the applicant, the authority is normally entitled to reconsider it,[75] make further inquiries, issue a new set of reasons and, if necessary, change the decision itself; however, it seems on general administrative law principles that a decision that the applicant's homelessness is unintentional cannot later be reversed by the authority substituting a finding of intentional homelessness.[76] **4.166**

The duty imposed on the authority to "notify" the applicant of its decision and (where appropriate) its reasons does not have to be discharged by actually sending the relevant information to the applicant[77] (who may, of course, have nowhere to receive correspondence). If the information is "not received by [the applicant]," then it has to be "made available at the authority's office for a reasonable period for collection" by him or on his behalf.[78] In any event, the notification must be given in writing.[79] **4.167**

With regard to the content of the reasons, the Code simply advises that the reasons should be "sufficient and straightforward."[80] It has been recognised judicially that "[t]he purpose of the requirement to give reasons [in s.64(4)] is to enable the individual concerned to see whether the grounds given are valid or invalid, whether they can be challenged . . . in a court of law."[81] According to general administrative law principles, the reasons must be "proper, adequate and intelligible"[82]; although they can be "briefly stated,"[83] they must **4.168**

[74] H.A. 1985, s.64(4).

[75] *R.* v. *Hambleton D.C., ex p. Geoghan* [1985] J.P.L. 394 (D.C.).

[76] See, *e.g. Livingstone* v. *Westminster Corpn.* [1904] 2 K.B. 109; *Re 56 Denton Road, Twickenham, Middlesex* [1953] Ch. 51; *Rootkin* v. *Kent C.C.* [1981] 2 All E.R. 227, 233 (C.A.).

[77] Compare the separate notification rules concerning the authority's responsibilities with regard to the protection of the applicant's property, see below, para. 5.91.

[78] H.A. 1985, s.64(5).

[79] *Ibid.*

[80] *Op. cit.* para. 2.24.

[81] *Per* Megaw L. J. in *Thornton* v. *Kirklees M.B.C.* [1979] 2 All E.R. 349, 354 (C.A.).

[82] *Per* Lord Scarman in *Great Portland Estates* v. *Westminster C.C.* [1984] 3 All E.R. 744, 752 (H.L.).

[83] *Ibid.*

"deal with the substantial points that have been raised."[84] The relevant question is whether the process of reasoning "was sufficiently apparent from the decision letter, assuming a careful, unpedantic and well-tutored reader."[85] It has been suggested that the authority should expressly state in its reasons that it is "satisfied" on the relevant points (as sections 65 and 66 require it to be), rather than use weaker phraseology such as that the applicant "be considered" to come within the relevant category.[86]

4.169 Where inadequate reasons are given, the applicant may seek (*inter alia*) an order (via a claim for judicial review in the High Court[87]) setting aside the authority's decision and remitting the case to the authority in order that it may provide proper reasons[88]; although the authority may subsequently be able to cure the defects in its reasons by issuing a correctly-worded decision in the light of the court's judgement, the applicant will at least normally get the benefit of the relevant duty to accommodate him in the meantime.[89] Sometimes, however, the courts have taken a benevolent attitude to the authority's stated reasons in homelessness cases, and have been prepared in effect to "re-write" them in order to fit within the wording of the Act.[90]

[84] *Re Poyser and Mills' Arbitration* [1963] 1 All E.R. 612, 616 (*per* Megaw J.); see also *Givandan & Co.* v. *Minister of Housing and Local Government* [1967] 1 W.L.R. 250; *French Kier Developments Ltd.* v. *Secretary of State for the Environment* [1977] 1 All E.R. 296; *Guppy's Properties Ltd.* v. *Knott* (1979) 253 E.G. 907; *Bone* v. *Mental Health Review Tribunal* [1985] 3 All E.R. 330, 333; *R.* v. *Mental Health Review Tribunal, ex p. Pickering* [1986] 1 All E.R. 99, 102(D.C.).

[85] *London Residuary Body* v. *Secretary of State for the Environment, The Times*, March 30, 1988 (D.C.), *per* Simon Brown J.; see, *e.g. R.* v. *L.B. of Hillingdon, ex p. H* (1988) 20 H.L.R. 554 (D.C.) (reasons stating merely that applicant could have continued to occupy his council house held insufficient to support finding of intentional homelessness).

[86] *Islam* v. *Hillingdon L.B.C.* [1981] 3 All E.R. 901, 910 (H.L., *per* Lord Lowry).

[87] The methods of challenging the authority's decision are discussed in detail in Chap. 6.

[88] See, *e.g. Brayhead (Ascot) Ltd.* v. *Berks C.C.* [1964] 1 All E.R. 149, 154; *R.* v. *L.B. of Hillingdon, ex p. H,* see above; *R.* v. *L.B. of Tower Hamlets, ex p. Monaf* (1988) 20 H.L.R. 529 (C.A.).

[89] Pursuant to H.A. 1985, s.63.

[90] See, *e.g. De Falco* v. *Crawley B.C.* [1980] Q.B. 460 (C.A.); *R.* v. *Swansea C.C., ex p. John* (1982) 9 H.L.R. 58 (D.C.); *R.* v. *L.B. of Wandsworth, ex p. Wells,* November 23, 1983 (D.C., unreported); *Mazzaccherini* v. *Argyll & Bute D.C.* [1987] 9 C.L. 679 (Ct. of Session: O.H.); but *cf.* the stricter approach adopted in, *e.g. Thornton* v. *Kirklees M.B.C.* [1979] 2 All E.R. 349, 354 (C.A.); *R.* v. *Reigate and Banstead B.C., ex p. Paris* (1984) 15 Fam. Law 28 (D.C.); *R.* v. *L.B. of Tower Hamlets, ex p. Monaf,* see above.

5 Discharge of the Duty to Secure Accommodation

The previous chapter considered in outline the general duties owed by the authority, and in detail the key concepts which govern the extent of those duties. This chapter will discuss aspects of the authority's duties which arise once a decision has been reached that the authority is under an obligation to secure accommodation for the applicant. 5.01

1. *The Length of Time for which Accommodation must be Provided*

(a) *Where the homelessness is intentional*

We have seen that where the authority is satisfied that the applicant is homeless, in priority need, but intentionally homeless, it must not only offer advice and assistance, but must also secure that accommodation is made available for the applicant for such a period as it considers will give him a reasonable opportunity of himself securing accommodation for his occupation.[1] 5.02

In deciding on the period of time to allow an applicant in this situation, authorities are advised by the Code that they "should not arbitrarily nor too quickly withdraw the provision of accommodation."[2] It would clearly be wrong[3] for authorities to impose inflexible "blanket" rules, offering for example 28 days in "bed and breakfast" for intentionally homeless families regardless of the diffi- 5.03

[1] H.A. 1985, s.65(3); see above, para. 4.08.

[2] Para. 4.01.

[3] *Bristol C.C.* v. *Stockford,* June 25, 1973 (Ch.D., unreported); a decision on the former temporary housing duty in the National Assistance Act 1948, s.21(1)(*b*).

culties which they may experience in rehousing themselves. However, there would appear to be nothing to prevent an authority from adopting a general policy of applying a pre-determined fixed period, provided this period is reasonable and individual consideration is given to each case in order to establish whether the fixed period is in fact appropriate.[4]

5.04 The courts have decided that, as regards the London area, a short period such as 14 or 28 days is normally insufficient to allow for the finding of family accommodation,[5] and that a period of three to four months or even longer might reasonably be required.[6] Outside the London area, the time allowed to a family in temporary accommodation might legitimately be shorter where appropriate. Although periods as diverse as 14 days and two months have been considered appropriate for provincial authorities,[7] each case depends on its own facts; and it has indeed been argued that if the applicant, at the end of the period allowed by the authority, has still not found accommodation despite constant searching, then this provides prima facie evidence that the original period fixed by the authority must have been too short.[8]

5.05 In determining the reasonableness of the period for which accommodation is offered to an intentionally homeless person, it is obviously crucial to decide the correct date from which that period starts to run. It has been suggested that the "reasonable period" can, in an appropriate case, actually ante-date the communication to the applicant of the authority's decision on intentionality, so that account can be taken of the time allowed in temporary housing provided under section 63 prior to the decision being reached.[9] However, the better view[10] is that the period can only commence when the authority's decision on intentionality is communicated to the applicant, for until that time the responsibility for finding accommo-

[4] See, *e.g. British Oxygen Co. Ltd.* v. *Minister of Technology* [1971] A.C. 610 (H.L.); *Roberts* v. *Dorset C.C.* (1977) 75 L.G.R. 462; *R.* v. *Rochdale M.B.C., ex p. Cromer Ring Mill* [1982] 3 All E.R. 761, 766 (D.C.); *Eastleigh B.C.* v. *Betts* [1983] 2 All E.R. 1111, 1119 (H.L.); *Findlay* v. *Secretary of State for the Home Dept.* [1984] 3 All E.R. 801, 828 (H.L.).

[5] *Fanning* v. *Wandsworth L.B.C.* [1980] L.A.G. Bull. 16 (Cty. Ct.); *Lally* v. *Kensington and Chelsea B.C., The Times*, March 27, 1980.

[6] *Lally* v. *Kensington and Chelsea B.C., ibid.*

[7] *R.* v. *Slough B.C., ex p. Ealing L.B.C.* [1981] 1 All E.R. 601, 612 (C.A.); *R.* v. *Southampton C.C., ex p. Ward* (1984) 14 H.L.R. 114, 138 (D.C.).

[8] R. Carnwath, *A Guide to the Housing (Homeless Persons) Act 1977* (1978), pp. 46–47.

[9] *De Falco* v. *Crawley B.C.* [1980] 1 All E.R. 913 (C.A.).

[10] See the dissenting opinion of Bridge L.J. in *De Falco, ibid.* p. 925.

dation does not rest with him. It is at least clear that time can start running for these purposes from a merely informal communication of the authority's decision on intentionality, even though this is later followed by a formal notification.[11]

Even where the period allowed by the housing authority has been exhausted, if the applicant has dependent children he could consider an approach to the social services authority pursuant to section 1(1) of the Child Care Act 1980, since this provision allows assistance to be given in order to diminish the need to receive children into care, even though the parents have been judged intentionally homeless by the housing authority.[12] **5.06**

(b) *Where the homelessness is unintentional*

It was noted in the previous chapter that where the authority is satisfied that the applicant is homeless, in priority need, and unintentionally homeless, then it owes the full duty to secure that accommodation becomes available for his occupation.[13] No time-limit is specified in this connection, and none is to be implied: the applicant is entitled to be provided with accommodation "indefinite in length," regardless of any lack of security of tenure affecting his previous accommodation,[14] although the authority is permitted to provide the accommodation in stages (so that the first stage may be, for example, bed and breakfast accommodation).[15] **5.07**

2. *Preventative Measures where the Applicant is Threatened with Homelessness*

It will be recalled that where the applicant is unintentionally threatened with homelessness and in priority need, the authority must take reasonable steps to secure that accommodation does not cease to be available for his occupation.[16] It appears that this in fact imposes a two-fold duty on the authority. **5.08**

[11] *Dyson* v. *Kerrier D.C.* [1980] 1 W.L.R. 1205 (C.A.).

[12] *Tilley* v. *Wandsworth L.B.C.* [1981] 1 All E.R. 1162 (C.A.); *R.* v. *L.B. of Tower Hamlets, ex p. Monaf* (1988) 20 H.L.R. 529 (C.A.); see above, para. 4.163.

[13] H.A. 1985, s.65(2); see above, para. 4.14.

[14] *R.* v. *L.B. of Camden, ex p. Wait* (1986) 18 H.L.R. 434 (D.C.); however, in considering the *type* of accommodation to offer, the authority can have regard to the degree of security afforded by the applicant's previous accommodation, *R.* v. *Westminster C.C., ex p. Tansey*, March 6, 1987 (D.C., unreported).

[15] *R.* v. *East Hertfordshire D.C., ex p. Hunt* (1985) 1 F.L.R. 431 (D.C.); see below, paras. 5.78–5.80.

[16] H.A. 1985, s.66(2): see above, para. 4.12.

5.09 First, the authority must in an appropriate case take reasonable steps to try to preserve the applicant's current accommodation for him; this may involve, for example, the housing authority persuading the social services authority to provide financial assistance under section 1(1) of the Child Care Act 1980 where children are involved[17]; or the housing authority may be able to arrange a remortgage[18] for an owner-occupying mortgagor on more favourable terms than those which are currently causing his mortgage default.

5.10 Where, however, the authority decides that it cannot prevent the loss of the applicant's existing accommodation, it appears to be under a second, quite separate duty to take reasonable steps to keep, in effect, a "safety net" under the applicant, so that when he loses his existing accommodation, other accommodation can immediately be made available, thus ensuring that accommodation does not cease to be available for his occupation. It is significant that the duty relates to securing "accommodation" in a wide sense, and not to "his" (*i.e.* current) accommodation. Thus an applicant in this situation should not actually become statutorily "homeless" at all.[19] This "cumulative duty" approach to persons threatened with homelessness becomes important in the context of the "local connection" provisions, since (as will be seen) these provisions can only operate where the full duty is owed to a *homeless* person.[20]

3. *Refusal by the Applicant of the Authority's Offer of Accommodation*

5.11 We have seen that a refusal by the applicant of the authority's offer of accommodation cannot of itself constitute intentional homelessness.[21] However, if the applicant unreasonably refuses a suitable[22] offer from the authority, then the authority will nevertheless have performed its duty[23]; in addition, it will be absolved from having to

[17] See above, para. 4.163.
[18] Pursuant to H.A. 1985, ss.435(1), 439(3).
[19] But note that, following the introduction of the "reasonableness" criterion into s.58, an applicant may sometimes now be statutorily "homeless" in a situation where previously he would have been regarded as "threatened with homelessness": see above, paras. 4.42–4.48.
[20] See below, paras. 5.14, 5.34.
[21] See above, paras. 4.145–4.146.
[22] For a discussion of the relevant considerations in deciding whether the offer is suitable, see below, paras. 5.68–5.71.
[23] *R.* v. *Westminster C.C., ex p. Chambers* (1983) 18 L.G.R. 401 (D.C.); see above, para. 4.146.

make any further offer to the applicant so long as there have been no material changes in his circumstances,[24] even if the fresh application has not been made directly to it by the applicant but has been referred to it by another authority under the local connection provisions.[25]

In this context it is necessary to distinguish between a refusal of an authority's offer by the applicant and a mere request by him that the authority should reconsider its decision: in the latter situation, the authority continues to owe the original duty to the applicant.[26] The authority must also give the applicant a proper opportunity to consider the offer, by giving him sufficient details about the property and a reasonable time to decide whether to accept it.[27] **5.12**

Where the applicant has unreasonably refused the authority's offer of accommodation, and he re-applies to the same authority at a later date, the authority will become subject to a fresh duty to offer him accommodation if there has been a change in the material circumstances which causes the previous offer of accommodation to be unsuitable, even though the change of circumstances does not actually amount to a new incidence of homelessness.[28] **5.13**

4. *Transfer of Responsibility under the "Local Connection" Provisions*

(a) *General*

We have seen that an authority, when interviewing an applicant, may make inquiries as to whether he has a local connection with the area of another housing authority.[29] Sections 67 and 68 of the Act try to ensure that in cases where the full duty to secure accommodation under section 65(2) would otherwise be imposed, but the applicant has no "local connection" with the authority to which he applies, and he has such a connection with another authority, then that latter authority should ultimately accept responsibility if the **5.14**

[24] *R.* v. *Westminster C.C., ex p. Chambers, ibid.*, as modified by *R.* v. *Ealing L.B.C., ex p. McBain* [1985] 1 W.L.R. 1351 (C.A.).

[25] *R.* v. *Hammersmith & Fulham L.B.C., ex p. O'Brian* (1985) 84 L.G.R. 202 (D.C.); see below, para. 5.43.

[26] *R.* v. *L.B. of Wandsworth, ex p. Lindsay* (1986) 18 H.L.R. 502 (D.C.); see also *Parr* v. *Wyre B.C.* (1982) 2 H.L.R. 41, 71 (C.A.).

[27] *Parr* v. *Wyre B.C., ibid.* p. 72; *R.* v. *L.B. of Wandsworth, ex p. Lindsay*, see above.

[28] *R.* v. *Ealing L.B.C., ex p. McBain*, see above, modifying the principle laid down in *R.* v. *Westminster C.C., ex p. Chambers*, see above; in *McBain* the accommodation originally offered to the applicant when she was pregnant with her first child was no longer suitable for her following her second pregnancy.

[29] H.A. 1985, s.62(2); see above, para. 4.30.

former authority wishes it to do so; but, pending a decision on this point, the authority to which the application was initially made must normally provide temporary accommodation for the applicant.

5.15 The relevant material is scattered among the Act,[30] the Code,[31] two statutory instruments,[32] and a formal agreement entered into in 1979 by the three local authority associations[33] and entitled *The Agreement on Procedures for Referrals of the Homeless—Revised* (hereafter referred to as the "1979 Agreement").

5.16 The 1979 Agreement is not authorised by the 1985 Act: it does not form part of any "arrangements" directed by Ministerial order to deal with disputes between authorities pursuant to the Act,[34] nor is it Ministerial guidance falling within section 71.[35] Despite its lack of precise legal status, the 1979 Agreement is in practice a useful aid for councils in England and Wales[36] to the interpretation of the sometimes rather vague "local connection" provisions; the House of Lords has decided that a council is free to apply the "eminently sensible and proper" guidelines in the 1979 Agreement, provided it does not close its mind to considerations as to the suitability or otherwise of the guidance to the particular facts of each individual case.[37]

5.17 There is also a digest of Referees Decisions published by the London Boroughs Association, which sets out the decisions of referees appointed to resolve disputes between authorities pursuant to arrangements prescribed under the Act[38]; this is hereafter referred to as the "Digest."

[30] Particularly ss.61, 67 and 68.

[31] *Op. cit.* paras. 2.21–2.23, 5.1–5.6.

[32] The Housing (Homeless Persons) (Appropriate Arrangements) Order 1978 (S.I. 1978 No. 69), and the Housing (Homeless Persons) (Appropriate Arrangements) (No. 2) Order 1978 (S.I. 1978 No. 661); both were issued pursuant to what is now H.A. 1985, s.67(4)–(6), and remain in force under the Housing (Consequential Provisions) Act 1985, s.2.

[33] Association of District Councils, Association of Metropolitan Authorities, and London Boroughs Association.

[34] *Cf.* the statutory instruments referred to in n. 32 above.

[35] See above, para. 4.03, n. 5.

[36] Scottish authorities are not parties to the 1979 Agreement; the Convention of Scottish Local Authorities has produced its own, somewhat different, agreement (see N. Finnis, *Roof*, September 1978, pp. 139–140); where a Scottish and an English or Welsh authority are in dispute, the referee who has to decide the matter (see below) is therefore normally restricted to the wording of the Act itself.

[37] *Eastleigh B.C.* v. *Betts* [1983] 2 All E.R. 1111 (H.L.); *R.* v. *L.B. of Waltham Forest, ex p. Koutsoudis*, September 1, 1986 (D.C., unreported).

[38] See n. 32 above.

In practice, "local connection" transfers do not appear to be implemented very frequently; most applicants become homeless in the area where they have previously been resident for a considerable period, thus preventing any referral under section 67 (since, as will be seen, responsibility cannot be transferred to another authority where there is a "local connection" with the authority to which the initial application was made). **5.18**

(b) *The meaning of "local connection"*

"Local connection" is defined by section 61: a person can establish a local connection with an area because he is, or in the past was, normally resident in it of his own choice, or because he is employed in it, or because of family associations with it, or because of special circumstances.[39] But whichever limb is being relied on, the local connection must be sufficiently built up and established, so that it may be that there is (for example) "normal residence" which does not on the facts suffice to establish a local connection.[40] **5.19**

(i) Residence. The word "reside" is not defined, but would appear to mean "to have one's settled or usual abode."[41] The residence must be "normal," which appears to mean habitual, lawful and settled, disregarding temporary or occasional absences[42]; referees have taken the view that "visitors, guests or wanderers settling temporarily," and occupiers of "temporary welfare accommodation," are not "normally" resident.[43] **5.20**

The residence must also be of a person's "own choice." The Act specifies that this requirement will not be satisfied if the person becomes resident in the area because he or a person who might reasonably be expected to reside with him is serving in the regular armed forces or is detained under the authority of any Act of Parliament[44] (for example, because he is a mental patient detained under **5.21**

[39] H.A. 1985, s.61(1).

[40] *Eastleigh B.C.* v. *Betts*, see above; discussed below, para. 5.24.

[41] *Per* Viscount Cave L.C. in *Levene* v. *I.R.C.* [1928] All E.R. Rep. 746, 749 (H.L.); applied in *Fox* v. *Stirk* [1970] 2 Q.B. 463 (C.A.); *Brokelmann* v. *Barr* [1971] 2 Q.B. 602; *Shah* v. *Barnet L.B.C.* [1983] 2 A.C. 309 (H.L.).

[42] *Shah* v. *Barnet L.B.C.*, *ibid.*; *Eastleigh B.C.* v. *Betts*, see above, at p. 1120.

[43] Digest, Cases No. 5 and 8; *cf.* Case No. 9, where the applicant was sharing accommodation with friends with the intention that the arrangement would continue indefinitely, but later the friends decided to sell the house, and the referee held that this arrangement constituted "normal residence," since it was "not of a transient nature."

[44] H.A. 1985, s.61(2)(*b*), (3).

the Mental Health Act 1983, or because he is serving a sentence of imprisonment). The Minister can add to the excluded categories of residence.[45]

5.22 It appears that the statutory exclusions will apply even though the person in question would in any event have chosen to reside in the area had the prescribed circumstances not compelled him to do so. However, local residential ties which have already been built up before the prescribed "compulsory residence" began can be counted for local connection purposes[46]; and where an applicant's "compulsory residence" ends (for example because he ceases to serve in the armed forces), then even in the absence of any previous residential ties a relevant fresh period of residence in the area may in an appropriate case be established (even in the same unit of accommodation), which will count for local connection purposes.[47] Where someone is discharged from the armed forces but does not on the facts have a local connection with the area of his choice, the 1979 Agreement suggests that the relevant authority should nevertheless be prepared to accept a local connection on the ground of "special circumstances."[48]

5.23 The 1979 Agreement also suggests that residence is not of a person's "own choice" if it is in hospital or in "an institution in which households are accepted only for a limited period (*e.g.* mother and baby homes, refuges, rehabilitation centres)"[49]; but it would seem that students should not necessarily be prevented from acquiring a local connection through residing in university or college accommodation, even though this is situated in a different area from that in which their parents live.[50]

5.24 The Act is silent as to the length of time for which "normal residence" must have lasted before a local connection can be acquired. The House of Lords has held that a local connection (whether by way of normal residence, employment, family associations or special circumstances) has to have been sufficiently built up and established in real terms, so that, as regards "normal residence," while it would be possible for an applicant to be (in one sense) "normally resident" in an area after living there for only one day, this would not suffice to

[45] H.A. 1985, s.61(4)–(5).
[46] *R.* v. *Vale of White Horse D.C., ex p. Smith and Hay* (1985) 83 L.G.R. 437 (D.C.).
[47] *Ibid.*
[48] *Op. cit.* para. 2.5(iv).
[49] *Op. cit.* para. 2.6(iii)–(iv).
[50] *Fox* v. *Stirk*, see above; *Shah* v. *Barnet L.B.C.*, see above.

show that the applicant had actually built up and established a *local connection* through his residence.[51]

The 1979 Agreement suggests as a "working definition" of normal residence that the household must have been residing in the area in question for at least six out of the past 12 months, or at least three out of the past five years, or both[52]; however, in order primarily to safeguard the position of "seaside" authorities, the 1979 Agreement adds the proviso that "residence up to 6 months under one or more tenancies subject to Case 13 of Schedule 15 of the Rent Act 1977 should be disregarded for the purpose of defining 'normal residence' "[53]; the effect is to leave out of account periods of residence of up to six months under "winter lets."[54] These guidelines on periods of residence can be safely followed by authorities, provided they are treated only as "norms" and consideration is given in each case as to whether they should be departed from having regard to the particular facts.[55] **5.25**

(ii) Employment. The 1979 Agreement provides that in "employment" cases the relevant authority should "satisfy itself by confirmation from the employer that the person is in his employment and that the employment is not of a casual nature."[56] Particular problems can however arise in the case of employees who are permanent but "mobile," for example bricklayers who move from one building site to the next, in a variety of areas, but work throughout for the same employer: in such cases the place of employment is arguably either where the contract of employment with the mobile worker was made, or where the head office of the firm is situated.[57] **5.26**

The Act provides that service in the regular armed forces is not to be regarded as employment for these purposes (and permits the Minister to add further excluded categories of employment).[58] **5.27**

[51] *Eastleigh B.C.* v. *Betts*, see above; see also *Brooks* v. *Midlothian D.C.* (1986) 37 Housing Aid 4 (Ct. of Session); *R.* v. *L.B. of Islington, ex p. Adigun* (1988) 20 H.L.R. 600 (D.C.).

[52] *Op. cit.* para. 2.5(i).

[53] *Ibid.*

[54] In the case of post-January 15, 1989 tenancies which are "assured," the "winter let" ground is contained in H.A. 1988, Sched. 2, Pt. I, gd. 3; see above, para. 4.141, n. 32.

[55] *Eastleigh B.C.* v. *Betts*, see above; *R.* v. *Waltham Forest, ex p. Koutsoudis*, see above.

[56] *Op. cit.* para. 2.5(ii).

[57] L. Culley, *Roof*, November 1978, p. 190; *cf.* Digest, Cases No. 17, 21 and 25.

[58] H.A. 1985, ss.61(2)(*a*), (4)–(5).

5.28 Only *present* employment is relevant for the purpose of giving rise to a local connection under this head, so that someone who leaves the armed forces and obtains a civilian job in the same area can claim to have established a local connection thereby regardless of the past service in the armed forces.[59] However, where the person in question has no current employment in the area, a lengthy period of past employment there may give rise to a local connection on the ground of "special circumstances."[60]

5.29 **(iii) Family associations.** Again, this term is not defined by the Act. According to the 1979 Agreement, family associations "normally arise where an applicant, or member of his household, has parents, adult children or brothers or sisters currently residing in the area and these relatives have been resident for a period of at least 5 years, and the applicant indicates a wish to be near them."[61] The Agreement adds that the residence of relatives other than parents, adult children or brothers or sisters should be taken to establish a local connection "[o]nly in exceptional circumstances," and emphasises that applicants should not be referred to another area on the ground of family associations if they object.[62]

5.30 **(iv) Special circumstances.** According to the 1979 Agreement, an authority is at liberty to conclude that an applicant has a local connection with its *own* area "for any reason it may decide," although the authority cannot impose a "special circumstance" local connection on *another* authority without that authority's consent.[63] The examples given in the 1979 Agreement of "special circumstances" justifying acceptance of a local connection, even though the normal criteria ((i)-(iii) above) are not satisfied, are where the household returns from abroad, or where an applicant is discharged from the armed forces, or where an applicant wishes to return to an area where he was brought up or had lived for a considerable time in the past, though he has not lived there in recent years.[64] The assessing authority must give proper consideration to

[59] *R.* v. *Vale of White Horse D.C., ex p. Smith and Hay*, see above.
[60] See below, para. 5.30.
[61] *Op. cit.* para. 2.5(iii).
[62] *Ibid.*
[63] *Op. cit.* para. 2.5(iv).
[64] *Ibid.*

the possibility of a local connection by virtue of "special circumstances," where appropriate.[65]

In the case of a dispute between authorities, the referee may be prepared to take a flexible approach in deciding that there is a local connection by virtue of special circumstances with one of the authorities involved.[66] **5.31**

(c) *Implementation of the transfer provisions*

(i) The relevant conditions. The transfer provisions can only be operated where the authority to which the application is made is satisfied[67] that the applicant is homeless and in priority need, and is not satisfied that he became homeless intentionally (so that the "full duty" is prima facie owed), *and* the authority is of the opinion that the following additional conditions are satisfied: neither the applicant nor any person who might reasonably be expected to reside with him has a local connection with its area; the applicant or a person who might reasonably be expected to reside with him has a local connection with another authority's area; and neither the applicant nor any person who might reasonably be expected to reside with him will run the risk of domestic violence in that other authority's area.[68] All of these conditions must be satisfied, and each warrants separate analysis. **5.32**

Even where all the conditions are satisfied, there is no requirement that the transfer provisions should be operated, but merely a power to implement them. The 1979 Agreement urges authorities to "try to avoid disruption to the household, which may result from the operation of the [local connection] criteria."[69] **5.33**

The "full duty" condition. It is clear that the transfer provisions cannot be used where the applicant is found, by the authority to which he applies, to be either intentionally homeless, or merely threatened **5.34**

[65] *R.* v. *L.B. of Waltham Forest, ex p. Koutsoudis*, see above.

[66] See, *e.g.* Digest, Case No. 3.

[67] Thus there can be no referral under these provisions where the authority has not yet completed its inquiries under s.62: *R.* v. *Crawley B.C., ex p. L.B. of Brent*, March 24, 1983 (D.C., unreported); the authority must have made proper inquiries on the relevant issues, which were appropriate to resolve any factual disputes, before a referral can be made, *R.* v. *Tower Hamlets L.B.C., ex p. Camden L.B.C., The Times*, December 12, 1988 (D.C.).

[68] H.A. 1985, s.67(1)–(2).

[69] *Op. cit.* para. 4.6.

with homelessness.[70] If an applicant who was formerly found to be threatened with homelessness and in priority need actually loses his accommodation, it seems that the transfer provisions still cannot be used, because he should never be allowed by the authority to become statutorily "homeless" at all in this situation, and the authority should not be able to engineer a local connection transfer through initially defaulting in its duties owed to those threatened with homelessness.[71]

5.35 *The condition of no local connection with the determining authority.* With regard to the condition that neither the applicant nor any person who might reasonably be expected to reside with him[72] must have any local connection with the area of the authority to which the application was made, it is clear that if there *is* any such local connection, there is no question of a transfer of responsibility to another authority under the local connection provisions[73] on the ground that there happens to be a greater connection with that other authority's area.[74]

5.36 *The condition of local connection with another authority.* Turning to the condition that either the applicant or a person who might reasonably be expected to reside with him has a local connection with another authority's area, it frequently happens that an applicant and his family unit appear to have local connections with the areas of more than one other authority (for example, he may apply to authority A, with which he has no local connection, and authority A may discover that he has spent six out of the last 12 months in the area of authority B, and three out of the last five years in the area of authority C). In such a case, the Code states that the authority to which the initial application is made should take account of the household's wishes in deciding which authority to notify[75]; and the 1979 Agreement suggests that another relevant factor in deciding which auth-

[70] H.A. 1985, s.67(1)(*a*); *Delahaye* v. *Oswestry B.C.*, *The Times*, July 29, 1980; *Williams* v. *Exeter C.C.* [1981] L.A.G. Bull. 211 (Cty. Ct.).

[71] H.A. 1985, s.66(2); see above, para. 5.10.

[72] The importance of considering not just the applicant's position, but also that of any other person who might reasonably be expected to reside with him, was emphasised in *R.* v. *Mr. Referee McCall, etc., ex p. Eastbourne B.C.* [1981] L.A.G. Bull. 210 (D.C.).

[73] The other authority may however be prepared voluntarily to accept responsibility under H.A. 1985, ss.69(1) and 72: see below, paras. 5.53, 5.62.

[74] Code, para. 2.21; *R.* v. *Eastleigh B.C.*, *ex p. Betts* [1983] 2 All E.R. 481, 491 (C.A.).

[75] *Op. cit.* para. 5.3; applied in *R.* v. *Mr. Referee McCall*, see above.

ority to notify in a "multiple local connection" case would be "the degree of strength of the residential local connection in relation to connections established by virtue of employment and family ties."[76]

It may also sometimes happen that an applicant and the members of his family unit (where applicable) have no local connection with the area of any housing authority (as, for example, in the case of gypsies, "gentlemen of the road," and certain lawful immigrants[77]). In such cases the Code makes clear that the duty to secure accommodation (assuming the relevant conditions in section 65 are satisfied) rests with the authority to which the applicant actually applies.[78] It may be that this authority discovers that he has previously applied to another authority which wrongly refused to accept responsibility for him. Nevertheless, there being no "local connection" with that authority's area, the applicant cannot be referred back there under these provisions. Thus conscientious authorities may have to accommodate applicants in respect of whom other authorities have neglected their duties. **5.37**

The condition of no risk of domestic violence. The final condition is that neither the applicant nor any person who might reasonably be expected to reside with him will run the risk of domestic violence in the other authority's area; if there is such a risk, the transfer provisions cannot be operated even if the person concerned is prepared to accept that risk and is willing to return to that other authority's area. **5.38**

For these purposes, a person runs the risk of domestic violence if he runs the risk of violence from a person with whom (but for the risk of violence) he might reasonably be expected to reside, or from a person with whom he formerly resided, or if he runs the risk of threats of violence from such a person and the threats are likely to be carried out.[79] This definition refers to the "risk" of domestic violence, whereas the extended definition of homelessness in section 58(3) refers to the "probability" of violence,[80] which suggests that under section 67 there may be no probability of violence in the other authority's area, but merely a risk that this may occur, and yet this will suffice to bar any transfer of the applicant (and his family unit) to that area. **5.39**

[76] *Op. cit.* para. 3.6.
[77] See above, para. 4.40.
[78] *Op. cit.* para. 5.5.
[79] H.A. 1985, s.67(3).
[80] See above, paras. 4.89–4.91.

5.40 In order to establish the relevant "risk" of violence or threats of violence, it is certainly not essential to show that actual violence or actual threats of violence have already occurred in the past.[81] Nevertheless, the limited case law on the issue of "risk" in this context has adopted a hard line, showing a marked unwillingness to interfere with the authority's own assessment that there will be no risk involved in a transfer even where there have been actual incidents of past violence.[82]

5.41 **(ii) The transfer machinery.** Assuming that the "exporting" authority is of the opinion that all the above conditions are satisfied, then, in order to operate the transfer provisions, it must notify the "importing" authority of the situation.[83] The "exporting" authority will however remain under a duty to secure accommodation for the applicant and his family unit pending acceptance of responsibility by the "importing" authority[84]; and if it later transpires that the conditions for transfer were not in fact all satisfied, the responsibility for securing accommodation remains with the "exporting" authority.[85] Furthermore, once the "exporting" authority decides that the applicant is homeless and writes to the "importing" authority pursuant to these provisions, the "exporting" authority cannot later change its mind and deny any responsibility for the applicant on the ground that, after all, he is *not* homeless.[86]

5.42 The "exporting" authority must also notify the applicant in writing that it is operating the "transfer" provisions, together with its reasons for doing so[87]; and it must notify the applicant in writing of the result of the referral when this is known, together with the reasons therefor.[88] The accommodation duties imposed on the "exporting" authority are independent of, and arise prior to, any

[81] See *Kelly* v. *Monklands D.C.* 1986 S.L.T. 169 (Ct. of Session: O.H.); see above, para. 4.107.

[82] *R.* v. *Bristol C.C., ex p. Browne* [1979] 3 All E.R. 344, 350–351 (D.C.); *R.* v. *L.B. of Islington, ex p. Adigun* (1988) 20 H.L.R. 600 (D.C.); *cf.* the more flexible approach indicated by the Code, para. 2.21, and by the decision in *McCartney* v. *McCartney* [1981] 2 W.L.R. 184 (concerning the grant of an exclusion order under the Domestic Proceedings and Magistrates' Courts Act 1978, s.16(3)).

[83] H.A. 1985, s.67(1).

[84] *Ibid.* s.68(1).

[85] *Ibid.* s.68(2).

[86] *R.* v. *Beverley B.C., ex p. McPhee* (1978) 122 S.J. 760 (D.C.); see, *e.g. Livingstone* v. *Westminster Corpn.* [1904] 2 K.B. 109.

[87] H.A. 1985, s.64(3)(*b*), (4)–(5).

[88] *Ibid.* s.68(3)–(4).

notification to the applicant of the position concerning the local connection procedures.[89]

(iii) The responsibilities of the "importing" authority. Turning to the position of the "importing" authority, it must normally secure accommodation for the applicant if all the conditions referred to above are satisfied.[90] However, if the "importing" authority has on a previous occasion offered accommodation to the applicant under section 65(2) (the general "full duty" provision), which the applicant unreasonably refused, and there has been no change in the applicant's material circumstances, then the "importing" authority is not under any obligation to house the applicant: the reason is that the local connection housing duty owed by the "importing" authority is not a separate duty from the duty imposed by section 65(2), but is all part of the same obligation, so that the position of the "importing" authority is treated as being the same as if the applicant had remained in its area throughout.[91] **5.43**

The 1979 Agreement urges "importing" authorities to "accept the facts of the case relating to residence, employment, family ties, etc., as stated by the ['exporting'] authority unless they have clear provable evidence to the contrary," since "[i]t is the ['exporting'] authority's duty to investigate the household's circumstances with their usual degree of care and thoroughness before making a referral . . . ."[92] **5.44**

The "importing" authority cannot refuse to accept the "exporting" authority's decision that the applicant is homeless, in priority need, and unintentionally homeless, for these issues are not normally relevant for consideration by the "importing" authority,[93] but only by the "exporting" authority.[94] Thus if the "exporting" authority decides, for example, that the applicant is not intentionally homeless, the "importing" authority normally cannot refuse to accept responsibility on the ground that the applicant's homeless- **5.45**

[89] *R.* v. *Beverley B.C., ex p. McPhee*, see above.

[90] H.A. 1985, s.68(2).

[91] *R.* v. *Hammersmith & Fulham L.B.C., ex p. O'Brian* (1985) 84 L.G.R. 202 (D.C.); with regard to "changes in material circumstances," see *R.* v. *Ealing L.B.C., ex p. McBain* [1985] 1 W.L.R. 1351 (C.A.), discussed above, para. 5.11.

[92] *Op. cit.* para. 4.3.

[93] H.A. 1985, s.68(2); however, the "importing" authority may be able to block the referral by showing that the "exporting" authority has not made proper inquiries on the relevant issues, *R.* v. *Tower Hamlets L.B.C., ex p. Camden L.B.C.*, *The Times*, December 12, 1988 (D.C.).

[94] H.A. 1985, s.67(1).

ness was in fact intentional. Indeed, the "importing" authority will not normally be permitted formally to dispute the issue of intentionality on a section 67 transfer even if that authority had itself decided that the applicant's homelessness was intentional following an original application made to it by the applicant on a previous occasion.[95] In effect, therefore, sections 67 and 68 provide for a "merry-go-round," which can be boarded by the applicant at any point where some authority can be persuaded to accept the applicant as unintentionally homeless, following which he can be referred back to the authority with which he has a local connection but which may previously have denied permanent responsibility for him on the ground that he was intentionally homeless.[96] In practice, therefore, the concept of intentionality may vary in the rigour or otherwise with which it is applied, depending on whether the authority making the decision will ultimately be charged with the burden of rehousing.[97]

5.46 Where there is a successful referral, in the sense that the "importing" authority accepts responsibility, then the 1979 Agreement allows that authority a period of up to 14 days from the date of the initial notification to it in which to make arrangements for the accommodation of the applicant,[98] and it must normally reimburse the "exporting" authority for all expenses which the latter authority may have incurred through the provision of temporary accommodation.[99] However, where the "exporting" authority delays unduly (*i.e.* normally, for more than 14 days) in notifying the "importing" authority of its intention to make a local connection referral of the applicant, then the "importing" authority is only to be responsible for expenses incurred after the receipt of the notification.[1]

(d) *Disputes between authorities concerning the transfer provisions*

5.47 The Act provides that any question relating to the three referral conditions (*i.e.* absence of local connection with the "exporting" authority, presence of local connection with the "importing" authority, and absence of risk of domestic violence in the area of the

[95] *R.* v. *Slough B.C., ex p. Ealing L.B.C.* [1981] 1 All E.R. 601 (C.A.); *R.* v. *Tower Hamlets L.B.C., ex p. Camden L.B.C., ibid.*
[96] *R.* v. *Slough B.C., ex p. Ealing L.B.C., ibid.* p. 616.
[97] See P. J. Woodward and E. M. Davidge, [1982] J.P.L. 158, 165.
[98] *Op. cit.* para. 5.2.
[99] *Op. cit.* para. 5.4.
[1] *Ibid.*

"importing" authority), "shall be determined by agreement" between the authorities concerned, or, in default of such agreement, in accordance with "arrangements" prescribed by statutory instrument.[2] The 1979 Agreement provides for a "negotiation period" of 21 days running from the notification by the "exporting" authority to the "importing" authority, within which the two authorities must try to agree upon whether or not responsibility is to be transferred,[3] failing which the prescribed "arrangements" will have to be operated in order to resolve the dispute. In the meantime, the "exporting" authority remains responsible for securing accommodation for the applicant.[4]

The "arrangements" are prescribed by statutory instrument for authorities in England and Wales,[5] and provide for any relevant disputed question to be determined by a person mutually agreed upon as referee by the local authorities involved; if however the authorities cannot even agree on the choice of referee, then the dispute is to be determined by a person appointed by the chairmen of the associations representing those authorities, from a panel drawn up by the local authority associations. **5.48**

It is clear from the wording of the Act[6] that the referee is restricted to determining issues concerning local connections, so that he cannot investigate the question of whether the full duty to accommodate is owed to the applicant at all, for example because he is alleged to be intentionally homeless.[7] **5.49**

The referee cannot automatically refer to the contents of the 1979 Agreement in reaching his decision, since after the authorities involved have failed to arrive at a solution by reference to the 1979 Agreement, its effect is spent, and the referee must normally apply the words of the Act and the Code alone.[8] Nevertheless, if the authorities concerned agree, whether expressly or by implication, that the referee should apply the criteria in the 1979 Agreement, then **5.50**

[2] H.A. 1985, s.67(4).

[3] *Op. cit.* para. 6.

[4] H.A. 1985, s.68(1).

[5] See n. 32 above; separate arrangements are made by the Housing (Homeless Persons) (Appropriate Arrangements) (No.2) Order 1978 (S.I. 1978 No. 661) for cases involving only Scottish authorities, and for cases involving disputes between Scottish authorities and authorities in England and Wales.

[6] H.A. 1985, s.67(4).

[7] *R.* v. *Slough B.C., ex p. Ealing L.B.C.*, see above; the issues of homelessness, priority need and "unintentionality" fall to the "exporting" authority alone to decide, see above, para. 5.45.

[8] *R.* v. *Mr. Referee McCall, etc., ex p. Eastbourne B.C.*, see above.

(and only then) may he do so.[9] It is clearly a "very sensible approach"[10] for the authorities concerned to agree to allow the referee to decide the dispute having full regard to the 1979 Agreement since, as has been seen, the provisions of the Act and the Code concerning "local connection" are very vague, and it would be difficult for the referee to reach a sensible decision if he were to be precluded from using the same "rules of thumb" (concerning, for example, length of residence) as those which the authorities themselves adopted in their efforts to resolve the dispute.

5.51 The actual disputes procedure is broadly left to the discretion of the individual referee, but he must take into account relevant representations from the authorities involved together with any relevant information from the applicant himself, supplied in response to an invitation which the referee must extend to him to provide information on specified matters.[11] Neither the authorities nor the applicant have any right to an oral hearing as such.

5.52 The 1979 Agreement provides that, following the referee's decision, the costs already incurred in providing temporary accommodation for the household are to be borne by the "losing" authority.[12]

5. *Who is to Offer the Accommodation?*

(a) *General*

5.53 Assuming that an authority is under one of the duties to "secure" that accommodation is made available for the occupation of the applicant (and, where appropriate, for the occupation of members of his family unit[13]), then the authority need not offer its own accommodation if it can ensure that some other person (which can include a body corporate[14]) offers it to the applicant. Section 69(1) states that where an authority is under a duty to secure that accommodation becomes available for an applicant under section 65 or section 68, that duty may be discharged by the authority making one of its own suitable dwellings available, or securing that he obtains suitable accommodation from some other person, or giving him such

[9] *R.* v. *Mr. Referee McCall, etc., ex p. Eastbourne B.C.*, see above.
[10] *Ibid.*
[11] Housing (Homeless Persons) (Appropriate Arrangements) Order 1978 (S.I. 1978 No. 69), Sched., para. 6(3)–(4).
[12] *Op. cit.* para. 5.4.
[13] See H.A. 1985, s.75, discussed below, paras. 5.65–5.67.
[14] Interpretation Act 1978, Sched. 1.

advice and assistance as will secure that he obtains suitable accommodation from some other person. The distinction between the last two options appears to be that:

> "in the former case, the authority will be directly responsible to the owner of the property for payment of rent, etc.; whereas, in the latter, the applicant will be personally responsible, even though he may be assisted by the authority."[15]

In an appropriate case, the advice and assistance may be directed towards the applicant acquiring a house by purchase.[16]

Section 69(1) makes no express reference to the preliminary duty to accommodate in section 63,[17] but the Court of Appeal has decided that even as regards this preliminary duty, the authority can either make its own accommodation available, or use the agency of any other person or body.[18] **5.54**

Whichever method of arranging accommodation the authority chooses to adopt, it must, in order to "secure" the availability of the accommodation, itself take the necessary active steps; it cannot rely on accommodation obtained by the applicant himself, which it has taken no part in securing, as being a discharge of its own duty.[19] **5.55**

In a situation where the applicant's homelessness arises because, although he has a legal right to occupy accommodation, he is treated as having no accommodation because it is not accommodation which it would be reasonable for him to continue to occupy,[20] it would seem that the authority may in an appropriate case discharge its duty to "secure" that accommodation becomes available for him by taking the necessary remedial measures to ensure that it becomes reasonable for him to continue to occupy it.[21] Such action would secure that he "obtains suitable accommodation" within section 69(1), in the sense that, once it is again reasonable for him to occupy the accommodation, that accommodation will begin to "count" for the purposes of the Act so that his "homelessness" will cease. **5.56**

15 R. Carnwath, *op. cit.* p. 72.
16 Code, para. A2.3.
17 See above, para. 4.02.
18 *Family Housing Association* v. *Miah* (1982) 5 H.L.R. 94.
19 *R.* v. *Ealing L.B.C., ex p. Sidhu* (1982) 80 L.G.R. 534 (D.C.).
20 H.A. 1985, s.58(2A), see above, paras. 4.42–4.48.
21 There is an analogy here with the position where the applicant is "threatened with homelessness": see above, paras. 5.08–5.09.

(b) *The provision of council housing*

5.57 The relationship between the duties in Part III of the 1985 Act and the use of local authority accommodation which might otherwise be made available to families on the general council house waiting list is dealt with by section 22, which requires authorities, in effect, to give a "reasonable preference" in the allocation process to (*inter alios*) " . . . persons towards whom the authority are subject to a duty under section 65 or 68," *i.e.* persons found to be homeless (whether or not in priority need or intentionally homeless). The detailed operation of this "reasonable preference" obligation as regards the homeless has already been discussed.[22]

5.58 Where the authority has decided to offer its own accommodation, it need only make a single offer,[23] provided the accommodation offered is "suitable."[24]

(c) *The provision of accommodation by "some other person"*

5.59 If the authority decides to discharge its duty by securing that the accommodation is forthcoming from a source other than its own housing stock, then although in practice the "some other person" from whom the accommodation is to be obtained will normally be in the area of the housing authority in question, this is not essential, and an authority's decision to arrange accommodation a considerable distance away from its area will not necessarily be upset.[25]

5.60 However, the accommodation must be "suitable,"[26] not just as to the house itself, but also as to "other factors such as the nature of the

[22] See above, paras. 2.17–2.22; it may be that an authority has disposed of its entire stock under one of the privatisation schemes discussed in Chap. 15: in such a case the authority will nevertheless retain its statutory duties towards the homeless, but it may be able to enter into contracts with the new landlord(s) for the provision of the necessary accommodation: see above, para. 3.04, n. 6.

[23] *R.* v. *Westminster C.C., ex p. Chambers* (1982) 6 H.L.R. 24 (D.C.); *R.* v. *Wandsworth L.B.C., ex p. Lindsay* (1986) 18 H.L.R. 502 (D.C.); *cf.* the advice given in the Scottish Code of Guidance, para. 4.18, to the effect that the homeless should be entitled to the same number of offers as other applicants for council housing.

[24] See below, paras. 5.68–5.71.

[25] *R.* v. *Bristol C.C., ex p. Browne* [1979] 1 W.L.R. 1437 (D.C.), where the council's decision to return the applicant to Tralee (where she had formerly lived) was upheld on the facts despite her expressed fears of domestic violence (as to which see above, paras. 5.38–5.40); the "local connection" provisions could not be operated, since Tralee was not a relevant "local housing authority" (see H.A. 1985, s.1).

[26] See below, paras. 5.68–5.71.

area and . . . employment prospects"[27]; furthermore, "the wishes of the applicant [are] one of the things to be taken into account if it [is] proposed to send him to an area far distant from that where he ha[s] a local connection,"[28] and the authority should if possible "avoid undue disruption of education . . . or other ties of this kind."[29]

(d) *Co-operation between authorities*

A separate method whereby the authority to which the appli- **5.61**
cation is made can discharge a duty to secure accommodation for the applicant, without actually having to provide that accommodation itself, is by arranging for another public or quasi-public body to provide the accommodation pursuant to the "co-operation" provisions in section 72. These provisions are quite separate from the "local connection" transfer procedure, which as we have seen can be used to *compel* another authority to take over long-term responsibility for housing an applicant.[30]

Section 72 provides for co-operation between housing authorities **5.62**
and various other prescribed bodies, so that a housing authority can ask such a body to help it to discharge its functions under any of sections 62 to 63, 65 to 68, or 70,[31] and the body to which the request is made must "co-operate in rendering such assistance . . . as is reasonable in the circumstances." The Code attaches importance to these provisions, and asks authorities to consider making greater use of them.[32] If an authority manages to operate these somewhat vague provisions successfully, by ensuring that some other body takes over responsibility for securing suitable accommodation for the applicant, then the authority will itself have discharged its duty to secure accommodation, since it will have secured that the applicant "obtains . . . accommodation from some other person" within section 69(1).

The prescribed bodies for the purposes of section 72 are: local **5.63**
housing authorities in England, Wales or Scotland (regarding the

[27] *R.* v. *Wyre B.C., ex p. Parr* (1982) 2 H.L.R. 71, 72 (C.A., *per* Lord Denning M.R.); here the authority decided to rehouse an applicant, who was homeless in Fleetwood, by arranging accommodation in Birmingham even though he had no connections with Birmingham. The court held, on the facts, that the accommodation offered was "inappropriate," so that the housing duty had not been discharged.

[28] *Ibid.* at 72.

[29] Code, para. A2.1.

[30] See above, paras. 5.14, 5.43.

[31] s.70 relates to protection of property, and is discussed below, paras. 5.87–5.91.

[32] *Op. cit.* para. 7.1.

discharge of functions under sections 62 to 63, 65 to 68, and 70); and social services authorities in England, Wales or Scotland, new town corporations, registered housing associations, Housing Action Trusts, and Scottish Homes (regarding the discharge of functions under sections 62 to 63 and 65 to 68).

5.64 With regard to co-operation with social services authorities, the Code recognises that where (following a reference made by the housing authority) a social services authority offers the applicant accommodation pursuant to (for example) the National Assistance Act 1948,[33] this can be an appropriate discharge of the housing authority's own duty under Part III of the 1985 Act.[34] More generally, the Code emphasises that these co-operation arrangements under section 72 should only be made after "taking full account of the wishes of the applicant"[35] and should "avoid undue disruption."[36]

6. *The Nature of the Accommodation to be Offered*

(a) *The accommodation must be available*

5.65 Where an authority is under one of the duties to secure that accommodation is made "available" for an applicant's occupation, then, under section 75, accommodation must be made available for occupation both by him and by "any other person who might reasonably be expected to reside with him." In the particular context of deciding whether a cohabitee might reasonably be expected to reside with the applicant, if the relationship is an established one then the authority cannot take the view that residence together is unreasonable merely on the grounds of "morality."[37] The notification duties in section 64[38] do not however require an authority to give reasons for its decision to exclude people from the "family unit" under section 75.

5.66 The Code spells out very clearly, in the context of section 75, that the old practice adopted by some authorities of splitting up homeless families for the purposes of accommodating them is normally no longer acceptable, even for short periods.[39] More specifically, the

[33] N.A.A. 1948, s.21(1)(*a*): see above, paras. 2.05–2.11.
[34] *Op. cit.* para. 4.4.
[35] *Op. cit.* para. 2.22.
[36] *Op. cit.* para. A2.1; see also *Wyness* v. *Poole B.C.* [1979] J.S.W.L. 368 (Cty. Ct.); *R.* v. *Wyre B.C., ex p. Parr*, see above.
[37] See above, paras. 3.17, 4.66, 4.151.
[38] See above, paras. 4.164–4.169.
[39] *Op. cit.* para. 4.2.

Code emphasises that children should not be received into care save in the exceptional case where professional social work advice is that there are compelling reasons for doing so quite apart from the homelessness.[40] Furthermore, the exclusion of one partner from the accommodation offered is likewise unacceptable unless there are "sound reasons," such as where a woman seeks temporary shelter after suffering violence from another member of her household[41]; another such example of a "sound reason" for exclusion might be where the applicant is a girl under 16, who requests accommodation in which she can live together with her boyfriend: even if she is already pregnant by him (and thus clearly in priority need), it may be proper for the authority to refuse to accommodate the boyfriend while the girl remains under the age of consent, since otherwise it might be seen to be encouraging unlawful sexual intercourse.[42]

Considerable problems can arise regarding the extent of the authority's obligations to rehouse large "extended" families, particularly where the applicant comes from overseas; bearing in mind that most of the accommodation which can be offered will not be suitable for the use of very large families, the authority must do the best it can, which may involve accommodating the family members in two or more adjacent flats or houses, or even separating various units of the family group for accommodation purposes provided the distances between the units are not, on the facts, excessive.[43] **5.67**

(b) *The accommodation must be "suitable"*

(i) The "suitability" criterion in section 69(1). The poor quality of the accommodation which some authorities have secured for the homeless has frequently been commented upon.[44] **5.68**

The Code contains very little specific material relating to the standard of the accommodation to be provided: authorities are asked to "bear in mind relevant provisions of general housing and public **5.69**

40 *Op. cit.* para. 4.2.

41 *Ibid.*

42 See Sexual Offences Act 1956, s.6.

43 *R.* v. *Lambeth L.B.C., ex p. Ly* (1987) 19 H.L.R. 51 (D.C.): applicant was a Vietnamese refugee, whose family group comprised 11 members; on the particular facts the court upheld the council's decision to separate the group into two units, and accommodate the respective units two miles apart.

44 See, *e.g.* S. Billcliffe, *Roof*, July 1981, p. 8; A. Grosskurth and J. Stearn, *Roof*, January 1986, p. 9; *Court* v. *Court* [1982] 2 All E.R. 531, 533; see above, paras. 3.20–3.21.

health legislation,"[45] and are reminded that "mobile homes are not satisfactory for families with children or as a form of interim accommodation for homeless people."[46]

5.70 There were sweeping *dicta* from the House of Lords in *Puhlhofer* v. *Hillingdon L.B.C.*[47] to the effect that considerations relating to the "appropriateness" or "reasonableness" of accommodation, and the statutory criteria relating to unfitness or overcrowding, were not to be imported into Part III of the 1985 Act, even as regards the type of accommodation to be secured for the applicant by the authority in discharge of its duties. However, section 69(1) was amended by the Housing and Planning Act 1986,[48] to the effect that any duty to secure accommodation under section 65 or 68 of the 1985 Act[49] will only be discharged if the accommodation secured is "suitable," and "in determining whether accommodation is suitable [the authority] shall have regard to Part IX (slum clearance), X (overcrowding) and XI (houses in multiple occupation) of [the 1985] Act."

5.71 These listed matters are not exhaustive: thus consideration should be given, where appropriate, to such issues as statutory unfitness within the terms of Part VI of the 1985 Act,[50] and the "statutory nuisance" provisions in the Public Health Act 1936.[51] However, a dwelling which merely requires substantial repairs to bring it up to a reasonable standard,[52] without being either unfit or a statutory nuisance, may rank as "suitable" (depending on the facts),[53] and it appears that lower standards may be regarded as acceptable (provided the accommodation does not actually infringe the criteria which are specified in section 69(1)[54]) where the property is provided under the temporary housing duties, as opposed to the perma-

[45] *Op. cit.* para. 4.3.
[46] *Op. cit.* para. A2.8.
[47] [1986] 1 All E.R. 467, 474; these *dicta* were applied in *R.* v. *L.B. of Wandsworth, ex p. Lindsay* (1986) 18 H.L.R. 502 (D.C.).
[48] H.P.A. 1986, s.14(3).
[49] Although the amended s.69(1) refers only to the rehousing duties under ss.65 and 68, and not expressly to the temporary rehousing duty in s.63, the courts could well import the "suitability" requirement into s.63 also: see *Family Housing Association* v. *Miah* (1982) 5 H.L.R. 94 (C.A.), discussed above, para. 5.54.
[50] Pt. VI applies where the authority is satisfied that a dwelling is unfit but capable of being rendered fit at reasonable expense; *cf.* Pt. IX, above, which deals with dwellings which are unfit and incapable of being rendered fit at reasonable expense.
[51] See below, para. 5.72.
[52] *I.e.* within the terms of H.A. 1985, ss.190 (1)(*a*), (1A)(*a*).
[53] See *R.* v. *Exeter C.C., ex p. Glidden and Draper* [1985] 1 All E.R. 493 (D.C.).
[54] See *Brown* v. *Hamilton D.C.* 1983 S.L.T. 397, 403 (Ct. of Session: 2nd Div.).

nent housing duties.[55] It would seem, from other areas of housing law, that the courts may not be very anxious to interfere with the exercise of an authority's discretion on the "suitability" issue.[56]

(ii) General remedies for poor housing conditions. The occupier may in any event have various remedies in relation to the state of the property, irrespective of whether the authority is in breach of Part III of the 1985 Act in securing that property for him in the first place. Where appropriate, a private law action may lie for breach of contract[57] or in tort[58] against the landlord. Where the accommodation in question has been provided by the council, it is usually impossible to secure action by the environmental health department under the Public Health Act 1936[59]; and it is clear that the machinery of the unfitness provisions of the Housing Act 1985 is not designed to be operated by a local authority against itself.[60] Nevertheless, even occupiers of council property can instigate private proceedings in the magistrates' court for "statutory nuisance" under section 99 of the Public Health Act 1936.[61] **5.72**

With regard to overcrowding, it is significant that a local authority has been convicted of an offence contrary to Part X of the Housing Act 1985[62] for placing a homeless family in statutorily overcrowded accommodation.[63] **5.73**

The multiple occupation provisions[64] can in principle be used by local authorities in order to improve standards in private sector accommodation used for the homeless[65] and falling within the defi- **5.74**

55 Compare *Brown* v. *Hamilton D.C.* 1983 S.L.T. 397, 417 (H.L.) (s.63(1)), and *R.* v. *Exeter C.C., ex p. Glidden and Draper*, see above (s.65(3)(*a*)), with *R.* v. *Ryedale D.C., ex p. Smith* (1983) 16 H.L.R. 66 (D.C.) (s.65(2)).

56 See, *e.g. R.* v. *Bristol Corpn., ex p. Hendy* [1974] 1 W.L.R. 498 (C.A.) (Land Compensation Act 1973, s.39(1); see above, para. 2.35); *Savoury* v. *Secretary of State for Wales* (1976) 31 P. & C.R. 344 (H.A. 1985, s.289(4); see above, para. 2.15).

57 Under *e.g.* Landlord and Tenant Act 1985, ss.8, 11–16, or at common law; see below, paras. 12.09–12.39.

58 Under *e.g.* Defective Premises Act 1972, s.4: see below, paras. 12.40–12.41.

59 See, *e.g.* M. Cairns, J. McQuillan and D. Ormandy, *Roof*, September 1981, p. 12; see also by analogy the position regarding the unfitness provisions in H.A. 1985: *R.* v. *Cardiff C.C., ex p. Cross* (1983) 81 L.G.R. 105 (C.A.).

60 *R.* v. *Cardiff C.C., ex p. Cross, ibid.*

61 Discussed below, paras. 12.55–12.64; for the use of s.99 by a homeless family placed in interim accommodation which the council had acquired from the private sector as being unfit for habitation, see *Coventry C.C.* v. *Quinn* [1981] 2 All E.R. 184.

62 H.A. 1985, s.331.

63 *D.P.P.* v. *Carrick D.C.* (1985) 31 Housing Aid 5 (mags'. ct.).

64 H.A. 1985, Pt. XI.

65 See *Thrasyvoulou* v. *L.B. of Hackney* (1986) 18 H.L.R. 370 (C.A.).

nition[66] of housing in multiple occupation. However, it has been held[67] that a council cannot lawfully use these provisions in respect of a hotel on the grounds that it lacks the facilities of a house or flat, when the council itself, knowing of the lack of facilities in the hotel, has previously used it to accommodate its homeless families.

5.75 The local ombudsmen have been prepared to find maladministration in certain cases where poor quality accommodation has been secured for homeless people.[68]

(c) *Aspects of the use of temporary accommodation*

5.76 **(i) The accrual of security of tenure.** An offer of "temporary" accommodation, in the sense of accommodation (of whatever type) which the authority is making available to the applicant for only a limited period because it does not consider itself under the full (section 65(2)) duty to secure permanent accommodation, can only be justified in three cases: first, where the authority has reason to believe that the applicant may be homeless and in priority need, but it needs to make further inquiries before coming to a final decision[69]; secondly, where the authority is satisfied that the applicant is homeless and in priority need, but is also satisfied that he became homeless intentionally (here the accommodation need only be provided for such period as gives him a reasonable opportunity of himself securing his own accommodation[70]); and thirdly, where the authority is implementing the "local connection" transfer provisions (here the authority need only provide temporary accommodation until the "importing" authority takes over responsibility[71]).

5.77 In these three cases tenancies or licences granted by an authority (or by some other public body on its behalf) cannot become "secure" before the expiry of a period of 12 months after (normally) the notification of the authority's decision under section 64,[72] unless the tenant or licensee has, before the expiry of that period, been notified by the landlord or licensor that the tenancy or licence is to be

[66] H.A. 1985, s.345.

[67] *R.* v. *Hackney L.B.C., ex p. Evenbray Ltd.* (1987) 19 H.L.R. 557 (D.C.).

[68] See, *e.g.* Complaint No. 929/L/84 (applicants allocated property with defective sanitation and insufficient insulation, recommendation of *ex gratia* payment); Complaint No. 447/L/85 (applicants put into ex-guards room leased from the Admiralty, recommendation of *ex gratia* payment).

[69] H.A. 1985, s.63; see above, para. 4.02.

[70] *Ibid.* s.65(3); see above, paras. 4.08–4.11.

[71] *Ibid.* s.68(1); see above, para. 4.15.

[72] See above, para. 4.164.

regarded as "secure."[73] The detailed operation of this exemption from "secure" status is discussed later.[74]

5.78 **(ii) The provision of temporary accommodation as a prelude to more permanent accommodation.** Where the authority owes the full rehousing obligation in section 65(2) (*i.e.* the situation does not fall within one of the three "temporary housing" cases set out above), the applicant may still be placed initially in accommodation of a "temporary" type, provided the authority intends to move him to more permanent accommodation in due course. The Code states that where the full duty is owed, "[p]ermanent accommodation should be secured as soon as possible," and that "[h]omeless people should not be obliged to spend a certain period in interim accommodation as a matter of policy."[75] Yet the Code also recognises that it may not be possible to achieve a "long term solution" immediately, and that interim accommodation may sometimes need to be arranged in (for example) resettlement units (formerly known as reception centres), hostels, or women's refuges, or "as a last resort" in "lodgings, guest houses or hotels."[76] While people are thus kept in temporary accommodation, the Code suggests that they should "be included in housing lists, have their needs taken into account in the allocation process . . . and receive due priority in accordance with their circumstances."[77] Furthermore, in the case of women's refuges in particular, the Code points out that while these can be "a useful source of interim accommodation for women who have been subject to violence or are at risk of it," the authority will nevertheless "remain under the duty to secure permanent accommodation."[78]

5.79 The courts have made it clear[79] that the authority is entitled to provide accommodation under section 65(2) in stages, as contemplated by the Code; a person who has been placed in such initial "temporary" accommodation, pending rehousing, has been held to have accommodation which is sufficiently "settled" for the purpose

[73] H.A. 1985, s.79 and Sched. 1, para. 4.

[74] See paras. 7.38–7.41.

[75] *Op. cit.* para. 4.4.

[76] *Op. cit.* paras. A2.11, A2.13–A2.14; accommodation in hotels, hostels, etc. cannot *per se* be regarded as not "suitable" under the new s.69(1), see above; *R.* v. *Westminster C.C., ex p. Tansey*, March 6, 1987 (D.C., unreported).

[77] *Op. cit.* para. 4.5; see *Court* v. *Court* [1982] 2 All E.R. 531, 533–534.

[78] *Op. cit.* para. A2.13; see *R.* v. *Ealing L.B.C., ex p. Sidhu* (1982) 80 L.G.R. 534 (D.C.).

[79] *R.* v. *East Hertfordshire D.C., ex p. Hunt* (1986) 1 F.L.R. 431 (D.C.); this principle is unaffected by the introduction of the "suitability" requirement into s.69(1), *R.* v. *Westminster C.C., ex p. Tansey*, see above.

of breaking a chain of "*un*intentionality,"[80] and which suffices to satisfy the "occupation" requirement for a house in multiple occupation.[81]

5.80 The use of "bed and breakfast" accommodation, even by way of interim housing for those to whom the full rehousing duty is owed, has become an increasingly common response to the problems of the homeless.[82] The cost to authorities of such accommodation can be alarming,[83] although such expenditure is legally proper.[84]

5.81 **(iii) Financing for voluntary organisations.** Voluntary organisations concerned with homelessness may also be able to provide temporary accommodation on behalf of housing authorities under Part III of the 1985 Act. Both the central government and housing authorities have the power under section 73 to assist such organisations financially, by way of grants or loans.

7. *Charges for the Accommodation*

(a) *"Reasonable" charges*

5.82 Under section 69(2) of the Housing Act 1985, an authority which secures accommodation for an applicant under sections 63, 65 or 68 may require him to pay either such "reasonable charges" as it determines for the accommodation which it secures for him (whether the authority makes its own accommodation available or otherwise), or such "reasonable amount" as it determines in respect of sums payable by it for accommodation made available to the applicant by another person.

[80] *R.* v. *East Hertfordshire D.C., ex p. Hunt*, see above (applicant was placed in a hostel as the first stage of rehousing pursuant to s.65(2), but her licence to use the hostel was terminated, and possession obtained, due to her bad behaviour; held, the hostel counted as "settled accommodation," so that she could later be properly found intentionally homeless by virtue of the loss of the licence; the situation was regarded as the converse of that in *Lambert* v. *Ealing L.B.C.* [1982] 1 W.L.R. 550 (C.A.), see above, para. 4.141).

[81] *Thrasyvoulou* v. *L.B. of Hackney*, see above; H.A. 1985, ss. 345, 352.

[82] See, *e.g. The Times*, September 8, October 6, October 28, 1987; *Sunday Times*, May 29, 1988; P.Q. Watchman, [1988] J.S.W.L. 147, 148–149; Shelter, *Prescription for Poor Health* (1988).

[83] See n. 82.

[84] It is authorised by L.G.A. 1972, s.111(1), which permits authorities to do anything (whether or not involving expenditure) which is "calculated to facilitate or conducive or incidental to the discharge of" any of their functions; see also D.O.E. Circ. 166/77, para. 14.

Where the authority secures its own accommodation for the applicant, it is in any event subject to the more general provision in section 24 of the 1985 Act that it may make such "reasonable charges" as it may determine. The case law on this general "reasonableness" requirement, which is examined in detail later,[85] suggests that the courts will not be anxious to interfere with the discretion of authorities in respect of the sums which applicants are required to pay under Part III of the 1985 Act.[86] **5.83**

However, the charges should not be artificially inflated merely because the accommodation is being provided under the homelessness provisions.[87] Indeed, there is a logically strong argument for suggesting that where a homeless family is placed in spartan temporary accommodation, the charges should be appreciably *lower* than those imposed by the authority for its "normal" modern or modernised council housing stock. As regards bed and breakfast, which is a type of accommodation where the charges tend to be particularly heavy, it has been suggested that if the applicant has no entitlement to income support[88] then he should only be charged the average local authority dwelling rent for the area, and the authority should meet the remainder of the costs.[89] **5.84**

It appears that some authorities demand payment in respect of *past* rent arrears accrued in council property, before an offer of accommodation under Part III of the 1985 Act will be made (either under section 65(2), if the homelessness was unintentional, or under section 65(3), if it was intentional). There are no provisions outlawing requirements made by local authorities for the payment of sums which, in the case of certain private landlords, the law might regard as illegal "premiums."[90] It seems, however, that an offer under Part III of the 1985 Act which is made conditional upon the applicant **5.85**

[85] See paras. 10.30–10.37.

[86] But see [1986] S.C.O.L.A.G. 100, reporting a Sheriff court decision which interfered with a council's assessment of rent on the ground that it had not had proper regard to the individual financial circumstances of the homeless person.

[87] *R.* v. *Crawley B.C., ex p. L.B. of Brent*, March 24, 1983 (D.C., unreported).

[88] As to which see, *e.g.* J. Allbeson [1988] March Legal Action 9.

[89] Shelter, *Submission to the review of the Code of Guidance* (1978), p. 53.

[90] *Cf.* R.A. 1977, ss.119–120, 122, and 128, which broadly speaking outlaw "premiums" (capital sums in addition to rent) in the case of certain pre-January 15, 1989 private lettings; in *Hampstead Way Investments* v. *Mawdsley* [1980] 9 C.L. 115 (Cty. Ct.), it was held that a requirement that a tenant must discharge a previous tenant's arrears before taking over the tenancy constituted such an illegal premium. Premiums are not prohibited where the private letting is "assured" under H.A. 1988, Pt. I.

clearing arrears of rent under a previous tenancy (whether the arrears were those of the applicant himself or of someone else) would be in breach of that Act: for the duty (where appropriate) is to "secure accommodation," and the only power to require payment is in relation to *future* charges in respect of that accommodation under section 69(2). To allow the imposition of such conditions would render the limited duty towards intentionally homeless families in priority need (imposed by section 65(3)) totally inapplicable in the case of council house evictions for rent arrears.[91]

(b) *Assistance available from the social security and housing benefit schemes*

5.86 A successful applicant who has received accommodation under Part III of the 1985 Act may be able to obtain assistance from the D.S.S. or from the local housing authority (as appropriate) in meeting the costs of that accommodation. The precise form of this assistance (the details of which must be sought elsewhere[92]) depends upon the applicant's resources, whether he is eligible for income support, and the nature of the accommodation.

8. *Protection of Property*

5.87 If an authority has become subject to a housing duty under sections 63, 65(2), 65(3)(*a*), 66(2) or 68 of the 1985 Act, then under section 70, if the authority has reason to believe that there is a danger of loss of, or damage to, the personal property of the applicant or of any other person who might reasonably be expected to reside with him, because of his inability to protect or deal with it, and that no other suitable arrangements have been or are being made, it is subject to a further duty (whether or not the housing duty still subsists) to take reasonable steps to prevent the loss of or damage to that property.[93] The section 70 duty normally rests with the housing authority to which the application is made, even if the property in question is in another authority's area.[94] Shelter discovered that some authorities were "not carrying out their duties to protect property, with the

[91] See *Barry* v. *Newham L.B.C* [1980] L.A.G. Bull. 142 (Cty. Ct.); A. Arden, [1980] L.A.G. Bull. 295.

[92] See the Income Support (General) Regulations 1987 (S.I. 1987 No. 1967) reg. 17(e) and Sched. 3, and the Housing Benefit (General) Regulations 1987 (S.I. 1987 No. 1971); for a brief outline of the housing benefit scheme, see below, para. 10.48.

[93] H.A. 1985, s.70(1)–(2), (8).

[94] Code, para. 8.3.

result that some homeless people have had to sell all their furniture, at a considerable financial loss."[95]

However, where an authority is *not* under one of the above-stated duties to secure accommodation (as where the applicant is not in priority need or is intentionally threatened with homelessness), then it merely has the *power* to protect the applicant's property.[96] In practice, the common law responsibilities of authorities as bailees of goods might well dissuade them from deciding to exercise this power.[97] **5.88**

In pursuance of the duty or power (as appropriate) to protect property, the authority may enter "at all reasonable times" the premises in which the applicant currently resides or previously resided, and may "deal with" any relevant property of his (or of any person who might reasonably be expected to reside with him) "in any way which is reasonably necessary"[98]; such "dealings" can include the storage of the property,[99] which will be particularly relevant where the applicant is placed in bed and breakfast accommodation. **5.89**

Authorities may decline to discharge the section 70 duty or to exercise the section 70 power (as the case may be) "except upon such conditions as they consider appropriate," which may include conditions empowering the authority to recover its reasonable charges and to dispose "in such circumstances as may be specified" of the relevant property.[1] These conditions can apparently be imposed whether or not the applicant consents to them.[2] Reservation of a right of disposal might be appropriate where there is a danger that the authority might lose touch with the applicant and be unable to trace him after a specified period.[3] **5.90**

The duty or power (as the case may be) to protect property under section 70 ceases when the authority considers that there is no longer any reason to believe that there is a danger of loss of or damage to that property by reason of the owner's inability to protect or deal with it[4]; the property may however be kept in store where appropri- **5.91**

[95] *Submission to the review of the Code of Guidance*, *op. cit.* p. 41.
[96] H.A. 1985, s.70(2).
[97] See *Mitchell* v. *Ealing L.B.C.* [1979] Q.B. 1.
[98] H.A. 1985, s.70(3), (8).
[99] *Ibid.* s.70(3)(*b*).
[1] *Ibid.* s.70(4).
[2] See R. Carnwath, *op. cit.* p. 76.
[3] Code, para. 8.5.
[4] H.A. 1985, s.70(5).

ate even though the principal section 70 duty or power has ceased.[5] The authority must notify the applicant that the duty of protection (or power, if previously exercised) has ceased, and it must give its reasons.[6] This notification can only be given by delivering it to the applicant, or leaving it at his last known address, or sending it by post to him at that address[7]: compare the normal notification procedure in respect of other relevant matters under Part III of the 1985 Act, which requires the authority, where the applicant has not received the notification, to make the details available at its office for collection by or on behalf of the applicant.[8]

[5] H.A. 1985, s.70(5).
[6] H.A. 1985, s.70(6).
[7] *Ibid.* s.70(7).
[8] *Ibid.* s.64(5); see above, para. 4.167.

6 Challenges to the Authority's Decision[1]

1. *General*

(a) *Absence of any prescribed appeal procedure*

6.01 Although section 64[2] of the Housing Act 1985 provides for notification of the authority' s decision to the applicant, and also for notification of its reasons for findings which are adverse to him, the Act lays down no formal appeal procedure. The absence of any such procedure has meant that the courts have been prepared to intervene in an appropriate case without worrying about the long-established administrative law principle that where Parliament expressly provides a particular remedy for enforcing an individual statutory duty, that duty cannot normally be enforced other than by way of that stipulated remedy.[3] Indeed, Lord Lowry has recognised that Part III of the 1985 Act "has given rise to a volume of cases which is remarkable, having regard to . . . the extent of the discretion it confers and the absence of an ordinary right of appeal."[4] There have, however, been frequent demands for the introduction of a swift, cheap, independent and locally-based appeal mechanism for the review of

[1] Although this chapter is particularly concerned with challenges to homelessness decisions, much of it is also of relevance to decisions of authorities on several of the other housing issues discussed in this book.

[2] See above, paras. 4.164–4.169.

[3] *Doe d. Bishop of Rochester* v. *Bridges* (1831) 1 B. & Ad. 847, 859, applied in *e.g. Wyatt* v. *Hillingdon L.B.C.* (1978) 122 S.J. 349 (C.A.); the inapplicability of this principle to Part III of H.A. 1985 (due to its silence regarding remedies) was emphasised in *Thornton* v. *Kirklees M.B.C.* [1979] Q.B. 626 (C.A.).

[4] *Din* v. *Wandsworth L.B.C.* [1981] 3 All E.R. 881, 891 (H.L.); see Lord Bridge's reference in *Eastleigh B.C.* v. *Walsh* [1985] 2 All E.R. 112, 113 (H.L.) to the "now all too familiar" homelessness legislation.

homelessness decisions,[5] due to the drawbacks which currently affect recourse to court action in this area.

(b) *Drawbacks to court action*

6.02 As far as the applicant is concerned, there are several general drawbacks to court action as a remedy in homelessness cases. First, there is no guarantee that the applicant will even be aware of his right to challenge the authority's decision in court, since there is no obligation on the authority to inform him of possible remedies where he disagrees with that decision; perhaps a requirement should be introduced for the authority to include such information (in ordinary language) where it notifies the applicant of its reasons pursuant to section 64.[6] Secondly, although speed will normally be of the essence, it can in practice be difficult for the applicant to find a lawyer with the necessary expertise and motivation to obtain a swift (interlocutory) remedy in what can be very complicated proceedings. Thirdly, there may be difficulty in obtaining legal aid sufficiently quickly, or indeed at all.[7] Fourthly, legal action may mean attendant publicity, which the applicant may be unwilling to attract.[8] Finally, as will be seen, there are several technical problems involved in challenging an authority's decision in court, both as regards the grounds for intervention and the procedure to be adopted.

(c) *Non-judicial remedies*

6.03 The applicant has several methods of challenging the authority's decision which do not involve court action.[9] In particular, the authority may be asked to review its decision internally; and the local ombudsman may be prepared to intervene where there has been "maladministration."

[5] See, *e.g.* Council on Tribunals, *Annual Report 1984–85*, H.C.P. 54, para. 2.15; Law Centres Federation, *The Courts and the Housing Crisis* (1985), p. 10; Housing Courts Steering Group, *Housing Courts: The Issues* (1987); it appears that the D.O.E. is currently considering rights of appeal in homelessness cases as part of its review of the operation of H.A. 1985, Pt. III.

[6] For a suitable precedent, see the regulations prescribing the content of the notice of intended proceedings to be served on a "secure" council tenant from whom the authority seeks possession: see below, para. 8.19, n. 57.

[7] B. Widdowson, *Intentional Homelessness* (Shelter, 1981), p. 39; A. McAllister, [1987] May Legal Action 11.

[8] B. Widdowson, *loc. cit.*

[9] See B. Widdowson, [1982] L.A.G. Bull. 49.

(i) Internal review. In view of an authority's ability to delegate its functions,[10] many homelessness decisions are in practice initially taken at a fairly junior level. We have already seen, in the context of general allocation schemes,[11] that an authority may be prepared informally to review its decision,[12] for example by having it reviewed at a more senior level; we have also noted[13] that some authorities have introduced formal internal appeal mechanisms,[14] although there is at present no legal obligation to do so. **6.04**

(ii) Local ombudsmen. Mention of the role of the local ombudsmen in examining the decisions of housing authorities has already been made in the context of general allocation schemes.[15] As regards decisions taken by authorities in homelessness cases, there have been several instances where "maladministration" has been found by the ombudsmen[16]; in particular, it would seem that failure to follow the guidance in the Code can sometimes amount to maladministration,[17] so that a local ombudsman may take a more serious view of an authority's departure from clear guidance in the Code than the courts have tended to adopt.[18] **6.05**

2. *The Basic Grounds for Judicial Intervention: the "Administrative Law Principles"*

(a) *No "right of appeal" as such*

It is clear that there is no right of appeal as such to a court of law against an authority's decision on an application under Part III of the 1985 Act; the applicant must concentrate on the way in which the decision has been arrived at, and must seek to persuade the court that the authority, in the course of its decision-making process, has **6.06**

[10] L.G.A. 1972, s.101.
[11] See above, paras. 2.42–2.43.
[12] See, as regards homelessness, *R.* v. *Hambleton D.C., ex p. Geoghan* [1985] J.P.L. 394 (D.C.).
[13] See above, para. 2.42.
[14] See, as regards the review of homelessness decisions, D. Wright, [1985] L.S. Gaz. 3513, 3514.
[15] See above, paras. 2.44–2.45.
[16] See, *e.g.* above, para. 5.75.
[17] D. J. Hughes, *Public Sector Housing Law* (2nd ed., 1987), p. 180.
[18] See above, para. 4.03, n. 5.

broken what may be loosely termed the basic "administrative law principles."[19]

6.07 The most important duties in Part III of the 1985 Act are drafted, as we have seen, in *subjective* form: sections 65 and 66 talk of the authority being "satisfied" on the various key issues (compare section 63, which refers to the authority having "reason to believe" the appropriate matters and is thus couched in less subjective terms). Nevertheless, the subjective imposition of duties will not of itself exclude the courts from interfering where the "administrative law principles" have not been observed.[20]

(b) *The "administrative law principles"*

6.08 The classic statement of the "administrative law" grounds on which a public authority's decision may be attacked is contained in the judgment of Lord Greene M.R. in *Associated Provincial Picture Houses Ltd.* v. *Wednesbury Corpn.*[21] The courts can only interfere with an authority's decision if it can be shown that it has contravened the law. One way of demonstrating this is to establish bad faith or dishonesty. Even in the absence of bad faith or dishonesty, the authority's decision may still properly be challenged in court if it can be shown that the authority, in reaching the decision, has taken into account a factor which in law it should not have taken into account, or has omitted to take account of a factor which in law it should have taken into account. Even if the claimant cannot show specifically that a relevant matter has been erroneously taken into account or omitted from consideration, nevertheless, if the decision is so unreasonable that no reasonable authority could ever have come to it, then the courts can still intervene.

6.09 It is important to appreciate that even after the restrictive comments in *Puhlhofer* v. *Hillingdon L.B.C.*[22] about the use of judicial review in homelessness cases, all of the grounds of attack set out in

[19] See, *e.g. Thornton* v. *Kirklees M.B.C.* [1979] 2 All E.R. 349, 358 (C.A.); *Din* v. *Wandsworth L.B.C.* [1981] 3 All E.R. 881, 899 (H.L.); *Bromley L.B.C.* v. *G.L.C.* [1982] 1 All E.R. 129, 154 (H.L.). *Puhlhofer* v. *Hillingdon L.B.C.* [1986] 1 All E.R. 467, 474 (H.L.); *R.* v. *Gravesham B.C., ex p. Winchester* (1986) 18 H.L.R. 207, 215 (D.C.); *R.* v. *Westminster C.C., ex p. Tansey* (1988) 20 H.L.R. 520 (D.C.); *R.* v. *Wycombe D.C., ex p. Mahsood* (1988) 20 H.L.R. 683, 686 (D.C.).

[20] See, *e.g. Secretary of State for Education and Science* v. *Tameside M.B.C.* [1976] 3 All E.R. 665, 681–682 (H.L.); *R.* v. *Bristol C.C., ex p. Browne* [1979] 3 All E.R. 344, 352 (D.C.).

[21] [1947] 2 All E.R. 680, 682–683 (C.A.).

[22] [1986] 1 All E.R. 467, 474 (H.L.); see below, para. 6.19.

the *Wednesbury* case remain available where the circumstances are appropriate.[23]

The various "administrative law principles" tend to overlap considerably, and the details must be pursued elsewhere.[24] However, for present purposes in relation specifically to Part III of the 1985 Act, the more important of the grounds of attack can be further distilled as follows. **6.10**

(i) The authority has wrongly interpreted the law. Obviously, if the authority has misunderstood the relevant provisions of the Act in such a way as materially to affect its decision, that decision will not have been properly made and can be upset by the court.[25] **6.11**

(ii) The authority has taken into account irrelevant considerations, or omitted to take account of relevant considerations. With regard to the status of the Code, we have seen that, although its advice does not necessarily have to be followed by authorities, they must at least have regard to it pursuant to section 71.[26] Thus if an authority can be shown totally to have disregarded the Code, its decision may be upset,[27] although it may in practice be easier to show that the authority has failed to take account of relevant considerations because it has pursued inadequate inquiries.[28] **6.12**

In deciding whether the authority has had regard to irrelevant considerations, or has ignored relevant considerations, the court will examine the authority's decision as at the date when it was reached: the authority cannot rely in court on evidence which it has obtained subsequent to the date of its decision in order to justify that decision.[29] **6.13**

(iii) The authority has reached a decision which no reasonable authority could have reached. Although the burden of proof lying upon a plaintiff seeking to establish this particular ground of **6.14**

[23] See D. Watkinson, [1987] July Legal Action 23; discussed below, para. 6.19.

[24] See, *e.g. de Smith's Judicial Review of Administrative Action* (4th ed., 1980), Chap. 6.

[25] See, *e.g. Delahaye* v. *Oswestry B.C.*, *The Times*, July 29, 1980; *R.* v. *Hillingdon L.B.C., ex p. Streeting* [1980] 1 W.L.R. 1430 (C.A.); *R.* v. *Camden L.B.C., ex p. Wait* (1986) 18 H.L.R. 434 (D.C.).

[26] See above, para. 4.03, n. 5.

[27] See by analogy *R.* v. *Police Complaints Board, ex p. Madden* [1983] 2 All E.R. 353, 370 (D.C.).

[28] See above, paras. 4.19–4.29.

[29] *R.* v. *East Hertfordshire D.C., ex p. Bannon* (1986) 18 H.L.R. 515 (D.C.); *R.* v. *Warwick D.C., ex p. Wood*, August 15, 1983 (D.C., unreported).

attack is very heavy,[30] there have been homelessness cases where it has succeeded.[31]

6.15 **(iv) The authority has failed to act in accordance with the principles of natural justice.** It is one of the rules of natural justice that the decision-making body must give all relevant parties an opportunity fairly to state their case in order adequately to inform itself of the arguments.[32] Thus an authority's decision may be struck down where, for example, it has not given the applicant a proper opportunity to comment on material adverse information which it has received from third parties concerning his allegedly intentional homelessness.[33]

6.16 **(v) The authority has applied an inflexible "blanket" policy.** The authority must not unduly fetter its discretion by the adoption of general criteria.[34] We have seen[35] that while it is legitimate for an authority to adopt general policies in order to guide its officers in their decision-making, it is nevertheless essential that such general policies should be sufficiently flexible to allow consideration of their applicability or otherwise to the facts of each individual case.

6.17 **(vi) The authority has acted in bad faith or dishonestly.** There appears to have been no case on Part III of the 1985 Act in which an authority's decision has been successfully attacked on this ground.

(c) *The burden of proof*

6.18 The courts have frequently emphasised that the burden of proof lies firmly on the applicant who seeks to challenge the authority's decision[36]: in effect, he is faced with an initial presumption that the

[30] See *Associated Provincial Picture Houses Ltd.* v. *Wednesbury Corpn.* [1947] 2 All E.R. 680, 683 (C.A.).

[31] See, *e.g.* *Krishnan* v. *Hillingdon L.B.C.* [1981] L.A.G. Bull. 137; *Islam* v. *Hillingdon L.B.C.* [1983] 1 A.C. 688 (H.L.); *R.* v. *Westminster C.C., ex p. Ali* (1983) 11 H.L.R. 72, 83 (D.C.).

[32] See, *e.g.* *de Smith*, *op. cit.* Chap. 4.

[33] See, *e.g.* *Stubbs* v. *Slough B.C.* [1980] L.A.G. Bull. 16 (Cty. Ct.); *R.* v. *Gravesham B.C., ex p. Winchester* (1986) 18 H.L.R. 207 (D.C.); see above, paras. 4.22–4.23.

[34] See, *e.g.* *Tilley* v. *Wandsworth L.B.C.* [1981] 1 All E.R. 1162 (C.A.); see above, para. 4.163.

[35] See above, paras. 4.163, 5.03.

[36] See, *e.g.* *Cannock Chase D.C.* v. *Kelly* [1978] 1 W.L.R. 1 (C.A.); *Thornton* v. *Kirklees M.B.C.* [1979] 2 All E.R. 349, 355–356 (C.A.); *Tickner* v. *Mole Valley D.C.* [1980] L.A.G. Bull. 187, 188 (C.A.).

authority has properly arrived at its decision, and he sometimes has to face the further hurdle of the court's willingness benevolently to "re-write" the authority's reasons as originally stated, in order to make them comply with the Act.[37]

The burden appeared to have been dramatically increased following the decision of the House of Lords in *Puhlhofer* v. *Hillingdon L.B.C.*,[38] where Lord Brightman stated[39] that leave to apply for judicial review should no longer be granted for challenging decisions under Part III of the 1985 Act "save in the exceptional case"; and it indeed appears that, following *Puhlhofer*, leave for applications for judicial review in homelessness cases has been more difficult to obtain.[40] However, it is now clear that even after *Puhlhofer*, a court is not precluded from finding a decision to be void on any of the general "*Wednesbury*-type" principles[41]: in particular, despite the fact that there may be admissible factors on both sides of the question, if the weight of the factors in favour of a particular decision must be recognised by a reasonable council, properly informed as to its responsibilities, to be overwhelming, then a decision the other way can still be successfully challenged in court.[42] **6.19**

In view of the heavy burden of proof resting upon the applicant, it is obviously important for him to have a sight of relevant documentation in the council's possession, such as notes of interviews held with him, internal council memoranda, the minutes of the meetings of committees or sub-committees, etc. The applicant has statutory rights of inspection in relation to certain personal details recorded about him by the authority.[43] Certain other background information **6.20**

[37] See above, paras. 4.147, 4.169.

[38] [1986] 1 All E.R. 467.

[39] *Ibid.* at 474; applied in *R.* v. *Gravesham B.C., ex p. Winchester* (1986) 18 H.L.R. 207 (D.C.). For a similar restriction of judicial review to "exceptional" cases, in the context of appeals against decisions of immigration officers, see *R.* v. *Secretary of State for the Home Department, ex p. Swati* [1986] 1 W.L.R. 477 (C.A.); in immigration cases, however, there is normally an alternative remedy available.

[40] M. Sunkin, (1987) 50 M.L.R. 432, at 450, 466; A. McAllister, [1987] May Legal Action 11.

[41] *R.* v. *L.B. of Waltham Forest, ex p. Koutsoudis*, September 1, 1986 (D.C., unreported); *R.* v. *Wandsworth L.B.C., ex p. Henderson* (1986) 18 H.L.R. 522, 532 (D.C.); *West Glamorgan C.C.* v. *Rafferty* [1987] 1 All E.R. 1005, 1021 (C.A.); *R.* v. *Hillingdon L.B.C., ex p. Thomas* (1987) 19 H.L.R. 196, 200 (D.C.); *R* v. *Christchurch B.C., ex p. Conway* (1987) 19 H.L.R. 238, 245 (D.C.); *Hammell* v. *R.B. of Kensington and Chelsea* (1988) 20 H.L.R. 666, 680 (C.A.).

[42] *West Glamorgan C.C.* v. *Rafferty*, *ibid.*

[43] H.A. 1985, s.106(5); Data Protection Act 1984, ss.1(2)–(3), 2, 21 and Sched. 1; Access to Personal Files Act 1987, ss.1–3 and Sched. 1; see above, paras. 2.27–2.28.

in the shape of agenda, reports and minutes of council meetings must be made available for public inspection,[44] and these may provide the applicant with some "ammunition" relating to, for example, the general policies of the council.

6.21 The process of "discovery of documents" during court proceedings is of limited utility to the applicant in the present context, since, as will be seen, the procedure for judicial review under Order 53 of the Rules of the Supreme Court which must normally be adopted in homelessness cases is in two stages, the first of which is the application for leave to apply, and the second (assuming leave has been granted) being the application for judicial review itself. An order for discovery can only be granted at the second stage,[45] not the first, so that an application for leave may be dismissed without the applicant having had a chance of inspecting (*via* the discovery procedure) relevant documentation in the council's possession.[46]

3. *Court Proceedings: The Predominance of the Remedy by Way of Judicial Review*

(a) *Judicial review under R.S.C. Order 53*[47]

6.22 **(i) The distinction between "decision-making" and "executive" functions.** It is now clear that an applicant wishing to challenge an authority's decision must normally seek the public law remedy of judicial review in the Divisional Court of the Queen's Bench Division under Order 53 of the Rules of the Supreme Court (as codified by section 31 of the Supreme Court Act 1981); the remedies available on judicial review include the public law prerogative orders[48] of mandamus,[49] certiorari[50] and prohibition, and also

[44] See L.G.A. 1972, Pt. VA (introduced by Local Government (Access to Information) Act 1985, s.1).

[45] See R.S.C., Ord. 53, r. 8(1).

[46] See A. Arden, [1980] L.A.G. Bull. 14.

[47] For more detailed treatment, see, *e.g.* G. Aldous and J. Alder, *Applications for Judicial Review: Law and Practice* (1985); R. Gordon, *Judicial Review: Law and Procedure* (1985); R. Poynter, [1988] August Legal Action 11.

[48] Supreme Court Act 1981, s.29(1).

[49] If there is only one decision which the authority can properly reach in the circumstances, the court can by the use of mandamus order the authority to come to that decision, *e.g.* to the effect that the full s.65(2) duty is owed; in practice, however, the court will normally be content to make a declaration in such a case, rather than an order of mandamus, see, *e.g. R.* v. *Slough B.C., ex p. L.B. of Ealing* [1981] Q.B. 801 (C.A.).

[50] See, *e.g. R.* v. *Hillingdon L.B.C., ex p. Streeting* [1980] 1 W.L.R. 1430 (C.A.); the effect of quashing the authority's decision by certiorari will normally be that it will

(where appropriate) the private law remedies of an injunction, declaration, and damages. In *Cocks* v. *Thanet D.C.*[51] the House of Lords decided that an ordinary (private law) action for breach of statutory duty (whether in the High Court or a county court) can only be brought very rarely in homelessness cases.

In *Cocks* v. *Thanet D.C.* Lord Bridge drew a distinction[52] between an authority's *decision-making* functions on the one hand, and its *executive* functions on the other. The decision-making functions involve conclusions on the key concepts of homelessness, priority need and intentionality: these can properly be described as the authority's "public law functions" and are to be governed by the "administrative law principles" (above). By contrast, the executive functions of the authority involve matters like the duration of the accommodation provided for the applicant, and arise once the relevant primary duties under Part III of the Housing Act 1985 have been established, whereupon "rights and obligations are immediately created in the field of private law"[53]: these *private law*[54] rights and obligations can if necessary be enforced in an ordinary action for breach of statutory duty in the High Court or a county court by way of injunction, damages, etc. The scheme of Part III of the 1985 Act is such, however, that an appropriate *public law* decision must normally be arrived at by the authority (or, in effect, be imposed upon it by way of judicial review) as a necessary condition precedent to the establishment of these private law duties. **6.23**

become subject once more to the temporary housing duty in H.A. 1985, s.63 (see above, para. 4.02), until it reaches a proper, lawful decision.

[51] [1982] 3 All E.R. 1135 (applying *O'Reilly* v. *Mackman* [1982] 2 A.C. 237 (H.L.)).

[52] *Ibid.* at 1138.

[53] *Ibid.*; see also *South Holland D.C.* v. *Keyte* (1987) 19 H.L.R. 97, 102 (C.A.). However, it has been suggested that any objection regarding the "suitability" of the accommodation offered (see H.A. 1985, s.69, discussed above, paras. 5.68–5.71) relates to a *decision-making* function, which can only be challenged on judicial review (although once the authority decides to offer accommodation of a particular kind, the duty actually to offer that accommodation is an executive function capable of enforcement by private law proceedings): *R.* v. *Westminster C.C., ex p. Tansey* (1988) 20 H.L.R. 520 (D.C.); but the Court of Appeal refused to decide this issue, treating the judge's remarks as "both *obiter* and academic" because, on the facts, the applicant was only challenging a general, "in principle" resolution of the council (before it had decided any individual case): the issue was merely an "abstract question of law": *R.* v. *City of Westminster, ex p. Tansey* (1988) 21 H.L.R. 57 (C.A.).

[54] For examples of the application of this difficult distinction between "public law" and "private law" functions in other areas of the law, see *Davy* v. *Spelthorne B.C.* [1984] A.C. 262 (H.L.), *Gillick* v. *West Norfolk A.H.A.* [1985] 3 All E.R. 402, 416 (H.L.).

6.24 Sometimes, judicial review may be applied for purely in order to "enable later proceedings to be brought for damages for breach of the applicant's private rights"[55]; alternatively, the private law remedies can themselves be obtained as part of the judicial review proceedings (once the "public law" issues have been resolved in the applicant's favour).

6.25 It is normally crucial for the applicant correctly to make the initial decision as to whether the case is appropriate for judicial review or for an ordinary action for breach of statutory duty, since there is no general power for the court to treat a case which has been wrongly commenced as an ordinary action as if it was an application for leave for judicial review[56]; and it may be too late, by the time the error is detected, to make the initial application for judicial review.[57] However, it seems that if an ordinary action is initially brought and the authority does not object to it, then the court will not necessarily consider it appropriate to strike out the action: in such a situation of, in effect, "submission to the jurisdiction," the court may therefore allow the ordinary action to continue.[58]

6.26 **(ii) Procedure.** Judicial review proceedings are in two stages. First, the applicant must apply *ex parte* (*i.e.* without notice being given to the authority) for leave to bring the application; normally, this initial application is determined on the documentation alone, although an oral hearing may be requested.[59]

6.27 The initial application for leave "shall be made promptly and in any event within three months from the date when grounds for the application first arose unless the Court considers that there is good reason for extending the period . . . ."[60] Time normally runs from the date of notification of the authority's decision and reasons to the

[55] *Per* Woolf J. in *R.* v. *South Herefordshire D.C., ex p. Miles* (1983) 17 H.L.R. 82, 86 (D.C.).

[56] *R.* v. *Southampton C.C., ex p. Ward* (1984) 14 H.L.R. 89, 128 (D.C.).

[57] See below, para. 6.27.

[58] *O'Reilly* v. *Mackman* [1982] 3 All E.R. 1124, 1134 (H.L.).

[59] R.S.C., Ord. 53, r. 3; it has been argued that the need to seek leave to apply for judicial review should be removed, *Administrative Justice: Some Necessary Reforms: Report of the Committee of the JUSTICE—All Souls Review of Administrative Law in the United Kingdom* (1988), pp. 5–6, 152–155.

[60] R.S.C., Ord. 53, r. 4(1); it was made clear in *R.* v. *Stratford-on-Avon D.C., ex p. Jackson* [1985] 1 W.L.R. 1319 (C.A.) that it is the application for *leave* which is subject to the time-limit, not the substantive application for judicial review. The importance of adhering to the time-limit wherever possible was emphasised in *e.g. R.* v.

applicant pursuant to section 64.[61] Difficulty in obtaining legal aid which was not caused by the applicant may be regarded by the court as a sufficient reason for extending the three months' time-limit,[62] although, even if the time is extended, the delay may still influence the court's discretion in deciding whether to grant relief on the substantive application for judicial review, and if so on what terms.[63] It may also be appropriate to grant an extension of the time-limit where the applicant has been awaiting the result of an internal inquiry by the council.[64]

If the applicant obtains leave, the appropriate papers (including supporting affidavits) must be served on the authority[65] prior to the substantive application for judicial review itself, and the evidence will normally be restricted to affidavits alone[66]; discovery of documents can be obtained after leave to apply for judicial review has been given.[67] **6.28**

The first (application for leave) stage of judicial review has in practice become, since the *Puhlhofer* decision,[68] more crucial in many respects than the second (substantive application) stage, since the application for leave normally consists of the applicant's full written submissions, and is "in effect . . . a rehearsal of all the arguments and authorities which will, if leave is granted, be relied on at the substantive hearing."[69] **6.29**

It is essential for the applicant to specify with sufficient particularity the nature of the order sought: it is not enough, for example, simply to request mandamus in terms of "directing the respondent to carry out its statutory duties" under Part III of the Housing Act.[70] **6.30**

Rochester C.C., ex p. Trotman, The Times, May 9, 1983 (D.C.); *R.* v. *Southampton C.C., ex p. Ward* (1984) 14 H.L.R. 114, 138 (D.C.); *R.* v. *Hillingdon L.B.C., ex p. Thomas* (1987) 19 H.L.R. 197 (D.C.).

61 See above, paras. 4.164–4.169.

62 *R* v. *Stratford-on-Avon D.C., ex p. Jackson,* see above; *cf.* the stricter approach in the earlier decision in *Fezoui* v. *Torbay B.C.,* July 27, 1983 (C.A., unreported).

63 *R.* v. *Stratford-on-Avon D.C., ex p. Jackson,* see above.

64 See *R.* v. *Port Talbot B.C., ex p. Jones* [1988] 2 All E.R. 207, 215 (D.C.).

65 R.S.C., Ord. 53, r. 6.

66 *Ibid.* r. 8.

67 *Ibid.*

68 See above.

69 A. McAllister, [1987] May Legal Action 11.

70 *R.* v. *Beverley B.C., ex p. McPhee* [1978] L.A.G. Bull. 293 (D.C.).

(b) *Ordinary action for breach of statutory duty*

6.31 We have seen that ordinary actions for breach of statutory duty (which is a tort) will only lie in the rare cases where the purely "executive" functions of the authority are being challenged.[71]

6.32 The applicant can raise breach of statutory duty not merely in an action which he himself brings, but also (in an appropriate case) by way of defence or counterclaim where the authority is itself suing him and he has sufficient pre-existing private law rights to support the defence or counterclaim.[72] For example, if the applicant has been correctly found intentionally homeless, and the authority issues proceedings against him for the possession of premises temporarily allocated to him pursuant to section 65(3),[73] he may defend the action on the ground that the authority has not properly carried out its "executive" functions by accommodating him for a sufficient period to give him a "reasonable opportunity" of finding his own accommodation. On the other hand, if the applicant wishes to challenge the intentionality finding itself in the possession proceedings, then since this involves questioning the authority's "decision-making" function the appropriate course would normally be for the applicant to request an adjournment of the possession proceedings in the county court pending the result of judicial review proceedings which must be brought in the High Court under Order 53.[74]

(c) *Other types of court proceedings*

6.33 Other types of court proceedings besides judicial review and actions for breach of statutory duty may be brought where appropriate to challenge aspects of homelessness decisions. For example, the poor state of the property secured for the applicant may of itself give rise to an action in contract and/or tort, and to criminal prosecu-

[71] *South Holland D.C.* v. *Keyte* (1987) 19 H.L.R. 97 (C.A.); *Purves* v. *Midlothian D.C.* [1986] 120 S.C.O.L.A.G. 144 (Sh. Ct.); *R.* v. *Westminster C.C., ex p. Tansey* (1988) 20 H.L.R. 520 (D.C.) (see above, n. 53).

[72] *Cannock Chase D.C.* v. *Kelly* [1978] 1 W.L.R. 1 (C.A.); *Wandsworth L.B.C.* v. *Winder* [1985] A.C. 461 (H.L.); *West Glamorgan C.C.* v. *Rafferty* [1987] 1 W.L.R. 457 (C.A.); *Hammell* v. *R.B. of Kensington and Chelsea* (1988) 20 H.L.R. 666, 678 (C.A.); *cf. South Holland D.C.* v. *Keyte*, see above, where the defendant's counterclaim was rejected because it had been made very late in the proceedings, and would have been better dealt with by way of a separate action.

[73] See above, paras. 4.08–4.11.

[74] See *Wandsworth L.B.C.* v. *Winder* [1984] 3 All E.R. 83, 91 (C.A.); *Waverley B.C.* v. *Hilden* [1988] 1 All E.R. 807; *Avon C.C.* v. *Buscott* [1988] 1 All E.R. 841 (C.A.); I. McLeod, [1988] L.S. Gaz. 22.

tion[75]; furthermore, the general homelessness policies of a council might be challenged by way of a "relator action."[76]

(d) *General private law remedies: damages, injunctions and declarations*

Whether the applicant proceeds by way of judicial review or by way of ordinary action (in those exceptional cases where this course is still open), then he may claim (where appropriate) damages, an injunction and a declaration.[77] In the case of judicial review, an applicant may combine a claim for damages, an injunction, and a declaration (as appropriate) with his application for one or more of the prerogative orders.[78] **6.34**

(i) Damages. Special damages can be recovered for specific items such as financial loss incurred by the applicant having to stay in a hotel, or eat in restaurants, etc., although credit will have to be given for the outlay which the applicant would in any event have incurred (in terms of rent, etc.) had the authority properly carried out its duty to accommodate him. It has been pointed out that "[a]s authorities can charge for accommodation under the Act . . . and need not use their own accommodation, it by no means follows . . . that a refusal of accommodation will give rise to a claim for [special] damages."[79] **6.35**

It has been judicially recognised that if an applicant is "rendered homeless when he should have been housed" then this is "an injury which is sufficiently traumatic and hardly compensable in damages."[80] However, since breach of statutory duty is a tort, general damages will not normally be recoverable for mere general distress or inconvenience which falls short of nervous shock or men- **6.36**

[75] See above, paras. 5.72–5.75.

[76] The Attorney-General can seek an injunction restraining the council from continuing to act in a way that is detrimental to the public interest on the "relation" of some other person, or, indeed, on his own initiative; if he decides not to act, then a member of the public may institute a "relator action," but only with his consent, *Gouriet* v. *Union of Post Office Workers* [1978] A.C. 435 (H.L.); for an account of an effective threat to use this procedure in a homelessness context, see B. Martin, *Roof*, July 1979, p. 107.

[77] See, as regards judicial review, Supreme Court Act 1981, s.31, and R.S.C., Ord. 53, rr. 1(2), 7.

[78] R.S.C., Ord. 53, rr. 1–2, 7.

[79] A. Arden, [1982] L.S. Gaz. 593.

[80] *Per* Bridge L.J. in *De Falco* v. *Crawley B.C.* [1980] 1 All E.R. 913, 924 (C.A.).

tal trauma actually giving rise to a recognisable psychiatric illness.[81] The general level of damages awarded for breach of the statutory duties in Part III of the 1985 Act has tended to be low.[82] In those situations where county court proceedings are still available following *Cocks* v. *Thanet D.C.*,[83] it is in any event necessary to limit the damages claimed to the county court's jurisdictional ceiling (currently £5,000).

6.37 **(ii) Injunctions.** In order for the applicant to succeed in a claim for breach of statutory duty it seems that, even if he is seeking an injunction (or declaration) rather than damages, he must normally prove that he has "suffered damage which is regarded by the law as being the consequence of the breach of duty."[84] In addition, a claim for an injunction (or a declaration) will not normally be within the (now very limited[85]) jurisdiction of the county court (as opposed to the High Court) unless it is ancillary to a claim for damages.[86]

6.38 Obviously in a homelessness case the need for accommodation will normally be an urgent one, and the applicant will therefore usually wish to ask the court to grant him interlocutory relief by way of an interim mandatory injunction requiring the council to secure accommodation pending the final disposal of the action, under, for example, the preliminary duty to accommodate in section 63.[87] Interlocutory relief is available in judicial review proceedings,[88] and also in proceedings for breach of statutory duty.

[81] See, *e.g. Hinz* v. *Berry* [1970] 2 Q.B. 40 (C.A.); the authority's breach of duty was held to have contributed to the applicant's psychiatric illness in *Mallon* v. *Monklands D.C.* 1986 S.L.T. 347 (Ct. of Session: O.H.); *cf.* the more generous rule relating to damages for breach of contract, see, *e.g. Jarvis* v. *Swan Tours Ltd.* [1973] 1 Q.B. 233 (C.A.).

[82] See, *e.g. Lally* v. *Kensington & Chelsea B.C.*, *The Times*, March 27, 1980 (£30); *Mallon* v. *Monklands D.C.*, see above (£100).

[83] See above, paras. 6.22–6.23.

[84] *Per* Megaw L.J. in *Thornton* v. *Kirklees M.B.C.* [1979] 2 All E.R. 349, 355 (C.A.).

[85] See *Cocks* v. *Thanet D.C.*, above, paras. 6.22–6.23.

[86] See County Courts Act 1984, s.38; *Hatt & Co. (Bath) Ltd.* v. *Pearce* [1978] 1 W.L.R. 885 (C.A.); *Thornton* v. *Kirklees M.B.C.* [1979] 2 All E.R. 349, 351 (C.A.); C.C.A. 1984, s.22, which allows a county court to grant an injunction (or declaration) without a claim for damages in relation to any land, or in relation to the "possession, occupation, use or enjoyment of any land," will not normally be relevant, since it is restricted to claims concerning *specific* land, whereas the applicant will normally be claiming a *general* right to be housed.

[87] See above, para. 4.02; see, *e.g. R.* v. *Welwyn & Hatfield D.C., ex p. Holmes* [1988] June Legal Action 19 (D.C.); *Hammell* v. *R.B. of Kensington and Chelsea* (1988) 20 H.L.R. 666 (C.A.).

[88] R.S.C., Ord. 53, rr. 1, 8; see the cases in n. 87, above.

The normal rule relating to the grant of interlocutory injunctions is now to the effect that the plaintiff can succeed in gaining such an injunction on the "balance of convenience," without having to establish a prima facie case or a probability of success at the full trial of the action, so long as he can show that there is a "serious question" to be tried, in the sense that the claim is not "frivolous or vexatious."[89] **6.39**

However, for the purposes of Part III of the 1985 Act the courts have decided that a plaintiff must satisfy a more stringent test before he can claim a mandatory interlocutory injunction, namely that of establishing a "strong prima facie case."[90] The principal reason why the courts developed this distinction is because, in a homelessness case, the applicant cannot give any worthwhile undertakings as to the authority's damages in the event of him losing the action.[91] However, this approach is difficult to reconcile with that adopted in the latest cases[92]; and in any event it has been pointed out that it is hard to see what damages the authority would suffer if the interlocutory injunction is granted but the applicant loses the final action, since the applicant (or the housing benefit or income support schemes) will normally be paying rent for the accommodation until the disposal of the action.[93] **6.40**

There is a further restriction which the courts have imposed on the availability of interlocutory injunctions to compel authorities to perform their duties under Part III of the 1985 Act: such injunctions will not normally be granted *ex parte* (*i.e.* without notice to the authority), but only *inter partes* (*i.e.* after due notice to the authority).[94] **6.41**

(iii) Declarations. A declaration cannot be obtained on an interim application, but only at a full hearing. Furthermore, as with the remedy by way of injunction, a claim for a declaration will not normally be within the county court's jurisdiction (even assuming **6.42**

89 *American Cyanamid Co.* v. *Ethicon Ltd.* [1975] A.C. 396 (H.L.); *Fellowes* v. *Fisher* [1976] Q.B. 122 (C.A.).

90 *De Falco* v. *Crawley B.C.* [1980] 1 All E.R. 913 (C.A.); *Tickner* v. *Mole Valley D.C.* [1980] L.A.G. Bull. 187 (C.A.); see *Hanbury and Maudsley's Modern Equity* (12th ed., 1985), pp. 742–743. Nevertheless, despite the decision of the House of Lords in *Puhlhofer* v. *Hillingdon L.B.C.* (see above), it is not necessary for the applicant to show that the case is "exceptional" before an interlocutory injunction can be granted, *Hammell* v. *R.B. of Kensington & Chelsea* , see above.

91 See *De Falco, ibid.* at pp. 922, 924.

92 See *Allen* v. *Jambo Holdings Ltd.* [1980] 2 All E.R. 502, 505 (C.A.).

93 A. Arden, *Homeless Persons—The Housing Act 1985 Part III* (3rd ed., 1988), para. 3.63.

94 *Thornton* v. *Kirklees M.B.C.* [1979] Q.B. 626 (C.A.).

that the case can be brought within one of the exceptions to the general principle requiring judicial review to be used) unless it is added to a claim for damages.[95]

6.43 Although a declaration does not carry with it any direct method of enforcement, compliance by the authority with its terms will obviously be the normal result. Furthermore, where the applicant attaches a request for a declaration to a claim for judicial review, he may well find that the court is more prepared to grant the declaration than one or more of the prerogative orders, in view of the technicalities which still surround such orders.[96]

[95] See above, n. 86.

[96] See, *e.g. Islam* v. *Hillingdon L.B.C.* [1981] 3 All E.R. 901, 912 (H.L.); but *cf. Cocks* v. *Thanet D.C.* [1982] 3 All E.R. 1135, 1139 (H.L.).

Part III: The Management of Council Housing

7 The Nature of a "Secure" Tenancy

1. *The Basic Definition of a "Secure" Tenancy*

(a) *The definition in sections 79 to 81 of the Housing Act 1985*

The key concept of the "secure" public sector tenancy is dealt with by sections 79 to 81 of the Housing Act 1985; from this concept flow all the "tenants' charter" rights in the 1985 Act. The exemptions from the definition of the "secure" tenancy have been very tightly drafted, so that the vast majority of council tenancies are in fact "secure." **7.01**

The "tenants' charter" in the 1985 Act is best regarded as a self-contained legislative code.[1] Although several of the provisions have been "borrowed" from the Rent Act 1977 (such as certain of the grounds for possession), it can be misleading to try and draw too many parallels between the Rent Act regime (or the new regime for the private rented sector in the Housing Act 1988) and that in the Housing Act 1985. Moreover, the Court of Appeal has pointed out[2] that the public sector "tenants' charter" provisions were motivated by very different considerations from those underlying the early Rent Acts: the first Rent Acts were designed to deal with the urgent need to accommodate returning servicemen after the end of the Great War, whereas the "tenants' charter" provisions were not introduced to meet any such emergency, but were designed with the social aim of giving public sector tenants similar statutory security to that long enjoyed by tenants in the private sector. **7.02**

When deciding on the extent of the rights of a particular council tenant, the search for the appropriate "label" is normally not as dif- **7.03**

[1] See D.O.E. Consultation Paper, *Housing Management: Tenants' Rights: Security of Tenure for Public Sector Tenants* (1979), para. 3.
[2] *L.B. of Hammersmith & Fulham* v. *Harrison* [1981] 1 W.L.R. 650.

ficult a task as categorisation for the purposes of the private rented sector provisions in the Rent Act 1977[3] or the Housing Act 1988; in the public sector, the basic classification is simply between "secure" and "non-secure" tenancies, and tenancies can be "secure" whether granted before or after the date when the relevant statutory protection commenced.[4]

7.04 In order to be "secure," the tenancy (whether fixed-term or periodic) must satisfy the following requirements at the time when the question falls to be decided.[5]

7.05 **(i) Let "as a separate dwelling."** First, under section 79(1) the property (which may be a house or part of a house, such as a flat, and may include land let together with the dwelling even though physically separated from it[6]) must be let "*as a separate dwelling.*" This expression is not defined, but the courts have applied[7] relevant Rent Act decisions[8]: the result is that if the tenant shares living accommodation (such as a kitchen or a sitting-room, but not merely a bathroom or a toilet) with people other than those who are joint tenants with him or members of his household or his lodgers or sub-tenants,[9] then he cannot have a secure tenancy. In effect, therefore, the sharing of living accommodation by a tenant with other tenants removes security, unless the sharers are joint tenants with him: for example, an occupier of hostel accommodation who shares living facilities,[10] or a single parent or student sharing a house or flat with others though holding an individual licence,[11] does not hold under a "secure tenancy." There is no equivalent in the 1985 Act to section 22 of the Rent Act 1977 and section 3 of the Housing Act 1988,

[3] *Cf.* D. Tiplady, (1981) 44 M.L.R. 129, 130.
[4] *I.e.* October 3, 1980; and see H.A. 1980, s.47.
[5] See the words " . . . at any time when . . . " in H.A. 1985, s.79(1); in general, therefore, a tenancy can begin as secure, then cease to be secure, and then become secure again if not determined while insecure, *Crawley B.C.* v. *Sawyer* (1988) 20 H.L.R. 98, 100 (C.A.); see also *L.B. of Sutton* v. *Swann* (1986) 18 H.L.R. 140 (C.A.); but for exceptions to this principle, see H.A. 1985, ss.89(4), 90(4), 91(2), and 93(2) (below, paras. 9.18, 9.26, 9.39, 9.42).
[6] H.A. 1985, s.112.
[7] See, *e.g. Thompson* v. *City of Glasgow D.C.* 1986 S.L.T. 6 (Lands Trib.).
[8] See, *e.g. Baker* v. *Turner* [1950] 1 All E.R. 834, 854 (H.L.); *Goodrich* v. *Paisner* [1956] 2 All E.R. 176 (H.L.).
[9] Secure tenants are permitted to take in lodgers and (within limits) to sub-let part of the property: see H.A. 1985, s.93(1), discussed below, paras. 9.01–9.10.
[10] See above, *Thompson* v. *City of Glasgow D.C.*
[11] In certain circumstances, people holding licences can be treated as holding secure tenancies; see below, paras. 7.15, 7.23–7.24.

which provide that if a private tenant shares living accommodation with people other than the landlord, he can still enjoy statutory protection in relation to his separate (non-shared) accommodation.

The broad purpose behind the insertion of this "separate dwelling" requirement in the public sector provisions was apparently to avoid security attaching to "occupiers under . . . sharing arrangements, which are basically suitable only for households or individuals at a particular stage in their life-cycle," but to allow for security "where the sharing of some facilities such as bathroom or WC is only an incidental part of the provision of otherwise permanent accommodation to one household."[12] **7.06**

(ii) The "landlord condition." The second requirement for a secure tenancy is that the landlord's interest must belong to a prescribed public body; this is described as the "landlord condition."[13] The list of prescribed bodies includes[14] district councils, London borough councils, county councils, certain housing co-operatives, and housing action trusts. **7.07**

In the case of joint landlords, the tenancy will only be secure if *each* of the landlords satisfies the "landlord condition."[15] **7.08**

(iii) The "tenant condition." The third requirement for a secure tenancy is that the tenant must be an *individual* (not, for example, another public authority, a limited company, or a short-life housing organisation), who occupies the dwelling as his *only or principal home*; this is described as the "tenant condition."[16] In the case of a joint tenancy, each of the joint tenants must be an individual, and at least one must fulfil this occupation requirement.[17] **7.09**

The concept of occupation as the tenant's "only or principal home" is not defined. It is however clear that a secure tenant need not occupy the whole property, since the 1985 Act contemplates the subletting of part and the taking in of lodgers.[18] Furthermore, the **7.10**

[12] D.O.E. Consultation Paper, *op. cit.* para. 16.

[13] H.A. 1985, ss.79(1), 80(1).

[14] *Ibid.* ss.4(*e*), 80(1), (4); s.4(*e*) includes "joint authorities" established under L.G.A. 1985, Pt. IV; for discussion of housing co-operatives and housing action trusts, see Chaps. 13 and 15 respectively.

[15] *R.* v. *Plymouth C.C. and Cornwall C.C., ex p. Freeman* (1987) 19 H.L.R. 328 (C.A).

[16] H.A. 1985, ss.79(1), 81.

[17] *Ibid.* s.81.

[18] *Ibid.* s.93(1), see below, paras. 9.01–9.10; see also *Harris* v. *Swick Securities Ltd.* [1969] 3 All E.R. 1131 (C.A.).

Matrimonial Homes Act 1983[19] provides that a deserted spouse may, by remaining in occupation, keep the deserting spouse's secure tenancy alive notwithstanding the latter's departure.

7.11 The courts may be expected to refer in cases of difficulty to relevant decisions concerning similar expressions used in other legislation. Occupation is a matter of fact and degree, indicating something more than mere legal possession.[20] Temporary absences are likely to be disregarded where they have arisen because of (for example) holidays,[21] business commitments, ill-health,[22] or a short prison sentence.[23] Even in the case of a lengthy absence, the tenant might still be said to be occupying the dwelling as his only or principal home if he is keeping it ready for his renewed occupation[24]: this is shown by an intention to return, together with some physical signs of continued "occupation" by way of, for example, the leaving of furniture and other possessions in the dwelling, so that it can be occupied as a home[25]; but the onus lies firmly on the tenant to show that he has taken clear steps to maintain his occupation.[26]

7.12 If a sole tenant who is a cohabitee is excluded under the domestic violence legislation,[27] then the remaining cohabitee will not be able to keep the secure tenancy alive by virtue of his or her own occupa-

[19] M.H.A. 1983, s.1(6); this provision does not protect cohabitees, see below, para. 7.12.

[20] *Poland* v. *Earl Cadogan* (1980) 124 S.J. 575 (C.A); Leasehold Reform Act 1967, s.1(2).

[21] *Cf. Roland House Gardens Ltd.* v. *Cravitz* (1974) 119 S.J. 167 (C.A.), statutory tenancy under the Rent Acts.

[22] *Cf. Tomkins* v. *Rowley* [1949] E.G.D. 314 (C.A.), statutory tenancy under the Rent Acts.

[23] *Cf. Sumnall* v. *Statt* (1985) 49 P. & C.R. 367 (C.A), where, however, the tenant was required to "reside constantly at the farmhouse," which imposed a stricter requirement than that contained in H.A. 1985, s.81; *cf.* also *Brown* v. *Brash* [1948] 2 K.B. 247 (C.A.), statutory tenancy under the Rent Acts; for housing benefit purposes, a sentenced prisoner is normally treated as still occupying his dwelling as his home while "temporarily absent," if his sentence is not likely to exceed 52 weeks: see Housing Benefit (General) Regulations 1987 (S.I. 1987 No. 1971) reg. 5(8), and *R.* v. *Housing Benefits Review Board of the R.B. of Kensington & Chelsea, ex p. Robertson, The Times*, February 15, 1988 (D.C.).

[24] See, *e.g. Richards* v. *Green* (1984) 11 H.L.R. 1 (C.A.), a Rent Act case.

[25] *Crawley B.C.* v. *Sawyer* (1988) 20 H.L.R. 98, 102 (C.A), where it was pointed out (at p.101) that there is no material difference between occupying premises as a *home* and occupying them as a *residence*.

[26] *Poland* v. *Earl Cadogan*, see above; *Brickfield Properties Ltd.* v. *Hughes* (1988) 20 H.L.R. 108 (C.A).

[27] See below, paras. 11.21–11.27.

tion as such (since the Matrimonial Homes Act[28] does not apply to cohabitees); however, even in the case of a lengthy exclusion order[29] the courts are likely to avoid having to find that security has been lost due to the tenant's absence: some such concept as that of the tenant's "constructive occupation" could be relied on where the tenant has every intention of continuously occupying but is only prevented from doing so by virtue of a court order.[30]

The Housing Act makes it clear[31] that a person can "occupy" two or more different properties as his homes at the same time: thus actual physical occupation of each is not necessary.[32] In such a case, the question of which he occupies as his principal home cannot be decided solely by reference to the way he divides his time between the two,[33] although where a preponderance of time is spent at one particular property this can help to show that it is his principal home.[34] **7.13**

It is particularly important in this context to take care when seeking to rely on cases dealing with the Rent Act expressions "statutory tenancy" and "resident landlord," since the relevant provisions of the Rent Act 1977[35] refer to occupation "as his residence," whereas the Housing Act 1985 is much more narrowly drafted in its reference[36] to "only or principal home"; furthermore, it must be borne in mind that the mere failure to occupy by a Rent Act *protected*, *i.e.* contractual, tenant (as opposed to a Rent Act *statutory* tenant), is not necessarily inconsistent with the continuance of the tenancy.[37] **7.14**

[28] M.H.A. 1983, s.1(6), see above, para. 7.10.

[29] As in *Fairweather* v. *Kolosine* (1984) 11 H.L.R. 61 (C.A.), see below, para. 11.24.

[30] The House of Lords has emphasised that the domestic violence legislation cannot affect the property rights of cohabitees, but only the enjoyment of those rights, *Davis* v. *Johnson* [1979] A.C. 264 (H.L.); see below, paras. 11.24–11.26.

[31] 1985 Act, s.81, "only *or* principal home."

[32] *Crawley B.C.* v. *Sawyer* (1988) 20 H.L.R. 98, 101–102 (C.A.).

[33] *Frost* v. *Feltham* [1981] 1 W.L.R. 452 (house in Wales held on the facts to be the "only or main residence" of a publican working in Essex, for the purposes of mortgage interest tax relief under the Finance Act 1974, Sched. 1, para. 4(1), even though he only spent two or three days each month at the Welsh property).

[34] *Peabody Donation Fund Governors* v. *Grant* (1982) 6 H.L.R. 41 (C.A.), claimant spending four days per week at the flat in question held on the facts to satisfy the "only or principal home" requirement; *Camden L.B.C.* v. *Coombs* [1988] March Legal Action 17 (Cty. Ct.).

[35] R.A. 1977, ss.2, 12; as to statutory tenancies, see *Brickfield Properties Ltd.* v. *Hughes*, above.

[36] H.A. 1985, s.81; see *Crawley B.C.* v. *Sawyer* (1988) 20 H.L.R. 98, 100 (C.A).

[37] See, *e.g. Legg* v. *Coole and Sheaff* [1978] L.A.G. Bull. 189 (C.A.).

(b) *The lease/licence distinction*

7.15 **(i) Application of the secure tenancy provisions to licences.** The provisions in Part IV of the Housing Act 1985 relating to secure tenancies and the rights of secure tenants are expressed to apply "in relation to a licence to occupy a dwelling-house (whether or not granted for a consideration) as they apply in relation to a tenancy."[38] Throughout this book, references to secure "tenancies" are intended also to embrace licences, unless otherwise stated. However, following the important 1985 decision of the House of Lords in *Street* v. *Mountford*[39] many arrangements which would previously have been regarded as licences are now likely to be treated as *leases*, so that this particular provision probably now has only a limited scope.

7.16 **(ii) The test for deciding between a lease and a licence.** In *Street's* case it was decided that where there is the grant to an occupier of residential accommodation at a rent and with exclusive possession, then (whether the grant is for a fixed term or on a periodic basis) if there are no unusual circumstances, the legal result is a tenancy and not a licence, whatever label the parties may have attached to the transaction. The principal test for deciding the issue of exclusive possession was said to depend on whether the occupier is a "lodger": if so, there is no exclusive possession and the arrangement is a licence; but if the occupier is not a lodger, there will normally be exclusive possession and the arrangement will therefore be a lease.

7.17 The occupier is to be treated as a lodger if the landowner exercises a very high degree of control over the premises, which is normally indicated by the provision of attendance or services[40] which require

[38] H.A. 1985, s.79(3); although it was suggested in *Family Housing Association* v. *Miah* (1982) 5 H.L.R. 94, 101 (C.A.) that if a licensee is to be secure he must enjoy exclusive possession, the court was considering the narrower wording in H.A. 1980, s.48(1); the wording of s.79(3) of the 1985 Act would not appear to require exclusive possession.

[39] [1985] 2 All E.R. 289; see, *e.g.* N. Madge, [1985] Legal Action 77; R. Street, [1985] Conv. 328; D. Hoath, [1986] J.S.W.L. 46.

[40] "Attendance" is a narrower concept than "services": "attendance" is a personal service provided by the owner or his servant, such as cleaning the occupier's rooms, whereas "services" can include such non-personal matters as the general cleaning or carpeting of common parts, see, *e.g.* *Palser* v. *Grinling* [1948] A.C. 291 (H.L.)

him or his employees to exercise unrestricted access to and use of the premises. The access does not have to be constant, but the amount and frequency of the agreed attendance or services is relevant in applying the "lodger" test.[41]

The House of Lords in *Street*'s case also recognised, however, that in certain exceptional cases an occupier may be a licensee even if he does have exclusive possession, as where he is a service occupier pursuant to a contract of employment, or where he occupies under a contract for the purchase of the land,[42] or where the parties had no intention to create legal relations. **7.18**

The House of Lords in *Street*'s case went on to consider the status of so-called "non-exclusive licences," under which, typically, several intending occupiers are required to sign separate, individual agreements with the owner, which confer on each of them the right to live in the property, but in no particular part of it, together with such other people (including, often, the owner himself) as the owner may decide.[43] Judges have been urged to be astute in detecting shams or pretences in these cases,[44] so that sometimes the true arrangement will be found to be a joint tenancy rather than a series of non-exclusive licences.[45] **7.19**

(iii) Application of the lease/licence test to the public rented sector. *Street*'s case arose in the context of the private rented sector, and the House of Lords did not consider its implications for public landlords. After *Street* it has clearly become more difficult for an **7.20**

[41] *Crancour* v. *Da Silvaesa* (1986) 18 H.L.R. 265, 272–273 (C.A.), where it was acknowledged, on the facts, that if the real agreement between the parties required the owner to remove the occupier's rubbish daily, clean the occupier's accommodation weekly, and launder his sheets fortnightly, then the occupier would be a "lodger."

[42] See *Bretherten* v. *Paton* (1986) 18 H.L.R. 257 (C.A.).

[43] For an example of non-exclusive licences granted by a housing association, which were held on the facts not to attract statutory security, see *Family Housing Association* v. *Miah* (1982) 5 H.L.R. 94 (C.A.).

[44] See Lord Templeman in *Street*'s case, *ibid.* at 299, and in *Antoniades* v. *Villiers* [1988] 3 All E.R. 1058, 1067–1068 (H.L.); see also the discussion of "artificial schemes" in *Gisborne* v. *Burton* [1988] 3 W.L.R. 921 (C.A).

[45] *Antoniades* v. *Villiers* [1988] 3 All E.R. 1058 (H.L.): here, two cohabitees each signed identical purported "licence" agreements for the occupation of a one-bedroomed flat, and the landowner's reservation of the right to introduce further occupiers was held to be an ineffective attempt to disguise a true joint tenancy; but non-exclusive licences can still exist, even though the occupiers are not "lodgers," *Brooker Settled Estates* v. *Ayers* (1987) 19 H.L.R. 246 (C.A.); *Hadjiloucas* v. *Crean* [1987] 3 All E.R. 1008 (C.A.); *A G Securities* v. *Vaughan* [1988] 3 All E.R. 1058 (H.L): here a four-

authority to grant a licence rather than a lease.[46] However, it is possible (as an exception to the general principle in *Street*'s case) for an authority to grant a licence for a limited period, even though it confers exclusive possession, where this is done pursuant to the authority's statutory responsibilities towards the homeless in Part III of the 1985 Act.[47] Nevertheless, the restrictions indicated by *Street* on the use of non-exclusive licences would appear to be as relevant to councils as they are to private landowners.

7.21 Clearly, even if the situation does not fall within the "homelessness" category discussed above, an authority can effectively use a licence where it can satisfy the "lodger" test laid down in *Street*. However, despite the emphasis placed in *Street* on the payment of rent as an indicator of a tenancy, it now seems that short-term rent-free arrangements which are stated to be licences could nevertheless still be construed as leases where it is not a "homelessness" case, and the "lodger" test is not satisfied (so that there is exclusive possession): for the reservation of a rent is not legally necessary for the creation of a tenancy.[48]

7.22 In practice, it is frequently possible for authorities to avoid creating a "secure" arrangement regardless of whether it is technically a lease or a licence. For example, if the occupier shares living accommodation with others it may be that the "separate dwelling" requirement will not be satisfied anyway,[49] as in the case of many hostel arrangements; and even if the relationship (whether a lease or a licence) appears to satisfy all the basic requirements for security, it may nevertheless fall within one of the statutory exemptions from the definition of "secure tenancy" in the 1985 Act which will shortly be discussed.

bedroomed flat was occupied by four persons (who had previously been strangers) under separate and independent agreements, providing for different commencement dates and different monthly payments.

[46] See, *e.g. L.B. of Camden* v. *Shortlife Community Housing Ltd.* (*No.* 2) [1987] June Legal Action 17 (Ch.D.).

[47] *Ogwr B.C.* v. *Dykes, The Times*, November 10, 1988 (C.A.). Here a temporary licence granted to an intentionally homeless person was upheld notwithstanding the grant of exclusive possession. The court applied *dicta* from *South Holland D.C.* v.*Keyte* (1987) 19 H.L.R. 97, 101 (C.A.), and distinguished *Eastleigh B.C.* v. *Walsh* [1985] 1 W.L.R. 525 (H.L.); see below, paras. 7.38–7.41, and Chaps. 4–5 above.

[48] *Ashburn Anstalt* v. *Arnold* [1988] 2 W.L.R. 706 (C.A.); *cf.* N. Madge, [1986] Legal Action 97.

[49] H.A. 1985, s.79(1), see above, paras. 7.05–7.06.

(iv) Licences granted to former trespassers. Even if the basic requirements for a "secure" licence are satisfied,[50] there is a specific exemption from security in the 1985 Act where the licence is in effect a licensed squatting agreement, *i.e.* "a licence granted as a temporary expedient to a person who entered the dwelling-house or any other land as a trespasser (whether or not, before the grant of that licence, another licence to occupy that or another dwelling-house had been granted to him)."[51] **7.23**

It would seem that, for this exemption from "secure licence" status to apply, there must be some connection between the original trespass (even though this may relate to "any other land") and the current licence.[52] If a *lease*, rather than a licence, is granted to a former trespasser, then the tenancy will be "secure" (unless some other relevant exemption applies); and in the light of the *Street* decision, some purported non-secure "licences" granted to former trespassers in supposed reliance on this exemption may well now fall to be treated as secure leases. Where an effective licence to occupy short-life property is granted by an authority to someone who was not originally a trespasser, then again this particular exemption will not apply and security will *prima facie* attach, unless the arrangement falls within one of the standard exemptions dealt with below. **7.24**

2. *Exemptions from the Definition in section 79*

Assuming that the three basic conditions for a secure tenancy set out above are satisfied, the tenancy may nevertheless fail to be secure if it falls within one or more of various exemptions, most of which are listed in Schedule 1 to the 1985 Act.[53] An outline account of the more important of these exemptions now follows, but reference should be made to the wording of the statute for the details of each relevant exemption. **7.25**

[50] *I.e.* there is a licence which prima facie ranks as a secure tenancy under H.A. 1985, s.79(3), see above.

[51] H.A. 1985, s.79(4).

[52] Thus if the present licensee had happend to "gate-crash" a council committee meeting, his present security should not be affected!

[53] Quite separately, an originally secure tenancy may cease to be secure (*i.e.* it will lose statutory protection although the contractual term will continue) following certain acts of disposal: H.A. 1985, ss.79(2) (c), 91(2), and 93(2); see below, paras. 9.18, 9.25. Note also that there are several quite distinct exemptions from the right to buy, which is normally one of the rights enjoyed by secure tenants (see Chap. 14).

(a) *Long tenancies*

7.26 A tenancy granted for a term certain exceeding 21 years, or granted in pursuance of Part V of the 1985 Act (which covers the "right to buy," including the right to a "shared ownership lease") cannot be secure.[54]

(b) *Tenancies related to public employment*

7.27 **(i) Employees required to occupy dwellings under their contracts of employment.** A tenancy granted to an employee of the landlord authority, or to an employee of certain specified public bodies other than the landlord authority, is not secure if the contract of employment requires the employee to occupy the dwelling for the better performance of his duties.[55] This exemption would normally cover, for example, resident caretakers.

7.28 In applying this exemption, it will be relevant to consider the case law concerning the difficult distinction often made for Rent Act purposes between service occupiers (who are unprotected, because they are licensees required to occupy the property in order to carry out their duties), and service tenants (who are protected as tenants because they are merely permitted to reside in their employers' property)[56]; this is therefore one of the situations where it can still be relevant, for secure tenancy purposes, to distinguish between a lease and a licence as such.[57] When deciding whether the contract of employment actually requires an employee to occupy for the better performance of his duties, it is permissible to look beyond the express terms of the contract itself (whether oral or in writing[58]) and to have regard to the factual background which gave rise to the tenant's occupation.[59]

[54] H.A. 1985, s.115(1) and Sched. 1, para. 1; it will be seen in Chap. 14 that leases granted under Pt. V may sometimes be for terms not exceeding 21 years, but the effect of this exemption is that such leases are nevertheless not "secure."

[55] H.A. 1985, Sched. 1, para. 2(1).

[56] This distinction, which is often somewhat blurred in practice, is discussed in *e.g.* A. Arden, *Housing Act 1985* (Current Law Statutes Annotated Reprints), notes to H.A. 1985, Sched. 1, para. 2.

[57] *Cf.* H.A. 1985, s.79(3), see above, para. 7.15.

[58] H.A. 1985, Sched. 1, para. 2(5).

[59] *Campbell* v. *City of Edinburgh D.C.* 1987 S.L.T. 51 (Ct. of Session, 2nd Div.).

(ii) Rent- and rates-free accommodation for police officers. A tenancy granted to a member of a police force is not secure if the dwelling is provided for him free of rent and rates.[60] **7.29**

(iii) Employees of fire authorities. A tenancy granted to an employee of a fire authority is not secure if his contract of employment requires him to live in close proximity to a particular fire station, and the dwelling was let to him by the authority in consequence of that requirement.[61] **7.30**

(iv) Properties recently let on employment-related tenancies. A tenancy is not secure if: **7.31**

(a) within the period of three years immediately before the grant the property has been let on a tenancy falling within exemptions (i), (ii) or (iii) above;
(b) the periods during which the dwelling has been let otherwise than under a tenancy falling within those exemptions do not exceed three years in aggregate; and
(c) before the current grant the landlord notified the tenant in writing of the effect of this exemption.[62]

For this particular exemption to apply, the current tenant need not be an employee of a public body at all; but the exemption can only last for a maximum of three years in respect of the current lease, however long it may have been granted for.

(c) *Tenancies of land acquired for development*

A tenancy is not secure if the dwelling is on land which was initially *acquired* for development within the meaning of section 22 of the Town and Country Planning Act 1971 (as opposed merely to being currently *required* for such development), and the dwelling is used by the landlord authority, pending development, as temporary housing accommodation.[63] **7.32**

The problem with this exemption is that it does not cover short-life property as such; the authority must have acquired the property for development within the technical definition in section 22 of the 1971 Act ("the carrying out of building, engineering, mining, or **7.33**

[60] H.A. 1985, Sched. 1, para. 2(2).
[61] *Ibid.* Sched. 1, para. 2(3).
[62] *Ibid.* Sched. 1, para. 2(4).
[63] *Ibid.* Sched. 1, para. 3.

other operations . . . or the making of any material change in the use of any buildings or other land").

7.34 It is still not clear whether the complete demolition of a building would of itself be "development"[64]; and improvement work which does not materially affect the external appearance of the building is specifically exempted from the definition of development.[65] If, therefore, the authority acquired the land to do work which falls outside this technical definition of development, any short-term leases (or licences) would prima facie attract security (unless one of the other exemptions applies), and could therefore provide long-term difficulties for the authority.

7.35 This problem remains notwithstanding the availability of a special mandatory ground for possession against a secure tenant in this situation,[66] since before possession can be awarded on this ground the court has to be satisfied as to suitable alternative accommodation for the tenant.[67] There was a Ministerial statement in 1980 that the "acquisition for development" exemption was intended to facilitate developments such as road schemes, and not the normal improvement programmes of authorities, for which this special ground for possession was designed.[68]

7.36 There is thus a distinct danger that authorities may prove reluctant to lease (or licence) their short-life properties to someone who does not fall within one of the other exempt categories. It was originally suggested that one way out of this difficulty would be for the authority to grant a licence of the property to a special short-life borrowing agency, which would in turn licence the property to the intended occupants; if suitable precautions were taken, it was thought that security could thus be effectively avoided.[69]

7.37 However, the effect of the decision in *Street* v. *Mountford*[70] is that even such purported "licences" granted by authorities on a temporary basis to short-life borrowing agencies are likely in law to create leases.[71] This will not in practice usually have any adverse effects on

[64] See, *e.g.* A.E. Telling, *Planning Law and Procedure* (7th ed., 1986), pp. 82–83.
[65] T.C.P.A. 1971, s.22(2)(*a*).
[66] H.A. 1985, Sched. 2, Pt. II, gd. 10, see below, paras. 8.46–8.47.
[67] H.A. 1985, s.84(2)(*b*).
[68] *H.C. Standing Committee F on the Housing Bill*, April 24, 1980, cols. 2402–2403.
[69] See H.E.O. (Shelter), *The Housing Act 1980: Its implications for the short-term use of vacant property* (1981), pp. 23–25.
[70] [1985] 2 All E.R. 289, see above, paras. 7.15–7.21.
[71] See, *e.g.* *L.B. of Camden* v. *Shortlife Community Housing Ltd.* (*No.* 2) [1987] Legal Action 17 (Ch.D.).

the position as between the authority and the borrowing agency,[72] since if the latter is a company or friendly society it will not be able to satisfy the "tenant condition" of occupation as its only or principal home,[73] and therefore cannot hold either a secure tenancy under the Housing Act 1985 or an assured tenancy under the Housing Act 1988.[74] Furthermore, the fact that the head landlord is a local authority provides an additional reason why the head tenancy cannot be "assured" under the Housing Act 1988.[75] Nevertheless, the individual occupiers (*i.e.* the sub-tenants) could hold assured sub-tenancies under the Housing Act 1988 if the agency is not a relevant public landlord.[76] Yet the sub-tenancies would normally have to end on termination of the agency's head lease from the landlord authority, there being no statutory protection for the individual sub-tenants as against the head (council) landlord in this situation.[77]

(d) *Tenancies granted to certain homeless persons*

A tenancy granted in pursuance of the temporary housing duties[78] owed to certain homeless persons under Part III of the Housing Act 1985 will not be secure until the expiry of a period of 12 months after the notification to the tenant of the authority's decision[79] under Part III, unless he has, before the expiry of that period, been notified by the authority that the tenancy is to be regarded as secure.[80] **7.38**

It appears that the 12 months' period can normally only run, for the purpose of establishing eventual security, from the date of the actual notification of the authority's decision under Part III, and not **7.39**

[72] The implications of *Street*'s case as regards the use of authorities' short-life properties are fully discussed by N. Madge in [1986] Legal Action 97.

[73] H.A. 1985, s.81, see above, paras. 7.09–7.14; and see, *e.g. Carter* v. *S.U. Carburettor Co.* [1942] 2 All E.R. 228, 231 (C.A).

[74] H.A. 1988, s.1(1)(*b*).

[75] *Ibid.* Sched. 1, Pt. I, para. 12.

[76] *Cf. ibid.* Sched. 1, Pt. I, para. 12.

[77] Although the H.A. 1988, s.18, gives certain protection to sub-tenants on termination of the head tenancies, this provision cannot apply where (as here) the head tenancy falls outside the protection of H.A. 1988: H.A. 1988, s.18(2); see also *Acme Housing Association and R.B. of Kensington & Chelsea* v. *Chevska* [1987] June Legal Action 17 (Cty. Ct.), and below, para. 9.09.

[78] *I.e.* those in H.A. 1985, ss.63, 65(3) and 68(1), see above, paras. 4.02, 4.08, 4.15; where the accommodation is granted pursuant to the full rehousing duty in s.65(2), security will normally attach immediately if no other exemption applies: see above, para. 4.14.

[79] See H.A. 1985, s.64, discussed above, para. 4.164.

[80] H.A. 1985, Sched. 1, para. 4.

from any notional date by which it might be argued that the authority should have been in a position to give this notification (unless, possibly, there is very clear evidence that the authority could have come to its decision at an earlier date).[81] Moreover, even if a proper notification under Part III has been given, so that time can start to run for these purposes, if the contractual tenancy or licence is validly terminated by the council before the 12 months' period has elapsed then any subsequent occupation by the applicant will merely be in the capacity of a "tolerated trespasser," and will not count for security purposes by way of completing the 12 months' requirement.[82]

7.40 Although it is rare in these "temporary" cases for accommodation to be made available for more than 12 months from notification under Part III, authorities need to "diary ahead" if they are to ensure that security cannot arise; where necessary the tenant can then be switched to other accommodation before the deadline is reached, following service and expiry of a proper notice to quit[83] where the arrangement is a periodic tenancy. We have seen,[84] however, that an authority may validly grant a licence for a limited period to a homeless family under Part III, even though exclusive possession is conferred; in such a case, an informal notice can sometimes be served[85] to determine a periodic contract.

7.41 As regards those subsequently found to be entitled to permanent accommodation under the full rehousing duty[86] following a period of temporary accommodation under the interim housing duty[87] pend-

[81] *Family Housing Association* v. *Miah* (1982) 5 H.L.R. 94 (C.A): here an applicant had been in occupation of s.63 accommodation for more than 12 months, but security could not attach because the authority had not yet notified her of its decision under s.64.

[82] *Restormel B.C.* v. *Buscombe* (1982) 14 H.L.R. 91 (C.A.); this decision also reveals an extreme reluctance to allow occupation, initially permitted temporarily under s.65(3), subsequently to attract statutory security even though the terms of occupation have been subsequently varied, *e.g.* through the provision of a "rent card" containing new terms inconsistent with those originally agreed.

[83] For an awful warning of the problems which can arise where this procedure is not followed, see *Eastleigh B.C.* v. *Walsh* [1985] 1 W.L.R. 525 (H.L.); the appropriate formalities for a notice to quit are discussed below, paras. 8.81–8.82.

[84] See above, para. 7.20.

[85] As in *Ogwr B.C.* v. *Dykes, The Times,* November 10, 1988 (C.A.), see above, para. 7.20; however, in the case of certain periodic licences a formal notice to quit must now be served: see P.f.E.A. 1977, ss.3A, 5(1A)–(1B), 8(4), discussed below, para. 8.81, n. 6.

[86] Owed to those who are in priority need and unintentionally homeless: H.A. 1985, s.65(2).

[87] Owed to those who appear to be homeless and in priority need: H.A. 1985, s.63.

ing completion of the authority's inquiries, the position appears to be as follows[88]: in the initial period during which they are temporarily accommodated, they are not secure; once notification of their entitlement to full rehousing is given, the 12 months' period starts to run, and provided they are left in the same accommodation as that in which they were temporarily accommodated they are still not secure during that 12 months' period; but if they are rehoused after the notification, then they will become secure at once in their new accommodation, since this will not itself have been provided under the temporary housing duty at all, but rather under the full rehousing duty.

(e) *Tenancies granted to those securing employment*

A tenancy granted temporarily by an authority to someone who has already secured employment in its area or in the surrounding area, and who was not previously resident in the authority's area, will not normally be secure until the expiry of one year from the grant.[89] The authority must give prior written notice to the tenant explaining clearly that the proposed tenancy falls within the exemption,[90] otherwise security will attach immediately.[91] **7.42**

(f) *Tenancies granted under "North Wiltshire" schemes*

A sub-letting granted temporarily by an authority, pursuant to an arrangement with (normally) a private landlord under what is popularly called a "North Wiltshire"[92] scheme, will not be secure.[93] **7.43**

This scheme involves a short-term arrangement under which a dwelling is leased to the authority by (normally) a private landlord (*i.e.* not by another body capable of granting secure tenancies, although the landlord could be, for example, a government department such as the Crown Suppliers) with vacant possession, and for use as temporary housing accommodation on terms allowing the head landlord to obtain vacant possession from the authority on the expiry of a specified period or when required by him. The authority **7.44**

[88] See A. Arden, *op. cit.*, notes to H.A. 1985, Sched. 1, para. 4.
[89] H.A. 1985, Sched. 1, para. 5.
[90] *Ibid.*
[91] See *Campbell* v. *Western Isles Islands Council* 1988 S.L.T. 4 (Lands Trib.).
[92] The scheme originated in North Wiltshire in 1975, but was adopted by many other authorities; the viability of such schemes has been preserved by this exemption in the 1985 Act.
[93] H.A. 1985, Sched. 1, para. 6.

will then sub-let the property, with no danger of creating a secure (sub-) tenancy. Further encouragement to such schemes is afforded by a provision in the Landlord and Tenant Act 1985 which relieves the head landlord from complying with certain of the normal statutory repairing obligations.[94]

7.45 Thus a private landlord can avoid the security provisions in Part I of the Housing Act 1988 by (in effect) using the council as his letting agent.

(g) *Tenancies granted temporarily during works*

7.46 A tenancy is not secure if it is granted temporarily, during the period when works are being carried out on the tenant's previous dwelling, and the tenant was *not* a secure tenant of that previous dwelling.[95] This would cover, for example, a private sector tenant who has been temporarily displaced while his landlord carries out the work required by an authority's improvement notice served under Part VII of the Housing Act 1985. If such a temporarily "decanted" tenant was in fact a *secure* tenant of the previous dwelling, then the new tenancy will normally also be secure, although the council will have a discretionary ground for possession when the work on the previous dwelling is completed.[96]

(h) *Student tenancies*

7.47 Tenancies granted to students cannot normally be secure until six months from the end of the student's course.[97]

(i) *Tenancies granted following implementation of the "change of landlord" procedure*

7.48 Under section 101 of the Housing Act 1988, a tenancy granted by an authority cannot be secure where the relevant dwelling forms part of an estate in relation to which an application to purchase has been made under the "change of landlord" procedure (which is discussed later[98]). This exemption covers tenancies granted after the

[94] L. & T.A. 1985, s.14(4), see below, para. 12.26.
[95] H.A. 1985, Sched. 1, para. 7.
[96] *Ibid.* Sched. 2, Pt. I, gd. 8, see below, para. 8.43.
[97] H.A. 1985, Sched. 1, para. 10; the relevant courses are designated by the Secure Tenancies (Designated Courses) Regulations 1980 (S.I. 1980 No. 1407), which continue in force under the Housing (Consequential Provisions) Act 1985, s.2(2).
[98] See Chap. 15.

date of the relevant "change of landlord" application, and during such time as the application remains "live."[99]

3. *The Form of the Tenancy Agreement*

(a) *The requirement for written evidence of the tenancy terms*

Most council tenancies are periodic, being granted on a weekly basis. Under the general law, leases the length of which will not initially exceed three years need neither be under seal nor even in writing.[1] Oral council tenancies are still perfectly legal. The Housing Act 1985 does not require a written agreement as such,[2] but merely provides[3] that where under a secure tenancy there is no formal lease or tenancy agreement in writing, the authority must furnish the secure tenant with a written statement of all the terms of the tenancy other than those implied by law; where there is a formal lease or written tenancy agreement but it fails to set out all the terms agreed (for example, because it refers to a list of conditions kept at the authority's offices), then again a written statement of the omitted terms, other than those implied by law, must be supplied. **7.49**

This written statement must be furnished on the grant of the tenancy or as soon as practicable thereafter.[4] The court can pronounce by simple declaration on the accuracy of this written statement,[5] but the tenant cannot obtain the court's opinion as to the reasonableness of the stated terms of the tenancy as such (save in eviction proceedings[6]). **7.50**

Thus in practice the tenancy agreement itself will still often be made orally, but subject to certain conditions set out in some ancillary document such as the rent book.[7] Sometimes the tenant is required to sign these tenancy conditions[8]; but signature is not essential, since the tenant's acceptance of the conditions can be inferred merely from his entry into possession, and the conditions sometimes expressly provide that the tenant's possession of the property is conclusive evidence of his acceptance of those conditions. **7.51**

99 H.A. 1988, ss.93(5), 101(1), (4)(*f*).
1 Law of Property Act 1925, s.54(2).
2 *Cf.* Housing (Scotland) Act 1987, s.53(1).
3 H.A. 1985, s.104(2)(*b*).
4 *Ibid.* s.104(2).
5 *Ibid.* s.110(2)(*c*)
6 See *ibid.* s.84(2)(*a*) and Sched. 2, Pt. I, gd. 1, discussed below, paras. 8.31–8.36.
7 See below, paras. 7.53–7.55.
8 See, *e.g. Liverpool C.C.* v. *Irwin* [1976] 2 All E.R. 39, 43 (H.L).

(b) *Stamp duty*

7.52 If the document takes the form of a written lease or written tenancy agreement (as opposed to a printed list of conditions forming the basis of an oral or deemed acceptance by the tenant), then this can in theory actually prove disadvantageous to the tenant, since a written lease granting a periodic tenancy is subject to stamp duty at the rate of 50p per £50 where the rent exceeds £500 p.a.[9]; and even a written *contract* for such a tenancy must be stamped as if it were a lease.[10] In practice this requirement seems to be almost universally ignored in the context of council tenancies. Yet if a document subject to stamp duty is not properly stamped it is not admissible in court, save on a solicitor's undertaking to pay the duty and penalties for late stamping.[11]

(c) *Provision of a rent book*

7.53 Quite apart from the formalities considered so far, the authority must provide a "rent book" under the Landlord and Tenant Act 1985[12] where the rent is payable weekly (even if the tenancy itself is oral), unless the rent includes a payment in respect of board which forms a substantial proportion of the whole rent. The obligation to provide a rent book extends to contractual licences as well as tenancies.[13]

7.54 The rent book does not normally contain the tenancy agreement itself. Moreover, the Landlord and Tenant Act 1985 does not actually require even the recording of the rent payments in the rent book. Instead, the rent book is really more of a vehicle for the provision of information to the tenant,[14] although as regards secure tenants this role has been rather overshadowed by the provisions in the Housing Act 1985 relating to the supplying by the landlord of both a written statement of the tenancy terms[15] and explanatory information relating thereto.[16]

[9] Stamp Act 1891, Sched. 1; Finance Act 1974, s.49(1), Sched. 11, Pt. I, para. 10.
[10] Stamp Act 1891, s.75(1).
[11] Stamp Act 1891, s.14(1); *Parkfield Trust Ltd.* v. *Dent* [1931] 2 K.B. 579, 582.
[12] L. & T.A. 1985, s.4.
[13] *Ibid.* s.4(3)(*a*).
[14] See D.C. Hoath, [1978] J.S.W.L. 3.
[15] H.A. 1985, s.104(2), see above, paras. 7.49–7.50.
[16] H.A. 1985, s.104(1), see below, paras. 7.58–7.59.

The rent book must contain the landlord's name and address,[17] and a summary of the statutory provisions relating to overcrowding.[18] If the authority fails to provide a rent book when under an obligation to do so, or fails to include the relevant information therein, it is guilty of a criminal offence,[19] but it may still claim the rent from the tenant.[20] Although the information to be included in rent books by council landlords is much less than that required to be provided by certain private landlords,[21] nevertheless, since authorities have been urged by Ministerial Circular[22] to prosecute landlords contravening these requirements, they should themselves set a good example! **7.55**

4. *The Content of the Tenancy Agreement*

Prior to the statutory reforms of the 1980s, the terms of council tenancy agreements had frequently been criticised for their one-sidedness in setting out in detail the obligations of the tenant, without spelling out his rights as against the landlord.[23] The Housing Act 1985 still leaves most of the detailed tenancy terms to be decided by the individual authority in the exercise of its power of "general management, regulation and control" conferred by section 21, and many exotic or eccentric terms can be found[24]; moreover, the courts have no general discretion to interfere with oppressive tenancy conditions.[25] Nevertheless, the 1985 Act does regulate the terms relating to secure tenancies in the following ways. **7.56**

[17] L. & T.A. 1985, s.5(1).

[18] H.A. 1985, s.332(1).

[19] L. & T.A. 1985, s.7(1); H.A. 1985, s.332(2).

[20] *Shaw* v. *Groom* [1970] 2 Q.B. 504 (C.A.).

[21] L. & T.A. 1985, s.5; Rent Book (Forms of Notice) Regulations 1982 and 1988 (S.I. 1982 No. 1474, 1988 No. 2198); R.A. 1977, ss.14, 19(5)(*aa*); H.A. 1988, s.1(2) and Sched. 1, Pt. I, para. 12.

[22] M.H.L.G. Circ. 59/62, para. 3.

[23] See, *e.g. Liverpool C.C.* v. *Irwin* [1976] 2 All E.R. 39, 43 (H.L); National Consumer Council, *Tenancy Agreements* (1976), *passim*; H.S.A.G., *Tenancy Agreements* (1977), paras. 8–9.

[24] See, *e.g.* National Consumer Council, *op. cit.* pp.5, 13; *The Times*, July 21, 1983, July 26, 1983.

[25] *Cf.* Housing (Scotland) Act 1987, s.54, under which a tenant who wishes to vary any tenancy term which restricts his use or enjoyment of the property can take the matter to court, if the authority refuses to agree to the variation, and the court can make such order as it thinks reasonable.

(a) *Breach of the tenancy terms as a ground for possession*

7.57 Breach of the terms of the tenancy agreement will not automatically entitle the council to possession, since such a breach only provides a "reasonableness" ground.[26] Thus a court may ultimately have to consider with some care the implications of a particular tenancy term in deciding whether it is reasonable to make a possession order.

(b) *Provision of information concerning the terms of the tenancy*

7.58 In order to ensure that tenants are made aware of some of their basic rights, the 1985 Act imposes on authorities certain duties to provide their secure tenants with information about the terms of their tenancies.[27] We have noted that the Act imposes a duty to provide the secure tenant with a written statement of the terms of the tenancy (*i.e.* the actual terms, not merely a summary), in so far as these are not already set out in a formal lease or written tenancy agreement and are not implied by law.[28] There is also a quite separate obligation imposed on councils[29] under which they must from time to time publish up-to-date information about their secure tenancies, explaining "in simple terms"[30] the effect of:

(i) the express terms of such tenancies;
(ii) Parts IV and V of the Housing Act 1985 (*i.e.* the basic "charter" rights); and
(iii) sections 11 to 16 of the Landlord and Tenant Act 1985 (*i.e.* certain implied repairing obligations[31]).

A copy of this information, when published, must be supplied to every secure tenant.[32] There is evidence that some authorities have not been complying with these important "information" duties[33]; in cases of default, judicial review will lie.[34]

[26] See H.A. 1985, s.84(2)(*a*) and Sched. 2, Pt. I, gd. 1, discussed below, paras. 8.31–8.36.
[27] See C. Holmes, *Roof*, January 1982, p. 16.
[28] H.A. 1985, s.104(2)(*b*), see above, paras. 7.49–7.50.
[29] H.A. 1985, s.104(1).
[30] Thus merely photocopying the relevant statutory material will not suffice!
[31] See below, paras. 12.09–12.27.
[32] H.A. 1985, s.104(2)(*a*).
[33] See, *e.g.* A. Kay, C. Legg and J. Foot, *The 1980 Tenants' Rights in Practice* (Housing Research Group, City University, 1986); T. Shotton, *Roof*, July 1983, p. 5, September 1983, p.25.
[34] *R.* v. *Hackney L.B.C., ex p. Fleming* [1985] Legal Action 170 (D.C.).

However, the information which has to be provided under the Act is not comprehensive: thus the tenant does not have to be told of any implied terms beyond those in the Housing Act and the Landlord and Tenant Act which are specifically earmarked for the purposes of this publication duty, so that he need not be informed of (for example) the landlord's obligations concerning quiet enjoyment, non-derogation from grant, and certain additional repairing responsibilities[35]; nor need he be informed of his remedies for disrepair[36] (save for the statutory "right to repair"[37] in Part IV of the 1985 Act). Nevertheless, it is fair to point out that some authorities provide considerably more information for their tenants than the 1985 Act requires. **7.59**

(c) *Terms implied by the Housing Act 1985*

Certain specific provisions are in effect implied by the Housing Act 1985 into *every* secure tenancy, and therefore apply notwithstanding any stipulation to the contrary. These provisions (which are discussed in detail later) relate to the taking in of lodgers,[38] disposals *inter vivos*[39] and on death,[40] the "right to repair,"[41] and the right to carry out improvements.[42] **7.60**

5. *Variation of the Terms of the Tenancy*

At common law, a landlord cannot vary the terms of the tenancy without the agreement of the tenant. However, it was quite common before the introduction of the "tenants' charter" by the Housing Act 1980 for councils expressly to reserve the right to add to or vary the tenancy conditions,[43] and the courts had decided that such "unilateral variation clauses" were valid in the context of rent increases, provided reasonable notice of the variation had been given to the tenants.[44] In the absence of such a unilateral variation clause, prior **7.61**

[35] See below, paras. 12.28–12.35, 12.38–12.47.
[36] See below, paras. 12.51–12.80.
[37] H.A. 1985, s.96, see below, paras. 12.69–12.76.
[38] H.A. 1985, s.93(1)(*a*), see below, paras. 9.01–9.04.
[39] H.A. 1985, ss.91–94, see below, paras. 9.05–9.08, 9.20–9.23.
[40] H.A. 1985, ss.87–90, see below, paras. 9.27–9.42.
[41] H.A. 1985, s.96, see below, paras. 12.69–12.76.
[42] H.A. 1985, ss.97–101, see below, paras. 12.83–12.94.
[43] National Consumer Council, *op. cit.* p. 41.
[44] *G.L.C.* v. *Connolly* [1970] 2 Q.B. 100 (C.A.).

to the 1980 Act a council could only alter a term of the tenancy (other than the rent) by first ending the tenancy (if periodic) by notice to quit, and then offering a new tenancy incorporating the appropriate alterations[45]; but a special procedure, prescribed by the Prices and Incomes Act 1968,[46] allowed authorities to vary the rent by notice of increase without service of a notice to quit and even if the agreement contained no unilateral variation clause.

7.62 The Housing Act 1980 altered the common law variation rules so far as secure tenancies are concerned. As will be seen,[47] the authority will often be subject to preliminary consultation duties under section 105 of the Housing Act 1985 where the change relates to a matter of "housing management," but this expression does not include matters relating to rent or charges for services or facilities.[48] Assuming that such consultation, where applicable, has taken place, then section 102 of the 1985 Act provides that (except for a term of the tenancy which is implied by any enactment, for example under the Housing Act or the Landlord and Tenant Act), the terms of a secure tenancy can only be varied[49] by one of the three methods prescribed by the section. These methods do *not* include service by the authority of a notice to quit and the substitution of a new tenancy; indeed, as will be seen in the next chapter, a periodic secure tenancy cannot be ended by a notice to quit served by the landlord at all.

7.63 The three prescribed methods of variation are as follows.

7.64 First, *by ad hoc agreement* between the authority and the tenant.[50] This will usually only be feasible where the variation affects a very small number of tenants.

7.65 Secondly, *by the authority or the tenant alone* in accordance with any provision in the tenancy agreement (or any agreement varying it), but only to the extent that the variation relates to rent, rates or ser-

45 This practice had been disapproved of by the H.S.A.G., in view of the distress it often caused to tenants: *Tenancy Agreements, op. cit.* para. 19.

46 P. & I.A. 1968, s.12; this provision was repealed by the Housing (Consequential Provisions) Act 1985, s.3 and Sched. 1, and replaced by H.A. 1985, s.25, which does not apply to secure tenancies: see below, para. 10.19.

47 See below, paras. 13.08–13.13.

48 H.A. 1985, s.105(2).

49 "Variation" for these purposes includes addition and deletion, and the conversion of a monthly tenancy into a weekly tenancy or vice versa, but not a change in the premises let (H.A. 1985, s.102(2)); of course, the authority will need a possession order to compel a change of premises, and it will be seen in Chap. 8 that the offer of suitable alternative accommodation is not of itself a ground for possession.

50 H.A. 1985, s.102(1)(*a*).

vices[51]; thus a "unilateral variation clause" for a secure tenancy can now only be used in relation to these matters.[52]

Thirdly, *by the authority alone* in the case of a *periodic* secure tenancy, by a notice of variation served on the tenant.[53] Before serving the notice of variation, the authority must normally serve a preliminary notice giving the tenant information about the variation and an opportunity to comment thereon within a reasonable time[54]; and the authority must then consider any comments from the tenant regarding this preliminary notice.[55] Furthermore, the notice of variation itself must be accompanied by information as to the nature and effect of the variation.[56] The "information" duties relating to the preliminary notice of variation do not apply where the variation relates to the rent or to payments in respect of rates, services or facilities provided by the authority,[57] but even in these cases the actual notice of variation must inform the tenant of the nature and effect of the variation.[58] **7.66**

The notice of variation must also specify the variation and the date on which it takes effect, and the period between the date on which it is served and the date on which it takes effect must not be shorter than the rental period of the tenancy, nor shorter than four weeks.[59] Prior to the effective date of the variation, the tenant may serve a valid notice to quit,[60] whereupon the notice of variation will be ineffective (even for the remainder of the contractual tenancy) unless the tenant, with the authority's written consent, withdraws the notice to quit before the effective date of the variation.[61] But where the tenant uses this drastic method of avoiding the effect of the variation, there will of course no longer be any tenancy (secure or otherwise) once the notice to quit expires, so that if he fails to leave, the council can issue possession proceedings without having to establish a Housing Act ground. **7.67**

51 H.A. 1985, s.102(1)(*b*).
52 See below, para. 10.17.
53 H.A. 1985, s.102(1)(*c*), 103(1).
54 *Ibid.* s.103(2).
55 *Ibid.*
56 H.A. 1985, s.103(5).
57 *Ibid.* s.103(3).
58 *Cf.* the rather different wording of H.A. 1980, s.40(7).
59 H.A. 1985, s.103(4).
60 The notice to quit must be in writing, and be given not less than four weeks before the date on which it is to take effect (see P.f.E.A. 1977, s.5(1)); the notice must further expire at the end of a completed period of the tenancy.
61 H.A. 1985, s.103(6).

7.68 In order for a variation of an express term to be properly effected, it is essential that unambiguous use is made of one of the three methods prescribed by section 102.[62]

[62] *Palmer* v. *M.B. of Sandwell* (1988) 20 H.L.R. 74 (C.A.), where the sending by a council to each of its existing tenants of a booklet containing a proposed "Tenants' Handbook and Charter" and a new form of tenancy agreement was held to be insufficient to incorporate the new terms into the secure tenancies, in the absence of either notices of variation under s.103 or evidence that the tenants had clearly consented to the new terms under s.102(1)(*a*).

8 Security of Tenure

1. *The Termination of Secure Tenancies*

(a) *The introduction of statutory security*

The statutory security of tenure enjoyed by many private sector tenants has never extended to council tenants.[1] Although councils were subject at common law to the general administrative law principles in evicting their tenants, the practical burden of proving a breach of these principles was such that the courts exercised very little control over council evictions.[2] **8.01**

Statutory security of tenure was eventually conferred on most public sector tenants by the Housing Act 1980.[3] We shall initially consider the statutory security enjoyed by secure[4] council tenants (currently under the Housing Act 1985), and then turn to the much more limited protection afforded to non-secure council tenants. **8.02**

Where the tenancy is secure (and it will be recalled that a council *licensee* will sometimes be treated as a secure tenant[5]), then the authority can only regain possession by following carefully the prescribed procedure in the 1985 Act. Although there are some points of similarity with the security schemes in the Rent Act 1977[6] and the Housing Act 1988 which govern private sector tenants, the procedure in the Housing Act 1985 does differ in several important respects; in **8.03**

[1] R.A. 1977, ss.14, 19(5)(*aa*); H.A. 1985, s.612; H.A. 1988, Sched. 1, Pt. I, para. 12.

[2] See below, paras. 8.76 to 8.79.

[3] Those tenants whose tenancies had been terminated at common law by notice to quit prior to October 3, 1980, but in respect of whom the court's judgment in the possession proceedings was given after that date, did not attract security even as licensees, *L.B. of Hammersmith & Fulham* v. *Harrison* [1981] 1 W.L.R. 650 (C.A.); however, it is possible that former tenants against whom possession orders were made before October 3, 1980, may now have security where the authority has never sought to enforce the orders: J. Luba, [1984] Legal Action 28.

[4] For the definition of this term, see Chap. 7.

[5] H.A. 1985, s.79(3)–(4), see above, paras. 7.15–7.24.

[6] See *Fairweather* v. *Kolosine* (1982) 11 H.L.R. 61, 65 (C.A.).

particular, although some of the grounds for possession in the 1985 Act are the same as those in the Rent Act 1977 and the Housing Act 1988, it will be seen that there are several special grounds which are "tailor-made" for the public sector. Thus, although reference to the regimes in the 1977 and 1988 Acts can sometimes be helpful in interpreting the provisions of the 1985 Act, it can be misleading to try and draw too many parallels between the different systems.[7]

(b) *Termination by the tenant*

8.04 There is no restriction in the Housing Act 1985 on the *tenant* ending the secure tenancy by terminating the contract on which it depends; the principal ways in which this can be done at common law are by surrender, or service of a notice to quit. In addition, if the tenant ceases to occupy the dwelling as his only or principal home[8] the secure tenancy will end although the contractual tenancy may continue.

8.05 **(i) Surrender.** In order for there to be an effective express surrender, a deed is necessary even in the case of an oral tenancy.[9] However, there can be a surrender by operation of law where the parties have indicated their intention to end the lease and it would be inequitable for them to rely on the absence of a deed, as where the tenant gives up possession of the property and the landlord accepts the property back. A surrender by operation of law will not necessarily occur merely because the tenant has left the property owing rent and the landlord has purported to accept that the tenancy has terminated,[10] although where the authority can prove that the tenant has been absent for a substantial period and that there are considerable rent arrears then the inference of a surrender may properly be drawn.[11]

[7] See *L.B. of Hammersmith & Fulham* v. *Harrison* [1981] 1 W.L.R. 650 (C.A.); *Thompson* v. *Elmbridge B.C.* (1987) 19 H.L.R. 526, 530 (C.A.).

[8] See H.A. 1985, ss.79(1), 81, discussed above, paras. 7.09–7.14.

[9] L.P.A. 1925, s.52; in appropriate circumstances, the deed of surrender can be effective even though the tenant has not actually yielded up physical possession: *Dibbs* v. *Campbell* [1988] 30 E.G. 49 (C.A.).

[10] *Preston B.C.* v. *Fairclough* (1983) 8 H.L.R. 70 (C.A.).

[11] *Ibid.* at 73; see also *R.* v. *L.B. of Croydon, ex p. Toth* (1987) 20 H.L.R. 576 (C.A.): council entitled on the facts to accept surrender where tenant had left flat empty save for some bags of rubbish, notwithstanding tenant's later assertion that she had no intention of leaving permanently.

In order for the surrender of a joint tenancy to be effective, all the joint tenants (as well as the landlord) must concur.[12] **8.06**

(ii) Notice to quit. The tenant can unilaterally end a periodic secure tenancy by serving a notice to quit on the authority. The notice must expire at the end of a completed period of the tenancy; it must also normally be in writing, and be given not less than four weeks before the date on which it is to take effect.[13] **8.07**

Where there is a joint secure tenancy which is periodic, one or some of the joint tenants can effectively end the secure tenancy by serving a notice to quit[14] on the authority, without the concurrence of the remaining joint tenant(s).[15] This result occurs because at common law unanimity is essential for the continuation of a periodic contractual joint tenancy, and the statutory security of secure tenants depends in turn on the continued existence of the contract, there being no such concept in the Housing Act as the "statutory tenancy" provided for under the Rent Act 1977.[16] This can have important repercussions in cases of family breakdown.[17] **8.08**

However, joint tenants are in the position of trustees,[18] who are under a duty to safeguard the trust property.[19] It therefore seems that "for one co-owner to give such a notice [to quit] without the consent of the others might be a breach of the trusts now existing in **8.09**

[12] *Leek & Moorlands B.S.* v. *Clark* [1952] 2 All E.R. 492 (C.A).

[13] See P.f.E.A. 1977, s.5.

[14] For this device to succeed, the notice to quit must comply with the requirements in P.f.E.A. 1977, s.5, see above: *Wandsworth L.B.C.* v. *Brown* [1987] September Legal Action 13 (Cty. Ct.).

[15] *Greenwich L.B.C.* v. *McGrady* (1982) 46 P. & C.R. 223 (C.A.); the decision was criticised by F. Webb, [1983] Conv. 194, as being inconsistent with earlier Court of Appeal authority, but it was applied to a tenant's notice to quit in *Featherstone* v. *Staples* [1986] 1 W.L.R. 861 (C.A.), and was approved in *Wiseman* v. *Simpson* [1988] 1 All E.R. 245, 252 (C.A.); it has also been applied in the context of notices to quit served by some only out of several joint *landlords* (*Parsons* v. *Parsons* [1983] 1 W.L.R. 1390, *Leckhampton Dairies Ltd.* v. *Artus Whitfield Ltd.* (1986) 130 S.J. 225), and by one out of two joint *licensors* (*Annen* v. *Rattee* (1985) 17 H.L.R. 323 (C.A.)). But *cf. Community Housing Association* v. *Hoy* [1988] December Legal Action 18 (Cty. Ct.), where the tenancy agreement was construed as prohibiting one joint tenant from unilaterally serving notice to quit on the landlord.

[16] See R.A. 1977, s.2.

[17] See paras. 11.09, 11.46.

[18] L.P.A. 1925, s.36(1).

[19] See, *e.g. Hanbury & Maudsley's Modern Equity* (12th ed., 1985), by J.E. Martin, pp. 496–498.

cases of co-ownership"[20]; the giver of the notice may thus be liable to pay heavy compensation to his former joint tenant(s) for the loss of the former secure tenancy, and could be prevented by injunction from serving the notice at all if his intentions are discovered by the other joint tenant(s) in time.

8.10 **(iii) Cessation of occupation as the tenant's only or principal home.** Where the "tenant condition" for a secure tenancy (*i.e.* that the tenant occupies the dwelling as his only or principal home[21]) is no longer satisfied, then although the tenancy may remain on a purely contractual basis (if not surrendered), it will no longer be secure[22]; the tenancy can therefore be ended by the council serving an ordinary notice to quit[23] containing the prescribed information.[24]

(c) *Possession proceedings brought by the authority*[25]

8.11 **(i) Artificial continuation of the contractual tenancy.** Where it is the authority which seeks unilaterally to end the secure tenancy, the security of tenure system in the 1985 Act has "abolished . . . the common law principles on which contractual tenancies, both periodical and for a term certain, could be brought or come to an end."[26]

8.12 Where the secure tenancy is *periodic* (for example, weekly), it cannot be brought to an end by the authority except by the obtaining of a court order for possession of the dwelling,[27] which can only be granted on certain grounds,[28] whereupon the tenancy ends on the date on which the tenant is due to give up possession in pursuance of

[20] R.E. Megarry & H.W.R. Wade, *The Law of Real Property* (5th ed., 1984), p. 421; *cf.* L.P.A. 1925, s.26(3); see P. Matthews, [1983] L.S. Gaz. 603, 604–605.

[21] H.A. 1985, ss.79(1), 81, see above, paras. 7.09–7.14.

[22] As in *R.* v. *L.B. of Croydon, ex p. Toth* (1986) 18 H.L.R. 493 (D.C.), where the tenant left, taking virtually all her furniture and belongings with her; *cf. R.* v. *L.B. of Croydon, ex p. Toth* (1987) 20 H.L.R. 576, where the Court of Appeal held that the tenancy had in fact been surrendered.

[23] See *R.* v. *L.B. of Croydon, ex p. Toth* (D.C.), *ibid.* at 499.

[24] See below, para. 8.81.

[25] See, *e.g.* P. Walter and J. Harris, *Claims to the Possession of Land: The Law and Practice* (1987); G. Webber and R. Davidson, *Residential Possession Proceedings* (2nd ed., 1987); J. Luba, N. Madge & D. McConnell, *Defending Possession Proceedings* (1987); wide-ranging reforms of the way the courts handle housing cases, including possession actions, are proposed in the *Report of the Review Body on Civil Justice*, Cm. 394 (1988), Chap. 10.

[26] *Per* Brandon L.J. in *L.B. of Hammersmith & Fulham* v. *Harrison* [1981] 2 All E.R. 588, 597 (C.A.).

[27] H.A. 1985, s.82(1).

[28] *Ibid.* s.84; the grounds are discussed below, para. 8.25 *et seq.*

the order,[29] for example "forthwith," or "within 28 days." As will be seen, in the case of certain grounds for possession the court has wide powers to stay or suspend execution of a possession order or to postpone the date of possession[30]; where a suspended order has been made on the ground of rent arrears, postponing the date of possession for so long as the tenant pays the current rent together with a specified sum on account of the arrears, then the secure tenancy will terminate as soon as the tenant defaults in making any one payment,[31] unless the court grants a further suspension,[32] in which case the secure tenancy revives.

The secure tenancy ends on the date when the tenant is to give up possession in pursuance of the order,[33] rather than on the date when he is actually evicted by the bailiffs (if later): in between these two dates, he will in theory be a trespasser,[34] though protected from unlawful eviction by the Protection from Eviction Act 1977[35]; and even if, during such period, the authority purports to accept further "rent" from the former tenant (as opposed to "mesne profits"[36]), it is unlikely that a new tenancy (or even a licence[37]) will arise unless there is a very clear intention to that effect.[38] **8.13**

Where a secure tenancy is for a *fixed term* (for example, one year), and the term comes to an end by effluxion of time, security does not end as such: a periodic tenancy thereupon arises[39] (the periods being those of the rent payments of the former fixed-term tenancy). Moreover, a fixed-term secure tenancy which is prima facie subject to termination by the authority by way of forfeiture cannot in fact be so forfeited: on such a forfeiting event arising, the court cannot order possession on account of that forfeiting event as such, but if apart **8.14**

[29] H.A. 1985, s.82(2).

[30] *Ibid.* s.85(2).

[31] *Thompson* v. *Elmbridge B.C.* (1987) 131 S.J. 301 (C.A.); for a detailed criticism of the decision, see J. Driscoll (1988) 51 M.L.R. 371.

[32] See below, para. 8.65.

[33] H.A. 1985, s.82(2).

[34] *Landau* v. *Sloane* [1980] 2 All E.R. 539, 545 (C.A.); *cf.* Waller L.J. in *L.B. of Hammersmith & Fulham* v. *Harrison* [1981] 2 All E.R. 588, 601 (C.A.).

[35] P.f.E.A. 1977, s.3: see below, para. 8.16.

[36] See A. Arden, [1979] L.A.G. Bull. 44.

[37] *Cf.* H.A. 1985, s.79(3), see above, para. 7.15.

[38] See, *e.g. Musto* v. *Otiero* [1974] L.A.G. Bull. 278 (C.A.); *Longrigg, Burrough & Trounson* v. *Smith* (1979) 251 E.G. 847 (C.A.); *Cardiothoracic Institute* v. *Shrewdcrest Ltd.* [1986] 3 All E.R. 633, 642; N. Nardecchia, [1981] L.S. Gaz. 360.

[39] H.A. 1985, s.86.

from the Housing Act it would have ordered possession,[40] it must instead make an order terminating the fixed-term secure tenancy on a date specified in the order,[41] and from that date a periodic tenancy again normally arises.[42] Thus the forfeiting event is not itself a ground for possession: a separate statutory ground for possession under the Housing Act must be shown, and on such a ground being established the statutory periodic tenancy ends on the date specified for possession in the possession order, in accordance with the normal rule for periodic secure tenancies.[43] It seems clear[44] from other provisions in the Housing Act[45] that the statutory periodic tenancy[46] arising at the expiry of the fixed term, or following a court order for termination of the fixed term,[47] is itself secure.

8.15 The county court has jurisdiction over secure tenancies, whether periodic or for a fixed term[48]; and if the authority takes proceedings in the High Court which could have been taken in the county court, then it is not entitled to recover any costs.[49] Doubts have frequently been expressed, however, about the effectiveness of the county court from the unrepresented tenant's viewpoint.[50]

8.16 **(ii) Effect of the Protection from Eviction Act 1977.** We have seen that a secure tenancy continues on a contractual basis until the date fixed by the court for possession, and that terminated fixed-term secure tenancies are normally extended automatically as secure periodic tenancies. It follows that if the tenant remains in occupation[51] it will be a criminal offence under the Protection from Evic-

[40] The general provisions in L.P.A. 1925, s.146, relating to restrictions on and relief against forfeiture will also apply here (except for s.146(4), dealing with the protection of sub-lessees): H.A. 1985, s.82(4).

[41] H.A. 1985, s.82(1), (3).

[42] *Ibid.* s.86(1).

[43] See above, para. 8.12.

[44] See, *e.g.* J.E. Alder, [1982] Conv. 298, 304; but *cf.* D. Yates and A.J. Hawkins, [1982] Conv. 301.

[45] H.A. 1985, ss.83(5), 88(1)(*c*), 102(4) and 136(1).

[46] *Ibid.* s.86.

[47] *Ibid.* s.82(3).

[48] *Ibid.* s.110(1).

[49] *Ibid.* s.110(3).

[50] See, *e.g.* L. ffoulkes, [1983] March L.A.G. Bull. 9; J. Watts, [1984] October Legal Action 6, [1987] February Legal Action 6; M. Hill and A. Mercer, [1987] J.S.W.L. 237, 249; L. Burrows, *Rent arrears and the courts,* Lay Advocacy Service (1986); National Consumer Council, *Reform of Court Procedures for Housing* (1987).

[51] The P.f.E.A. cannot of course assist the tenant if he has ceased to occupy the premises as a residence: see s.1(1) thereof, and *R.* v. *L.B. of Croydon, ex p. Toth* (1986) 18 H.L.R. 493, 499 (D.C.).

tion Act 1977[52] to evict him, even by peaceful means, before the date fixed by the court for possession, since the tenant will until then be a " 'residential occupier' . . . occupying the premises as a residence . . . under a contract" within the terms of the Protection from Eviction Act[53]; and even after the date fixed by the court for possession, the former tenant who remains in occupation will normally be protected from eviction, save at the hands of the court bailiffs, by other provisions of the Protection from Eviction Act.[54]

However, once a secure tenancy has been terminated by court order obtained against the tenant, the bailiffs can evict all those found to be in occupation (such as the tenant's spouse or other members of his family), even though they have not themselves been made parties to the proceedings: the Protection from Eviction Act in effect normally requires a court order in relation to the premises in question, but does not require the authority to bring proceedings for possession against every occupier.[55] **8.17**

(iii) Procedure for possession: periodic secure tenancies. **8.18**
The procedure for obtaining possession differs depending on whether the secure tenancy is periodic, or for a fixed term.

In the case of periodic secure tenancies, instead of serving a notice to quit, the authority has to serve a special (untitled) notice which is in effect a "notice of intended proceedings"[56]: this notice has to specify the ground on which the court will be asked to make an order for possession, and must be in a prescribed form.[57] **8.19**

The authority must ensure that the notice of intended proceedings contains sufficient information in relation to the ground for possession which is being relied on: thus, in the case of breaches of **8.20**

52 P.f.E.A. 1977, s.1(2).

53 *Ibid.* s.1(1).

54 *Ibid.* ss.3, 3A, 8(1); *cf. Kyriacou* v. *Pandeli* [1980] C.L.Y. 1648 (Cty. Ct.).

55 *Thompson* v. *Elmbridge B.C.* (1987) 131 S.J. 1285 (C.A.), applying *R.* v. *Wandsworth County Court, ex p. L.B. of Wandsworth* [1975] 3 All E.R. 390, 394 (D.C.).

56 H.A. 1985, s.83.

57 *Ibid.* s.83(2); see Secure Tenancies (Notices) Regulations 1987 (S.I. 1987 No. 755); the legality of the initial regulations was established in *Wansbeck D.C.* v. *Charlton* (1981) 125 S.J. 148 (C.A.); the prescribed forms (in the Sched. to the 1987 regulations) state that the council must get a court order before the tenant can be evicted, and that he can get advice from a Citizens' Advice Bureau, Housing Aid Centre, Law Centre, or solicitor (if necessary with the help of legal aid, as to which see below, para. 8.29).

tenancy obligations,[58] the notice must not only specify the individual obligations which are alleged to have been broken, but must also give full particulars of the alleged breaches[59]; for example, in the case of rent arrears, particulars must be given of the amount claimed, so that the notice will not suffice if it merely states that "the reasons for taking this action are non-payment of rent."[60]

8.21 The notice must also specify the date after which proceedings for possession may be begun, and the date specified must not be earlier than the date on which the tenancy could, apart from the Housing Act, be ended by a notice to quit served on the same date as the notice of intended proceedings[61]; thus at least four weeks' notice must be given, in accordance with the Protection from Eviction Act 1977.[62]

8.22 Service of the notice is governed by a separate provision in the Local Government Act 1972,[63] which authorises (*inter alia*) service by post; however, if the notice is sent by ordinary post rather than by the registered or recorded delivery service, the tenant could defeat the notice by proving non-receipt.[64] If the tenant has left[65] and the authority is unable to discover his new address after reasonable inquiry, then it can affix the notice conspicuously to some part of the property.[66]

8.23 Proceedings must then be begun after the date specified in the notice, but within 12 months of the date so specified.[67] Failure to serve the correct notice, or an attempt to begin proceedings either before the date specified in the notice or after the notice has lapsed,[68] means that the court cannot entertain the possession proceedings.[69]

58 H.A. 1985, Sched. 2, Pt. I, gd. 1, see below, paras. 8.32 to 8.36.
59 See, *e.g. South Bucks C.C.* v. *Francis* [1985] 11 C.L. 152 (Cty. Ct.).
60 *Torridge D.C.* v. *Jones* (1985) 18 H.L.R. 107 (C.A.).
61 H.A. 1985, s.83(3).
62 P.f.E.A. 1977, s.5: see below, para. 8.81.
63 L.G.A. 1972, s.233.
64 Interpretation Act 1978, s.7.
65 In such a case the occupation requirement for continuation of a secure tenancy (see H.A. 1985, s.81, discussed above, paras. 7.09–7.14) may still be satisfied, *e.g.* because the tenant has left his wife in occupation: see M.H.A. 1983, s.1(6), discussed above, para. 7.10.
66 L.G.A. 1972, s.233(7).
67 H.A. 1985, s.83(3)–(4).
68 See *City of Edinburgh D.C.* v. *Davis* 1987 S.L.T. 33 (Sh. Ct.); in this situation a new notice can be served.
69 H.A. 1985, s.83(1), (4).

(iv) Procedure for possession: fixed-term secure tenancies. Where the council seeks possession of property let on a fixed-term secure tenancy while the original term is still on foot,[70] then again a "notice of intended proceedings" must be served[71]: here the notice has to specify the ground on which the court will be asked to terminate the tenancy[72]; again it must be in a prescribed form,[73] but this notice does not have to specify the date after which proceedings for possession may be begun.[74] The notice has effect also with regard to any periodic tenancy arising[75] on the termination of the fixed-term tenancy,[76] so that the authority may seek, all in the same proceedings, an order which both terminates the term certain and requires the tenant to give up possession (assuming an appropriate statutory ground can be established). But failure to serve the correct notice precludes the court from entertaining either the termination proceedings or the possession proceedings, as appropriate.[77] **8.24**

(v) Grounds for possession. Under section 84 of the 1985 Act, the court cannot make an order for the possession of a dwelling let under a secure tenancy (as opposed to an order for the termination of a fixed term tenancy), except on one or more of the grounds set out in Schedule 2 to the Act; and the court cannot make such an order unless the appropriate ground is specified in the notice of intended proceedings.[78] Although the grounds set out in this notice can be altered or added to with the leave of the court,[79] the court will not allow an extensive amendment which is applied for at a late stage in the proceedings.[80] **8.25**

Liability for costs. The grounds primarily involve considerations relating either to the misconduct of the tenant or the management needs of the authority. Both the authority and the tenant must bear in mind the implications of the rules relating to costs. The judge nor- **8.26**

[70] *Cf.* H.A. 1985, s.82(3) (above, para. 8.14).
[71] *Ibid.* s.83; see also n. 40 above.
[72] H.A. 1985, s.83(2)(*b*).
[73] *Ibid.* s.83(2)(*a*); see further n. 57 above.
[74] *Ibid.* s.83(5); *cf.* the notice relating to a periodic secure tenancy (see above, para. 8.21).
[75] *Ibid.* s.86 (see above, para. 8.14).
[76] *Ibid.* s.83(5).
[77] *Ibid.* s.83(1).
[78] *Ibid.* s.84(3).
[79] *Ibid.*
[80] *South Bucks C.C.* v. *Francis* [1985] 11 C.L. 152 (Cty. Ct.).

mally has a wide discretion to order that a party's costs must be paid by the other party, or to order that each party should bear his own costs.[81] The general rule is of course that the winning party should recover his costs from the losing party; where a "council's management" ground for possession is established, however, the court will often in its discretion refuse to order the tenant to pay the authority's costs unless there is some special reason why he should do so. More generally, where a possession order is made against a tenant who is receiving legal aid with a nil contribution, costs will frequently not be ordered against the tenant at all, and even where an order for costs is made against such a tenant, the court may stipulate that the costs cannot be enforced without further leave of the court; moreover, if the unsuccessful tenant is receiving legal aid subject to a contribution, any order for costs may well be limited to the amount of the defendant's contribution which is owing to the legal aid fund.[82] Thus "[a] legal aid certificate may . . . be some protection against an order for costs."[83] However, in possession proceedings there is no general rule limiting orders for the recovery of the landlord's costs merely because "people's homes are at stake."[84]

8.27 *"Consent" orders.* With regard to the making of possession orders with the "consent" of the tenant, the court will only be justified in making an order without a full investigation of the facts if there is not merely consent on the part of the tenant, but also an express admission of facts which, if they had been proved, would have given the court jurisdiction to make the order.[85]

8.28 *The three separate groups of grounds for possession.* In order fully to understand the grounds for possession, they are best discussed in three separate groups (among which "tenant's misconduct" grounds and "council's management" grounds are interspersed), since the conditions which must be met before the court can order possession on the various grounds may differ according to three separate criteria.

[81] C.C.R. 1981, Ord. 38, r. 1; see J. Luba, N. Madge & D. McConnell, *op. cit.* Chap. III.4.

[82] J. Luba, N. Madge & D. McConnell, *loc. cit.*

[83] J. Luba, N. Madge & D. McConnell, *op. cit.* p. 144.

[84] *Brown* v. *Sparrow* [1982] 1 W.L.R. 1269 (C.A.).

[85] *R.* v. *Bloomsbury & Marylebone County Court, ex p. Blackburne* [1985] 2 E.G. 1273 (C.A.); *Wandsworth L.B.C.* v. *Fadayomi* [1987] 1 W.L.R. 1473 (C.A.); *R.* v. *Newcastle-upon-Tyne County Court, ex p. Thompson* (1988) 20 H.L.R. 430 (D.C.); see also *Appleton* v. *Aspin* [1988] 1 W.L.R. 410 (C.A.).

We shall see that in the case of the grounds in two of these three groups, the judge is not permitted to make a possession order unless he considers it reasonable to do so.[86] Originally, it was difficult for tenants to obtain legal aid with a view to defending council possession proceedings, even where a "reasonableness" ground was in issue.[87] However, the criteria for the grant of legal aid include consideration of whether the claimant has "reasonable grounds" for defending an action and whether it is "reasonable" that he should receive legal aid[88]; such criteria will frequently be satisfied where the ground for possession involves consideration of the difficult issue of whether it is reasonable to make the order, and the revised notes for guidance, in connection with the criteria for granting legal aid, issued by the Law Society (prior to the transfer of the administration of the legal aid scheme to the new Legal Aid Board) emphasised the importance of carefully considering whether the tenant should be allowed legal aid in such cases (for example, involving rent arrears), in order to defend the action or to ask the court to stay or suspend execution of the order or postpone the date of possession, particularly "bearing in mind the formality of court proceedings and the seriousness to the tenant of possible homelessness."[89] **8.29**

GROUP A: Grounds on which the court can only make a possession order if it considers it reasonable to do so. These grounds largely relate to "tenant's misconduct," and it is important to note that where they apply, the court only has to be satisfied as to the reasonableness of making the order[90]; it does not[91] have to be satisfied that suitable accommodation will be available to the tenant when he is evicted. The authority may however be subject to its general homelessness duties under Part III of the 1985 Act towards the displaced tenant and his family (although the extent of these duties may be diminished by a finding of "intentional" homelessness where appropriate[92]). **8.30**

The relevant grounds in Group A (suitably paraphrased) are: **8.31**

[86] H.A. 1985, s.84(2); in deciding the question of reasonableness, it may be necessary (where appropriate) to consider a wide range of matters, such as the fact that the tenant has established the "right to buy": *Enfield L.B.C.* v. *McKeon* [1986] 2 All E.R. 730, 737 (C.A.).

[87] See N. Madge, [1982] June L.A.G. Bull. 14, 15.

[88] Legal Aid Act 1988, s.15(2)–(3).

[89] The Law Society, *Note for Guidance No. 9 (Criteria for the Grant of Legal Aid).*

[90] H.A. 1985, s.84(2)(*a*) and Sched. 2, Pt. I, gds. 1–8.

[91] *Cf.* the grounds in Groups B and C, see below.

[92] See Chaps. 4 and 5.

8.32 *Ground 1: Non-payment of rent*[93] *lawfully due or breach of any other (express*[94] *or implied*[95]*) obligation of the tenancy.* If rent arrears are alleged, they must still be due at the date when court proceedings are issued[96]; and although possession can be ordered where the tenant tenders the arrears *after* commencement of the proceedings, such an order will rarely be made.[97] There will be no arrears "lawfully due" where rent is being withheld in circumstances where the tenant is exercising a common law or equitable right of set-off,[98] or where he can show that the authority's rent-fixing decision was *ultra vires* and so void.[99]

8.33 Where the arrears have accrued due to an authority's delay in processing the tenant's claim for housing benefit (which is frequently dealt with by a separate department of the authority), then it has been suggested that the tenant should either ask the court to strike out the possession proceedings as an abuse of process, or enter a defence and counterclaim alleging breach of statutory duty.[1]

8.34 In deciding whether it is reasonable to order possession on the ground of rent arrears, it may be relevant to consider (where appropriate) such matters as whether the tenant has previously had a good rent record over a long period,[2] whether the arrears have arisen due to personal problems rather than wilfulness,[3] and whether the authority's financial interests are already being safe-

[93] See L. Burrows, *Rent arrears and the courts*, *op. cit.*

[94] This could include an obligation to pay to the landlord a sum representing some or all of the general rates, even if such payments cannot strictly be treated as "rent": see J. Luba, [1988] August Legal Action 20, 21.

[95] See, *e.g.* H.A. 1985, ss.93(1)(*b*) (below, paras. 9.05–9.08) and 97(1) (below, paras. 12.83–12.88).

[96] *Bird* v. *Hildage* [1948] 1 K.B. 91 (C.A.), where tender of the arrears before commencement of the proceedings precluded the court from ordering possession; see also *Johnson-Sneddon* v. *Harper* [1977] L.A.G. Bull. 114 (C.A.).

[97] *Dellenty* v. *Pellow* [1951] 2 K.B. 858 (C.A.); but see *Lee-Steere* v. *Jennings* (1988) 20 H.L.R. 1 (C.A.).

[98] See below, paras. 12.66–12.68.

[99] This issue can be raised as a defence to possession proceedings: the tenant is not required to resort to judicial review under R.S.C. Ord. 53: *Wandsworth L.B.C.* v. *Winder* [1985] A.C. 461 (H.L.); however, in this case the tenant eventually failed to show that the council's decision was *ultra vires: L.B. of Wandsworth* v. *Winder (No.2)* (1988) 20 H.L.R. 400 (C.A.); see further below, paras. 10.31–10.36.

[1] J. Luba, N. Madge & D. McConnell, *op. cit.* p. 162; under the Housing Benefit (General) Regulations 1987 (S.I. 1987 No. 1971) reg. 88(3), the authority has a duty to determine claims within 14 days, or, if this is not reasonably practicable, as soon as possible thereafter; see below, para. 8.65.

[2] See, *e.g. Woodspring D.C.* v. *Taylor* (1982) 4 H.L.R. 95 (C.A.).

[3] *Ibid.*

guarded through suitable arrangements having been made to clear the arrears (as where the tenant is claiming income support and the D.S.S. is operating the "arrears direct" scheme by paying a proportion of the tenant's social security entitlement direct to the council in order to help to pay off the arrears[4]). It is particularly important for the judge (and the authority) to understand the implications of the social security and housing benefit systems in such cases.[5] However, the mere fact that the consequences for the tenant of a possession order on the ground of rent arrears will inevitably be serious, in that he may well be found intentionally homeless under Part III of the Housing Act[6] and his creditworthiness will be greatly impaired, does not of itself necessarily mean that it is unreasonable to make the order.[7]

The court may sometimes consider it appropriate in rent arrears cases to give the authority a money judgment[8] for the arrears, but to refuse a possession order because this would not be reasonable having regard to the other ways in which the arrears may be recovered.[9] **8.35**

Even where the court considers it reasonable to make a possession order on the ground of rent arrears, the order will in practice often be suspended on payment of the current rent together with fixed instalments on account of the arrears[10]; however, where a suspended order is made the tenant may still be ordered to pay the authority's costs. **8.36**

Ground 2: The tenant or any other person residing in the dwelling has caused a nuisance or annoyance to neighbours (not necessarily the adjoining occupiers), or has been convicted of illegal or immoral user of the property. This ground has been used successfully by some authorities against tenants found **8.37**

[4] Under the Social Security (Claims and Payments) Regulations 1987 (S.I. 1987 No. 1968) reg. 35 and Sched. 9, paras. 2–3, 8: discussed below, n. 84; see, *e.g. Second W.R.V.S. Housing Society Ltd.* v. *Blair* (1987) 19 H.L.R. 104 (C.A.).

[5] *Second W.R.V.S. Housing Society Ltd.* v. *Blair, ibid.*

[6] See Chap. 4.

[7] *Lee-Steere* v. *Jennings* (1988) 20 H.L.R. 1 (C.A.).

[8] C.C.R. 1981, Ord. 24, Pt. II.

[9] See J. Luba, N. Madge & D. McConnell, *op. cit.* p. 18; see also, regarding alternative remedies to eviction, *Sutton Housing Trust* v. *Lawrence* (1987) 19 H.L.R. 520 (C.A.): injunction granted forbidding retention of pet in breach of tenancy agreement.

[10] *Second W.R.V.S. Housing Society Ltd.* v. *Blair* (1987) 19 H.L.R. 104, 107 (C.A.); see below, para. 8.64 *et seq.*

responsible for racial harassment on council estates.[11] It appears, however, that a tenant who is complaining of nuisance or annoyance on the part of neighbouring tenants cannot force the authority to take possession proceedings against them.[12]

8.38 *Grounds 3 and 4: Deterioration of the condition of the dwelling or of the common parts (or of any furniture provided by the authority for use in the dwelling or the common parts), due to the fault*[13] *of the tenant or of any other person residing in the dwelling (provided that, where the fault has been on the part of the tenant's sub-lessee or lodger, the tenant has not taken reasonable steps to evict that person).* The grounds so far considered (grounds 1–4) have broadly equivalent private sector counterparts in the Rent Act 1977 and the Housing Act 1988; in particular, most of the extensive case law on the Rent Act grounds will be relevant to secure tenancies.[14]

8.39 *Ground 5: The authority was induced to grant the tenancy by a false statement made knowingly or recklessly by the tenant.* This ground has no counterpart in the Rent Act 1977 or the Housing Act 1988. Mere non-disclosure is not covered, but the ground is nevertheless extensive in its scope: in theory, tenants can be evicted on account of statements[15] (relating, for example, to the size of their families) made many years previously, but this is of course a "reasonable-

[11] See, *e.g. Islington L.B.C.* v. *Isherwood, Islington L.B.C.* v. *Connor* [1987] June Legal Action 19 (Cty. Ct.); *cf. Camden L.B.C.* v. *Hawkins* [1988] March Legal Action 18 (C.A.), *Ealing Family Housing Association* v. *Taylor* [1987] December Legal Action 15 (Cty. Ct.); Commission for Racial Equality, *Living in Terror* (1987); D. Forbes, *Action on Racial Harassment: Legal Remedies and Local Authorities* (1988); E. Flegg, *Roof*, July 1988, p. 29; see above, paras. 3.26–3.28; some councils have inserted a specific clause in their tenancy agreements outlawing racial discrimination: breach of such a clause will come within gd. 1, above.

[12] *O'Leary* v. *Islington L.B.C.* (1983) 9 H.L.R. 81 (C.A.); but *cf. Hilton* v. *James Smith & Sons (Norwood)* (1979) 257 E.G. 1063 (C.A.), where the landlord was liable to the tenant for breach of the covenant for quiet enjoyment, and in nuisance, because it had adopted the acts of the other tenants.

[13] The tenant's implied repairing and maintenance obligations are discussed below, paras. 12.48–12.50; breach of the tenant's contractual obligations permits the authority also to proceed under gd. 1, above, but for the purposes of gds. 3 and 4 it is not necessary for the deterioration to amount to such a breach: see *Lowe* v. *Lendrum* (1950) 156 E.G. 423 (C.A.).

[14] See, *e.g.* A. Arden, [1978] L.A.G. Bull. 186, [1979] L.A.G. Bull. 11, 12; A. McAllister & S. McGrath, [1986] Legal Action 21; J. Luba, N. Madge & D. McConnell, *op. cit.* pp. 15–20, 79–82.

[15] See also the offence in H.A. 1985, s.74(1), of knowingly or recklessly making false statements in connection with a homelessness application (see above, para. 4.36).

ness" ground, and in any event the statement must have been material to the authority's decision to grant the tenancy.

In view of this ground, an applicant for council housing might consider it wise to exercise his right to require the authority to furnish him with details of the particulars given by him to the authority and recorded by it as relevant to his application,[16] so that any misunderstandings can be cleared up forthwith. **8.40**

Ground 6: The tenancy was assigned to the tenant (or to a predecessor in title who is a member of his family[17] and is residing in the dwelling) by an assignment pursuant to the statutory right to exchange,[18] and a premium (capital sum) was paid either in connection with that assignment (to the tenant or predecessor) or in connection with the assignment which the tenant or predecessor himself made by way of statutory exchange. This ground applies whether the tenant in question (or his predecessor) paid or received the premium, although it is of course a reasonableness ground and therefore the precise circumstances of the payment or receipt must be considered. **8.41**

Ground 7: The dwelling which is let forms part of (or is within the grounds of) a building which is held by the authority mainly for non-housing purposes and which consists mainly of non-housing accommodation, and the dwelling was let to the tenant or a predecessor in title in consequence of employment with a prescribed public body, and the tenant or a person residing in the dwelling has been guilty of conduct such that (having regard to the purpose for which the building is used) it would not be right for him to continue to occupy the dwelling. This ground is available in relation to the conduct of occupiers of dwellings held under certain job-related tenancies (such as school staff housed within the school grounds), but the reference to the dwelling forming part of or being within the grounds ("curtilage") of a *building* means that it will not be available where there is no such building, as in certain cases where the dwelling is merely situated within the grounds of a cemetery.[19] **8.42**

Ground 8: The tenant, having been a secure tenant of a dwelling on which works have been carried out, has been temporarily accommodated elsewhere during the works on the understanding that he would leave on their completion, and **8.43**

[16] H.A. 1985, s.106(5); Access to Personal Files Act 1987, ss.1–3 and Sched. 1; see above, paras. 2.27–2.28.

[17] See the definition in H.A. 1985, s.113, discussed below, paras. 9.31–9.33.

[18] *Ibid.* s.92, see below, paras. 9.20–9.23.

[19] In such a case gd. 12, see below, may be appropriate.

he now refuses to vacate this "temporary" accommodation even though the dwelling which he formerly occupied is ready for his renewed occupation. Although this is in effect a "council's management" ground, it is grouped with the "reasonableness" grounds because, if the works have taken a considerable time, it might not be reasonable to expect the "decanted" tenant to be displaced yet again.

8.44 *GROUP B: Grounds on which the court must make a possession order if it is satisfied as to suitable accommodation.* These are *mandatory* grounds (*i.e.* not depending on reasonableness as such), which apply provided that the court is satisfied that suitable accommodation will be available for the tenant when the order takes effect.[20] Three of these grounds are relevant to councils.

8.45 *Ground 9: Overcrowding, within the meaning of Part X of the 1985 Act, in such circumstances that the occupier is guilty of an offence.* This ground operates as a limitation on the "charter" rights for secure tenants to take in lodgers[21] and sub-let part of the dwelling.[22]

8.46 *Ground 10: The authority intends within a reasonable time of gaining possession to demolish or reconstruct the building (or part thereof) comprising the dwelling, or to carry out work thereon, and cannot reasonably do so without obtaining possession of the dwelling.* This ground applies where the tenant refuses to vacate in order for the work to be carried out on his dwelling; if he leaves voluntarily, he may be subject to the "reasonableness" ground 8 (above), in respect of the property into which he is "decanted."

8.47 The relevant time at which the authority's "intention" falls to be considered is the date of the hearing.[23] The authority must show, at that time, a "clearly defined and settled" intention to do the relevant work,[24] and also that the work cannot reasonably be done without obtaining possession by way of terminating the secure tenancy[25]; thus if the tenant is prepared to move out temporarily while the

[20] H.A. 1985, s.84(2)(*b*) and Sched. 2, Pt. II, gds. 9–10A.
[21] *Ibid.* s.93(1)(*a*), see below, paras. 9.01–9.04.
[22] *Ibid.* s.93(1)(*b*), see below, paras. 9.05–9.10; note the specific reference to overcrowding in s.94(3)(*a*).
[23] *Wansbeck D.C.* v. *Marley* (1988) 20 H.L.R. 247 (C.A.).
[24] *Ibid.* at 255.
[25] *Ibid.* at 257.

work is done, the ground may not (depending on the facts) be established.[26]

Ground 10A: The dwelling (or part thereof) is in an area which has been approved by the Minister under a "redevelopment scheme," and the authority intends within a reasonable time of obtaining possession to dispose of the dwelling (or part thereof) in accordance with the scheme. This ground is designed to cover the situation where the authority, rather than itself engaging upon demolition or reconstruction work relating to the dwelling,[27] intends to dispose of the dwelling (or part thereof) to a private developer in order that he may carry out demolition or reconstruction work. The "redevelopment scheme"must be approved by the Minister, and before seeking such approval the authority must notify and consult the affected tenants.[28] However, a "redevelopment scheme" is not restricted to groups of houses or estates: a scheme may be approved even for an area of land consisting of part of a single dwelling.[29] **8.48**

Compensation for eviction under ground 10 or ground 10A. Where the court orders possession under ground 10 or ground 10A, the displaced tenant will normally be entitled to a "home loss payment" under the Land Compensation Act 1973 representing (in general) three times the rateable value[30]; furthermore, where the authority obtains possession from a secure tenant by agreement, without the need for a court order, in a situation where ground 10 or ground 10A would otherwise have been appropriate, the authority *may* make the tenant a payment corresponding to a "home loss payment."[31] **8.49**

However, a tenant displaced under ground 10 or ground 10A will not normally be entitled to a "disturbance payment" under the Land Compensation Act (representing his reasonable expenses in removing from the land), because no "land" of his will have been "acquired" by the authority within the relevant provision,[32] since **8.50**

[26] See J. Luba, N. Madge & D. McConnell, *op. cit.* p. 24.
[27] As to which see gd. 10, above.
[28] H.A. 1985, Sched. 2, Pt. V; in such cases the general consultation duties concerning matters of "housing management," contained in s.105 (see below, paras. 13.08–13.13), are superseded: see Sched. 2, Pt. V, para. 2(3). Guidance as to the procedure for activating gd. 10A is contained in D.O.E. Circ. 14/87, paras. 4–19; the procedure is discussed in detail below, paras. 15.07–15.10.
[29] H.A. 1985, Sched. 2, Pt. V, para. 1(1).
[30] Land Compensation Act 1973, s.29(1)(*e*).
[31] *Ibid.* s.32(7B).
[32] *Ibid.* s.37.

the extinguishing of a tenancy does not result in the landlord "acquiring" any "land"[33] (as opposed to gaining vacant possession).

8.51 *Suitable accommodation.* We have seen that in order for any of the Group B grounds to apply, the court must be satisfied that suitable accommodation will be available for the tenant when the order takes effect.[34] It is important to appreciate that, unlike the position in the privately rented sector, the availability of suitable alternative accommodation is not of itself a ground for possession.[35]

8.52 For the purposes of the Housing Act 1985, "suitable accommodation" is defined in Part IV of Schedule 2: in essence, the available accommodation has to be let under a secure tenancy within the 1985 Act, or under a protected or assured tenancy (within the Rent Act 1977 or the Housing Act 1988) which is not subject to one of the mandatory grounds for possession (to avoid any "out of the frying-pan, into the fire" effect).

8.53 The accommodation also has to be "reasonably suitable to the needs[36] of the tenant and his family" (*not* his lodgers or sub-tenants), having regard (*inter alia*[37]) to various listed factors,[38] such as distance from place of work or education, distance from other close family members, and the means[39] and needs (as regards extent of accommodation) of the tenant and his family.

8.54 In the case of a joint secure tenancy where one (or some) of the joint tenants has (or have) ceased to occupy the dwelling before the

33 *R.* v. *Islington L.B.C., ex p. Knight* [1984] 1 All E.R. 154, 158 (D.C.); *cf. Newey* v. *Liverpool C.C.* [1982] L.A.G. Bull. 91.

34 H.A. 1985, s.84(2)(*b*).

35 *Cf.* R.A. 1977, s.98(1)(*a*), and H.A. 1988, Sched. 2, Pt. II, gd. 9, Pt. III, which respectively make the availability of such accommodation a "reasonableness" ground.

36 The tenant's need for a garden may be relevant, *L.B. of Enfield* v. *French* (1984) 17 H.L.R. 211 (C.A.).

37 The listed matters are not exhaustive, *L.B. of Enfield* v. *French, ibid.* at 215, 218–219.

38 For a discussion of the factors relating to "suitable alternative accommodation" for Rent Act purposes, much of which is relevant to the definition in H.A. 1985, see A. Arden, [1976] L.A.G. Bull. 280, 281–282; but the Rent Act cases may need to be approached with some caution in a secure tenancy context: see *L.B. of Enfield* v. *French, ibid.* at 216–217.

39 The fact that the alternative accommodation is subject to a higher rent does not *of itself* render it unsuitable: *cf. Cresswell* v. *Hodgson* [1951] 2 K.B. 92 (C.A.), a Rent Act case.

possession hearing,[40] it has been held that the alternative accommodation needs only to be suitable for the tenant or tenants remaining in occupation of the dwelling at the date of the hearing, so that an offer of accommodation which is large enough to accommodate the departed tenant(s) as well as the remaining tenant(s) may be rejected as unsuitable.[41] Although the outcome of this decision is sensible, its legal basis is questionable: unlike the Rent Act's "statutory tenancy,"[42] a secure tenancy depends on the subsistence of the contract, so that where the joint secure tenancy is still on foot at the date of the hearing,[43] the "tenant" for the purposes of Part IV of Schedule 2 (suitable accommodation) is surely an amalgam of *all* the secure tenants, regardless of whether some of them have left.

In considering whether the court can properly be satisfied that suitable accommodation will be available,[44] it is important to appreciate that a member of the tenant's family living in the dwelling of which possession is sought has a potential interest in the proceedings in the light of Part IV of Schedule 2, and therefore has the right to intervene in the action[45]; it may be, for example, that some member of the tenant's family wishes to be joined in the proceedings as a defendant in order to raise a matter concerning the availability or otherwise of suitable accommodation which the tenant himself does not wish to mention, and such an application will normally be allowed.[46] **8.55**

Unlike the definitions of suitable alternative accommodation in the Rent Act 1977 and the Housing Act 1988,[47] under the Housing Act 1985 the accommodation can be suitable even though it is not suited to the needs of the tenant and his family as regards its character,[48] so that the tenant can in effect be "downgraded." **8.56**

A special rule[49] regarding suitable accommodation applies where possession is sought under the "statutory overcrowding" ground (ground 9, above). Here the alternative accommodation can still be **8.57**

[40] The departure of some of the joint tenants will not affect the continuation of the secure tenancy: H.A. 1985, s.81 (see above, para. 7.09).
[41] *L.B. of Islington* v. *Metcalfe & Peacock* [1983] L.A.G. Bull. 105 (Cty. Ct.).
[42] *Cf. Lloyd* v. *Sadler* [1978] Q.B. 774 (C.A.).
[43] See H.A. 1985, s.81 (n. 40 above).
[44] *Ibid.* s.84(2), see above.
[45] *Wandsworth L.B.C.* v. *Fadayomi* [1987] 1 W.L.R. 1473 (C.A.).
[46] *Ibid.*
[47] R.A. 1977, Sched. 15, Pt. IV, para. 5; H.A. 1988, Sched. 2, Pt. III, para. 3.
[48] *Cf. e.g.*. the Rent Act cases of *Redspring* v. *Francis* [1973] 1 W.L.R. 134 (C.A.) and *Siddiqui* v. *Rashid* [1980] 1 W.L.R. 1018 (C.A.).
[49] H.A. 1985, Sched. 2, Pt. IV, para. 3.

suitable to the needs of the tenant and his family, even though it will still be overcrowded by the space standards in Part X of the Housing Act 1985[50] if all the existing occupiers move to it! This provision seems to have been designed to enable an authority to shift the occupants of a dwelling which is overcrowded due to the presence of lodgers or sub-tenants to smaller accommodation, so that the tenant is in effect compelled to jettison his lodgers or sub-tenants before moving to the new accommodation (the provision only refers to the suitability of the accommodation to the needs of the tenant and his family). Yet objection may still be raised as to the unsuitability of the new accommodation on the grounds of (for example) overcrowding due to the sleeping arrangements[51] (*i.e.* as opposed to the space standards), or the lack of amenities or services.[52]

8.58 *GROUP C: Grounds on which the court can only make a possession order if it considers it reasonable to do so and it is satisfied as to suitable accommodation.* The criteria for these grounds[53] combine the general requirements of Groups A and B above.[54] The Group C grounds are broadly concerned with tenants who do not satisfy the "purpose" for which the accommodation was originally provided; they are thus primarily (and in the case of ground 16, exclusively) concerned with statutory successors[55] of the original tenants.

8.59 Four of these grounds are relevant to council landlords, as follows.

8.60 *Ground 12: The dwelling forms part of, or is within the grounds of, a building which is held mainly for purposes other than housing purposes and consists mainly of accommodation other than housing accommodation, or is situated in a cemetery.*[56] In either case, the following additional conditions must be met: the authority reasonably requires the dwelling for occupation as a residence for some person who is either employed by the authority or another specified public body, or with whom, conditional on housing being provided, a contract for such employment has been entered into; the tenant or his predecessor in title was employed by the authority or another specified public body; the dwelling was let

[50] H.A. 1985, s.326.
[51] *Ibid.* s.325.
[52] *Ibid.* s.352.
[53] *Ibid.* s.84(2)(*c*) and Sched. 2, Pt. III, gds. 12–16.
[54] Thus the *character* of the accommodation, which (as has been seen) is excluded as a factor relating to "suitable accommodation," may nevertheless be considered as relevant to the issue of reasonableness.
[55] See below, paras. 9.29–9.40.
[56] *Cf.* gd. 7 (see above, para. 8.42).

to the tenant or his predecessor in consequence of that employment; and the tenant or predecessor has ceased to be in that employment.

Ground 13: The dwelling has features which are substantially different from those of ordinary dwellings and which are designed for a physically disabled person (not necessarily the tenant himself), there is no longer such a person in residence, and the authority requires the dwelling for occupation by such a person. This ground covers dwellings which are either purpose-built for, or adapted for, the physically disabled. The dwellings must however contain features which are *substantially* different from those of ordinary dwellings: in one case it was held that the provision of a third lavatory for the use of a disabled member of the tenants' family was not such a feature, although it was very unusual for the immediate area in question.[57] Furthermore, the requirement that the features must be "designed" for the physically disabled means that the features must have been architecturally formed (rather than merely intended) for such special use.[58] **8.61**

Ground 15: The dwelling is one of a group normally let to persons with special needs, a social services or special facility is provided nearby for the occupants, there is no longer a person with those special needs residing in the dwelling, and the authority requires it for occupation by such a person. The needs here do not necessarily have to be connected with old age[59]: the ground relates to "sheltered" housing in a wide sense. **8.62**

Ground 16: The accommodation afforded by the dwelling is more extensive than is reasonably required by the tenant, the tenancy vested in the tenant on the death of the previous tenant under the statutory succession provisions relating to periodic secure tenancies[60] as a member of the previous tenant's family[61] other than the spouse, and the notice of intended proceedings[62] was served more than **8.63**

[57] *Freeman* v. *Wansbeck D.C.* (1983) 127 S.J. 550 (C.A.), a case concerning the right to buy: see below, para. 14.17.

[58] *Ibid.*

[59] *Cf.* the exemption from the "right to buy" of certain old people's dwellings in H.A. 1985, Sched. 5, paras. 10–11 (see below, paras. 14.19–14.20).

[60] *Ibid.* s.89, see below, paras. 9.29–9.40; thus if the tenant succeeded to the tenancy at common law before the introduction of statutory security on October 3, 1980, this ground will not apply.

[61] See below, paras. 9.31–9.33.

[62] H.A. 1985, s.83 (see above, para. 8.19).

six months but less than 12 months[63] *after the date of the previous tenant's death.* This "under-occupation" ground is very narrowly defined: it cannot be used against an original tenant,[64] nor against a spouse-successor of an original tenant. Furthermore, the matters to be taken into account by the court in determining whether it is reasonable to make an order on this ground include the age of the tenant, the period during which the tenant has occupied the dwelling as his only or principal home, and any financial or other support given by the tenant to the previous tenant.[65] It is also a relevant consideration, in deciding the reasonableness issue, that the successor-tenant is exercising the right to buy.[66]

(vi) Adjournment, postponement and suspension.

8.64 *Grounds within Group A or Group C.* Where possession proceedings are brought on one or more of the grounds in Group A, above (*i.e.* the "reasonableness" grounds 1–8), or on one or more of the grounds in Group C, above (*i.e.* the "reasonableness plus suitable accommodation" grounds 12–16), then the court may adjourn the proceedings for such period or periods as it thinks fit[67] (for example, in order to allow the tenant to proceed with an application for legal aid). Furthermore, if it makes a possession order on any of these grounds, or at any time before the execution of the order, the court may postpone the date of possession, or stay or suspend execution of the order, again for such period or periods as it thinks fit.[68]

8.65 Where the power to postpone, stay or suspend is exercised, the secure tenancy will continue in the meantime, until the occurrence (if at all) of the "date on which the tenant is to give up possession in pursance of the order."[69] Where an order is suspended for so long as

[63] The prohibition against serving the notice within six months from the death is presumably for reasons of compassion, while the prohibition against serving it after 12 months from the death is no doubt intended to prevent hardship being caused to a successor who has "settled in" (see A. Arden, *Housing Act 1985*, Current Law Statutes Annotated Reprints, notes to Sched. 2, Pt. III, gd. 16). If an authority is going to be able to observe these time limits, it must have an efficient system of "diarying ahead."

[64] See below, para. 11.44.

[65] H.A. 1985, Sched. 2, Pt. III, gd. 16.

[66] *Enfield L.B.C.* v. *McKeon* [1986] 2 All E.R. 730, 737 (C.A.).

[67] H.A. 1985, s.85(1).

[68] *Ibid.* s.85(2); postponement of the date of possession can be made indefinite, *e.g.* (as regards gd. 2) "provided no further nuisance occurs" (*cf. Yates* v. *Morris* [1950] W.N. 409 (C.A.)).

[69] H.A. 1985, s.82(2), see above, para. 8.12.

the tenant complies with certain conditions (concerning, for example, the discharge of rent arrears[70]), the secure tenancy will prima facie terminate as soon as the tenant fails to comply with the conditions,[71] although he could still apply for a further suspension of the order[72] (which will revive the secure tenancy), or for a suspension of the warrant of execution. Where the failure to comply with the financial terms of a suspended order has been caused by delay in the processing of the tenant's claim for housing benefit,[73] it has been suggested that the tenant should consider serving a witness summons on a senior officer of the authority who is responsible for administering the scheme, requiring him to attend court in order to explain the delay![74]

In the county court, non-compliance with the terms of a suspended order means that the authority can issue a warrant for possession without any further court order,[75] unless the original order required the court's leave before the warrant could be issued; however, as explained above, the tenant can in any event apply to have the warrant suspended, as for example where he claims that he has not in fact infringed the terms of the suspended order. **8.66**

The power to postpone, stay or suspend can be exercised at any time before execution,[76] even if an absolute order was made at the original hearing.[77] Furthermore, a possession order (whether originally absolute or suspended) may in the court's discretion be set aside, together with the warrant for possession, even after the warrant has been both issued and executed.[78] **8.67**

Where the court makes a suspended order, the tenant will nevertheless generally be ordered to pay the authority's costs, just as in the case of an absolute order; however, tenants in receipt of legal aid **8.68**

[70] H.A. 1985, s.85(3)(*a*), see below, para. 8.69.

[71] *Thompson* v. *Elmbridge B.C.* (1987) 19 H.L.R. 526 (C.A.); see above, para. 8.12.

[72] *I.e.* under H.A. 1985, s.85(2), and C.C.R. 1981, Ord. 13, r. 4: see *R.* v. *Ilkeston County Court, ex p. Kruza* (1985) 17 H.L.R. 539 (D.C.).

[73] An unfortunately frequent occurrence. See D. Wright, [1983] November L.A.G. Bull. 14.

[74] N. Madge, [1984] January Legal Action 8, 9.

[75] C.C.R. 1981, Ord. 26, r. 17 and Form N.325.

[76] H.A. 1985, s.85(2).

[77] See *Birtwhistle* v. *Tweedale* [1954] 1 W.L.R. 190 (C.A.).

[78] *Governors of the Peabody Donation Fund* v. *Hay* (1987) 19 H.L.R. 145 (C.A.), applying C.C.R. 1981, Ord. 37, r. 8(3), and holding that the wording in H.A. 1985, s.85(2) ("at any time before . . . execution") does not deprive the court of its jurisdiction to *set aside* the order *after* execution; see also *Tower Hamlets L.B.C.* v. *McCarron* [1988] September Legal Action 13 (Cty. Ct.).

may be more fortunate in seeking to avoid or mitigate orders for costs.[79]

8.69 On any such adjournment, postponement, stay or suspension, the court *must* impose conditions regarding the payment by the tenant of arrears of rent (if any) and current[80] rent or mesne profits,[81] *unless* the court considers that to do so "would cause exceptional hardship to the tenant or would otherwise be unreasonable."[82] It appears that some county court judges have in fact been requiring council tenants in receipt of income support to pay unreasonable sums in order to clear their arrears, in breach of this provision,[83] and that insufficient account has been taken of the restriction under the social security "arrears direct" scheme on the amount of benefit that can be diverted for payment direct to the landlord in order to reduce the arrears.[84] Indeed, it can be argued that if the D.S.S. is already making "arrears direct" payments in accordance with this scheme, then it may be unreasonable for the court to make any possession order at all (even a suspended one) on the ground of rent arrears, since the authority's interests are already being protected.[85]

8.70 Conditions other than those relating to rent and/or mesne profits may be imposed if the court thinks fit.[86]

8.71 On compliance with the conditions imposed, the court may discharge or rescind the possession order.[87]

8.72 *Grounds within Group B.* The court's powers are much more restricted where it makes a possession order on one of the grounds in Group B, above (*i.e.* the "non-reasonableness" grounds 9–10A): here the court cannot postpone the giving up of possession (whether by the order or any variation, suspension or stay of execution) to a date later than 14 days after the making of the order, save in cases of

[79] See above, para. 8.26.
[80] *e.g.* in cases of adjournment of the proceedings, or in respect of the period up until the date fixed for possession: H.A. 1985, s.82(1)–(2), see above.
[81] *I.e.* for the period between the date fixed for possession and the actual eviction of the tenant (where later): H.A. 1985, s.82(1)–(2), see above.
[82] *Ibid.* s.85(3)(*a*).
[83] See L. ffoulkes, [1983] March L.A.G. Bull 9.
[84] See the Social Security (Claims and Payments) Regulations 1987 (S.I. 1987 No. 1968) reg. 35 and Sched. 9, paras. 2–3, 8; the maximum amount which can currently be diverted under this "arrears direct" scheme is £5.05 per week; see L. ffoulkes, *loc. cit.*, N. Madge, *loc. cit.*
[85] N. Madge, *loc. cit.*
[86] H.A. 1985, s.85(3)(*b*).
[87] *Ibid.* s.85(4).

exceptional hardship, where possession can be postponed for a maximum of six weeks from the making of the order.[88]

(vii) Right to security of the tenant's spouse.[89] The Housing Act also seeks to ensure that the position of the tenant's spouse is safeguarded where the authority obtains a possession order against the tenant, and, in particular, that the spouse's "rights of occupation" under the Matrimonial Homes Act 1983[90] are not inadvertently destroyed following the expiry of the time fixed for delivery of possession under a possession order made against the tenant alone. **8.73**

The 1985 Act[91] provides protection where possession proceedings are brought on one or more of the grounds in Group A or Group C, above, and the tenant's spouse, having rights of occupation under the Matrimonial Homes Act 1983, is then in occupation, and the tenancy is ended as against the tenant as a result of those proceedings. In these circumstances the tenant's spouse (so long as he or she remains in occupation) has the same rights to ask the court to adjourn the proceedings, postpone the date of possession, or stay or suspend execution of the order, as he or she would have if the rights of occupation under the 1983 Act were not affected by the ending of the tenancy.[92] **8.74**

This protection is not available to the tenant's cohabitee. **8.75**

2. *The Termination of Non-Secure Tenancies*

(a) *Relevance of the administrative law principles*

Those council tenants whose tenancies are not secure[93] do not of course enjoy statutory security of tenure, but they continue to have **8.76**

[88] H.A. 1980, s.89(1), (2)(*c*), which remains unrepealed; this "fourteen days" rule represents a tightening up of the old common law "four to six weeks" rule which applied where the landlord had a mandatory ground for possession (see, *e.g. McPhail* v. *Persons Unknown* [1973] 3 All E.R. 393, 399 (C.A.)). However, s.89 only restricts the postponement and suspension powers of *county courts*: the section does not affect the powers of High Court judges: *Bain & Co.* v. *Church Commissioners* (1988) 21 H.L.R. 29 (Ch.D.).

[89] Note also the position of the tenant's spouse regarding "suitable accommodation": see *Wandsworth L.B.C.* v. *Fadayomi* [1987] 1 W.L.R. 352 (C.A.), discussed above, para. 8.55.

[90] M.H.A. 1983, s.1: see below, paras. 11.12–11.16.

[91] H.A. 1985, s.85(5).

[92] *Cf.* the problems which had originally arisen in the private sector case of *Penn* v. *Dunn* [1970] 2 All E.R. 858 (C.A.).

[93] See Chap. 7.

the (relatively limited) protection which was available to all council tenants prior to the Housing Act 1980, primarily by virtue of general administrative law principles.[94] The details of this protection in the context of eviction must be sought elsewhere[95]; what follows is merely an outline of the position.

8.77 An authority, in deciding whether to evict a non-secure tenant by virtue of the power of "general management, regulation and control" of council housing vested in it by the Housing Act 1985,[96] must abide by the general administrative law principles: this primarily means that it must act "in good faith, taking into account relevant considerations and not irrelevant considerations."[97] If there has been a breach of these principles, the tenant will have a defence to the possession proceedings; he is not required to argue these "administrative law" points via an action for judicial review in the High Court under Order 53 of the Rules of the Supreme Court,[98] but can raise them by way of defence to the possession proceedings in the county court.[99] The "relevant considerations" to be taken into account by the authority in considering eviction can include Ministerial Circulars[1]; and the administrative law principles extend to the termination of council licences,[2] as well as council tenancies.

8.78 The major difficulty from the tenant's viewpoint, however, is that it may well be impossible to prove that the authority has failed to take these "relevant considerations" into account. A local "ombudsman"[3] may be able to do the necessary delving into an authority's

[94] These principles are discussed above, paras. 6.08–6.17.

[95] See, *e.g.* D. Hoath, *Council Housing* (1st ed., 1978), Chap. 7.

[96] H.A. 1985, s.21(1).

[97] *Bristol D.C.* v. *Clark* [1975] 3 All E.R. 976, 980 (C.A.), *per* Lord Denning M.R.; these administrative law principles do not apparently apply to evictions by housing associations, even though they may be in receipt of public funds: *Peabody Housing Association Ltd.* v. *Green* (1978) 122 S.J. 862 (C.A.); see also *Clays Lane Housing Co-operative Ltd.* v. *Patrick* (1984) 49 P. & C.R. 72 (C.A.).

[98] See above, paras. 6.22–6.30.

[99] *Cannock Chase D.C.* v. *Kelly* [1978] 1 W.L.R. 1 (C.A.); *Wandsworth L.B.C.* v. *Winder* [1984] A.C. 461 (H.L.), as interpreted in *West Glamorgan C.C.* v. *Rafferty* [1987] 1 All E.R. 1005, 1016 (C.A.), and *Avon C.C.* v. *Buscott* [1988] 1 All E.R. 841, 845 (C.A.).

[1] *e.g.* those dealing with the treatment of rent arrears: see below, paras. 10.40–10.42.

[2] *Cleethorpes B.C.* v. *Clarkson* [1978] L.A.G. Bull. 166 (C.A.); *cf.* the "secure licence" provisions in H.A. 1985, s.79(3) (see above, para. 7.15).

[3] See above, paras. 2.44–2.45; there have been some findings by local ombudsmen of "maladministration" concerning council evictions: see, *e.g.* Complaints No. 3917/S/77 and 1094/S/78.

administrative processes, but he would not be able to do so swiftly enough to provide the tenant with a defence to the possession proceedings.

The cases provide clear examples of the very heavy burden of proof which confronts a tenant who seeks to show a breach of the administrative law principles,[4] so that this protection can be regarded as having little value in practice where "run of the mill" possession actions are concerned. Although the protection extends equally to secure tenants, the extent of the security offered by the 1985 Act is such (particularly where a "reasonableness" ground is in issue) that it will be very unusual for a secure tenant to need to rely on these common law principles. **8.79**

(b) *The eviction process*

Assuming that the authority's initial decision to evict a non-secure tenant is unassailable, it may nevertheless be possible for the tenant to challenge the eviction process itself. **8.80**

Where the tenancy is periodic, a notice to quit must first be given.[5] This must expire at the end of a completed period of the tenancy; it must normally be in writing, be given at least four weeks before the date on which it is to take effect,[6] and inform the tenant of the need for a court order before he can lawfully be evicted, and of the availability of advice from a solicitor (under the legal aid scheme if necessary), or from a Citizens' Advice Bureau, Housing Aid **8.81**

[4] See, *e.g. Bristol D.C.* v. *Clark* [1975] 3 All E.R. 976 (C.A.); *Cannock Chase D.C.* v. *Kelly* [1978] 1 W.L.R. 1 (C.A.); *Cleethorpes B.C.* v. *Clarkson* [1978] L.A.G. Bull. 166 (C.A.); *Sevenoaks D.C.* v. *Emmott* (1979) 39 P. & C.R. 404 (C.A.); *cf.* the qualified successes achieved by the defendants in *Wandsworth L.B.C.* v. *Winder* [1984] A.C. 461 (H.L.), and *West Glamorgan C.C.* v. *Rafferty* [1987] 1 All E.R. 1005 (C.A.), both of which involved somewhat unusual features.

[5] If the periodic tenancy agreement restricts the authority's ability to serve notice to quit to specified situations arising due to the tenant's default, such as rent arrears, then this will nevertheless *not* be treated as a *forfeiture* provision merely because it operates on the tenant's default, so that the tenant cannot claim relief against forfeiture where such a notice to quit is served: *Clays Lane Housing Co-operative Ltd.* v. *Patrick* (1984) 49 P. & C.R. 72 (C.A.).

[6] P.f.E.A. 1977, s.5(1); this provision has been extended to licences (s.5(1A)), but it does not apply to "excluded tenancies" granted after January 15, 1989, nor to "excluded licences": ss.3A, 5(1B), 8(4).

Centre, etc.[7] Service of the notice is governed by the Local Government Act 1972.[8]

8.82 Even a technically valid notice to quit may be vitiated by a clearly unlawful purpose underlying it, such as the recovery of an invalid rent increase which is therefore *ultra vires* the authority.[9]

8.83 If the tenant refuses to leave after expiry[10] of a proper notice to quit, the authority normally cannot regain possession without a court order, since in most cases it will be bound by the unlawful eviction provisions in Part I of the Protection from Eviction Act 1977.[11] At the hearing, the authority need not prove that it requires the property for housing purposes.[12] It is entitled to a possession order as of right if the tenant has no viable defence,[13] although in rent arrears cases the tenant may be able to persuade the authority to accept a possession order which is suspended so long as the tenant pays off the arrears by agreed instalments.[14] The judge has some discretion in fixing the date for possession or suspending execution of the possession order,[15] but the giving up of possession cannot normally be postponed for more than 14 days.[16]

8.84 The protection against eviction afforded to secure council tenants under the 1985 Act is therefore much clearer and more wide-ranging than that available before statutory security was introduced in 1980, although only this latter protection can apply to those tenants (and licensees) who are not secure.

[7] P.f.E.A. 1977, s.5(1)–(2) (but see s.5(1B)); Notices to Quit etc. (Prescribed Information) Regulations 1988 (S.I. 1988 No. 2201); these information provisions also apply to notices to determine certain licences; if the notice does not contain the prescribed information, it is invalid and the landlord will not be entitled to possession on its expiry: *Shah* v. *Emmanuel* [1988] December Legal Action 17 (Cty. Ct.).

[8] L.G.A. 1972, s.233: see above, para. 8.22.

[9] *G.L.C.* v. *Connolly* [1970] 1 All E.R. 870, 875 (C.A.); see also *Wandsworth L.B.C.* v. *Winder* [1984] A.C. 461 (H.L.) (where, however, the tenancy was secure).

[10] A demand for the payment of *rent* (as opposed to mesne profits) after expiry of a notice to quit, but prior to the granting of a possession order, will only create a new periodic tenancy if there is very clear evidence that this is the intention of the parties; see above, para. 8.13.

[11] See P.f.E.A. 1977, ss.3, 3A and 8(1), discussed above, para. 8.16.

[12] *Bristol D.C.* v. *Clark* [1975] 3 All E.R. 976 (C.A.); *cf.* H.A. 1985, s.612.

[13] *Sheffield Corp.* v. *Luxford* [1929] 2 K.B. 180 (D.C.); *Bristol C.C.* v. *Rawlins* (1977) 34 P. & C.R. 12 (C.A.).

[14] See *Bristol C.C.* v. *Rawlins, ibid.*

[15] See C.C.R. 1981, Ord. 22, r. 3.

[16] H.A. 1980, s.89(1), see above, para. 8.72.

9 Dispositions By Secure Tenants

1. *Taking in Lodgers*

9.01 A "lodger" is someone who "is entitled to live in the premises but cannot call the place his own."[1] He is classified as a licensee rather than a tenant, since he lacks the exclusive possession necessary to support a tenancy, and he therefore does not normally hold any proprietary interest in the property. In such a case, the householder (owner or tenant) retains legal "possession" and the lodger merely obtains the use of the relevant premises. We have seen[2] that in order for a residential occupier to be a lodger, the householder must exercise a very high degree of control over the lodger's rooms, which is normally indicated by the provision of attendance or services which require the householder (or others acting on his behalf) to exercise unrestricted access to and use of those rooms in order to carry them out.[3]

9.02 At common law, if the lease is silent on the point, the tenant has complete freedom to take in lodgers. Nevertheless, prior to the Housing Act 1980 it was common for council tenancy agreements expressly to prohibit the taking in of lodgers without the authority's consent, and some authorities would only give consent if the tenant agreed to pay an additional "lodger charge."

9.03 The Housing Act 1985 provides[4] that it is a term of every secure council tenancy that the tenant may allow any persons to reside as lodgers in the dwelling, even without the authority's consent. It will be recalled, however, that if the dwelling becomes criminally over-

[1] *Street* v. *Mountford* [1985] 2 All E.R. 289, 293 (H.L.), *per* Lord Templeman.
[2] See above, paras. 7.16–7.17.
[3] *Street* v. *Mountford*, see above; *Crancour Ltd.* v. *Da Silvaesa* (1986) 18 H.L.R. 265, 272–273 (C.A.).
[4] H.A. 1985, s.93(1)(*a*).

crowded within the terms of Part X of the 1985 Act, then the authority has a ground for possession.[5] The increases in council rents in recent years could well have acted as an incentive for tenants to exercise their statutory right to take in lodgers.

9.04 The 1985 Act does not expressly prohibit the imposition of "lodger charges."[6] However, it seems that it is uncommon for authorities to impose such charges.[7] Moreover, the Act does not require the tenant even to inform the authority that he has taken in a lodger, so that the authority may well be unaware that an opportunity to claim a lodger charge has arisen (although the requirement to disclose lodgers could be imposed expressly by the tenancy agreement).

2. *Dispositions* Inter Vivos *of Part of the Dwelling by Sub-letting or Otherwise Parting with Possession*

(a) *Requirement for the council's consent*

9.05 If a lease contains no prohibition on sub-letting, then at common law the tenant may sub-let without the landlord's consent. However, prior to 1980 local authorities were obliged, pursuant to the Housing Act 1957,[8] to "make it a term of every letting that the tenant shall not assign, sublet or otherwise part with the possession of the premises, or any part thereof, except with the consent in writing of the authority"; and the insertion of such a "qualified" covenant against disposal attracted the implied proviso under the Landlord and Tenant Act 1927[9] that, notwithstanding any express provision to the contrary, the landlord's consent was not to be unreasonably withheld.

9.06 This provision in the 1957 Act was repealed in 1980.[10] Instead, the Housing Act 1985 states[11] that it is a term of every secure council tenancy that the tenant will not, without the written consent of the authority, sub-let part of the dwelling or otherwise part with the possession of part thereof. However, such consent (which may be retrospective) must not be unreasonably withheld or given subject to

[5] H.A. 1985, Sched. 2, Pt. II, gd. 9, see above, para. 8.45.
[6] Pursuant to the general rent-fixing power in H.A. 1985, s.24(1), see below, paras. 10.02, 10.30–10.37.
[7] D.O.E., *Housing Management: Consultation Paper on A Tenants' Charter* (1977), Annex 4, paras. 4–5.
[8] H.A. 1957, s.113(5).
[9] L. & T.A. 1927, s.19(1)(*a*).
[10] H.A. 1980, s.35(4) and Sched. 26.
[11] H.A. 1985, s.93(1)(*b*).

conditions[12] (for example, as to rent levels for a sub-lease); if consent is unreasonably withheld or given subject to conditions, it shall be treated as given, or given unconditionally, as the case may be.[13] It therefore remains important here to distinguish between the taking of lodgers (*i.e.* a licence), for which (as has been seen) no consent is needed, and a sub-letting of part of the property (*i.e.* a disposal conferring a proprietary interest), for which consent is required[14]; even though for many other purposes relating to secure tenancies the distinction between a lease and a licence has been removed by the 1985 Act.[15]

Thus, following a disposition of part of the property, the original tenancy remains secure, but if the authority's consent was not requested or was properly withheld, a "reasonableness" ground for possession arises.[16] The burden lies on the authority to show that the consent was reasonably withheld,[17] and the following matters (*inter alia*) are relevant[18]: that statutory overcrowding[19] would result if consent were to be given, or that the authority proposes to carry out works which will affect the accommodation likely to be used by the proposed sub-tenant. Although the authority normally has to consider only its own relevant interests in deciding whether to refuse consent, it may nevertheless also have to consider the detriment which the tenant would suffer on refusal if that detriment would be extreme and disproportionate in relation to the benefit gained by the authority.[20] **9.07**

[12] H.A. 1985, s.94(2), (4)–(5); s.94(5) would also appear to preclude the insertion by the authority of an "Adler"-type clause, whereby the tenant must first offer to surrender the tenancy to the landlord before applying for a licence to sub-let: *cf. Adler* v. *Upper Grosvenor Street Investment* [1957] 1 W.L.R. 227; *Bocarda S.A.* v. *S. & M. Hotels* [1980] 1 W.L.R. 17 (C.A.); C. G. Blake, [1980] Conv. 418, 426.

[13] H.A. 1985, s.94(2), (5).

[14] For the distinction between a lease and a licence, see above, paras. 7.15–7.24; in practice, the authority may have difficulty in establishing that the tenant of a small house or flat has taken in a *sub-tenant*, rather than a lodger.

[15] H.A. 1985, s.79(3); see above, para. 7.15.

[16] H.A. 1985, Sched. 2, Pt. I, gd. 1; see above, para. 8.31.

[17] H.A. 1985, s.94(2); *cf.* L. & T.A. 1927, s.19(1)(*a*), see above, under which it is clear that the burden lies on the *tenant* to show that the withholding of consent was unreasonable (see, *e.g. Shanly* v. *Ward* (1913) 29 T.L.R. 714; *International Drilling Fluids* v. *Louisville Investments (Uxbridge)* [1986] 1 All E.R. 321, 325 (C.A.)). Although s.94 of the 1985 Act does not expressly exclude the 1927 Act, the "burden" rule in s.94(2) must clearly prevail here regarding partial disposals.

[18] H.A. 1985, s.94(3).

[19] Within the meaning of H.A. 1985, Pt. X.

[20] *International Drilling Fluids* v. *Louisville Investments (Uxbridge)*, see above (a case concerning a qualified covenant against assignment).

9.08 The tenant must be given written reasons for any refusal of consent, and if the authority fails to respond to the tenant's request for consent within a reasonable time then the consent is taken to have been withheld.[21] The county court has jurisdiction to decide this consent issue by simple declaration.[22]

(b) *Position of sub-tenants*

9.09 Whether or not the sub-letting is with consent, a sub-tenant cannot normally gain any security against the authority after the ending[23] of the head tenant's tenancy, since the Act does not exclude the basic common law rule that an interest derived out of the tenant's estate will fall with the tenancy.[24] Furthermore, if in breach of the statutory provisions the authority's consent to the sub-letting has not been obtained, the authority may secure the swift eviction of the sub-tenant (following termination of the head lease) by using the "squatters" possession procedure.[25] However, it appears that if the head tenant voluntarily surrenders the tenancy to the authority, or gives notice to quit to the authority, then the sub-lease (even if it was not granted with the authority's consent) will be capable of binding the authority,[26] and the portion of the property sub-let will become subject to a direct secure tenancy provided that the "separate dwelling" requirement[27] is satisfied.

9.10 Whether or not the sub-tenancy was lawfully granted, the sub-tenant's position as against the head tenant is not affected while the head tenancy is on foot: if the sub-tenancy was granted before January 15, 1989, it will normally be classed as a "resident landlord"

[21] H.A. 1985, s.94(6)(*b*); note that L. & T.A. 1988 (which imposes tortious liability for breach of statutory duty on a landlord who does not respond within a reasonable time to a tenant's application for consent to a sub-lease or other parting with possession) does *not* apply to secure tenancies: L. & T.A. 1988, s.5(3).

[22] H.A. 1985, s.110(2)(*b*).

[23] While the head tenancy is still on foot, the authority has no *locus standi* to claim possession from the sub-tenant, even if the sub-letting was without its consent: *Wirral B.C.* v. *Smith and Cooper* (1982) 80 L.G.R. 628 (C.A.); *Preston B.C.* v. *Fairclough* (1983) 8 H.L.R. 70 (C.A.).

[24] Applied to secure tenancies in *Acme Housing Association and R.B. of Kensington & Chelsea* v. *Chevska* [1987] June Legal Action 17 (Cty. Ct.); see also *Harrison* v. *Wing, The Times*, April 6, 1988 (C. A.); *Gisborne* v. *Burton* [1988] 3 All E.R. 760, 763 (C.A.).

[25] R.S.C., Ord. 113, or C.C.R. 1981, Ord. 24: see *Moore Properties (Ilford)* v. *McKeon* [1976] 1 W.L.R. 1278.

[26] *Mellor* v. *Watkins* (1874) L.R. 9 Q.B. 400; *Parker* v. *Jones* [1910] 2 K.B. 32; *Brown* v. *Wilson* (1949) 208 L.T. 144; see also W. Birtles, [1987] L.G.C., September 18, p.12.

[27] H.A. 1985, s.79(1), see above, paras. 7.05–7.06.

tenancy, and will therefore receive limited protection as a "restricted contract" under the Rent Act 1977,[28] unless substantial board is provided (*i.e.* meals of an adequate nature)[29]; if, however, the sub-tenancy was granted after January 15, 1989, it cannot rank as a "restricted contract,"[30] nor is it protected under the "assured tenancy" provisions in the Housing Act 1988.[31]

3. *Dispositions* Inter Vivos *of the Whole of the Dwelling by Assignment, Sub-letting or Otherwise Parting with Possession*

No matter what the terms of the tenancy may provide, the 1985 Act prevents the tenant from transferring his secure tenancy (and the package of "charter" rights which it comprises) to whomever he pleases. The reason for this is that the tenant's chosen recipient may not be a person in need of the accommodation at all, whereas it is felt that there should be some restrictions on the disposal of public housing stock. Thus secure council tenants "have no ordinarily saleable interest."[32] **9.11**

The provisions relating to assignment are rather more complicated than those dealing with the sub-letting or otherwise parting with possession of the whole dwelling. **9.12**

(a) *Assignments*

(i) General. Even where an assignment is permitted by the 1985 Act, the necessary formalities must be complied with before it will be effective at law. A deed is required before the legal estate can pass by way of assignment,[33] even where the lease is periodic and has been granted orally. An oral assignment, or one which is in writing but not under seal, will be effective in equity as a contract to assign as between the assignor and the assignee if adequately evidenced in writing[34] or supported by part performance[35]; however, such an **9.13**

[28] R.A. 1977, ss.12, 20.

[29] *Ibid.* s.19(5)(*c*).

[30] H.A. 1988, s.36(1).

[31] *Ibid.* Sched. 1, para. 10.

[32] *Per* Ralph Gibson L.J. in *Wiseman* v. *Simpson* [1988] 1 All E.R. 245, 251 (C.A.).

[33] L.P.A. 1925, s.52(1); a deed of assignment was duly used by the secure tenant in *Governors of the Peabody Donation Fund* v. *Higgins* [1983] 3 All E.R. 122 (C.A.); *cf.* *Newham L.B.C.* v. *Bennett* [1984] C.L.Y. 1960 (Cty. Ct.), where no deed was used, and the purported assignment was held to be ineffective.

[34] L.P.A. 1925, s.40(1).

[35] *Ibid.* s.40(2).

informal assignment will not normally be effective as between the landlord and the assignee,[36] unless for example the doctrine of estoppel can operate.[37]

9.14 The original version of the scheme establishing the rights of secure tenants in the Housing Act 1980 did not seek either to permit or to prohibit assignments as such, but rather spelled out the consequences if an assignment took place.[38] The current scheme in the 1985 Act takes a rather more complicated approach regarding assignments.

(ii) Assignments of periodic secure tenancies, or of fixed-term secure tenancies granted on or after November 5, 1982

9.15 *The general rule.* If a secure tenancy is periodic (whenever granted), or has been granted for a fixed term on or after November 5, 1982, then the normal rule[39] is that the tenancy is not capable of being assigned: the tenant cannot even dispose of the contractual tenancy by way of assignment,[40] regardless of whether assignment is permitted by the tenancy agreement. This is in marked contrast to the common law position, under which an assignment will be effective even if it is made in breach of a covenant against assignment, although the assignee may face possession proceedings or a claim for damages for breach of the covenant.[41]

9.16 *The three exceptional cases.* There are three exceptional cases where secure tenancies which are periodic, or for a fixed term granted on or after November 5, 1982, can be assigned[42]: first, where the assignment complies with the statutory rules regarding assignments by way of exchange[43]; secondly, where the assignment is made pursuant to a court order under section 24 of the Matrimonial Causes

[36] *Newham L.B.C.* v. *Bennett*, see above.

[37] See R. E. Megarry and H. W. R. Wade, *The Law of Real Property* (5th ed., 1984), pp. 665–666.

[38] H.A. 1980, s.37(1).

[39] H.A. 1985, s.91(1).

[40] *Cf.* the original version of H.A. 1980, s.37(1), which provided that if a secure tenancy was assigned, it would generally cease to be secure, but the contractual tenancy would pass.

[41] *Old Grovebury Manor Farm* v. *W. Seymour Plant Sales & Hire* (*No.2*) [1979] 1 W.L.R. 263 (C.A.).

[42] H.A. 1985, s.91(3); an assignment by deed is necessary, since s.91(3) does not cover assignments which are only effective in equity: *Newham L.B.C.* v. *Bennett*, see above.

[43] H.A. 1985, s.92, see below, paras. 9.20–9.23.

Act 1973[44]; and thirdly, where the assignment is made to a member of the tenant's family who would be qualified to succeed the tenant under the statutory succession provisions[45] if the tenant had died immediately before the assignment.

9.17 With regard to an assignment within the third permitted category (*i.e.* one made to a potential "successor"), the secure tenancy will pass even if the tenancy agreement contains an absolute prohibition against assignment[46]; and although the authority could seek possession in such a case on the "reasonableness" ground of breach of tenancy obligation,[47] such an action would be very unlikely to succeed: since the defendant would *ex hypothesi* have been entitled to take the tenancy if the tenant had died, it would generally not be reasonable to order possession against him. It can be advantageous, from the potential assignee's viewpoint, for the tenant to make a permitted *inter vivos* assignment to him as the tenant's potential successor (rather than relying on the statutory succession provisions vesting the secure tenancy in him on the tenant's death), because the "under-occupation" ground for possession[48] can apply to a statutory successor following the original tenant's death, but it cannot apply to an assignee under an *inter vivos* assignment.

(iii) Assignments of fixed-term secure tenancies granted before November 5, 1982

9.18 *The general rule.* If a secure tenancy is for a fixed term which was granted before November 5, 1982, then the normal rule is that the contractual tenancy is capable of being assigned, but on assignment the tenancy ceases to be secure[49]: thus the package of "charter" rights disappears, although the common law tenancy itself will continue on a purely contractual basis. A tenancy which ceases to be secure under this provision cannot subsequently become secure

[44] The jurisdiction concerns property adjustment orders relating to certain matrimonial proceedings, and is discussed in detail in Chap. 11; it was not necessary for s.91(3)(*b*) specifically to exempt transfers made by court order pursuant to M.H.A. 1983, Sched. 1 (discussed in Chap. 11), since these do not operate by way of assignment by the tenant but purely "by virtue of the [court's] order and without further assurance" (M.H.A. 1983, Sched. 1, Pt. II, para. 2(1)).

[45] H.A. 1985, s.87 (see below, para. 9.29 *et seq.*).

[46] *Governors of the Peabody Donation Fund* v. *Higgins* [1983] 3 All E.R. 122 (C.A.).

[47] *Ibid.*

[48] H.A. 1985, Sched. 2, Pt. III, gd. 16, see above, para. 8.63.

[49] H.A. 1985, s.91(2).

again,[50] even though (for example) the authority accepts rent from the assignee.

9.19 *The three exceptional cases.* The three exceptional cases[51] discussed above apply also where the tenancy is for a fixed term granted before November 5, 1982: in this context, if any of the three exceptions operates, the effect will be that the assignment[52] will pass the secure tenancy and not just the contractual tenancy.

9.20 **(iv) Assignments by way of exchange.** One of the three exceptional cases (see above) where the secure tenancy can be preserved on its assignment is where the assignment complies with the statutory rules governing assignments by way of exchange.[53] Originally, the result of a "swap" between secure tenants was that under the Housing Act 1980 both tenancies ceased to be secure, so that they could both be terminated by notice to quit.[54] However, the Housing Act 1985 provides[55] that it is now a term of every secure tenancy that the tenant may, with the written consent of his landlord, assign the tenancy to any person who is himself a secure tenant and who has the written consent of *his* respective landlord to assign *his* tenancy either to the first assignor-tenant or to another secure tenant who satisfies the same condition; this provision therefore contemplates either a straight exchange between two secure tenants, or an arrangement whereby secure tenant A assigns to secure tenant B who in turn assigns to secure tenant C, etc.

9.21 Consent to such an assignment can only be withheld on one or more of the grounds set out in Schedule 3 to the Act, and if it is withheld otherwise than on one of these grounds, it is treated as having been given.[56] Moreover, an authority can only rely on a Schedule 3 ground if, within 42 days after the tenant's application for consent, it serves on him a notice specifying the ground and giving particulars

[50] H.A. 1985, s.91(2).
[51] H.A. 1985, s.91(3).
[52] A deed must be used; s.91(3) does not cover assignments which are only effective in equity: *Newham L.B.C.* v. *Bennett* [1984] C.L.Y. 1960 (Cty. Ct.).
[53] H.A. 1985, ss. 91(3)(*a*), 92.
[54] *Warwick D.C.* v. *Smith & Benton, Roof*, March 1982, p. 5 (Cty. Ct.); *Norwich C.C.* v. *Secretary of State for the Environment* [1982] 1 All E.R. 737, 744 (C.A.); but note the effect of Housing (Consequential Provisions) Act 1985, Sched. 4, para. 8: see below, para. 9.24.
[55] H.A. 1985, s.92(1)–(2).
[56] *Ibid.* s.92(3).

of it.[57] No conditions can be attached to the consent, other than one requiring the tenant to pay rent arrears or otherwise remedy any breach of the tenancy agreement.[58]

The grounds on which consent to an "exchange" assignment can be withheld include the following[59]: the tenant or proposed assignee is obliged (or will on a specified date be obliged) to give up possession of his dwelling in pursuance of a court order; proceedings for possession have been commenced against the tenant or the proposed assignee on one or more of grounds 1 to 6 in Part I of Schedule 2,[60] or notice of intended proceedings has been served specifying one or more of these grounds; the dwelling is too large for the reasonable requirements of the proposed assignee. The county court has jurisdiction to decide whether any requisite consent was withheld otherwise than on one or more of the prescribed grounds.[61] **9.22**

While there is no specific prohibition on the payment of premiums on assignment of secure tenancies,[62] in the case of an "exchange" assignment the payment or receipt of a premium provides the authority with a "reasonableness" ground for possession.[63] **9.23**

(v) Assignments effected before August 26, 1984. A special rule now governs assignments of secure tenancies which were effected before August 26, 1984 (the date when the current provisions were first introduced), whether the tenancies are periodic or for a fixed term. The original rule in the Housing Act 1980,[64] to the effect that (with exceptions) a secure tenancy which was assigned would thereupon cease to be secure, is now "deemed never to have applied in relation to the assignment of secure tenancies."[65] This remarkable provision means that a pre-August 26, 1984 assignment of a secure tenancy to *anyone* is retrospectively deemed effectively to have transferred the secure tenancy (even if, originally, security had **9.24**

[57] H.A. 1985, s.92(4); L. & T.A. 1988 (which imposes tortious liability for breach of statutory duty on a landlord who does not respond within a reasonable time to the tenant's application for consent to an assignment) does *not* apply to secure tenancies: L & T.A. 1988, s.5(3).

[58] H.A. 1985, s.92(5)–(6).

[59] *Ibid.* Sched. 3, gds. 1–3.

[60] See above, paras. 8.31–8.41.

[61] H.A. 1985, s.110(2)(*a*).

[62] *Cf.* the prohibitions on premiums in connection with protected tenancies and certain restricted contracts, imposed by R.A 1977, ss.119–120, 122.

[63] H.A. 1985, Sched. 2, Pt. I, gd. 6: see above, para. 8.41.

[64] H.A. 1980, s.37.

[65] Housing (Consequential Provisions) Act 1985, Sched. 4, para. 8(1).

been lost due to the operation of the assignment provisions in the 1980 Act); however, notices to quit and forfeiture notices served before August 26, 1984 have not been affected.[66]

(b) *Sub-letting or otherwise parting with possession of the whole of the dwelling*

9.25 If a secure tenant sub-lets the whole of the dwelling, or parts with the possession of the whole of the dwelling other than by way of sub-letting or assignment, then the tenancy will cease to be secure,[67] whether the tenancy agreement permitted or prohibited the disposition; the tenancy will then continue on a purely contractual basis. Here it matters not whether the sub-tenant or new possessor happens to be the tenant's spouse or other "member of his family."[68] This rule is consistent with the basic "tenant condition" for a secure tenancy,[69] which requires that the tenant himself must normally occupy the dwelling as his only or principal home.[70]

9.26 Where a tenancy ceases to be secure under this provision following a disposal of the whole by way of sub-letting or otherwise parting with possession, that tenancy cannot later become secure again[71] (even if, for example, the sub-letting is ended).

4. *Dispositions on Death*

(a) *General*

9.27 A bequest of a tenancy in the tenant's will cannot be a breach of a covenant against assignment.[72]

9.28 Prior to the introduction of the statutory "charter" rights in 1980, the lack of security for council tenants gave authorities considerable control in practice over the tenant's choice of successor, although the deceased tenant's spouse or adult child was often permitted to retain

[66] Housing (Consequential Provisions) Act 1985, Sched. 4, para. 8(2).
[67] H.A. 1985, s.93(2).
[68] *Cf.* the exception in H.A. 1985, s.91(3)(*c*), see above, relating to assignments.
[69] H.A. 1985, s.81.
[70] See above, paras. 7.09–7.14.
[71] H.A. 1985, s.93(2).
[72] See, *e.g. Crusoe d. Blencowe* v. *Bugby* (1771) 3 Wils. K.B. 234, 237. Even a weekly tenancy can in law be disposed of by the tenant's will or under his intestacy (see, *e.g. Youngmin* v. *Heath* [1974] 1 W.L.R. 135 (C.A.)); but possibly the assent by the tenant's personal representatives giving effect to the bequest, or on the intestacy, might break a covenant against assignment.

the tenancy. The 1985 Act[73] now regulates succession to a *secure* council tenancy. It is necessary to consider the position regarding *periodic* secure tenancies separately from the position regarding *fixed-term* secure tenancies.

(b) *Periodic secure tenancies*

(i) The basic requirements for statutory succession. Where the deceased tenant's secure tenancy is periodic, the secure tenancy vests by virtue of the Housing Act 1985 (regardless of the terms of the tenant's will and even though the tenancy must remain contractual[74]), in a "member of his family" who can satisfy certain stipulated residence requirements,[75] *i.e. either* he (or she) is the tenant's spouse and he (or she) occupied the dwelling as his (or her) only or principal home at the time of the tenant's death; *or* (failing such spouse) he (or she) is some other prescribed "member of the tenant's family," and as non-spouse successor he (or she) has not only occupied the dwelling as his (or her) only or principal home at the time of the secure tenant's death, but has also resided with the secure tenant throughout the period of 12 months before the death and (throughout that period) has resided in the same dwelling as that which the tenant held on lease when he (or she) died[76] (or, possibly, in two or more council dwellings successively[77]). **9.29**

The burden of proof (on the balance of probabilities) rests with the claimant as regards the "only or principal home" requirement and, in the case of non-spouse claimants, the 12 months' residence requirement.[78] The former requirement is the same as that imposed by the "tenant condition" of the definition of a secure tenancy,[79] **9.30**

[73] H.A. 1985, ss.87–90.

[74] The Rent Act concept of the "statutory tenancy" is inapplicable: see above, paras. 7.14, 8.12; the succession scheme in the 1985 Act is an improvement on the Rent Act's provisions, since it avoids the awkward separation between the statutory and contractual tenancies which can follow on the death of a Rent Act tenant (see, *e.g.* J. E. Alder, [1982] Conv. 298, 300, n. 11).

[75] H.A. 1985, ss.87, 89(1)–(2).

[76] The requirement for a 12 months' connection with the relevant dwelling is not expressly imposed by the statute, but was established by *South Northamptonshire D.C.* v. *Power* [1987] 3 All E.R. 831 (C.A.), where for part of the relevant 12 months' period the claimant had lived with the tenant as cohabitee in a private sector dwelling, and therefore failed to establish statutory succession.

[77] This was left open in *Power's* case, *ibid.*

[78] *Peabody Donation Fund Governors* v. *Grant* (1982) 6 H.L.R. 41 (C.A.); *L.B. of Lewisham* v. *Marsh*, October 2, 1986 (C.A., unreported).

[79] H.A. 1985, s.81, see above, paras. 7.09–7.14.

while the latter requirement has been said to involve the establishing of a "sufficient measure of . . . factual community of family living and companionship" over the 12 months' period.[80]

9.31 **(ii) "Members of the family."** To be a "member of the tenant's family," the claimant must be the tenant's spouse, parent, grandparent, child, grandchild, brother, sister, uncle, aunt, nephew, niece, or a person who lived together with the tenant "as husband and wife."[81] With regard to cohabitees,[82] they may still be "living together" for this purpose even if their relationship has broken down, if their accommodation is so small that they cannot live separate lives within it.[83] However, "gay" relationships (whether homosexual or lesbian) do not count for statutory succession, since the parties cannot " live together as husband and wife" within the wording of the statute.[84]

9.32 Relationships by marriage or the half-blood count as full relationships, as do step-relationships and illegitimate relationships[85]; adopted children are treated as the natural children of the adopters under separate provisions in the Adoption Act 1976.[86]

9.33 A county court case[87] has decided that foster-children who had been treated as if they were the natural children of the tenant, although not formally adopted by him, were entitled to succeed to his secure tenancy because they had been "adopted *de facto*"; this is questionable, since the Housing Act 1985 (in marked contrast to the

[80] *Peabody Donation Fund Governors* v. *Grant*, *ibid.* at 45.

[81] H.A. 1985, s.113(1).

[82] For analogous Rent Act cases concerning statutory succession by heterosexual cohabitees see, *e.g. Dyson Holdings* v. *Fox* [1976] Q.B. 603 (C.A.); *Helby* v. *Rafferty* [1979] 1 W.L.R. 13 (C.A.); *Carega Properties S.A.* v. *Sharratt* [1979] 1 W.L.R. 928 (H.L.); *Watson* v. *Lucas* [1980] 1 W.L.R. 1493 (C.A.); see also B. Berkovits, [1981] J.S.W.L. 83.

[83] *Adeoso* v. *Adeoso* [1980] 1 W.L.R. 1535 (C.A.); it is significant that the issue of "living together" relates in the present context primarily to the termination of that state, rather than its inception: *cf. Crake* v. *S.B.C.* [1982] 1 All E.R. 498, 502; see also, as regards analogous supplementary benefit cases, T. Lyon, [1981] J.S.W.L. 372.

[84] *Harrogate B.C.* v. *Simpson* (1986) 2 F.L.R. 91 (C.A.); Ms. Simpson's subsequent complaint to the European Commission of Human Rights was similarly unsuccessful: *Application No.11716/85* v. *U.K.*

[85] H.A. 1985, s.113(2).

[86] A.A. 1976, s.39.

[87] *Reading B.C.* v. *Ilsley* [1981] C.L.Y. 1323.

Rent Act 1977[88]) appears to have provided an exhaustive list of "family members."[89]

(iii) Competing claimants. Where there are two or more claimants, the spouse has priority,[90] and as regards other competing members of the family the authority can decide the matter if the relevant members cannot agree which one of them is to succeed.[91] This jurisdiction is probably unwelcome to most authorities, and it contrasts with the statutory succession provisions in the Rent Act 1977,[92] under which such disputes are decided by the county court. The wording of the Housing Act[93] makes it clear that there cannot be joint statutory succession. **9.34**

(iv) The "one succession stage only" rule. Only one statutory "succession stage" is possible, for statutory succession cannot apply if the deceased tenant was himself a "successor,"[94] an expression which is very widely defined.[95] The effect[96] is that under a periodic secure tenancy the dead tenant is normally treated as himself having been a (first) "successor" (so that no further statutory succession is permitted on his death) if the tenancy vested in him under the statutory succession provisions relating to periodic secure tenancies,[97] or if he was a joint tenant and became the sole tenant (for example, on the death of the other joint tenant), or if he became the tenant on the tenancy being assigned to him or on its being vested in him on the death of the previous tenant. However, a tenant to whom the **9.35**

[88] See R.A. 1977, Sched. 1 (as amended by H.A. 1988, s.39 and Sched. 4, Pt. I), where the expression "member of the [tenant's] family" is left undefined, save for the express inclusion of surviving spouses and cohabitees.

[89] *Harrogate B.C.* v. *Simpson*, see above; see also the general comments on statutory interpretation, where a relevant issue is governed by a comprehensive legislative code, in *Pioneer Aggregates (U.K.)* v. *Secretary of State for the Environment* [1985] A.C. 132 (H.L.), a planning case.

[90] H.A. 1985, s.89(2)(*a*).

[91] *Ibid.* s.89(2)(*b*); in cases of agreement, the authority does not have to be notified before the agreement becomes valid: see *General Management Ltd.* v. *Locke* (1980) 255 E.G. 155 (C.A.).

[92] R.A. 1977, Sched. 1, para. 3; see also H.A. 1988, s.17(5), under which the county court decides disputes between potential cohabitee-successors to an assured periodic tenancy.

[93] H.A. 1985, s.89(2) ("vests . . . in the *one* to be preferred"); but *cf.* *Reading B.C.* v. *Ilsley*, see above, where this point appears to have been overlooked.

[94] H.A. 1985, s.87.

[95] *Ibid.* s.88.

[96] *Ibid.* s.88(1).

[97] *I.e.* under *ibid.* s.89.

tenancy was assigned pursuant to an order under section 24 of the Matrimonial Causes Act 1973[98] is only treated as a "successor" for these purposes if the other party to the marriage was originally a "successor"[99]; and a tenant to whom the tenancy was assigned pursuant to the statutory exchange provisions[1] is only treated as a "successor" if he was a successor in relation to the tenancy which he himself assigned.[2]

9.36 A separate provision deals with the situation where, within six months of the ending of a periodic secure tenancy, the tenant becomes a tenant under another periodic secure tenancy, he was a "successor" as regards the former tenancy, and under the new tenancy either the dwelling or the landlord (or both) is (or are) the same as under the former tenancy: in this situation the tenant is a successor in respect of the *new* tenancy also (thus prohibiting any statutory succession on his death), unless the new tenancy agreement otherwise provides.[3] This devious provision, whereby successorship may be carried forward from one tenancy to another, will often operate in practice where the former tenancy has been ended by a possession order obtained on the "under-occupation" ground.[4]

9.37 **(v) The position where there is no statutory successor.** Where there is no member of the dead tenant's family who is qualified to succeed to the periodic secure tenancy under these provisions, and the tenancy is accordingly dealt with in the course of the administration of the dead tenant's estate, then the tenancy generally ceases to be secure.[5]

98 See Chap. 11; similarly, where the secure tenancy is transferred by court order pursuant to Sched. 1 to M.H.A. 1983 (see Chap. 11), and the former tenant-spouse was a "successor" for the purposes of H.A. 1985, s.88, then (and only then) is the transferee also deemed to be a successor: M.H.A. 1983, Sched. 1, Pt. II, para. 2(3).

99 H.A. 1985, s.88(2). An example may help. Assume that Y, who satisfies the 12 months' residence requirement, wishes to take the secure periodic tenancy of her dead mother, Mrs. X, a widow. Y will be eligible if Mrs. X was the original tenant or gained the tenancy from her husband Mr. X under M.C.A. 1973, s.24, where he was the original tenant; but Y will not be eligible if Mrs. X gained the tenancy from Mr. X on his death, or if she gained the tenancy from him under s.24 of the 1973 Act but he was then himself a "successor," *e.g.* through having taken the secure tenancy on his mother's death. Y therefore had some interest in fomenting matrimonial discord between her parents!

1 H.A. 1985, s.92; see above, paras. 9.20–9.23.

2 H.A. 1985, s.88(3).

3 *Ibid.* s.88(4).

4 *Ibid.* Sched. 2, Pt. III, gd. 16, see above, para. 8.63.

5 H.A. 1985, s.89(3).

However, there is an exception to this rule applying where the secure tenancy is disposed of by the personal representatives in pursuance of an order made under section 24 of the Matrimonial Causes Act 1973.[6] This exception deals with the situation where the divorce court has previously made an order regulating what is to happen to the secure tenancy in the event of the tenant's death: for example,[7] the divorce court may have ordered the secure tenancy to be transferred forthwith from the former husband to the former wife, but with the proviso that on the former wife's death the secure tenancy is to be revested in the former husband if he is then still alive. By virtue of this exception, the *secure* tenancy can be duly transferred to the former husband on the former wife's death. **9.38**

Where a tenancy ceases to be secure following the tenant's death, it cannot subsequently become secure again,[8] and it continues as an ordinary contractual tenancy at common law until terminated in one of the appropriate ways, such as surrender or notice to quit.[9] While the (now non-secure) tenancy is still on foot following the tenant's death, the council has no *locus standi* to institute possession proceedings against third parties found in the dwelling, such as squatters[10] or sub-tenants[11] of the deceased tenant. **9.39**

(vi) Comparison with the succession scheme under the Rent Act. These complicated succession provisions differ significantly from those in the Rent Act 1977[12] (where "members of the family" are not comprehensively defined, the residence requirement for a claimant who is neither the spouse nor the cohabitee of the dead tenant is two years, and a second statutory succession stage is permitted). It is suggested that excessive difficulties are caused by the prohibition in the Housing Act 1985 of a second succession to a per- **9.40**

[6] H.A. 1985, s.89(3); for M.C.A. 1973, s.24, see Chap. 11.

[7] See J. Luba, N. Madge and D. McConnell, *Defending Possession Proceedings* (1987), p. 11.

[8] H.A. 1985, s.89(4).

[9] Where the authority wishes to serve a notice to quit, this should be served on the deceased tenant's executor (if any); if there is no executor, then the administrator is the appropriate recipient if a grant of letters of administration has been obtained, failing which, the notice to quit should be served on the President of the Family Division of the High Court: see Administration of Estates Act 1925, s.9; *Practice Direction*, [1985] 1 All E.R. 832; *Wirral B.C.* v. *Smith and Cooper* (1982) 80 L.G.R. 628 (C.A.).

[10] *Wirral B.C.* v. *Smith, ibid.*

[11] *Preston B.C.* v. *Fairclough* (1983) 8 H.L.R. 70 (C.A.).

[12] R.A. 1977, Sched. 1 (as amended by H.A. 1988, s.39 and Sched. 4, Pt. I).

iodic secure tenancy, and by the wide definition of "successor" in the Act.[13] A second succession stage should be permitted, as in the Rent Act: authorities would then still be adequately safeguarded against under-occupation by non-spouse successors, through the availability of the "under-occupation" ground for possession.[14]

(c) *Fixed-term secure tenancies*

9.41 Where the secure tenancy is for a fixed term, and the tenant dies, the tenancy will cease to be secure[15] if *either*:

(i) the tenancy is disposed of by the tenant's personal representatives to someone who is neither a member of the tenant's family who is "qualified to succeed" him[16] nor a person to whom the personal representatives are disposing of the tenancy pursuant to a court order under section 24 of the Matrimonial Causes Act 1973[17]; *or*
(ii) it is known that when the tenancy has been so disposed of, it will not pass to such a person.

Thus, broadly speaking, if the relevant beneficiary is a member of the tenant's family who is qualified to succeed him, the *secure* tenancy (and not merely the contractual tenancy) will pass following the death; while if the relevant beneficiary is not so qualified, the *secure* tenancy will end, but the *contractual* tenancy will pass, so that the authority will not normally be entitled to possession until the end of the fixed term.

9.42 Where a fixed-term secure tenancy ceases to be secure under these provisions following the tenant's death, then it cannot subsequently become secure again.[18]

[13] H.A. 1985, s.88, see above, para. 9.35.
[14] H.A. 1985, Sched. 2, Pt. III, gd. 16.
[15] *Ibid.* s.90.
[16] *I.e. ibid.* s.87, see above.
[17] See above, para. 9.38.
[18] H.A. 1985, s.90(4).

10 Rent Fixing

1. *The Relationship between Law and Policy*

(a) *The legal framework*

The legal framework within which local authorities can fix and subsequently increase the rents of their properties is very flexible, although in practice (as will be seen) this flexibility is more apparent than real, in view of the financial controls which central government is now able to exert. **10.01**

Authorities are exempt from all the detailed provisions for rent-fixing which govern the private sector.[1] Instead, they have a very wide power under the Housing Act 1985[2] to "make such reasonable charges as they may determine," and we shall see that the courts have proved most reluctant to interfere with the exercise of this power. However, the Local Government and Housing Bill 1989 provides for the amending of the 1985 Act by the addition of a requirement that, in determining their rents, authorities must "have regard in particular to the principle that the rents of [dwellings] of any class or description should bear broadly the same proportion to private sector [market] rents as the rents of [dwellings] of any other class or description."[2a] This means that authorities would have to consider, for example, the desirability of keeping the ratio between council rents and private sector market rents in relation to modern terraced housing in line with the ratio between council rents and private sector market rents in relation to purpose-built flats, and if a council could be shown completely to have failed to consider this "relati- **10.02**

[1] See R.A. 1977, ss.14, 19(5)(*aa*); H.A. 1988, Sched. 1, Pt. I, para. 12.

[2] H.A. 1985, s.24(1).

[2a] L.G. & H.B. 1989, cl. 129, adding new subss. (3)–(4) to H.A. 1985, s.24; the new s.24(4) defines "private sector rents" for this purpose as the rents recoverable if the dwellings were let on private sector "assured" tenancies under H.A. 1988, Pt. I, which in turn provides for *market* rents (H.A. 1988, s.14(1)); H.A. 1985, s.24 refers to "houses," but this expression is defined (in *ibid.* s.56) to include flats.

vity" principle, then its rent determinations would be open to challenge. This new amendment does not require that council rents should be the same as private sector market rents for comparable dwellings: the principle is concerned with relative proportions as between the different classes or descriptions of dwellings in the public and private sectors respectively.

10.02a An authority is normally precluded from increasing the rent on account of a tenant's improvements.[3] Furthermore, the Minister can make an order restricting the amount of rent which would otherwise be payable on new lettings of dwellings, or restricting or preventing rent increases[4]; but such an order can only so provide "generally or in relation to any specified description of dwelling,"[5] and thus cannot be aimed at an individual council or council house. No such orders are currently in force.

10.03 The general legal freedom regarding the fixing of initial rents also extends to the determination of rent increases: authorities are merely required to review their rents "from time to time," and to make "such changes . . . as circumstances may require."[6]

10.04 Authorities have to maintain a "Housing Revenue Account,"[7] into which is paid the rent income, together with subsidies from central government and contributions from the general rates; and out of which must be taken the sums necessary for the capital repayments and interest on loans raised, together with the cost of management, repairs and maintenance. Any deficits in the Housing Revenue Account must be met from the general rate fund.[8] There is also a general power to carry to the credit of the Housing Revenue Account "such further amounts, if any, as [the authority] may think fit" out of the general rate fund[9]; this general power can be exercised before the end of the relevant financial year, and it is not a precondition of its exercise that a contribution has already had to be made in order to remedy a deficit in the account.[10] The account can be allowed to

[3] H.A. 1985, s.101, see below, paras. 12.91–12.94.
[4] L. & T.A. 1985, s.31(1).
[5] *Ibid.*
[6] H.A. 1985, s.24(2).
[7] *Ibid.* ss.417–418, and Sched. 14.
[8] *Ibid.* Sched. 14, Pt. IV, para. 4(1); however, a new housing revenue account regime has been introduced by cll. 63–65 and Sched. 4 of the Local Government and Housing Bill 1989, under which authorities will no longer be able to make any contributions from their general funds into the housing revenue account; in many areas, the effect of this reform will be to compel authorities to increase rents.
[9] H.A. 1985, Sched. 14, Pt. IV, para. 4(2); but see n. 8 above.
[10] *Hemsted* v. *Lees and Norwich C.C.* (1986) 18 H.L.R. 424.

show a profit, (*i.e.* there is now no restriction to a mere working balance in the account); any such profit must either be carried forward into the next accounting period, or credited to the general rate fund (*i.e.* to non-housing expenditure).[11]

(b) *Practical problems*

The fixing of council rents has always been an intensely political matter, which "perhaps attract[s] more discussion—and dissension—than any other aspect of local authority housing policy."[12] Until recently, the structure of public housing finance largely depended on Exchequer subsidies; but it is now common for individual housing authorities outside the London area to receive either very little central government subsidy,[13] or indeed no general housing subsidy[14] at all, and such authorities are consequently often forced to borrow heavily in order to "balance the books." **10.05**

Council rent-fixing has never been an exact science: considerable regional variations have long been apparent, and councils have been accused of deciding their rents against a backdrop of "untested assumptions, expediency, convention and lack of basic data."[15] The inter-relation of council rents with authorities' mandatory rent rebate schemes, and with the income support system, is examined later in this chapter; in fixing their rents, councils share a basic dilemma with the D.S.S. in its administration of welfare benefits: "principles must be reconciled with some degree of administrative convenience and simplicity . . . A highly complex scheme may be very fair, but also virtually incomprehensible."[16] **10.06**

Although the fluctuations between the rent levels of different authorities can be dramatic, the rents of the various types of dwellings within the same individual authority may not differ as much as **10.07**

[11] H.A. 1985, Sched. 14, Pt. V, para. 1; however, under the new housing revenue account scheme in the Local Government and Housing Bill 1989, profits on the account will no longer be transferable to the credit of the authority's general funds: such profits must instead be retained within the housing revenue account and carried forward into the next accounting period under that account, unless the profits are creamed off by the Minister "in accordance with such formulae as [he] may . . . determine" (Sched. 4, Pts. I–II); thus the Minister could utilise profits on housing revenue accounts to subsidise more needy authorities.

[12] J. B. Cullingworth, *Housing and Local Government* (1960), p. 172; this statement was of course made before the introduction of the "right to buy"!

[13] See, *e.g.* *Hemsted* v. *Lees and Norwich C.C.* (1986) 18 H.L.R. 424.

[14] *I.e.* as opposed to rent rebate subsidy.

[15] R. A. Parker, *The Rents of Council Houses* (1967), p. 72.

[16] J. B. Cullingworth, *loc. cit.*

might be expected, due to the system known as "rent pooling," whereby the rents of the newer properties are subsidised by the older properties.[16a] The suggestion that rent-pooling should be operated on a nationwide basis was rejected by the government in 1977[17] on the ground that the expense of subsidising high housing costs should fall on the community as a whole, and not solely on council tenants elsewhere who happen to enjoy low housing costs.

10.08 To these recurrent problems have been added, over the past 15 years or so, acute difficulties resulting from escalating Housing Revenue Account costs, particularly the interest repayments on loans taken out to finance capital expenditure.

(c) *Recent changes in policy*

10.09 Against this background, it may be useful briefly to review the quite dramatic changes in policy affecting council rents over the last two decades.

10.10 By 1971, the chaotic system of council rent-fixing and the variations between the rent rebate schemes adopted by different authorities was causing considerable concern to the then Conservative government; in particular, the government felt that the system of housing subsidies was reducing council rents without paying proper regard to tenants' incomes. The government accordingly proposed, in a 1971 White Paper, the introduction of a uniform nationwide council rent-fixing scheme, geared to private sector "fair rent" principles, together with *mandatory* national rent rebate and allowance schemes for both public and private sector tenants, and a revamping of the subsidies system[18]; the "central policy" of the proposals was described as one of "subsidising people, not bricks and mortar."[19]

10.11 These proposals became law in the Housing Finance Act 1972. The provisions relating to mandatory rent rebates and allowances have since been carried forward, substantially amended, in the Social Security Act 1986[20] and consequential regulations; but the mandatory "fair rents" scheme for council tenants[21] generated

[16a] However, the ability of councils to operate "rent pooling" schemes will to some extent be curtailed by the new s.24(3)–(4) of H.A. 1985, introduced by L.G. & H.B. 1989: see above, para. 10.02.

[17] Green Paper on *Housing Policy*, Cmnd. 6851, p. 87.

[18] White Paper, *Fair Deal for Housing*, Cmnd. 4728.

[19] *Op. cit.* p. 11.

[20] See below, paras. 10.48 to 10.49.

[21] For an account of the workings of the scheme see, *e.g.* D. Yates, (1972) 36 Conv. (N.S.) 402.

intense opposition, and was repealed, following a change of government, by the Housing Rents and Subsidies Act 1975. The 1975 Act broadly restored to authorities their pre-1972 freedom to fix rents as they wished,[22] although it did not affect their duty to operate a rent rebate scheme. The Act also severely limited the extent to which authorities could make a profit from council housing, by restricting the surplus in Housing Revenue Accounts to a "working balance," although (as we have seen) this restriction has since been removed.[23]

By 1980, after another change of government, steps were once **10.12**
more taken to interfere with the discretion of authorities in the field of rent-fixing, but this time the methods adopted in order to reimpose a measure of central control over rent levels were much more subtle than those employed in the Housing Finance Act 1972. The Housing Act 1980 retained[24] the discretion in law for councils to fix their own rents, but it provided a new system of housing subsidies (since re-enacted in the Housing Act 1985[25]) which provided the means for rents to be raised indirectly, in such a way that central government can call the tune but councils have to field the brickbats. Basically, in order to receive general housing subsidy from the government, authorities have to raise rents to levels decided upon by the Minister (after consultation with the local authority associations), and spend no more on repairs and maintenance than the Minister authorises (after such consultation), failing which they will lose some or all of this government subsidy and will often have to make good any shortfall from the general rates.[26]

The result of this scheme has been that (as noted earlier) most **10.13**
authorities no longer receive general housing subsidies from the government. However, even where the Minister's "persuasion" regarding rent levels and repair and maintenance costs is no longer relevant because the particular authority is not receiving subsidy

[22] See D. Yates, (1975) 39 Conv. (N.S.) 387.

[23] H.A. 1985, Sched. 14, Pt. V, para. 1, see above, para. 10.04.

[24] In Pt. VI.

[25] In Pt. XIII; for a straightforward account of the workings of the current scheme, see H. Aughton, *Housing Finance—A Basic Guide* (1986), Chap. 3.

[26] For a practical illustration, see the facts of *Hemsted* v. *Lees and Norwich C.C.* (1986) 18 H.L.R. 424; but see n. 8, above. L.G. & H.B. 1989, Pt. VI, introduces a new "Housing Revenue Account Subsidy" to replace the housing subsidy scheme in H.A. 1985; however, in calculating this "Housing Revenue Account Subsidy" the Minister may similarly determine a formula by reference to amounts which he *assumes* authorities *ought* to have raised, by way of (for example) rental income: see cl. 69(3).

anyway, the Minister has a further subtle method of "persuasion" regarding rate support grant affecting general expenditure (*i.e.* expenditure not specifically related to housing) under Part VI of the Local Government, Planning and Land Act 1980[27]: this gives the Minister power to penalise a council in terms of rate support grant if the average levels of its rents are lower than the regional average; although this particular power has not in practice been exercised by the Minister recently, it was used shortly after the Local Government, Planning and Land Act came into force and it could be reactivated at any time.

10.14 Councils are therefore currently placed in an unenviable position concerning rent increases: in law, the decision is theirs alone, but in practice the decision to put up the rent will very often be forced upon them, since they would otherwise run the risk of losing valuable subsidies. There has been a marked change of emphasis from the general subsidising of the "bricks and mortar" of council houses to the subsidising of individual council tenants through means-tested rent rebates and income support. In the course of proposing yet further reforms in local authority housing finance, the government stated in July 1988 that one objective of the new scheme would be that "[r]ents generally should not exceed levels within the reach of people in low paid employment, and in practice they will frequently be below market levels"[28]; this passage implies that "market" council rents will not be at all unusual in the near future.

2. *The Machinery for Implementing Rent Increases*

10.15 If an authority has decided in its "discretion" to increase its rents (albeit after Ministerial prompting), it must next ensure that the appropriate formalities are observed in order that the increase can take effect; whether or not the tenancy is secure, there is no system of "phasing" increases in order to ease the burden on the tenant.[29]

[27] A thorough explanation of the rate support grant system is contained in the judgment of Ackner L.J. in *R.* v. *Secretary of State for the Environment, ex p. Brent L.B.C.* [1983] 2 Q.B. 593 (D.C.).

[28] D.O.E., *New Financial Regime for Local Authority Housing in England and Wales: A Consultation Paper*, para. 11.

[29] *Cf.* the phasing rules formerly governing the private sector under R.A. 1977, s.55 and Sched. 8; these private sector phasing rules have, however, now been withdrawn in most cases (see S.I. 1987 No. 264, and H.A. 1988, Sched. 17, para. 24).

(a) *Secure tenancies*

At common law, it is clear that "a landlord cannot, *in the absence of agreement*, increase the rent, against the will of the tenant, unless he gives notice to quit and determines the tenancy."[30] However, we have seen[31] that under the Housing Act 1985 authorities cannot use a notice to quit as a method of determining secure periodic tenancies, and we have also noted[32] the provisions in the 1985 Act[33] whereby the express terms of a secure tenancy can only be varied by one of three methods, *i.e.*: (i) by ad hoc agreement; (ii) by virtue of a provision in the tenancy agreement permitting unilateral variation; or (iii) by statutory notice of variation. **10.16**

With regard to the second method, this in effect gives statutory validity to the common law's recognition of a "unilateral variation clause" under which the rent could be increased on the giving of reasonable notice by the landlord[34]; the requirement of reasonable notice of the increase is not spelled out in the 1985 Act, but is clearly implicit. We have seen[35] that the 1985 Act[36] in fact restricts these unilateral variation clauses, as regards secure tenancies, to matters concerning rent, rates or services. **10.17**

As regards the third statutory method of variation, that of notice of variation (of at least four weeks) where the tenancy is periodic, we have noted[37] that in the case of a variation relating to the rent or rates or to payments in respect of services or facilities provided by the authority, no preliminary notice need be served on the tenant (giving him information about the nature and effect of the variation and an opportunity to comment),[38] although the notice of variation itself has to be accompanied by information about its nature and effect.[39] As we have already seen,[40] the tenant can prevent the notice of variation from taking effect by giving a notice to quit before the effective date of the notice of variation (whereupon the notice of vari- **10.18**

30 *Per* Lord Denning M.R. in *G.L.C.* v. *Connolly* [1970] 1 All E.R. 870, 873 (C.A.), italics supplied.
31 See above, para. 8.19.
32 See above, paras. 7.62–7.66.
33 H.A. 1985, ss.102–103.
34 *G.L.C.* v. *Connolly* [1970] 1 All E.R. 870, 873 (C.A.).
35 See above, para. 7.65.
36 H.A. 1985, s.102(1)(*b*).
37 See above, para. 7.66.
38 H.A. 1985, s. 103(2)–(3); this is consistent with the general exemption of rent-fixing from the consultation process: see s.105(2), discussed below, para. 13.09.
39 H.A. 1985, s.103(5).
40 See above, para. 7.67.

ation can only be effective if the tenant, with the authority's written agreement, withdraws the notice to quit)[41]; the tenant does not have to be told in the notice of variation of his right to end the tenancy by notice to quit.[42]

(b) *Non-secure tenancies*

10.19 Where the tenancy is not secure, the variation rules in the 1985 Act (which we have just considered) cannot apply. Here the authority may increase the rent by one of the following methods:

(i) by ad hoc agreement;
(ii) by common law unilateral variation clause[43];
(iii) by notice to quit and substitution of a fresh tenancy agreement providing for the increased rent; or
(iv) by the special procedure in the 1985 Act[44] relating to non-secure tenancies, which enables authorities to serve on the tenant a notice of increase (at least four weeks in advance) without serving a notice to quit, although the tenant must be told of his right to end the tenancy by notice to quit if he wishes.[45]

3. *Challenges to the Rent*

10.20 The rent-fixing process for council housing is much less regulated and standardised than the schemes designed for the private sector (where tenants may have their rents considered, where appropriate, by Rent Officers, Rent Assessment Committees or Rent Tribunals). Even a secure tenant has no right to be consulted or to be heard in relation to rent fixing.[46] Originally, under the Housing Act 1957,[47] the Minister had the power to hold a local inquiry into a council's rents; but this power was removed by the Local Government Act 1972.

10.21 If a council tenant (or other ratepayer) wishes to challenge the authority's rents as being unreasonable, he might of course try infor-

[41] H.A. 1985, s.103(6).
[42] *Cf.* H.A. 1985, s.25(3)(*b*), which concerns notices of increase relating to non-secure tenancies: see below, para. 10.19.
[43] See *G.L.C.* v. *Connolly* [1970] 1 All E.R. 870, 873 (C.A.)
[44] H.A. 1985, s.25.
[45] *Ibid.* s.25(3)(*b*); this last requirement (formerly contained in the Prices and Incomes Act 1968, s.12(3)) was not satisfied in *Connolly's* case, see above, n. 43.
[46] H.A. 1985, ss.103(3), 105(2).
[47] H.A. 1957, ss.171–176, 181.

mal pressure on local councillors. If this proves unsuccessful, then there are nevertheless three principal challenges which the council may have to face.

(a) *Audit*

Official intervention may occur through the medium of an ordinary audit of the authority's accounts under Part III of the Local Government Finance Act 1982: the auditor (who is appointed by the Audit Commission) might decide that a particular rent scheme is unreasonable and *ultra vires* because (for example) it unreasonably increases the deficit on the Housing Revenue Account,[48] in which case he may apply to the High Court or a county court for a declaration that the scheme is "contrary to law"[49] (excessive expenditure or the improper exercise of discretion can be "contrary to law"[50]). Any local government elector for the relevant area can make objections to the auditor regarding the authority's accounts,[51] and if he remains dissatisfied by the auditor's decision, the elector may appeal to the High Court or a county court,[52] which can then make the necessary declaration. Furthermore, the Audit Commission has the power, on the application of a local government elector, to order an auditor to hold an extraordinary audit of the authority's accounts.[53] **10.22**

(b) *Local ombudsman*

Failure by an authority to deal properly with a tenant's rent problems can amount to "maladministration," allowing an appeal to be made to a local ombudsman under Part III of the Local Government Act 1974.[54] **10.23**

[48] See "The Case of the St. Pancras Rents," *The Listener*, May 26, 1960, p. 919 (quoted by R. A. Parker, *op. cit.* p. 11).
[49] L.G.F.A. 1982, s.19(1), (6).
[50] *Roberts* v. *Hopwood* [1925] A.C. 578 (H.L.); *Taylor* v. *Munrow* [1960] 1 W.L.R 151 (D.C.).
[51] L.G.F.A. 1982, s.17(3).
[52] L.G.F.A. 1982, s.19(4), (6); see, *e.g. Hemsted* v. *Lees and Norwich C.C.* (1986) 18 H.L.R. 424.
[53] L.G.F.A. 1982, s.22(1).
[54] See above, paras. 2.44–2.45; see also Complaint No. 1094/S/77.

(c) *Court action*

10.24 The cases decided on council rent-fixing are few compared with the decisions on private sector rents, and do not hold many prizes in store for the disgruntled council tenant or other ratepayer who wishes to challenge the rent in the courts merely on the ground of unreasonableness (as opposed to the presence of some defect in the authority's own internal decision-making procedure[55]).

10.25 **(i) Getting the case to court.** The question of whether the authority's rents are "reasonable" will normally be brought before the court by a disgruntled tenant on the ground that they are too high, although the rents may also be challenged by a non-tenant ratepayer on the ground that they are too low[56]; such a ratepayer will normally only have *locus standi* to bring an ordinary action in his own name if he obtains the consent of the Attorney-General to relator proceedings.[57]

10.26 The usual remedy sought is a declaration that the rent scheme is unreasonable, so that it is *ultra vires* the authority and so void.[58] An injunction may also be claimed, where appropriate, to restrain the authority from carrying out the scheme.[59] Where the authority is claiming possession from a tenant on the ground of rent arrears, the tenant may challenge the validity of the rent by way of defence to the possession proceedings, relying on his existing private law rights as tenant, and he is not required to raise this issue by separate proceedings for judicial review under Order 53 of the Rules of the Supreme Court.[60]

[55] See, *e.g.* the case briefly reported in *The Times*, February 14, 1981, where Forbes J. decided that a council's rent increase was invalid because the housing committee had adjourned the matter to another place (because of rowdy behaviour in the public gallery to the council chamber) before reaching its decision, whereas under the council's standing orders the committee could only adjourn the matter to another time, and not to another place.

[56] See, *e.g.* *Evans* v. *Collins* [1964] 1 All E.R. 808 (D.C.); *Hemsted* v. *Lees and Norwich C.C.* (1986) 18 H.L.R. 424.

[57] *Barrs* v. *Bethell* [1982] Ch. 294; in this case the Attorney–General's consent was subsequently given: *The Times*, July 17, 1981.

[58] *Smith* v. *Cardiff Corpn.* [1955] 1 All E.R. 113.

[59] *Belcher* v. *Reading Corpn.* [1949] 2 All E.R. 969.

[60] *Wandsworth L.B.C.* v. *Winder* [1985] A.C. 461 (H.L.); see above, para. 8.32, n. 99.

English court procedure (unlike that in parts of the United States[61]) does not permit a comprehensive "class action" to be brought where numerous people (such as the tenants of a council) have suffered the same wrong.[62] Nevertheless, if the tenants of an authority have a sufficient "common interest" or "common grievance" in relation to the fixing of their rents, then it may not be necessary for each tenant to proceed as an individual against the authority: in this situation, one or more of them may be permitted to bring a "representative action" on behalf of the others, claiming relief beneficial to all[63] (typically, a declaration and/or an injunction[64]). It will not always be the case, however, that council tenants will have a sufficient "unanimity of interest" for a representative action.[65] **10.27**

Where such a representative action does lie, it appears that in an appropriate case even damages may be recovered by a plaintiff in his representative capacity, if the same damage has been suffered by all members of the particular class and those members have consented to all pecuniary remedies being granted to the plaintiff in respect of the action brought on their behalf[66]; in such a case the plaintiff will hold the appropriate sums recovered on trust for the other members of the class.[67] **10.28**

A tenant seeking to challenge the authority's rent may encounter grave difficulties in obtaining legal aid: for example, in one case[68] two tenants who wanted to apply for judicial review of their council's decision on their rent were refused legal aid, on the ground (*inter alia*) that the proposed claim was essentially a representative action, **10.29**

[61] See G. Van Bueren, [1983] August L.A.G. Bull. 7; S. Hughes, [1988] May Legal Action 8.

[62] See R. Campbell & W. Morrison, [1987] L.S.Gaz. 2585; Sir John Donaldson M.R. has recommended consideration of the need for introducing a class action: see *Davies* v. *Eli Lilley & Co.* [1987] 3 All E.R. 94, 96 (C.A.).

[63] R.S.C., Ord. 15, r. 12; C.C.R. 1981, Ord. 5, r. 5.

[64] See *John* v. *Rees* [1969] 2 W.L.R. 1294.

[65] See, *e.g. Smith* v. *Cardiff Corpn.* [1953] 2 All E.R. 1373 (C.A.), where the tenants were complaining about a "differential rent scheme" (as to which see below, para. 10.35) which would have benefited some 5,000 of them and adversely affected the other 8,000; but *cf. Pan Atlantic Insurance Co.* v. *Pine Top Insurance Co., The Times*, May 23, 1988.

[66] *E.M.I. Records* v. *Riley* [1981] 1 W.L.R. 923; but *cf. Prudential Assurance Co.* v. *Newman Industries (No. 1)* [1980] 2 W.L.R. 339.

[67] *E.M.I. Records Ltd.* v. *Riley, ibid.*

[68] See letter in [1985] June Legal Action 13.

in respect of which a refusal would not substantially prejudice the rights of the particular tenants.[69]

10.30 **(ii) The difficulty of proving unreasonableness.** It is clear that the burden of proving that the rent scheme is unreasonable[70] lies firmly on the tenant (or other challenger[71]). The courts have emphasised that rent-fixing often involves matters which concern "social policy,"[72] and which are therefore seen as "not really matters of law at all."[73] Indeed, it appears that there is only one reported case in which a court has struck down an authority's rent as being unreasonable[74]; this decision was unsurprising, given that it was concerned with an increase in the rent of an ordinary council house from £7.71 per week to £18,000 per week![75]

10.31 **(iii) Specific principles.** Apart from indicating the heavy burden involved in proving the "unreasonableness" of an authority's rents, and the "social policy" dimensions of the rent-fixing process, the cases have also laid down various specific principles.

10.32 The rents must be objectively reasonable, and not merely reasonable in the authority's opinion.[76] Furthermore, there is a duty on the authority to consider the interests of its tenants as a whole, and those of the "general body of ratepayers"[77]: a balance must be maintained between the *interests* of these two "sections of the local com-

[69] See Legal Aid Regulations 1980 (S.I. 1980 No. 1894) reg. 33(2); in November 1988 the Lord Chancellor asked the new Legal Aid Board (set up under the Legal Aid Act 1988) to consider fresh procedures whereby actions raising "common problems" (*i.e.* joint actions) could be more effectively brought under the legal aid scheme: *The Times*, November 14, 1988.

[70] "Unreasonableness" is tested in accordance with the administrative law principles laid down in *Associated Provincial Picture Houses* v. *Wednesbury Corpn.* [1948] 1 K.B. 223 (C.A.), see above, paras. 6.08–6.21; see also *L.B. of Wandsworth* v. *Winder (No.2)* (1987) 19 H.L.R. 204, 208–209 (Ch.D.), (1988) 20 H.L.R. 400, 402–403 (C.A.).

[71] See, *e.g. Smith* v. *Cardiff Corpn.* [1955] 1 All E.R. 113, 121; *R.* v. *G.L.C., ex p. R.B. of Kensington & Chelsea, The Times,* April 7, 1982 (D.C.).

[72] *Evans* v. *Collins* [1964] 1 All E.R. 808, 812 (D.C.); *Hemsted* v. *Lees and Norwich C.C.* (1986) 18 H.L.R. 424, 430; *Mandeville* v. *G.L.C., The Times,* January 28, 1982.

[73] *Evans's* case, *loc. cit.*

[74] *Backhouse* v. *Lambeth B.C., The Times,* October 14, 1972.

[75] This bizarre arrangement was designed to bring the authority's rent total above the figure which would exempt it from making the general increases in rent otherwise required by the Housing Finance Act 1972, ss.62(1)–63(1).

[76] *Smith* v. *Cardiff Corpn.* [1955] 1 All E.R. 113, 121.

[77] *Belcher* v. *Reading Corpn.* [1949] 2 All E.R. 969, 983; *Hemsted* v. *Lees and Norwich C.C.* (1986) 18 H.L.R. 424, 428.

munity,"[78] but there is no obligation to consider the relative *means* of those two groups.[79]

There is no duty to fix "economic" rents,[80] (*i.e.* the rents at which dwellings must be let if they are to cover the costs of loan repayments, management, repairs and maintenance), nor to make a profit out of the tenants by charging market rents.[81] Conversely, there is "no justification in the Housing Acts" for "the notion that a council house . . . must necessarily be run at a loss,"[82] and the idea that tenants who have occupied council houses for a long time should be immune from rent increases "has no justification at all."[83] Prior to the Local Government and Housing Bill 1989 the authority was not obliged to consider legislation regarding private sector rents[84]; however, the 1989 Bill introduces the principle of "proportionality" with private sector rents for "assured" tenancies under Part I of the Housing Act 1988.[85] **10.33**

The authority may fix rents by reference to the needs and capacities of tenants in broad groups, rather than by reference to the needs of individual tenants, provided a balance is kept between the tenants and the ratepayers.[86] A "pooling" system may be operated whereby the rents of older housing subsidise those of the newer properties[87]; moreover, rents may be geared to the rateable values of the houses,[88] **10.34**

[78] *Ibid.*; see also *Mandeville* v. *G.L.C., The Times* January 28, 1982; national statistics of a very general nature are not of any real value in this balancing exercise, *L.B. of Wandsworth* v. *Winder (No. 2)* (1988) 20 H.L.R. 400, 407 (C.A.).

[79] *L.B. of Wandsworth* v. *Winder (No. 2)* (1987) 19 H.L.R. 204, 215 (Ch.D.), (1988) 20 H.L.R. 400, 406 (C.A.).

[80] *Summerfield* v. *Hampstead B.C.* [1957] 1 All E.R. 221, 225–226; *L.B. of Wandsworth* v. *Winder (No. 2)* (Ch.D.), *ibid.* p. 215.

[81] *Evans* v. *Collins* [1964] 1 All E.R. 808, 811–812 (D.C.); *Hemsted* v. *Lees and Norwich C.C.* (1986) 18 H.L.R. 424, 430; but note the new duty on authorities to have regard to the principle of "proportionality" with private sector market rents, introduced by the Local Government and Housing Bill 1989, and discussed above, para. 10.02.

[82] *Per* Harman J. in *Summerfield* v. *Hampstead B.C.* [1957] 1 All E.R. 221, 226; and see now H.A. 1985, Sched. 14, Pt. V, para. 1, discussed above, para. 10.04.

[83] *Per* Romer J. in *Belcher* v. *Reading Corpn.* [1949] 2 All E.R. 969, 981.

[84] *L.B. of Wandsworth* v. *Winder (No. 2)* (1987) 19 H.L.R. 204, 216 (Ch.D.).

[85] See above, para. 10.02.

[86] *Evans* v. *Collins* [1964] 1 All E.R. 808, 814 (D.C.); see also *Mandeville* v. *G.L.C., The Times,* January 28, 1982 (lettings at double the normal rent to tenants who were prospective "right to buy" purchasers upheld).

[87] *Summerfield* v. *Hampstead B.C.* [1957] 1 All E.R. 221, 225–226; but see above, n. 16A.

[88] *Luby* v. *Newcastle-under-Lyme Corpn.* [1964] 3 All E.R. 169, 173 (C.A.).

and many authorities do in practice use rateable values in order conveniently to adjust rent levels as between properties of various types.

10.35 There is no duty to subsidise rents, whether generally[89] or through the operation of a differential rent scheme[90] (*i.e.* a scheme where the rent is adjusted to the individual tenant's income and needs). But differential rent schemes have long been judicially sanctioned,[91] and the discretion to provide them survives[92] the introduction of a mandatory rent rebate scheme by the Housing Finance Act 1972[93] (the current statutory scheme is prescribed by the Social Security Act 1986). The mandatory rent rebate scheme[94] has diminished the importance of differential rent schemes generally, and the impact of the current rent rebate system in reducing or cancelling the effects of rent increases on housing benefit claimants must, it seems, be considered when fixing general rent levels.[95] It also appears that the authority must consider in general terms the incidence of government subsidy, both in the shape of general housing subsidy (if any) and rent rebate subsidy, in so far as this affects any particular rent scheme which it plans to introduce[96]; at the other extreme, if an authority were to adopt a rent-fixing scheme solely in order to obtain an increased government subsidy, the decision might well be open to attack on the ground of improper purpose, although the heavy burden of proving bad faith on the part of the decision-makers would have to be discharged.[97] Where appropriate, the

[89] *L.B. of Wandsworth* v. *Winder (No. 2)* (1987) 19 H.L.R. 204, 215 (Ch.D.).

[90] *Evans* v. *Collins* [1964] 1 All E.R. 808, 812 (D.C.); *Luby* v. *Newcastle-under-Lyme Corpn.* [1964] 3 All E.R. 169, 173 (C.A.)

[91] See, *e.g. Leeds Corpn.* v. *Jenkinson* [1935] 1 K.B. 181 (C.A.); *Summerfield* v. *Hampstead B.C.* [1957] 1 All E.R. 221, 225–226.

[92] The contrary view, expressed in *Evans* v. *Collins* [1964] 1 All E.R. 808, 810, that the discretion to provide differential rent schemes came from the former power to grant rebates (n. 93), appears to be incorrect: *Luby* v. *Newcastle-under-Lyme Corpn.* [1964] 3 All E.R. 169, 172.

[93] Previously there was merely a *power* to grant rebates (see H.A. 1957, s.113(3)).

[94] Discussed below, paras. 10.48 to 10.49; the practical distinction between a differential rent scheme (defined above) and a rent rebate scheme is that "... in rent rebate schemes a standard rent is fixed and is generally related to some kind of concept of what the average tenant pays and deductions are made from it; whereas in differential rent schemes [the] maximum rent, being a full economic rent, may be very much higher" (D.O.E., *The Administration of the Rent Rebate and Rent Allowance Schemes* (1976), p. 21).

[95] *L.B. of Wandsworth* v. *Winder (No. 2)* (1987) 19 H.L.R. 204, 215 (Ch.D.).

[96] *R.* v. *Secretary of State for Health and Social Security, ex p. City of Sheffield* (1985) 18 H.L.R. 6, 21 (D.C.).

[97] *Ibid.*

authority must have regard to the fact that rate fund contributions will have to be increased if the rent is not put up.[98]

The rate of inflation need not be regarded as an "overriding consideration"[99]; and the mere fact that an increase in rent is very great is certainly no indication in itself that the authority's decision is unreasonable on *Wednesbury* principles.[1] **10.36**

Finally, it appears that the small number of council tenants who do not hold under secure tenancies[2] cannot claim that their lack of statutory security of tenure should be reflected in the fixing of lower rents for their dwellings than those fixed for their "secure" neighbours.[3] **10.37**

4. *Rent Arrears*

(a) *The extent of arrears*

Despite the help available to impecunious tenants by way of welfare benefits, particularly under the housing benefit scheme,[4] rent arrears pose a growing problem for many councils; even where tenants are entitled to housing benefit, many are ignorant of their rights and so do not claim. A survey by the D.O.E. published in 1987 revealed a figure of £211m. worth of arrears owed to English councils in 1986[5]; and in 1987 it was also estimated that nearly one in ten council tenants were then in arrears.[6] Studies have indicated that where individual tenants owe substantial sums, the causes are fre- **10.38**

[98] *L.B. of Wandsworth* v. *Winder (No. 2)* (1987) 19 H.L.R. 204, 216 (Ch.D.); but see above, n. 8, regarding the new housing revenue account scheme contained in L.G. & H.B. 1989.

[99] *L.B. of Wandsworth* v. *Winder (No. 2)* (1987) 19 H.L.R. 204, 216 (Ch.D.).

[1] *Ibid.*; see also *L.B. of Wandsworth* v. *Winder (No. 2)* (1988) 20 H.L.R. 400, 409 (C.A.): in the *Wandsworth* case, the increase was 37 per cent. at a time when inflation was only running at 10.5 per cent.; see also *Ricketts* v. *Havering L.B.C., The Times,* July 17, 1980 (charges for market stalls under Food and Drugs Act 1955, s.52(1)); *R.* v. *Waltham Forest L.B.C., ex p. Waltham Forest Ratepayers Action Group, The Times,* July 31, 1987 (D.C.), determination of general rates.

[2] See above, paras. 7.25–7.48.

[3] See by analogy *Palmer* v. *Peabody Trust* [1974] 3 All E.R. 355 (D.C.), where the housing trust in question was exempt from the security provisions in R.A. 1977 (under s.15 thereof), but the court refused to regard this as relevant to the fixing of the rent.

[4] See below, paras. 10.48 to 10.49.

[5] *The Times,* May 11, 1987.

[6] C.I.P.F.A., *Arrears Statistics* (March 1987).

quently low incomes or personal difficulties rather than any deliberate irresponsibility.[7]

(b) *Remedies for arrears*

10.39 **(i) Preliminary information duties.** Before attempting to recover arrears of rent or other sums (such as service charges), the authority must of course ensure that the relevant sums are legally due. Under the Landlord and Tenant Act 1987, any written demand for rent, service charges or other sums due under the tenancy must include the council's name and address[8]; failure to provide this information means that any relevant sum by way of *service charge* is treated as not being due from the tenant so long as the council remains in default, but this result only occurs in relation to *service charges*, as opposed to demands for rent *per se*.[9] Quite separately, however, the authority must, pursuant to the 1987 Act, furnish each tenant with an address at which notices may be served on it by him,[10] and if this address is not provided then any relevant service charge *or rent* is treated as not being due from the tenant so long as the authority's default continues.[11] These provisions in the 1987 Act apply to both secure and non-secure leases, but not to licences.[12]

10.40 **(ii) Methods of recovery.** Housing departments have been given detailed advice in government circulars and reports regarding alternatives to eviction in the case of rent arrears, and this guidance remains relevant even though, in the case of secure tenants, the authority is prevented by the Housing Act 1985 from actually recovering possession on the ground of rent arrears unless the court considers this to be reasonable.[13]

10.41 Some of this advice has merely been platitudinous[14]; but other suggestions have been more specifically helpful, drawing the atten-

[7] See, *e.g.* L. Alpren, *The Causes of Serious Rent Arrears* (1977), pp. 46–47; A. Harvey, *Remedies for Rent Arrears* (Shelter, 1979), p. 48; S. Duncan & K. Kirby, *Preventing Rent Arrears* (D.O.E., 1983); N. Fielding, *Roof*, May 1984, p. 23; see also D.O.E., *Housing (Homeless Persons) Act 1977 Code of Guidance (England & Wales)* (2nd ed., 1983), para. A1. 14.

[8] L. & T.A. 1987, s.47(1).

[9] *Ibid.* s.47(2).

[10] *Ibid.* s.48(1).

[11] *Ibid.* s.48(2).

[12] *Ibid.* s.59(1)–(2).

[13] H.A 1985, Sched. 2, Pt. I, gd. 1, above, paras. 8.31–8.36.

[14] See, *e.g.* M.H.L.G. Circ. 62/67, para. 7.

tion of authorities to (for example) the remedy of attachment of earnings under the Attachment of Earnings Act 1971,[15] and the special procedure for a rent action in the county court[16] whereby rent can be recovered quite simply from a tenant who is still in occupation, without the need for possession proceedings.[17] A somewhat more wide-ranging circular in 1974[18] detailed a series of eight possible measures.

The most comprehensive guidance yet, incorporating and expanding many of the previous suggestions, is contained in the Annex to the *Housing (Homeless Persons) Act 1977 Code of Guidance (England and Wales)*.[19] This Annex emphasises that rent arrears "call for a variety of approaches,"[20] and it then details 12 possible measures[21] which can be used to control arrears, including the checking of the tenant's entitlement to rent and rate rebates, financial support from social services authorities by way of rent guarantees or payment of the arrears, the direct payment of a standard contribution towards rent arrears by the D.S.S. to the housing authority in the case of tenants in receipt of income support,[22] and setting the debt aside for a period in order to give the tenant a chance to put his finances in order. The Code regards eviction as a final step, only to be taken when "unavoidable" after all the other preventive measures have failed.[23] **10.42**

The statutory security of tenure now enjoyed by most council tenants should in principle ensure that the commencement of possession proceedings is not treated by the authority as an automatic process even in the case of persistent defaulters. Some concern has however been expressed that in practice the security safeguards in the 1985 Act are often not fully effective[24]; yet in 1983 the D.O.E. estimated that on average less than one tenant in every 1,000 was actually being evicted each year for rent arrears, and urged auth- **10.43**

[15] Discussed in D.O.E. Circ. 83/72.
[16] C.C.R. 1981, Ord. 24, Pt. II.
[17] Discussed in D.O.E. Circ. 83/72.
[18] D.O.E. Circ. 18/74, App., paras. 3–4.
[19] *Op. cit.*.
[20] Para. A1.13.
[21] Para. A1.15.
[22] See above, paras. 8.34, 8.69.
[23] Para. A1. 16; see also D.O.E. Circ. 18/87, paras. 28–29, 32, describing repossession as "the ultimate sanction," which is only to be used "[w]here other methods have failed."
[24] See above, para. 8.15, n. 50.

orities to "review their rent arrears procedures if they have a significantly higher rate of evictions."[25]

(c) *"Distress"*

10.44 The advice in the Annex to the Code of Guidance[26] made no mention of the archaic remedy of "distress." This remedy has not been affected by the Housing Act 1985, and indeed has been enjoying something of a renaissance since the introduction of statutory security in 1980. It therefore merits separate treatment.

10.45 "Distress" is a form of self-help under which the landlord can take and detain his tenant's goods until the rent arrears are paid, failing which the goods may be sold. The details of this procedure may be found elsewhere[27]; but it is important to note that while private landlords cannot distrain for rent owed by protected or statutory tenants (within the Rent Act 1977) or by assured tenants (within the Housing Act 1988) unless they first obtain the leave of the county court,[28] a council can institute distress without a court order: it can simply write a "distress warrant" authorising its bailiff to distrain (although the bailiff must be "certificated," *i.e.* authorised to act by a county court judge[29]).

10.46 Notwithstanding the publication of guidelines by the A.D.C. in 1983,[30] this procedure has been repeatedly criticised[31] and its abolition has been recommended in government-sponsored studies.[32] Even if abolition is to be delayed, there would at least be a strong case for requiring authorities to obtain a court order before the right is exercised; the unregulated use of distress is surely contrary to the spirit (though not the letter) of the "tenants' charter" in the 1985 Act.

[25] *Housing (Homeless Persons) Act 1977 Code of Guidance, op. cit.* para. A1. 16.
[26] *Loc. cit.*
[27] See, *e.g.* A. Arden & M. Partington, *Housing Law* (1983), Chap. 5.
[28] R.A. 1977, s.147; H.A. 1988, s.19.
[29] Law of Distress Amendment Act 1888, s.7; Distress for Rent Rules 1988 (S.I. 1988 No. 2050).
[30] A.D.C., *Distress for Rent*; not all councils appear to be observing these guidelines: see, *e.g.* M. Friel, *Roof*, July 1984, p. 4.
[31] See, *e.g.* National Consumer Council, *Behind With the Rent* (1976); Shelter, *In Distress Over Rent* (1978); National Consumer Council, *Distress for Rent* (1986).
[32] See *Enforcement of Judgment Debts*, Report of the Payne Committee, Cmnd. 3909 (1969); Law Commission's Working Paper on *Distress for Rent* (Law Comm: No. 97, 1986).

(d) *Harassment of rent defaulters*

Some rather more unorthodox methods of collecting rent arrears have been considered by individual authorities, such as the use of "shame vans."[33] Before introducing such novel methods, authorities should bear in mind that it is an offence under the Administration of Justice Act 1970 for any person "with the object of coercing another person to pay money claimed from the other as a debt due under a contract" to "harass . . . the other with demands for payment which, in respect of their frequency or the manner or occasion of making any such demand, *or of any threat or publicity by which any demand is accompanied,* are calculated to subject him or members of his family or household to alarm, distress *or humiliation.*"[34] **10.47**

5. *Welfare Benefits*

A mandatory housing benefit scheme is administered by local authorities; it is contained in the Social Security Act 1986 and the Housing Benefit (General) Regulations 1987.[35] The details of the scheme must be sought elsewhere.[36] Basically, rent rebate entitlement depends on a comparison between the claimant's net income (after deduction of tax and National Insurance contributions), and the income support level to which he is entitled. If the income is less than or equal to the income support entitlement, then the claimant receives the maximum level of assistance: this means that he is not required to pay any of the rent, but has to pay 20 per cent. of the general rates. If, however, the claimant's income exceeds the relevant income support level, then, for every pound of the excess, the maximum level of benefit assistance is reduced by 65p for rent and 20p for general rates. **10.48**

The authority receives subsidy from central government to cover rent and rate rebates: the subsidy is currently 80 per cent. of the relevant costs. **10.49**

Quite separately from the housing benefit scheme administered by local authorities, low-income tenants may be entitled in certain narrowly-defined circumstances to payments from the D.S.S. in con- **10.50**

[33] *I.e.* vans which advertise the fact that they are involved in collecting arrears: see, *e.g. Roof,* July 1977, p. 105; *The Times,* June 22, 1978.

[34] A.J.A. 1970, s.40(1); italics supplied.

[35] S.I. 1987 No. 1971.

[36] See, *e.g.* S.H.A.C./Institute of Housing, *Guide to Housing Benefit* (1988); J. Allbeson, [1988] June Legal Action 9.

nection with their housing costs.[37] We have already noted[38] that, subject to certain conditions, a prescribed amount can be deducted from social security benefits by the D.S.S. and paid direct to the landlord in order to discharge rent arrears.[39]

6. *District Heating Schemes*

10.51 Authorities frequently make "heating charges" for heat which they produce and supply to their tenants; typically, a "district heating scheme" will cover all dwellings on an individual estate or in a block of flats. The charges are either paid as part of the rent, or collected separately under a collateral agreement.

10.52 Considerable concern has been expressed at the high heating charges imposed by some authorities. The Housing Act 1985[40] enables the Minister to make regulations conferring certain rights on secure tenants in respect of "heating charges" payable to a "heating authority." "Heating charges" are defined[41] for this purpose as "amount[s] payable to a heating authority in respect of heat produced . . . and supplied . . . including . . . such an amount payable as part of the rent"; while a "heating authority" is defined[42] as a housing authority which "operate[s] a heating installation and suppl[ies] to premises heat produced at the installation."

10.53 The relevant regulations (which have yet to be made) may require heating authorities to "adopt such methods for determining heating charges payable by [the relevant] tenants as will secure that the proportion of heating costs borne by each of those tenants is no greater than is reasonable"[43]; the relevant "heating costs" are the "expenses incurred by a heating authority in operating a heating installation."[44] It is significant that the regulations are concerned merely to ensure a reasonable apportionment of heating costs between the individual tenants: they cannot require that the costs themselves be reasonable in relation to the amount of heat actually supplied. The regulations may also entitle the secure tenants to

[37] See the Income Support (General) Regulations 1987 (S.I. 1987 No. 1967) reg. 17(e) and Sched. 3.

[38] See above, paras. 8.34, 8.69.

[39] Social Security (Claims and Payments) Regulations 1987 (S.I. 1987 No. 1968) reg. 35 and Sched. 9, paras. 2–3, 8.

[40] H.A. 1985, s.108.

[41] *Ibid.* s.108(5)(*d*).

[42] *Ibid.* s.108(5)(*a*).

[43] *Ibid.* s.108(2).

[44] *Ibid.* s.108(5)(*e*).

require the heating authority to give them prescribed information regarding heating charges and heating costs, and to permit them to inspect and copy accounts and other documents supporting such information.[45] Any question arising under these provisions is to be decided by the county court.[46]

[45] H.A. 1985, s.108(3).
[46] *Ibid.* s.110(1).

11 The Effects of Family Disputes

1. *The Authority's Role where Family Disputes arise*

11.01 Considerable difficulties can occur where a council property is occupied by spouses or cohabitees, and the relationship breaks down. The Housing Act 1985 contains several important provisions which cater for the special interests of the secure tenant's "family" even where there has been no discord between the spouses or cohabitees, particularly as regards assignments,[1] succession rights,[2] and the "right to buy"[3]; however, the security of tenure provisions in the 1985 Act[4] have caused particular complications in cases of relationship breakdown which did not exist prior to the introduction of statutory security in 1980.

11.02 The resolution of the problem of deciding what is to be done with a council dwelling on relationship breakdown demands just as much care on the part of those advising the parties as if the dwelling were owner-occupied, since the result can be of equally crucial importance: it has been judicially recognised that a council house tenancy provides vital protection by way of "solving the difficulties which people who are not in affluent circumstances must face otherwise in endeavouring to establish a home and bring up young children,"[5] and the economic value of a council tenancy has been greatly

[1] See above, paras. 9.16–9.17, 9.19.
[2] See above, paras. 9.29–9.40.
[3] See below, Chap. 14.
[4] See above, Chap. 8.
[5] *Ainsbury* v. *Millington* [1986] 1 All E.R. 73, 77 (C.A., *per* Dillon L.J.); see also *Browne* v. *Pritchard* [1975] 3 All E.R. 721, 725 (C.A.).

enhanced by the very generous "right to buy" provisions in the 1985 Act.[6] More generally, it may well be that the introduction of the statutory "charter" in 1980 has caused a greater awareness among council tenants and their partners that such tenancies attract "rights," so that legal advice may now be sought more swiftly following the breakdown of the relationship.

The imminent allocation of council housing to one of the spouses may also prove relevant in settling a dispute involving a former matrimonial home which is either owner-occupied[7] or privately rented. **11.03**

In viewing a council dwelling as a family home, there has long been the fundamental problem that the interests of at least one of the parties to the dispute may well differ from the interests of the local authority, which may for example be particularly concerned to avoid "under-occupation" following the departure of one or more of the family members from the dwelling. It will be seen that the discretion of authorities in situations of family breakdown has been substantially curtailed by the introduction of statutory security of tenure; conversely, we shall see that the role of the courts has been substantially increased in this area as a result of changes in family legislation. Thus the emphasis is currently placed rather more on the views of the court than on the views of the council, with the result that the "housing management" aspects of the problem of deciding the destination of a council dwelling in a case of family breakdown have been largely subordinated to the "family welfare" aspects.[8] **11.04**

We shall consider separately the position of the spouses or cohabitees *inter se*, before turning to the position of the authority itself (although in practice, of course, these two issues cannot be viewed entirely separately, since for example the authority's views will be considered by the court in deciding the destination of the tenancy following divorce). **11.05**

[6] See below, Chap. 14.

[7] See, *e.g. Browne* v. *Pritchard* [1975] 3 All E.R. 721 (C.A.); *Martin* v. *Martin* (1978) 122 S.J. 366 (C.A.).

[8] See, *e.g. Buckingham* v. *Buckingham & London Brick Co. Ltd.* (1979) 129 N.L.J. 52 ((Cty. Ct.), a case involving a Rent Act statutory tenancy); for earlier judicial examples of two very different approaches to the problem, compare *Brent* v. *Brent* [1974] 2 All E.R. 1211, 1216 (Dunn J.) with *Hutchings* v. *Hutchings* (1976) 237 E.G. 571, 573 (C.A., Ormrod L.J.).

2. *Relief Available to the Parties to the Dispute*[9]

(a) *General*

11.06 We shall see that as regards secure tenancies Parliament has in effect removed the power which authorities previously enjoyed at common law to intervene at an early stage after the breakdown of the relationship by "switching" the tenancy from one spouse or cohabitee to the other (by way of determination and re-grant). Thus a spouse or cohabitee must rely on the normal legal remedies available in respect of the "family" home: in the case of a spouse, these remedies may be either short-term or long-term, whether or not he or she currently has an interest in the tenancy; but in the case of a cohabitee, only short-term remedies are normally available unless he or she already has an interest in the tenancy. These remedies will now be examined, with particular emphasis on those aspects most relevant to council housing. As a preliminary issue, however, the significance of joint tenancy agreements will be briefly discussed.

(b) *Joint tenancy agreements*

11.07 Where a council tenancy is granted for the purposes of occupation as a matrimonial home, it seems to have become the standard practice for the agreement to vest the tenancy in the joint names of the spouses, rather than in the husband's name alone.[10] In the case of cohabitees, however, some authorities remain reluctant to grant joint tenancies.

11.08 Where the spouses or cohabitees do hold under a joint tenancy, the tenancy will be "secure" if at least one of them occupies the dwelling as his or her "only or principal home,"[11] providing the other conditions for security[12] are satisfied; the "right to buy" can be exercised either jointly by both of the tenants, or by one of them following an agreement to that effect[13]; and on the death of one joint tenant the other will take the secure tenancy automatically under

[9] See, *e.g.* S. M. Cretney, *Principles of Family Law* (4th ed., 1984), Pts. III and V; for a discussion of the available relief placed in the specific context of council housing, see, *e.g.* C. Williams, [1988] Fam.Law 438.

[10] See also Sex Discrimination Act 1975, s.30, which makes it unlawful to discriminate in the disposal or management of premises against a man or woman on the ground of his or her sex.

[11] H.A. 1985, s.81, see above, paras. 7.09–7.14.

[12] See above, paras. 7.01–7.08, 7.25–7.48.

[13] H.A. 1985, ss.118(2), 132(2), see below, para. 14.40.

the common law right of survivorship rather than under the statutory succession provisions in the 1985 Act,[14] although in such a case the survivor is treated as a statutory "successor,"[15] so that there can be no transmission of the *secure* tenancy to a "member of [his or her] family" on his or her own death.[16]

Views have differed as regards the extent to which the existence of a joint tenancy may be advantageous to the "weaker" partner.[17] In the case of *spouses*, although the holding of a joint tenancy may have an important psychological effect on the "weaker" partner if the relationship breaks down (in that he or she may be more reluctant to leave merely at the "stronger" partner's bidding), we shall see that in terms of legal remedies (whether of a short-term or long-term nature) it may make little difference whether the spouses hold as joint tenants or whether the tenancy is solely in one partner's name. However, in the case of *cohabitees*, while joint tenancies are of no inherent advantage where short-term legal remedies are sought, we shall see that as regards long-term remedies the broad matrimonial jurisdiction under which the court can "switch" the tenancy from one partner to the other does not apply, since it only extends to spouses; thus as regards long-term remedies joint tenancies can be a great advantage for the "weaker" cohabitee.[18] Nevertheless, the supposed protection afforded to the "weaker" party to a relationship by a joint tenancy may actually prove rather fragile, since the "stronger" party can unilaterally serve a notice to quit on the council, thereby ending the secure tenancy and depriving the other joint tenant of protection[19] unless the council is prepared to grant a new secure tenancy to the "weaker" party. **11.09**

Under the general law, where there is a joint tenancy each tenant is of course jointly and severally liable to the landlord for the rent even if arrears have arisen solely due to the "fault" of the other(s); whereas if the tenancy is in the name of one partner alone, the non- **11.10**

[14] H.A. 1985, s.89, see above, para. 9.29.

[15] H.A. 1985, s.88(1)(*b*), see above, para. 9.35.

[16] H.A. 1985, s.87, see above, para. 9.35.

[17] See, *e.g.* H.S.A.G., *Tenancy Agreements* (1977), p. 5: "as many arguments in favour of, as there are against, tenancies in joint names"; S.H.A.C., *Violence in Marriage* (1977): "the availability of joint tenancies is not the issue most crucial to a wife's rights"; *cf.* H.S.A.G., *The Housing of One Parent Families* (1978), para. 3.29: "strong advantages to joint tenancies."

[18] See 1978 H.S.A.G. Report, *op. cit.* para. 3.30.

[19] See *Greenwich L.B.C.* v. *McGrady* (1982) 6 H.L.R. 36 (C.A.); *Wiseman* v. *Simpson* [1988] 1 All E.R. 245, 252 (C.A.); see above, paras. 8.08–8.09.

tenant partner (whether spouse or cohabitee) is under no legal liability for rent arrears.

(c) *Short-term remedies*

11.11 **(i) Spouses.** Whether the tenancy is in the joint names of both spouses or in the sole name of one spouse, each has the right to remain in occupation until a court orders otherwise. This right exists at common law, either by virtue of any proprietary interest the spouse may have,[20] or by virtue of the husband's duty to provide a roof over his wife's head regardless of whose name the house is in.[21]

11.12 *The Matrimonial Homes Act 1983, section 1.* The right to remain in occupation has been separately conferred by statute. The Matrimonial Homes Act 1983 confers[22] "rights of occupation" on spouses who are not entitled to a legal estate in the dwelling either solely or as joint tenant.[23] Furthermore, an occupying spouse may keep the secure council tenancy of the other spouse "alive" even though the latter spouse has deserted the occupying spouse, since a spouse's occupation under the Matrimonial Homes Act is to be treated as occupation by the tenant-spouse[24] for the purposes of the requirement in the Housing Act 1985[25] that a secure tenant must *occupy* the dwelling. The occupying non-tenant spouse is also entitled to pay the rent due from the other spouse,[26] so that rent arrears and the consequent threat of possession proceedings may be avoided; and where possession is sought on one of the grounds involving "reasonableness,"[27] and the tenancy is terminated as a result of those proceedings as against the secure tenant, then the tenant's spouse, if

[20] See, *e.g. Bull* v. *Bull* [1953] 3 W.L.R. 326 (C.A.).

[21] See, *e.g. National Provincial Bank Ltd.* v. *Ainsworth* [1965] 2 A.C. 1175 (H.L.); *Gurasz* v. *Gurasz* [1969] 3 All E.R. 822, 823 (C.A.).

[22] M.H.A. 1983, s.1(1).

[23] M.H.A. 1983, s.1(11); a spouse who has the legal estate will of course have equivalent rights of occupation at common law; in the case of legal joint tenants, these common law rights can be enforced or controlled under separate powers in M.H.A. 1983, s.9 (see below, para. 11.14).

[24] M.H.A. 1983, s.1(6).

[25] H.A. 1985, s.81 (see above, paras. 7.09–7.14).

[26] M.H.A. 1983, s.1(5).

[27] See above, paras. 8.30, 8.58.

exercising rights of occupation under the Matrimonial Homes Act, has the same rights to ask the court to adjourn the proceedings, postpone the date of possession or stay or suspend execution of the possession order as he or she would have if those rights of occupation were not affected by the termination of the tenancy.[28]

The effect on the non-tenant spouse's occupation rights of a purported surrender of the secure tenancy by the tenant-spouse to the authority, or of a notice to quit served by the tenant-spouse on the authority, is not clear. The concept of the Rent Act "statutory tenancy"[29] does not apply to a "secure" tenancy, in which security attaches to and is dependent upon the subsistence of the contractual rights,[30] so that the Rent Act cases which preserve a statutory tenancy for the benefit of the tenant's occupying spouse in the teeth of a purported surrender[31] or service of a notice to quit by the tenant cannot strictly be applied. It has nevertheless been suggested[32] that the purported surrender or determination by notice to quit of a secure tenancy in this situation without the consent of the other spouse would likewise be ineffective; yet the courts' insistence on applying the common law termination rules where one of two or more joint tenants has sought to end the secure tenancy by notice to quit[33] indicates that the purported surrender or service of a notice to quit by a sole tenant may indeed operate, despite unfortunate consequences for the non-tenant spouse, unless he or she manages to apply for a transfer of the secure tenancy under the matrimonial jurisdiction[34] prior to the attempt of the tenant-spouse to end the tenancy.[35] **11.13**

Where one spouse is exercising these statutory "rights of occupation" under the Matrimonial Homes Act, either spouse may apply to the court for an order "declaring, enforcing, restricting or termi- **11.14**

[28] H.A. 1985, s.85(5), see above, paras. 8.73–8.75.

[29] R.A. 1977, s.2; for a recent example of the interplay between the R.A. "statutory tenancy" and the M.H.A. occupation rights, see *Griffiths* v. *Renfree*, *The Times*, March 4, 1989 (C.A.).

[30] See above, paras. 8.12, 8.14.

[31] *Middleton* v. *Baldock* [1950] 1 K.B. 657 (C.A.); *Hoggett* v. *Hoggett* (1979) 39 P. & C.R. 121 (C.A.).

[32] A. Arden and M. Partington, *Housing Law* (1983), p. 1140.

[33] *Greenwich L.B.C.* v. *McGrady* (1982) 6 H.L.R. 36 (C.A.); *Wiseman* v. *Simpson* [1988] 1 All E.R. 245, 252 (C.A.); see above, para. 11.09.

[34] See the long-term remedies, discussed below.

[35] See *Lewis* v. *Lewis* [1985] 2 All E.R. 449, 451–452 (H.L.), discussed below, para. 11.29.

nating those rights, or . . . prohibiting, suspending or restricting the exercise by either spouse of the right to occupy . . . or . . . requiring either spouse to permit the exercise by the other of that right"[36]; and a power of arrest may be attached to an injunction in cases of violent behaviour.[37] The reference to "prohibiting" occupation shows that, a least in theory, the court now has power to grant a permanent exclusion order under the Matrimonial Homes Act. Similar statutory powers are available to the court where the spouses jointly hold the legal estate.[38] The powers conferred on the court by the Matrimonial Homes Act have apparently displaced the court's general jurisdiction under the Supreme Court Act 1981[39] to exclude a spouse from the matrimonial home, in so far as there might otherwise be any overlap.[40]

11.15 In exercising its powers under the Matrimonial Homes Act, the court may make such order as it thinks just and reasonable, having regard to the conduct of the spouses, their respective needs and financial resources, the needs of any children, and "all the circumstances of the case"[41]; none of these specifically listed factors has priority over any of the others, so that there is no principle in ouster cases under the Matrimonial Homes Act that the welfare of the children should be the first and paramount consideration.[42]

11.16 However, the statutory rights of occupation under the Matrimonial Homes Act will cease on the death of the tenant or on the termination of the marriage *inter vivos*, unless the court has ordered otherwise during the subsistence of the marriage.[43]

[36] M.H.A. 1983, s.1(2).

[37] See the general power in D.V.M.P.A. 1976, s.2(1).

[38] *Ibid.* s.9.

[39] S.C.A. 1981, s.37 (applicable to county courts also, under the County Courts Act 1984, s.38).

[40] See *Richards* v. *Richards* [1983] 2 All E.R. 807, 815 (H.L.); *cf. Webb* v. *Webb* [1986] 1 F.L.R. 541 (C.A.), where the general jurisdiction had to be resorted to in order to grant an ouster order *after* decree absolute of divorce; however, it seems that in any event the general jurisdiction cannot now be used unless the plaintiff has some legal right in the property: *Ainsbury* v. *Millington* [1987] 1 W.L.R. 379 (C.A.); *M.* v. *M.* [1987] September Legal Action 13 (C.A.).

[41] M.H.A. 1983, s.1(3).

[42] *Richards* v. *Richards* [1983] 2 All E.R. 807 (H.L.).

[43] M.H.A. 1983, s.2(4); but where the former spouses are still living in the former matrimonial home following divorce, the court has inherent jurisdiction to exclude one party if this is necessary for the welfare of the children: see, *e.g. Wilde* v. *Wilde* [1988] 2 F.L.R. 83 (C.A.).

The Domestic Violence and Matrimonial Proceedings Act 1976. Quite apart from the Matrimonial Homes Act, one spouse can seek a county court injunction against the other under the Domestic Violence and Matrimonial Proceedings Act 1976,[44] without the need to claim any further relief in the proceedings, which can have the effect of (*inter alia*) excluding him or her from the matrimonial home, and to which in certain circumstances a power of arrest may be attached. The Domestic Violence and Matrimonial Proceedings Act can usually provide speedier relief than that obtainable under the Matrimonial Homes Act.[45] Despite the title of the Domestic Violence and Matrimonial Proceedings Act, no violence needs to be shown before an exclusion order (as opposed to a power of arrest) can be granted[46]; and it is immaterial which spouse has the legal interest in the dwelling.[47] **11.17**

The principles to be applied in deciding whether to grant ouster injunctions under the Domestic Violence and Matrimonial Proceedings Act are those set out in the Matrimonial Homes Act.[48] Ouster orders are of a drastic nature; they are only to be made in cases of real necessity, and not simply as a matter of housing policy.[49] If, however, the court is satisfied that the husband's violence is uncontrollable, and that an ouster order would expose the wife to severe risk of attack because he would know where to find her, then in the wife's own interests the court may refuse to make the order.[50] The housing needs of the parties may be relevant in deciding whether to make an ouster order: thus if the housing authority would be under an obligation to rehouse the wife and children under Part III of the Housing Act 1985, but would owe no such duty to the husband if he **11.18**

[44] D.V.M.P.A. 1976, ss.1–2; it appears that the county courts' jurisdiction under this Act in relation to spouses has not been affected by the decision in *Richards* v. *Richards*, see above, n. 42; see R. Hamilton, [1984] Legal Action 25.

[45] R. Hamilton, *loc. cit.*

[46] See, *e.g.* *Spindlow* v. *Spindlow* [1979] Ch. 52 (C.A.); *Fairweather* v. *Kolosine* (1982) 11 H.L.R. 61 (C.A.); *Wiseman* v. *Simpson* [1988] 1 All E.R. 245, 250 (C.A.); all these cases involved council housing.

[47] *Davis* v. *Johnson* [1979] A.C. 264 (H.L.), another council housing case.

[48] *Richards* v. *Richards*, [1983] 2 All E.R. 807, 829–830; for the relevant principles see M.H.A. 1983, s.1(3), discussed above.

[49] *Burke* v. *Burke* [1987] 2 F.L.R. 71 (C.A.); *Summers* v. *Summers*, *The Times*, May 19, 1987 (C.A.); *Wiseman* v. *Simpson* [1988] 1 W.L.R. 35 (C.A.); *Tuck* v. *Nicholls*, *The Times*, November 21, 1988 (C.A.).

[50] *Charles* v. *Charles* [1984] Legal Action 81 (C.A.); the implications of this decision as regards the authority's rehousing obligations in H.A. 1985, Pt. III are discussed above, para. 4.54.

is ousted, then it may not be considered appropriate to order him out and thereby render him homeless.[51]

11.19 The Domestic Violence and Matrimonial Proceedings Act cannot be used for the benefit of a spouse who has no intention (at least in the short-term) of re-occupying the matrimonial home.[52] A further restriction is that the Act is designed to provide essentially short-term remedies as far as spouses are concerned,[53] in contrast to the Matrimonial Homes Act 1983[54] and the Matrimonial Causes Act 1973.[55] Practice Notes from the Family Division have accordingly indicated that ouster orders and powers of arrest granted under the Domestic Violence and Matrimonial Proceedings Act in the case of spouses should not initially exceed three months in duration unless the circumstances are unusual.[56] These Practice Notes only cover the matrimonial home, with regard to which spouses have other remedies available which are of a long-term nature; in the case of cohabitees, however, it will be seen that there are normally no long-term remedies available, so that the courts have sometimes been tempted to extend ouster orders under the Domestic Violence and Matrimonial Proceedings Act over a lengthy period.

11.20 *The Domestic Proceedings and Magistrates' Courts Act 1978.* There is a completely separate jurisdiction relating to short-term remedies conferred on *magistrates' courts* under the Domestic Proceedings and Magistrates' Courts Act 1978,[57] whereby orders may be made

[51] See *Wooton* v. *Wooton* [1984] F.L.R. 871 (C.A.); but *cf. Thurley* v. *Smith* [1984] F.L.R. 875 (C.A.); see M. Bryan, [1985] J.S.W.L. 372. The various issues affecting the question of whether either party is entitled to rehousing under H.A. 1985, Pt. III (*e.g.* "deemed homelessness" in cases of actual or threatened violence, and "priority need"), are fully discussed in Chap. 4 above.

[52] *Warwick* v. *Warwick* (1982) 3 F.L.R. 393 (C.A.); the particular "obscure housing policy game" (*per* Ormrod L.J. at p. 395) which was unsuccessfully tried in this (joint tenancy) case would have stood more chance of technical success if it had utilised the principle in *Greenwich L.B.C.* v. *McGrady*, see above, n. 33.

[53] See, *e.g. Hopper* v. *Hopper* [1979] 1 All E.R. 181 (C.A.).

[54] We have seen that there is power to grant a *permanent* exclusion order under M.H.A. 1983, s.1(2); the separate power in M.H.A. 1983, Sched. 1, enabling the court to order the transfer of a secure tenancy from one spouse to the other, is discussed below.

[55] M.C.A. 1973, s.24, see below.

[56] *Practice Notes* in [1978] 2 All E.R. 1056 (injunctions), and [1981] 1 All E.R. 224 (powers of arrest).

[57] D.P.M.C.A. 1978, s.16.

excluding one spouse from the matrimonial home, even though no other matrimonial proceedings have been begun: but here the applicant must normally be able to show that the respondent has committed an act of violence and that the applicant or a child of the family is in danger of being physically injured by the respondent.[58] As with the Domestic Violence and Matrimonial Proceedings Act, a power of arrest may be attached under the Domestic Proceedings and Magistrates' Courts Act in certain circumstances,[59] and the procedure is designed to secure speedier relief than that normally obtainable under the Matrimonial Homes Act.[60]

(ii) Cohabitees. Of the short-term remedies available to spouses which have just been discussed, neither the Matrimonial Homes Act 1983[61] nor the Domestic Proceedings and Magistrates' Courts Act 1978[62] offer any protection to cohabitees. However, the Domestic Violence and Matrimonial Proceedings Act 1976[63] applies equally to those "living with each other in the same household as husband and wife" at the time of the incidents giving rise to the application,[64] although they are unmarried.[65] **11.21**

Even if the relationship has broken down, the parties may still be "living with each other" for these purposes if their accommodation is so small that they cannot live separate lives.[66] However, if the "cohabitees" are no longer in fact living with each other in the same household as husband and wife at the relevant time, then the applicant will frequently be in a "limbo" position: an ouster injunction cannot be granted under the Domestic Violence and Matrimonial Proceedings Act 1976, nor under the Guardianship of Minors Act 1971 even if children are involved (because the proceedings do not **11.22**

[58] D.P.M.C.A. 1978, s.16(3); see, *e.g. McCartney* v. *McCartney* [1981] 2 W.L.R. 184 (D.C.).

[59] D.P.M.C.A. 1978, s.18.

[60] D.P.M.C.A. 1978, ss.16(5), 17(2); *cf.* M.H.A. 1983, s.1.

[61] M.H.A. 1983, ss.1–2.

[62] D.P.M.C.A. 1978, ss.16–18.

[63] D.V.M.P.A. 1976, ss.1–2.

[64] They need not (and frequently in practice will not) be still actually living together at the time when the application is made to the court: *Davis* v. *Johnson* [1978] 1 All E.R. 841, 850 (C.A.); but they must have been cohabiting "shortly before" the application: see *Harrison* v. *Lewis, R.* v. *S.* [1988] 2 F.L.R. 339 (C.A.), concerning powers of arrest.

[65] D.V.M.P.A. 1976, ss.1(2), 2(2); see also *Davis* v. *Johnson* [1978] A.C. 264 (H.L.).

[66] *Adeoso* v. *Adeoso* [1981] 1 W.L.R. 1535 (C.A.); a case concerning cohabitees who were joint tenants of a one-bedroomed council flat.

directly relate to the custody or upbringing of a minor as such)[67]; and although it is sometimes possible for an ouster order to be made as a last resort under the general powers to grant injunctions contained in the Supreme Court Act 1981,[68] this can only be done if the applicant already has a relevant legal right in the property, and a mere right as joint tenant will apparently be insufficient, because neither joint tenant has the right to occupy to the exclusion of the other.[69]

11.23 Where there is jurisdiction to make an ouster order against a cohabitee under the Domestic Violence and Matrimonial Proceedings Act 1976, the principles to be applied are those concerning rights of occupation under the Matrimonial Homes Act 1983,[70] even though cohabitees do not of course fall within the terms of the 1983 Act as such.

11.24 Cohabitees have sometimes been excluded from council dwellings under the Domestic Violence and Matrimonial Proceedings Act 1976 for lengthy periods, far in excess of the maximum initial period of three months recommended for spouses in normal cases.[71] Thus in one case,[72] the male cohabitee, who was the sole tenant of a council dwelling, was excluded by the Court of Appeal for a period of five years (*i.e.* until the youngest child was 16), even though there had been no violence; the female cohabitee was ordered to indemnify him for the rent which he would remain contractually liable to pay. However, the court chose not to express any opinion on the question of whether the tenancy would remain "secure" during his absence; arguably, security would cease once the tenant had failed to occupy the dwelling as his "only or principal home,"[73] but it may be expected that the courts would strive to avoid such a draconian

[67] *Ainsbury* v. *Millington* [1987] 1 W.L.R. 379 (C.A.): a case concerning joint tenants of a council house, in which the authority subsequently obtained a possession order and granted the applicant a tenancy of a different council house: [1987] 1 All E.R. 929 (H.L.); see also *M.* v. *M.*, *The Times*, June 23, 1987 (C.A.); *Tuck* v. *Nicholls*, *The Times*, November 21, 1988 (C.A.).

[68] S.C.A. 1981, s.37 (applicable to county courts also, by virtue of the County Courts Act 1984, s.38).

[69] *Ainsbury* v. *Millington* (C.A.), see above, n. 67; *cf. Re W (a minor)* [1981] 3 All E.R. 401 (C.A.), where the successful applicant was *sole* tenant of the council flat in question.

[70] M.H.A. 1983, s.1(3), as applied in *Richards* v. *Richards*, see above, n. 42, and treated as relevant to ouster injunctions affecting cohabitees in *Lee* v. *Lee* (1983) 12 H.L.R. 116 (C.A.) and *Wiseman* v. *Simpson* [1988] 1 W.L.R. 35 (C.A.).

[71] See the *Practice Notes* referred to in n. 56, above.

[72] *Fairweather* v. *Kolosine* (1982) 11 H.L.R. 61 (C.A.).

[73] H.A. 1985, s.81, see above, paras. 7.09–7.14.

result, perhaps relying on a concept of "constructive occupation" where the tenant has every intention of occupying but is only prevented from doing so by virtue of a court order.[74]

This particular decision is in any event somewhat unreliable as a precedent, since the Court of Appeal treated the secure tenancy rather dismissively as a "very limited property right,"[75] placed great emphasis on the welfare of the child (an approach subsequently disapproved of by the House of Lords[76]), and in any event regarded the circumstances as unusual. **11.25**

In a later case,[77] however, involving cohabitees of a council house who were joint tenants, the male cohabitee (who had been violent) was eventually excluded (following two three-month orders) "until further order," and emphasis was placed on the fact that the Practice Notes[78] relating to short-term exclusions referred only to spouses, who had other remedies of a long-term nature available to them. In this case the lengthy exclusion of the male partner could not have affected the subsistence of the secure tenancy as such, since the parties were joint tenants and the partner remaining in occupation could thereby keep the secure tenancy alive[79]; but she remained at risk of losing the secure tenancy if the ousted partner had decided unilaterally to serve notice to quit on the authority.[80] **11.26**

By contrast, in yet another Court of Appeal decision,[81] which involved the exclusion of the male cohabitee who was sole tenant of a council house, it was stated that ouster orders in cases where the woman has no proprietary interest in the home should be temporary and subject to a fixed time limit even where the parties are cohabitees and therefore have no recourse to the matrimonial legislation; the court here fixed a time limit of one month in the ouster order, and pointed out that the ultimate responsibility for rehousing the woman and her children lay with the council. It is submitted that this decision represents the orthodox approach to exclusion orders **11.27**

[74] See above, para. 7.12; it is significant that the House of Lords emphasised in *Davis* v. *Johnson* [1978] A.C. 264 that the D.V.M.P.A. cannot affect the *property rights* of cohabitees, but only the *enjoyment* of those rights.

[75] (1982) 11 H.L.R. 61, 70 (*per* Lawton L.J.).

[76] See *Richards* v. *Richards*, above, n. 42.

[77] *Spencer* v. *Camacho* (1983) 127 S.J. 155 (C.A.), applied in *Galan* v. *Galan* [1985] F.L.R. 905 (C.A.).

[78] See above, n. 56.

[79] H.A. 1985, s.81; see above, para. 7.09.

[80] *Greenwich L.B.C.* v. *McGrady*, see above, n. 33.

[81] *Freeman* v. *Collins* (1983) 13 Fam.Law 113 (C.A.).

as between cohabitees, and that lengthy exclusion orders are likely to be increasingly difficult to obtain.

(d) *Long-term remedies*

11.28 **(i) Spouses.** If a long-term solution is sought regarding the destination of the council tenancy following marriage breakdown, then the parties may be able to agree between themselves as to which of them should retain or gain the tenancy: if so, then the Housing Act 1985[82] provides, broadly speaking, that an assignment from one spouse to the other shall not cause any cessation of the secure tenancy. Failing any such agreement, however, the introduction of statutory security of tenure has meant that the authority cannot now itself terminate a secure tenancy and "switch" it to the "deserving" spouse; only the *court* can decide the ultimate destination of the tenancy under Schedule 1 to the Matrimonial Homes Act 1983 or section 24 of the Matrimonial Causes Act 1973, and (in either case) only where a decree of divorce, nullity or judicial separation is granted.

11.29 *The Matrimonial Homes Act 1983, Schedule 1.* Under Schedule 1 to the Matrimonial Homes Act the court, on granting a decree of divorce, nullity or judicial separation, or (with leave of the court) at any time thereafter, may order the transfer of the interest of one spouse under a secure council tenancy (whether as sole or joint tenant) to the other spouse.[83] The secure tenancy must still be in existence at the date of the application to the court for a transfer[84]; if the secure tenancy is subsisting at the date of the application, the court cannot be deprived of jurisdiction by a subsequent attempted termination of the tenancy by the tenant (for example, by way of surrender), before the application comes before the court.[85] Although there is a power (with leave of the court) to entertain an application even after the granting of the decree of divorce, nullity or judicial separation,[86] this may prove illusory where a decree has been obtained and the non-tenant ex-spouse continues in sole occupation of the former matri-

[82] H.A. 1985, s.91(3)(*c*).

[83] M.H.A. 1983, Sched. 1, paras. 1–2, 8(2); under the Matrimonial and Family Proceedings Act 1984, s.22, a transfer order relating to a secure tenancy can also be made where a spouse applies for certain forms of "financial relief."

[84] *Lewis* v. *Lewis* [1985] 2 All E.R. 449 (H.L.), statutory tenancy under R.A. 1977; *Thompson* v. *Elmbridge B.C.* (1987) 131 S.J. 1285 (C.A.), secure council tenancy.

[85] *Lewis* v. *Lewis* [1985] 2 All E.R. 449, 451–452 (H.L.).

[86] M.H.A. 1983, Sched. 1, paras. 1(1), 8(2).

monial home: for, unless the court has directed[87] during the subsistence of the marriage that the wife's statutory rights of occupation[88] should outlast the termination of the marriage, the "tenant condition" of a secure tenancy that the tenant must occupy the dwelling as his only or principal home[89] will no longer be satisfied after the marriage has been terminated[90]; thus there may no longer be any secure tenancy left to transfer.

Where the court makes an order under Schedule 1 to the 1983 **11.30** Act, the transfer of the secure tenancy operates "by virtue of the order and without further assurance"[91]; the secure tenancy is *not assigned* by the existing tenant-spouse, so that the court's power to order the transfer will not be affected by the presence in the tenancy agreement of a prohibition against assignments,[92] whether drafted in absolute or qualified form.[93] Nevertheless, although the authority's consent is not required, it has the right to be given notice of the application and the right to be heard by the court before any such order is made[94]; the court has to balance the interests of the wife (and children, if any) against the claims of the authority, and the interests of the former may in the event be held to prevail notwithstanding the authority's objections: the authority merely has a right to be heard, it does not have a right of veto.[95]

It would not normally be appropriate for an authority to demand **11.31** that the transferee-spouse (not being an existing joint tenant) should discharge rent arrears due from the other spouse,[96] although such demands are not illegal *per se*.[97] One spouse certainly has no inherent legal obligation to pay the arrears of the other spouse where the latter was the sole tenant, and Schedule 1 to the Matrimonial

[87] Pursuant to M.H.A. 1983, s.2(4).

[88] M.H.A. 1983, s.1(1), see above, paras. 11.12–11.16.

[89] H.A. 1985, s.81: see above, paras. 7.09–7.14.

[90] See A. Arden, [1982] Conv. 334, 342–344; *Lewis* v. *Lewis*, see above, n. 85.

[91] M.H.A. 1983, Sched. 1, para. 2(1).

[92] *Buckingham* v. *Buckingham & London Brick Co.* (1979) 129 N.L.J. 52 (Cty. Ct.).

[93] See above, paras. 9.05, 9.17.

[94] M.H.A. 1983, Sched. 1, para. 8(1); Matrimonial Causes Rules 1977 (S.I. 1977 No. 344) r. 107(4); see, *e.g. Lewis* v. *Lewis* [1985] 2 All E.R. 449, 451 (H.L.).

[95] *Buckingham* v. *Buckingham & London Brick Co.*, see above, n. 92.

[96] See H.S.A.G., *The Housing of One Parent Families* (1978), para. 4.24.

[97] *Cf.* the private sector "premium" provisions in R.A. 1977, ss.119, 128, as interpreted in *Hampstead Way Investments* v. *Mawdsley* [1980] 9 C.L. 115 (Cty. Ct.); *cf.* also the Housing (Scotland) Act 1987, s.20(2)(*a*), which makes it illegal for an authority to refuse to house a person until he or she has repaid rent arrears attributable to any tenancy of which he or she was not a tenant.

Homes Act expressly provides[98] that the other spouse is only exempt from liability under the terms of the lease in respect of obligations falling due on or after the date of transfer. Requirements that a wife should discharge her estranged husband's rent arrears in order to retain or obtain council accommodation have been held by local ombudsmen[99] to amount to "maladministration."[1]

11.32 *The Matrimonial Causes Act 1973, section 24.* Under section 24 of the Matrimonial Causes Act the court has a general power to order that one spouse shall transfer to the other (or to or for the benefit of a child of the family) "such property as may be so specified."[2] In making such an order the court must take into account "all the circumstances of the case," including certain specified matters, for example the "income, earning capacity, property and other financial resources" of the parties and the appropriateness or otherwise of the "clean break" principle, but "first consideration" must be given to the welfare of any infant children.[3]

11.33 Both secure and non-secure[4] council tenancies may be the subject of transfer of property orders under section 24; the specific jurisdiction in Schedule 1 to the Matrimonial Homes Act relating to secure tenancies (discussed above) in no way precludes the use of the general jurisdiction in section 24 of the Matrimonial Causes Act in relation to such tenancies.[5] If the tenancy is no longer secure at the date of the application, then the court can only order the transfer of the non-secure tenancy.[6] The order can be made on granting the decree or (with leave of the court) at any time thereafter.[7]

[98] M.H.A. 1983, Sched. 1, para. 2(2).
[99] The general role of the local ombudsmen is discussed above, paras. 2.44–2.45.
[1] See, *e.g.* Complaint Nos. 1854/(C) H/76, 4692/H/77, referred to by D.J. Hughes and S.R. Jones, [1979] J.S.W.L. 273, 286–287.
[2] M.C.A. 1973, s.24(1)(*a*).
[3] M.C.A. 1973, ss.25–25A; the duty to give "first consideration" to the welfare of the children does not however mean that this consideration is paramount: thus it does not necessarily override other considerations pointing to a just result: *Suter* v. *Suter* [1987] 2 All E.R. 336 (C.A.).
[4] See, *e.g.* *Rodewald* v. *Rodewald* [1977] 3 W.L.R. 9 (C.A.).
[5] See *Hale* v. *Hale* [1975] 2 All E.R. 1090, 1094 (C.A.), a case concerning the transfer of a protected tenancy under the Rent Act.
[6] *Cf.* *Lewis* v. *Lewis*, see above, n. 85; *Thompson* v. *Elmbridge B.C.*, see above, n. 84.
[7] M.C.A. 1973, ss.24(1), 26(2); Matrimonial Causes Rules 1977 (S.I. 1977 No. 344) r. 68(2); in the case of a post-decree application, security may already have been irretrievably lost (see above, para. 11.29), so that only the non-secure tenancy can be transferred.

The authority has no statutory right to be heard in section 24 proceedings.[8] Nevertheless, the almost invariable practice is for the court to direct that notice of the section 24 application is served on the authority,[9] and the court tends carefully to consider the authority's views before making a transfer order. **11.34**

The court's order under section 24 can only be effected by the assignment of the tenancy by the tenant.[10] It is therefore relevant to consider whether the court's powers can be in any way limited by the presence of an absolute or qualified covenant against assignment in the tenancy agreement. Under the now-repealed Housing Act 1957,[11] authorities had to make it a term of every letting that the tenant could not assign (or sub-let) without the authority's written consent. After the statutory reforms effected by the Housing Act 1980, a council tenancy agreement may now unreservedly permit, or indeed absolutely prohibit, assignments of the tenancy[12]; but there are many council tenancy agreements entered into prior to October 3, 1980 which (until they are varied[13]) are expressly subject to the qualified prohibition on assignments formerly required to be inserted by the Housing Act 1957. Where absolute or qualified prohibitions on assignment are still encountered, the old problems concerning the courts' powers to order the transfer of the tenancy will, at least in theory, remain relevant.[14] **11.35**

In practice, however, the use of the court's enlarged jurisdiction under Schedule 1 to the Matrimonial Homes Act, which relates specifically to secure tenancies, will frequently prove much more appropriate than the more general jurisdiction in the Matrimonial Causes Act. In particular, use of the powers in Schedule 1 to the Matrimonial Homes Act does not depend on the assignment of the tenancy by the tenant, so that any covenant against assignment need **11.36**

[8] *Cf.* M.H.A. 1983, Sched. 1, para. 8(1), see above, para. 11.30.

[9] See, *e.g.* M. Petley, [1983] Law Notes 331, 333.

[10] *Cf.* M.H.A. 1983, Sched. 1, para. 2(1), see above, para. 11.30.

[11] H.A. 1957, s.113(5); see, *e.g. Regan* v. *Regan* [1977] 1 W.L.R. 84; for a discussion of the general problems which s.113(5) presented in this context, and of the relevance of L. & T.A. 1927, s.19(1)(*a*) (which provides that the landlord's consent to an assignment, when required, cannot be unreasonably withheld), see D. Yates, (1977) 41 Conv. (N.S.) 309, 313–317, and D. Hoath, *Council Housing* (1st ed., 1978), pp. 57–59.

[12] See above, paras. 9.14–9.15.

[13] See H.A. 1985, ss.102–103, discussed above, paras. 7.61–7.68.

[14] Note also the Sex Discrimination Act 1975, s.31, which makes it unlawful for a landlord to discriminate on the ground of sex against a woman (or man) by withholding consent to (*inter alia*) the assignment of the lease to her (or him).

not as such prove an insuperable hurdle, despite the authority's right to be heard in the transfer proceedings.[15] Since the courts bear in mind broadly the same criteria in deciding on transfers under the Matrimonial Homes Act as those specifically listed in the Matrimonial Causes Act,[16] it is difficult to see what advantage an applicant would normally gain by seeking a transfer under the Matrimonial Causes Act rather than under the "purpose-built" procedure in the Matrimonial Homes Act. Obviously, if the tenancy is not "secure,"[17] the transfer jurisdiction in the Matrimonial Homes Act will not be available; and if a transfer of the tenancy is sought to a "child of the family," only the Matrimonial Causes Act can be used, and not the Matrimonial Homes Act; but apart from such cases, section 24 of the Matrimonial Causes Act has now been rather eclipsed, as far as council housing is concerned, by the jurisdiction in Schedule 1 to the Matrimonial Homes Act.

11.37 Where a transfer is nevertheless ordered under section 24 of the Matrimonial Causes Act, then the tenancy will remain secure following the assignment (assuming it was secure prior to the assignment) in view of the specific "saving" reference to this jurisdiction in the Housing Act 1985,[18] as an exception to the normal prohibition on the assignment of secure tenancies.[19] Furthermore, even if the assignment takes place in technical breach of covenant, the secure tenancy will nevertheless pass,[20] and the authority's only remedy is to seek possession from the assignee-spouse on the "reasonableness" ground of breach of the tenancy agreement[21]; since *ex hypothesi* the assignment would have been made pursuant to a court order, it is difficult to see how such possession proceedings could succeed.

11.38 It is possible[22] that the presence in a tenancy agreement of an absolute[23] prohibition against assignment may persuade a court

[15] See *Buckingham* v. *Buckingham & London Brick Co.*, see above, n. 92.

[16] M.C.A. 1973, s.25, see above; see the Law Commission's *Third Report on Family Property Law* (Law Comm: No. 86, 1978), pp. 251–252.

[17] See above, paras. 7.01–7.48.

[18] H.A. 1985, s.91 (3)(*b*), see above, paras. 9.16, 9.19.

[19] H.A. 1985, s.91(1)–(2), see above, paras. 9.15, 9.18.

[20] See *Governors of the Peabody Donation Fund* v. *Higgins* [1983] 3 All E.R. 122 (C.A.); this case involved an absolute prohibition against assignment, and is discussed above, para. 9.17.

[21] H.A. 1985, Sched. 2, Pt. I, gd. 1, discussed above, para. 8.31.

[22] See, *e.g.* *Regan* v. *Regan* [1977] 1 All E.R. 428, 429, which involved the old "qualified" covenant prescribed by H.A. 1957, s.113(5), prior to the introduction of statutory security.

[23] In the case of a qualified prohibition, L. & T.A. 1927, s.19(1)(*a*) would apply, see n. 11 above.

that it should not actually make an order under section 24 of the Matrimonial Causes Act at all, even though (as we have just seen) the covenant is in any event unlikely to have any adverse consequences on such an order if it were to be made. It is suggested, however, that there are several reasons why the presence of a prohibition against assignment in the tenancy agreement should not now deter the court from making the order if it is otherwise fair to do so.

First, the specific recognition in the assignment provisions of the **11.39**
Housing Act 1985[24] of the role of the courts under section 24 of the Matrimonial Causes Act surely indicates that on the grounds of public policy this matrimonial jurisdiction cannot be evaded by councils through the facile device of introducing covenants against assignment. Secondly, the earlier reluctance[25] of the court to become a party to a breach of covenant, in view of the ease with which the authority could at common law speedily end a tenancy transferred to an "unwelcome" spouse, should no longer persist now that statutory security of tenure has been introduced (and, indeed, attaches to the tenancy in the hands of the assignee-spouse even if the assignment was in breach of covenant[26]). Thirdly, it is arguable that a transfer by a tenant pursuant to a court order under section 24 of the Matrimonial Causes Act cannot in any event involve the tenant in breach of a covenant against assignment, because in reality the transfer takes effect by operation of law, and there is support for the proposition that there will only be a breach of such a covenant if there is some *voluntary* dealing with the property *inter vivos*.[27]

We have already noted that it would normally not be appropriate **11.40**
for an authority to impose liability on an assignee-spouse for the previous tenant-spouse's rent arrears.[28]

(ii) Cohabitees. Neither Schedule 1 to the Matrimonial Homes Act **11.41**
1983 nor section 24 of the Matrimonial Causes Act 1973[29] extend to cohabitees. Thus the court cannot order the transfer of the tenancy from one cohabitee to the other, and the long-term rights of a party

[24] H.A. 1985, s.91 (3)(*b*), see above, para. 9.16.

[25] See, *e.g. Regan* v. *Regan* [1977] 1 All E.R. 428, 429; *Thompson* v. *Thompson* [1975] 2 All E.R. 208, 213 (C.A.).

[26] See above.

[27] See, *e.g. Slipper* v. *Tottenham & Hampstead Junction Ry. Co.* (1867) L.R. 4 Eq. 112, where a compulsory sale of a lease pursuant to a statute was held to be outside the scope of an absolute covenant against assignment; see also (1977) 96 Law Notes 86, 87.

[28] See above, para. 11.31.

[29] See *Mossop* v. *Mossop* [1988] 2 All E.R. 202 (C.A.).

in respect of the tenancy on the breakdown of the relationship depend, not on any "matrimonial" jurisdiction as such, but primarily on whether he or she already has a proprietary interest in that tenancy, failing which he or she can only try and persuade the other partner to assign the secure tenancy to him or her,[30] or to surrender it to the authority with a view to a re-grant to him or her.[31]

3. *Implications for the Authority*[32]

(a) *Position where no court order is made pursuant to Schedule 1 to the Matrimonial Homes Act or section 24 of the Matrimonial Causes Act*

11.42 Prior to the introduction of statutory security of tenure in 1980, the authority itself could intervene in an appropriate case to "switch" the tenancy from one spouse or cohabitee to the other even in advance of any court order being obtained by the parties (under, for example, the Domestic Violence and Matrimonial Proceedings Act 1976[33]). This could be achieved by way of simple determination by the authority of the existing tenancy by notice to quit and the grant of a new tenancy to the appropriate party (who would normally be the spouse or cohabitee who was taking care of the children, if any).

11.43 This power was particularly useful when exercised in favour of an ousted cohabitee, who was (and is) unable to apply under the "transfer" jurisdiction in the Matrimonial Homes Act or Matrimonial Causes Act described above; but such transfers were often also beneficial from the authority's viewpoint, since it could thereby try to ensure, for example, that a council tenant whose wife and children had left him did not continue to under-occupy a large council house, either right up until divorce proceedings or indeed indefinitely where no divorce proceedings were to be instituted.[34] Moreover, the courts had often emphasised the particular relevance of this

[30] See H.A. 1985, s.91(3)(*c*), discussed above, paras. 9.16–9.17; in order for security to be retained under this provision following assignment, the cohabitees must "live together as husband and wife" at the time it is executed (see ss.87, 113(1)(*a*)); thus the assignment should take place before, or at the latest very shortly after, they separate: see J. Luba, [1981] L.A.G. Bull. 211.

[31] See below, para. 11.45.

[32] See, *e.g.* D.Pearl, *Essays in Family Law 1985* (ed. M.D.A. Freeman), pp. 20–33; F. Logan, *Homelessness and Relationship Breakdown*, Brunel Socio-Legal Working Paper (1987), Chap. 6.

[33] See above, paras. 11.17–11.19.

[34] See, *e.g. Sales* v. *Sales* (1980) 10 Fam.Law 115 (C.A.); *Spindlow* v. *Spindlow* [1979] 1 All E.R. 169, 173 (C.A.).

"switching" power possessed by authorities, when cases arose concerning the grant of exclusion orders under the Domestic Violence and Matrimonial Proceedings Act 1976 against council tenants: judges were prepared in appropriate cases to exclude the tenant (whether spouse or cohabitee) for a sufficient period to allow for the "switching" of the tenancy by the authority.[35]

After the introduction of statutory security of tenure in 1980, this power of early intervention which authorities had possessed, whereby the tenancy could be "switched" in cases of family disputes, is generally no longer exercisable in the case of secure tenancies. There is no obviously relevant statutory ground for possession,[36] and the government seems to have been content to leave such matters to be decided by the courts.[37] Although it has been suggested[38] that authorities could insert a "Thou shalt not beat thy wife"-type condition in their tenancy agreements, breach of which might give rise to a "reasonableness" ground for possession,[39] it is most unlikely that a court would be persuaded to treat family breakdown as a mere breach of a tenancy condition in this way. As has been seen,[40] the offer by the authority of suitable alternative accommodation is not of itself a "reasonableness" ground for possession (unlike the position under the private sector regimes in the Rent Act 1977 and the Housing Act 1988[41]); and the "under-occupation" ground[42] is of no avail even against a tenant who is grossly under-occupying following the departure of his wife or cohabitee and children, because this ground only applies where the secure tenancy has vested in the current tenant on the death of the previous tenant under the statutory succession provisions, as a member of the previous tenant's family other than the spouse. Indeed, as has been **11.44**

35 See, *e.g. Davis* v. *Johnson* [1978] 1 All E.R. 1132, 1152 (H.L.); *Spindlow* v. *Spindlow*, see above, n. 34; *Sales* v. *Sales*, see above, n. 34; *Harding* v. *Harding* (1980) 10 Fam.-Law 146, 147 (C.A.).

36 The various grounds (in H.A. 1985, Sched. 2) are discussed above, paras. 8.25–8.63; *cf.* the purpose-built "family breakdown" ground for possession in Housing (Scotland) Act 1987, s.48 and Sched. 3, Pt.I, para. 16; despite considerable demand (primarily from women's groups) for the introduction of such a ground into the Housing Bill 1980, the Housing and Building Control Bills of 1983 and 1984, and the Housing and Planning Bill 1986, no action has been taken; see D. Pearl, *op.cit.* pp. 31–32.

37 See, *e.g.* H.L. Deb., July 21, 1980, col. 140 (Lord Mowbray and Stourton).

38 See, *e.g.* J. Luba, [1981] L.A.G. Bull. 82, 85.

39 *I.e.* under H.A. 1985, Sched. 2, Pt. I, gd. 1 (see above, para. 8.31).

40 See above, para. 8.51.

41 See R.A. 1977, s.98(1); H.A. 1988, Sched. 2, Pt. II, gd. 9.

42 H.A. 1985, Sched. 2, Pt. III, gd. 16 (see above, para. 8.63).

seen,[43] the authority may be under a separate duty in such a case to find accommodation for the displaced spouse or cohabitee and the children under Part III of the Housing Act 1985.

11.45 The old power of an authority to "switch" the tenancy on its own initiative can thus normally only now be used in the case of non-secure tenancies. However, even if the tenancy is secure, the authority can still "switch" the tenancy where the tenant-spouse or tenant-cohabitee is prepared voluntarily to surrender it to the authority, or to serve notice to quit; the authority can then grant a new tenancy to the other partner. Alternatively, an authority may perhaps be able indirectly to put pressure on a grossly under-occupying tenant in this situation, by way of legitimately increasing the rent[44]; gross under-occupation would appear to be a proper consideration for rent-fixing purposes.[45]

11.46 Furthermore, where the parties to the marriage or cohabitation are *joint* secure tenants under a periodic council tenancy, the "deserving" party and the authority may choose to collaborate in employing a particularly devious solution whereby the authority's pre-1980 freedom of intervention can be restored. The "deserving" party (whether spouse or cohabitee) can determine the secure joint tenancy by giving a notice to quit to the authority, even without the concurrence of the other joint tenant, which will be effective to determine the contractual tenancy on which the secure tenancy depends,[46] since (as we have seen[47]) the courts have been prepared to apply to secure tenancies the common law rule that unanimity is necessary for the continuation of a periodic joint tenancy. Thus, on expiry of the notice to quit, security will cease, and the authority can then grant a new tenancy in the old way to the "deserving" partner alone, save that the new tenancy can itself be secure. Nevertheless, we have also seen[48] that a joint tenant who serves a unilateral notice to quit in this situation could well be regarded in equity as committing a breach of trust, giving rise to a claim for substantial compensation on the part of the evicted party; and if the "undeserving" party discovers the "deserving" party's intentions in time, he or she

[43] In Pt. II of this book.
[44] See C.H.A.C., *Transfers, Exchanges and Rents* (1953), pp. 3–4.
[45] For a discussion of the width of the discretion conferred on authorities with regard to rents, see above, paras. 10.01–10.03, 10.30.
[46] *Greenwich L.B.C.* v. *McGrady* (1982) 46 P. & C.R. 223 (C.A.); see above, paras. 8.08–8.09.
[47] See above, para. 8.08.
[48] See above, para. 8.09.

may be able to obtain an injunction preventing service of the notice to quit. Having regard to the present uncertain state of the law, therefore, this particular method of "switching" the tenancy cannot be unreservedly recommended.

Another possible method of enabling the authority to "switch" a secure tenancy currently held in the name of one partner alone is for the "deserving" partner, if he or she is a cohabitee,[49] to obtain a lengthy[50] exclusion order against the other partner under the Domestic Violence and Matrimonial Proceedings Act 1976; if the effect of such a lengthy ouster is to render the excluded tenant-partner no longer capable of occupying the dwelling as his "only or principal home,"[51] then the tenancy will no longer be secure, and the authority can terminate it by notice to quit and grant a new (secure) tenancy on its own initiative to the "deserving" partner. However, we have seen[52] that it is now difficult to obtain lengthy exclusion orders under the Domestic Violence and Matrimonial Proceedings Act, and that even where such a lengthy ouster is secured, the courts may well be reluctant to hold that the ousted party has thereby lost his or her secure tenancy. **11.47**

(b) *Position where a court order is made pursuant to Schedule 1 to the Matrimonial Homes Act or section 24 of the Matrimonial Causes Act*

We have seen that a *spouse* (but not a cohabitee) can obtain a transfer of the secure tenancy by virtue of a court order under Schedule 1 to the Matrimonial Homes Act or section 24 of the Matrimonial Causes Act. Whichever jurisdiction is exercised, it has been suggested earlier that there is little scope for objections on the part of councils: an authority has no right to prevent an order made under the Matrimonial Homes Act from taking effect (although it has the right to be heard by the court); and although the power of the court to order an assignment of the secure tenancy under the Matrimonial Causes Act is technically liable to be affected by the presence of a covenant against assignment in the lease, it has been argued above that the courts should be able to surmount any such prohibitive covenants. **11.48**

[49] And thus not capable of preserving the secure tenancy by virtue of his or her own occupation: *cf.* M.H.A. 1983, s.1(6).

[50] As in *Spencer* v. *Camacho* (1983) 127 S.J. 155 (C.A.), see above, para. 11.26.

[51] H.A. 1985, s.81.

[52] See above, para. 11.27.

12 The Condition of the Dwelling: Repairs and Improvements

1. *General*

12.01 There is considerable evidence relating to the bad condition of many council estates.[1] The difficulties presented by novel construction methods (especially those used in "tower" blocks[2]) have proved particularly acute, often presenting an unhappy combination of vandalism, high heating charges, condensation, noise, and psychological problems; several "tower" blocks have been demolished,[3] while others have been sold off at low figures for renovation by private developers.[4]

12.02 The severe restraints on expenditure imposed on councils in recent years, together with the effects of the statutory "right to buy"[5] in creaming off the better-quality housing stock and leaving councils with their unpopular estates, have exacerbated the problems of disrepair. Yet, at the same time, large increases in council rents[6] have resulted in tenants becoming more insistent on their

[1] See, *e.g.* National Consumer Council, *Soonest mended* (1979), *Cracking up* (1982); *English House Condition Survey 1981* (H.M.S.O., 1982); D.O.E., *An Inquiry into the Condition of the Local Authority Housing Stock in England: 1985*; D. Hughes, [1984] J.S.W.L. 137.

[2] See, *e.g.* D.O.E. Survey, *Families in Flats* (1981); C. McKean, *The Times*, March 28, 1983; Association of Metropolitan Authorities, *Defects in Housing, Part 2: Industrialised and System Built Dwellings of the 1960s and 1970s* (1984).

[3] See, *e.g. The Times*, May 17, 1982.

[4] See, *e.g. Roof*, November 1982, p. 32; the privatisation of whole council estates is discussed in Chap. 15.

[5] See Chap. 14.

[6] See above, para. 10.14.

"pound of flesh" in terms of the enforcement of their landlords' repairing obligations.

In some cases councils may have "inherited" defective housing through having acquired it from the private sector. Where a council has acquired a building which may be made suitable for housing, it must make it so suitable "forthwith," and any house or building suitable for housing which is acquired by the council must be used as housing accommodation "as soon as practicable after the acquisition or . . . after the completion of the necessary works."[7] These provisions are intended as "one statutory reflection of the need for unoccupied property in areas of housing shortage to be brought into use as soon as practicable."[8] However, if such "municipalised" properties are allowed subsequently to deteriorate to the extent that they become statutorily unfit,[9] then the council may eventually decide to include them in a clearance area[10] with a view to their ultimate demolition; and in making such a decision the council is not obliged to take account of the fact that the properties may have become unfit through its own neglect, so that the inclusion of such properties in the clearance area cannot be challenged on this ground.[11] **12.03**

Against this background, the present chapter looks at the implied obligations relating to the repair and maintenance of council housing, together with the legal remedies available against the council where they are not complied with. **12.04**

2. *The Respective Liabilities of Council and Tenant*

(a) *The tenancy agreement*

It is important to appreciate that repairs may need doing, and yet neither the landlord nor the tenant may be liable for the repairs *vis-à-vis* the other party to the lease. At common law, no covenants are normally implied on the part of either the landlord or the tenant relating to the repair of the dwelling, or its fitness for habitation or **12.05**

[7] H.A. 1985, s.18.
[8] D.O.E. Circ. 160/74, para. 14.
[9] *I.e.* within the terms of H.A. 1985, s.604(1).
[10] See *ibid.* ss.289–290, 293.
[11] *A.-G. ex rel. Rivers Moore* v. *Portsmouth C.C.* (1978) 76 L.G.R. 643.

for any other purpose for which it may be let.[12] This basic principle is however subject to exceptions imposed both by the common law and (particularly) by statute, but when dealing with disrepair problems it remains important initially to inspect the tenancy agreement in order to discover what obligations (if any) it expressly imposes on the parties.

12.06 Council tenancy agreements used to be notorious for their silence regarding the landlord's repairing obligations.[13] This problem has been partly met by a statutory requirement[14] for councils to give their secure tenants information explaining "in simple terms" the effect of (*inter alia*) the express terms of the tenancy, the landlord's implied repairing obligations in the Landlord and Tenant Act 1985 relating to short leases,[15] and the secure tenant's statutory "right to repair" where the council has failed to carry out its repairing obligations.[16] However, the information to be provided relating to the council's repairing obligations is not comprehensive, since the implied terms concerning repairs other than those applicable to short leases (such as those concerning fitness for habitation and common law liability for the common parts) do not have to be brought to the tenant's attention, nor need he be informed of his common law and equitable remedies for disrepair.

12.07 As regards the tenant's responsibilities concerning the condition of the property,[17] it is common for the tenancy agreement expressly to require him to carry out internal decorations.[18]

12.08 Apart from considering the relevant liabilities (if any) expressly imposed on the parties by the tenancy agreement, it is necessary to appreciate the impact of various implied responsibilities imposed by the general law concerning the repair and maintenance of council housing; sometimes, indeed, these implied responsibilities will prevail even in the teeth of contractual terms to the contrary.

[12] See, *e.g.* Law Commission, *Report on Obligations of Landlords and Tenants* (Law Comm: No. 67, 1975), p. 28; *Duke of Westminster* v. *Guild* [1984] 3 All E.R. 144, 149 (C.A.); in the case of a *licence*, however, a warranty may sometimes be implied that the property is of sound construction and reasonably suitable for the licensee's purposes: *Wettern Electric* v. *Welsh Development Agency* [1983] Q.B. 796 (licence to use factory unit newly constructed by licensor).

[13] See, *e.g. Liverpool C.C.* v. *Irwin* [1975] 3 All E.R. 658, 663 (C.A.), [1976] 2 All E.R. 39, 43 (H.L.).

[14] H.A. 1985, s.104, see above, para. 7.58.

[15] L. & T.A. 1985, ss.11–16, see below, paras. 12.09–12.27.

[16] H.A. 1985, s.96, see below, paras. 12.69–12.76.

[17] See below, paras. 12.48–12.50.

[18] See, *e.g.* National Consumer Council, *Tenancy Agreements* (1976), p. 15.

(b) *The council's implied contractual obligations*

(i) The dwelling itself: sections 11 to 16 of the Landlord and Tenant Act 1985

General. Sections 11 to 16 of the Landlord and Tenant Act 1985 **12.09** impose significant repairing and maintenance covenants on landlords in the case of most short leases. The fact that the landlord is a council rather than a private landlord does not affect the construction of these statutory obligations, so that, in particular, a higher standard cannot be imposed on a council landlord than that required of a private landlord.[19]

The conditions which must be satisfied. In order that these covenants **12.10** can apply, three basic conditions must be satisfied. First, there must be a lease or agreement for a tenancy of a "dwelling-house," which may be a house or part of a building, such as a flat[20]; thus these provisions only cover leases and tenancy agreements, not licences.[21] Secondly, the letting must be for an initial term of less than seven years[22]; since most council tenancies are on a weekly periodic basis, this requirement will normally be satisfied. Thirdly, the letting must commence on or after October 24, 1961.[23] Where the letting precedes this date, then in the case of weekly tenancies there appears to be an implied term that the property will be kept in "reasonable and habitable condition," if at all, by the landlord rather than by the tenant: this absolves the tenant from doing the repairs, but does not actually make the landlord responsible for them.[24] However, if a pre-October 24, 1961 tenancy agreement expressly imposes a liab-

19 *Wainwright* v. *Leeds C.C.* (1984) 82 L.G.R. 657 (C.A.).

20 L. & T.A. 1985, ss.11(1), 16(*b*), and 36(2); see also *Brikom Investments* v. *Seaford* [1981] 1 W.L.R. 863 (C.A.).

21 *Cf.* H.A. 1985, s.79(3), which makes many of the provisions of the H.A. applicable to licences: see above, para. 7.15.

22 L. & T.A. 1985, s.13(1); *Brikom Investments* v. *Seaford*, see above, n. 20.

23 L. & T.A. 1985, s.13(1); where the rent payable by a tenant who took up occupation *before* October 24, 1961 has been increased *after* that date by the pre-1980 method of notice to quit followed by re-grant (see above, paras. 10.16, 10.19), then the re-granted tenancy will attract the statutory repairing covenants: see, *e.g. Benson* v. *Liverpool C.C.* [1989] March Legal Action 22 (Cty. Ct.).

24 *Mint* v. *Good* [1950] 2 All E.R. 1159, 1162 (C.A.); *Sleafer* v. *Lambeth B.C.* [1960] 1 Q.B. 43 (C.A.).

ility on the tenant to do internal repairs, but makes no express provision for external and structural repairs, then the agreement may be construed, in order to give it business efficacy, as impliedly obliging the *landlord* to do the external and structural repairs.[25]

12.11 *The items covered by the covenants.* Where these conditions are satisfied, covenants are implied on the part of the landlord to keep in repair the structure and exterior of the dwelling (including drains, gutters and external pipes), and to keep in repair and proper working order the installations in the dwelling for the supply of water, gas and electricity, for sanitation (including basins, sinks, baths and sanitary conveniences), and for space heating or water heating.[26] Any tenant's repairing covenant is ineffective in so far as it relates to these items,[27] and any attempt to exclude the statutory provisions is void,[28] save that county courts may with the consent of the parties allow the exclusion or modification of the statutory provisions if they consider it reasonable to do so.[29]

12.12 Difficult questions of fact may need to be resolved regarding whether an item falls within these implied covenants. It seems that wallplaster can be treated as part of the "structure."[30] Windows appear to be part of the "exterior"[31] (though probably not part of the "structure"[32]). Steps and flagstones used for access to the dwelling have been held to be part of its "exterior"[33]; but paving slabs which are not a necessary means of access to the dwelling have been held, on the facts, not to be part of the "exterior"[34] (despite the absence of any mention in the statute of the relevance of access ways). The covenants appear to impose an obligation on the land-

[25] *Barrett* v. *Lounova (1982)* (1988) 20 H.L.R. 584 (C.A.).
[26] L. & T.A. 1985, s.11(1).
[27] *Ibid.* s.11(4).
[28] *Ibid.* s.12(1); *R.* v. *Secretary of State for Health and Social Security, ex p. City of Sheffield* (1985) 18 H.L.R. 6, 13 (D.C.).
[29] L. & T.A. 1985, s.12(2).
[30] See *Quick* v. *Taff Ely B.C.* [1986] Q.B. 809 (C.A.), where the point was conceded by the council.
[31] *Ball* v. *Plummer* (1879) 23 S.J. 656 (express covenant to do "outside" repairs); *McKay* v. *Horwell* [1983] L.A.G. Bull. 35 (Sh.Ct.); *Hastie* v. *Edinburgh D.C.* 1981 S.L.T. 61 (Sh.Ct.).
[32] *McKay* v. *Horwell*, see above, n. 31; *Holiday Fellowship* v. *Hereford* [1959] 1 W.L.R. 211 (C.A.).
[33] *Brown* v. *Liverpool Corpn.* [1969] 3 All E.R. 1345 (C.A.).
[34] *Hopwood* v. *Cannock Chase D.C.* [1975] 1 W.L.R. 373 (C.A.).

lord to decorate the exterior if this is necessary to "keep" it in repair in order to prevent deterioration of the fabric of the dwelling,[35] but not merely for cosmetic reasons.

The obligation to "keep" in repair the structure, exterior, and relevant installations imposes a liability first to *put* the house into repair if it is in disrepair at the commencement of the tenancy.[36] In the case of the specified installations, the obligation is not merely to keep them in repair, but also in proper working order. However, the reference to "proper working order" apparently relates merely to the physical or mechanical condition of the installation: thus it has been held that there is no obligation on a landlord to lag water pipes in order to guard against frost damage, so that if they become frozen the council will not be responsible for any water damage caused by a resulting burst.[37] Nevertheless, the council will be liable to repair the pipe itself, following the burst, unless the burst can be attributed to the tenant's default[38]; and the council may be tortiously liable to the tenant in negligence for damage caused by the burst if it failed to respond adequately to the tenant's request for advice about how he should deal with the frozen pipes.[39] **12.13**

In the case of blocks of flats, there are particular problems in deciding the scope of the implied covenants in respect of an individual flat within a block. It appears that the relevant "structure" extends to the structural framework and beams directly supporting the floors, ceilings and walls of the individual flat[40]; the relevant "exterior" extends to the outside walls of the individual flat (even though those walls are not included in the letting), the outside of the inner party walls of that flat, and the outer sides of the horizontal divisions between that flat and the flats above and below it[41]; while the relevant "installations" are restricted to those within the physical confines of the individual flat.[42] Repairs to other parts of the block or to installations outside the individual flat (such as a central **12.14**

[35] See *Monk* v. *Noyes* (1824) 1 C. & P. 265; *Crawford* v. *Newton* (1886) 2 T.L.R. 877 (C.A.).
[36] *Proudfoot* v. *Hart* (1890) 25 Q.B.D. 42 (C.A.); *Liverpool C.C.* v. *Irwin* [1976] 2 All E.R. 39, 57 (H.L.).
[37] *Wycombe A.H.A.* v. *Barnett* (1982) 5 H.L.R. 84 (C.A.).
[38] See below, para. 12.49.
[39] *Stockley* v. *Knowsley M.B.C.* [1986] 2 E.G.L.R. 141 (C.A.).
[40] *Campden Hill Towers* v. *Gardner* [1977] Q.B. 823 (C.A.).
[41] *Ibid.*
[42] *Ibid.*

heating boiler in the basement of the block[43]) are generally not covered by the statutory obligations where the lease was entered into before January 15, 1989,[44] although it may be possible to treat the portion of the roof above a top-floor flat as part of the structure or exterior of that flat, even though the roof does not form part of the demise, and whether or not it is pitched rather than level.[45]

12.15 *Restrictions on the landlord's liability*. There are several restrictions on the landlord's liability:

12.16 (i) The "knowledge" requirement. The council will not be in breach of the implied covenants unless it knows of the defect,[46] and a reasonable time has also elapsed after the receipt of such knowledge within which it could have had the repairs carried out[47]; this "knowledge" limitation (the introduction of which by the courts has been much criticised[48]) applies even where the defect was latent, so that the tenant was unable to tell the landlord about it.[49] The burden lies on the tenant to show knowledge of the defect on the part of the landlord.[50]

12.17 The necessary "knowledge" can however arise from a source other than the tenant himself: it may come from an independent third party, such as the district valuer[51]; and where the landlord's employee is aware of the defect, then

[43] *Cf. Parker* v. *Camden L.B.C.* [1986] Ch. 162 (C.A.), where the council had entered into an *express* covenant concerning the heating and hot water services in the block; however, the court could decide that there is a collateral contract with an *implied* term entitling the tenants to a reasonable degree of heat from an estate heating system: *Collins* v. *Northern Ireland Housing Executive* [1988] September Legal Action 15 (C.A.(N.I.)).

[44] *Campden Hill Towers* v. *Gardner*, see above, n. 40; where the lease is entered into on or after January 15, 1989, then the s.11 obligations extend to certain other parts of the block: see below, paras. 12.36–12.37.

[45] *Douglas-Scott* v. *Scorgie* [1984] 1 W.L.R. 716 (C.A.).

[46] *O'Brien* v. *Robinson* [1973] 1 All E.R. 583 (H.L.).

[47] *Calebar Properties Ltd.* v. *Stitcher* [1983] 3 All E.R. 759, 769 (C.A.); *McGreal* v. *Wake* (1984) 13 H.L.R. 107 (C.A.); *Morris* v. *Liverpool C.C.* (1988) 20 H.L.R. 498 (C.A.).

[48] See, *e.g. McGreal* v. *Wake*, (1984) 13 H.L.R. 107, 109; J.I. Reynolds, (1974) 37 M.L.R. 377; *cf.* M. J. Robinson, (1976) 39 M.L.R. 43, Law Commission, *Report on Obligations of Landlords and Tenants*, *op. cit.* pp. 33–36.

[49] *O'Brien* v. *Robinson*, see above, n. 46.

[50] *Hughes* v. *Liverpool C.C.*, *The Times*, March 30, 1988 (C.A.).

[51] *Dinefwr B.C.* v. *Jones* (1987) 19 H.L.R. 445 (C.A.); see also *Hall* v. *Howard* (1988) 20 H.L.R. 566 (C.A.), where the landlord was held to have notice of defects which had been referred to in a valuation report sent by the tenant's surveyor to the landlord's agents, in connection with a proposed purchase.

the landlord will be liable even if the information is not in fact relayed to it by the employee[52] and even though the employee may have been inspecting the dwelling for some purpose other than that of ascertaining its state of disrepair.[53]

The "knowledge" requirement is satisfied if the landlord is aware in broad terms of the defect in question: it need not know of the precise nature or degree of the disrepair.[54] **12.18**

The need for the landlord to have "knowledge" is particularly significant where there has been consequential injury or damage caused by the disrepair, and the question arises as to whether the landlord was in breach at the relevant time (*i.e.* when the injury or damage occurred). It may, however, be possible for the plaintiff to circumvent the "knowledge" rule by bringing an action in tort under the Defective Premises Act 1972.[55] **12.19**

(ii) The "age, character, prospective life and locality" qualifications. The statute provides that, in determining the standard of repair required by the implied repairing covenant, "regard shall be had to the age, character and prospective life of the dwelling-house and the locality in which it is situated."[56] This can sometimes be applied to the council's considerable advantage: thus it appears that if the property is very old and with a short life, the council cannot be compelled to carry out substantial repairs.[57] Indeed, it has been suggested[58] that if demolition is imminent, the standard of repair required should be nil; this construction may be doubtful, since it renders the statutory covenants completely useless in such a case. If, however, the dwelling **12.20**

[52] *Dinefwr B.C.* v. *Jones*, see above, n. 51 (inspection by one of the council's environmental health officers); *Sheldon* v. *West Bromwich Corpn.* (1973) 117 S.J. 486 (C.A., knowledge of corporation's plumber sufficient); *Daejan Properties Ltd.* v. *Elliott* [1977] L.A.G. Bull. 208 (Cty. Ct., knowledge of landlord's resident caretaker sufficient).

[53] *Dinefwr B.C.* v. *Jones*, see above, n. 51 (inspection for purpose of checking cleanliness of dwelling).

[54] *Al Hassani* v. *Merrigan* (1988) 20 H.L.R. 238, 244 (C.A.), where, however, the relevant letter written by the tenant's solicitors was too ambiguous to fix the landlord with "knowledge."

[55] D.P.A. 1972, s.4: see below, para. 12.40.

[56] L. & T.A. 1985, s.11(3).

[57] *L.B. of Newham* v. *Patel* [1979] J.P.L. 303 (C.A.).

[58] *Ibid.*

has not yet reached the end of its life, and the costs of repair would be modest, then the courts will not be anxious to allow the council to rely on this qualification.[59]

12.21 (iii) The distinction between the concept of repair, and that of renewal or improvement. A covenant to "repair," such as that imposed by section 11 of the Landlord and Tenant Act, does not go so far as to require the landlord in substance to renew or improve the property. Nevertheless, works of repair will frequently involve elements of renewal or improvement, particularly where the only effective way of remedying the disrepair is by the introduction of something "new" such as a damp-proof course. There is no rule that inherent defects automatically fall outside a repairing covenant: it is a question of degree whether the work in question "can properly be described as repair," or whether it involves the production of "a wholly different thing from that demised"[60] (in which case the work falls outside the repairing obligation), and in deciding this question "the proportion which the cost of the disputed work bears to the value or cost of the whole premises, may sometimes be helpful as a guide."[61]

12.22 Thus where items such as roofs, damp-proof courses or exterior doors are defective, and have caused the dwelling to fall into disrepair,[62] then complete replacement by materials complying with appropriate modern standards may, where appropriate, be required as part of the "repairing" covenant.[63] Where disrepair has been caused by rising damp, then even if the dwelling lacks any damp-proof course at all, the insertion of an efficient modern damp-proofing system (rather than, for example, simple replastering) may nevertheless (depending on the facts) be within the scope of a "repairing" covenant,[64] though the

[59] *McClean* v. *Liverpool C.C.* [1987] 2 E.G.L.R. 56 (C.A.).
[60] *Ravenseft Properties* v. *Davstone (Holdings)* [1979] 1 All E.R. 929, 937 (*per* Forbes J.); see also *McDougall* v. *Easington D.C., The Times*, February 2, 1989 (C.A.).
[61] *Ravenseft Properties* v. *Davstone (Holdings), ibid.*; see, on the cost factor, *Elite Investments* v. *Bainbridge Silencers* (1986) 280 E.G. 1001.
[62] Water penetration of itself is not disrepair: see below, para. 12.24.
[63] See, *e.g. Elmcroft Developments* v. *Tankersley-Sawyer* (1984) 15 H.L.R. 63 (C.A.); *Stent* v. *Monmouth D.C.* (1987) 19 H.L.R. 269 (C.A.); *cf. Murray* v. *Birmingham C.C.* [1987] 2 E.G.L.R. 53 (C.A.), where the condition of the roof in question was not yet, on the facts, so bad as to require total replacement.
[64] See by analogy *Ravenseft Properties* v. *Davstone Holdings* [1979] 1 All E.R. 929, 937.

position may be otherwise where the house is old, run-down, and of little value.[65]

It appears that these problems concerning the scope of the obligation to "repair" do not arise where the tenant's complaint relates to the landlord's failure to keep a relevant *installation* "in proper working order"[66]: this obligation is more far-reaching than simply keeping the installation in repair,[67] and may involve the complete replacement of faulty items. **12.23**

(iv) The need to show *dis*repair. Breach of the statutory covenant to "keep in repair the structure and exterior"[68] will only occur where there is *dis*repair of the structure or exterior[69]; for example, rotted doors[70] or window frames[71] or damaged plaster[72] will constitute "disrepair," but the mere fact that the dwelling has severe condensation[73] or is regularly flooded[74] or suffers from rising damp[75] will not of itself necessarily mean that "disrepair" of the structure or exterior has resulted, in the absence of corruption of the structure or exterior. A house may actually be unfit for habitation because of damp, and yet there may be no relevant *dis*repair.[76] **12.24**

(v) Breach of the tenant's own obligations, and the effects of inevitable accident. The statutory covenants do not require the council to do repairs for which the tenant is liable under his obligation to use the premises in a "tenant-like manner,"[77] nor to rebuild or reinstate the premises in cases of destruction or damage by fire, or by tempest, flood, or other inevitable accident,[78] nor to repair or main- **12.25**

[65] *Wainwright* v. *Leeds C.C.* (1984) 82 L.G.R. 657 (C.A.).
[66] *I.e.* within L. & T.A. 1985, s.11(1)(*b*)–(*c*), see above.
[67] *Liverpool C.C.* v. *Irwin* [1976] 2 All E.R. 39, 57 (H.L.).
[68] L. & T.A. 1985, s.11(1)(*a*), see above.
[69] *Quick* v. *Taff Ely B.C.* [1985] Q.B. 809 (C.A.); *Post Office* v. *Aquarius Properties* [1987] 1 All E.R. 1055 (C.A.).
[70] *Stent* v. *Monmouth D.C.*, see above, n. 63.
[71] *Mitchell* v. *L.B. of Brent* [1984] Legal Action 53 (Cty. Ct.); *Palmer* v. *Sandwell M.B.C.* (1988) 20 H.L.R. 74 (C.A.).
[72] *Quick* v. *Taff Ely B.C.*, see above, n. 69; *Palmer* v. *Sandwell M.B.C.*, see above, n. 71.
[73] *Quick* v. *Taff Ely B.C.*, see above, n. 69.
[74] *Post Office* v. *Aquarius Properties*, see above, n. 69.
[75] *London Congregational Union Inc.* v. *Harriss and Harriss* [1988] 1 All E.R. 15 (C.A.).
[76] *Quick* v. *Taff Ely B.C.*, see above, n. 69.
[77] L. & T.A. 1985, s.11(2)(*a*); see below, paras. 12.49–12.50.
[78] *Ibid.* s.11(2)(*b*).

tain anything which the tenant is entitled to remove from the property.[79] However, there appears to be no exemption from liability on the part of the landlord for disrepair caused by acts of vandalism beyond the tenant's own control.[80]

12.26 (vi) Leases *to* councils. The statutory covenants do not apply to leases granted after October 3, 1980, *to* certain public bodies including local authorities[81]: this exemption only applies to short leases *to* these public bodies, not short leases *by* them, and it is designed to encourage private owners to release their properties to public bodies for short-term lettings falling outside the definition of a "secure tenancy."[82]

12.27 *The effects of breach of the covenants.* On breach of these covenants, the tenant may claim (*inter alia*[83]) damages and specific performance. The tenant cannot however repudiate the lease on account of the disrepair, since the statute implies covenants rather than conditions[84]; nevertheless, it would of course be open to the tenant to determine the tenancy (if periodic) by serving a notice to quit.

(ii) The dwelling itself: section 8 of the Landlord and Tenant Act 1985

12.28 *General.* The implied obligations in section 8 of the Landlord and Tenant Act 1985 are of rather less relevance to council tenancies, in view of the restrictive conditions governing their applicability. Where they can apply, the obligations relate to fitness for habitation rather than to simple disrepair as such.

12.29 *The conditions which must be satisfied.* In order for section 8 to apply, there must be a contract for the letting (rather than the licensing) of a house or part of a house, at a rent which did not exceed, *at the date of the making of the contract,* £80 per annum in Inner London or £52 per annum elsewhere (or half these figures if the letting began before

[79] L. & T.A. 1985, s.11(2)(*c*).
[80] See below, para. 12.50; see also *Morris* v. *Liverpool C.C.* (1988) 20 H.L.R. 498 (C.A.), where the court accepted that a landlord may be liable under s.11 to repair a flat door broken by firemen when dealing with a fire in the block.
[81] L. & T.A. 1985, s.14(4).
[82] See H.A. 1985, Sched. 1, para. 6, discussed above, paras. 7.43–7.45.
[83] The range of remedies open to the tenant is discussed below, paras. 12.51–12.80.
[84] See *Surplice* v. *Farnsworth* (1844) 7 M. & G. 576.

July 6, 1957).[85] Despite these very low rent ceilings,[86] it seems that if the rent under the tenancy was originally within the relevant limit, it is immaterial that it is later increased under the tenancy agreement to a figure exceeding that limit (since increases in the rent merely have the effect of varying the tenancy terms, rather than of giving rise to surrenders and regrants).[87]

The effect of section 8. Where these conditions are satisfied, then, notwithstanding any contrary stipulation, a condition is implied that the house is fit for human habitation at the start of the tenancy, coupled with an undertaking that it will be kept fit by the landlord during the tenancy.[88] **12.30**

"Fitness for habitation" is defined by the Landlord and Tenant Act 1985[89]: a house is unfit for human habitation for these purposes if, and only if, it is defective in respect of certain prescribed[90] matters (repair, stability, freedom from damp,[91] etc.) to such an extent that it is not reasonably suitable for occupation in that condition. This definition has been amplified by ministerial Circulars,[92] but the standard remains a low one, and is arguably inadequate for modern housing needs.[93] A 1985 Green Paper[94] proposed a new statutory fitness standard, which would include requirements for a fixed bath or shower and inside toilet, but in other respects would actually be more restrictive than the current standard: thus disrepair would **12.31**

[85] L. & T.A. 1985, s.8(1), (3)–(4), (6); "rent" for these purposes means the figure actually contracted to be paid to the landlord, and will therefore include the rates where these are recovered from the tenant as part of the rent: *Rousou* v. *Photi* [1940] 2 All E.R. 528 (C.A.).

[86] Parliament's failure to sanction any increase in these figures since 1957 was commented on with surprise in *Quick* v. *Taff Ely B.C.*, see above, n. 69.

[87] See, *e.g. Gable Construction Co.* v. *I.R.C.* [1968] 1 W.L.R. 1426; *Jenkin R. Lewis & Son* v. *Kerman* [1971] Ch. 477 (C.A.); *Smirk* v. *Lyndale Developments* [1975] Ch. 317 (C.A.).

[88] L. & T.A. 1985, s.8(1).

[89] *Ibid.* s.10.

[90] The nine prescribed matters are often referred to by environmental health officers as the "nine-point standard."

[91] See, *e.g. Quick* v. *Taff Ely B.C.*, see above, n. 69, where it was recognised that a house suffering from very severe condensation could well come within s.8 as being unfit (although on the facts the section could not apply, because the rent exceeded the statutory limit).

[92] M.H.L.G. Circs. 55/54, 69/67, and 68/69.

[93] See, *e.g.* D. Ormandy [1977] L.A.G. Bull. 206; for example, such problems as infestation by bugs, the risk of disease, the absence of an inside toilet, and the absence of an electricity or gas supply, are all outside the statutory standard.

[94] *Home Improvement—a New Approach*, Cmnd. 9513.

only be relevant if it constituted "dangerous structural disrepair or instability," and dampness would only be relevant if "so pervasive as to be a threat to the health of the occupants."[95] Under the current standard, the fact that the defect may be quickly and cheaply remedied is irrelevant to the question of unfitness,[96] and there is no requirement that the specified matters must be dangerous to health.

12.32 *Restrictions on the landlord's liability*. As with the covenants in section 11 of the Landlord and Tenant Act, the courts have decided that knowledge of the defect on the part of the landlord is a precondition of section 8 liability.[97] Furthermore, although there is no equivalent in section 8 to the "age, character and prospective life" qualification in section 11,[98] it has been decided that liability under section 8 can only arise if the house is capable of being made fit at reasonable expense.[99]

12.33 There are two other exclusions which are imposed by the statute: first, section 8 will not apply if the dwelling is let for three years or more on terms that the tenant will render it fit for human habitation[1]; and secondly, the section will not apply where the council is retaining, pursuant to powers in the Housing Act 1985, seriously unfit housing which is nevertheless capable of providing accommodation which is adequate for the time being.[2]

12.34 *The effects of breach of the section 8 obligations*. Breach of the condition or undertaking in section 8 allows the tenant to choose (*inter alia*[3]) the remedies of damages and specific performance. He may also

[95] *Home Improvement—a New Approach*, Cmnd. 9513, Annex II.
[96] *Summers* v. *Salford Corpn.* [1943] A.C. 283 (H.L.), defective sash cord held to render the house unfit.
[97] *McCarrick* v. *Liverpool Corpn.* [1946] 2 All E.R. 646 (H.L.).
[98] L. & T.A. 1985, s.11(3), see above, para. 12.20.
[99] *Buswell* v. *Goodwin* [1971] 1 W.L.R. 92 (C.A.); this decision is questionable, particularly in view of H.A. 1985, s.302, which excludes L. & T.A. 1985, s.8, where the council is exercising its statutory powers to retain unfit housing which is beyond repair at reasonable expense but is capable of providing accommodation which is adequate for the time being: the fact that s.8 is expressly excluded in such cases indicates that it would otherwise have applied, even though *ex hypothesi* the dwelling is incapable of being made fit at reasonable expense.
[1] L. & T.A. 1985, s.8(5).
[2] H.A. 1985, ss.300–302; see n. 99 above.
[3] Remedies for disrepair are discussed in detail below, paras. 12.51–12.80.

repudiate the tenancy for breach of the *condition*,[4] but is unlikely to wish to take this course.

(iii) The dwelling itself: furnished property. There is a quite separate condition implied at common law that on the letting of a *furnished* dwelling the property will be reasonably fit for human habitation at the start of the tenancy[5]; however, since furnished lettings of council properties are very rare, this common law fitness condition will not be further dealt with here.[6] 12.35

(iv) The common parts: extension of section 11 liability. Where the dwelling in question forms part only of a building, then in the case of leases entered into after January 15, 1989, the covenants in section 11 of the Landlord and Tenant Act 1985 extend beyond the dwelling itself to include the "structure and exterior" of any part of that building in which the landlord has an interest, and also to include relevant "installations" which directly or indirectly serve the dwelling and are *either* installations forming part of any portion of the building in which the landlord has an interest *or* installations owned by the landlord or under the landlord's control.[7] 12.36

However, this extension of the section 11 covenants only applies where the defect in question affects the tenant's enjoyment of the dwelling or of the relevant common parts (including structure, exterior and common facilities) of the building of which the dwelling forms part[8]; moreover, the landlord has a defence where it does not have a sufficient right in the relevant part of the building or the relevant installation to enable it to carry out the necessary work, and it was unable, after using all reasonable endeavours, to obtain the necessary rights to enable it to do the work.[9] 12.37

(v) The common parts: common law liability. At common law, if the council retains in its occupation or control such common parts of the building (for example roofs, stairways or lifts) as are essential to the enjoyment of the property let, then it owes to the tenant an implied contractual obligation to use reasonable care to maintain those common parts in a reasonably safe and fit condition, so that 12.38

[4] Compare the breach of a mere repairing *covenant*, which does not permit repudiation of the tenancy; see above, para. 12.27.
[5] See, *e.g. Smith* v. *Marrable* (1843) 11 M. & W. 5.
[6] See, *e.g.* A. Arden and M. Partington, *Housing Law* (1983), pp. 651–652.
[7] L. & T.A. 1985, s.11(1A); H.A. 1988, s.116(4).
[8] L. & T.A. 1985, s.11(1B).
[9] *Ibid.* s.11(3A).

they do not cause injury, inconvenience or discomfort to the tenant, or damage to his property, or damage to the dwelling which is let to him.[10] The council's liability in relation to property kept under its control is not dependent on it receiving notice of the defect.[11]

12.39 However, this implied obligation is not absolute: it only imposes a duty to take reasonable care.[12] Furthermore, authorities may seek expressly to exclude this common law liability in their tenancy agreements to the extent permitted by the Unfair Contract Terms Act 1977.

(c) *The council's liability in tort*

12.40 **(i) The dwelling itself: the Defective Premises Act 1972.** Under the Defective Premises Act 1972,[13] where premises are let *either* under a tenancy which puts on the landlord an obligation to the tenant for the maintenance or repair of the premises (including[14] the statutory obligations imposed by the Landlord and Tenant Act 1985[15]), *or* under a tenancy which gives the landlord an express or implied right to enter[16] in order to maintain[17] or repair,[18] then the landlord owes, to all persons (including the tenant) who might reasonably be expected to be affected by defects in the maintenance or repair of the premises, a duty to take reasonable care to see that

[10] See, *e.g. Hargroves, Aronson & Co.* v. *Hartopp* [1905] 1 K.B. 472; *Dunster* v. *Hollis* [1918] 2 K.B. 795; *Cockburn* v. *Smith* [1924] 2 K.B. 119 (C.A.); *Liverpool C.C.* v. *Irwin* [1976] 2 W.L.R. 562 (H.L.), where it was decided that the obligation can be broken if the common parts are not reasonably fit for the tenant's use even though neither injury nor damage has yet occurred; compare the refusal to extend the *Irwin* principle to defective drains in *Duke of Westminster* v. *Guild* [1984] 3 All E.R. 144, 151 (C.A.).

[11] *Melles & Co.* v. *Holme* [1918] 2 K.B. 100.

[12] See, *e.g. Liverpool C.C.* v. *Irwin* [1976] 2 W.L.R. 562 (H.L.), where the council was held on the facts to have taken such care.

[13] D.P.A. 1972, s.4(1).

[14] *Ibid.* s.4(5).

[15] See above, paras. 12.09–12.34.

[16] D.P.A. 1972, s.4(4); see, *e.g. Smith* v. *Bradford M.C.* (1982) 126 S.J. 624 (C.A.); *Barrett* v. *Lounova (1982)* [1988] June Legal Action 20 (Cty. Ct.).

[17] An express reservation of the right to do *maintenance* work (which is wider than a right to repair), could give rise to tortious liability under s.4 even though there is as yet no disrepair, for example in cases where the tenant's health or possessions have been affected by severe condensation dampness: see D. Watkinson, [1986] Legal Action 49, 50; *cf.* the contractual position established in *Quick* v. *Taff Ely B.C.* [1985] Q.B. 809 (C.A.).

[18] Weekly tenancies are subject to an *implied* term that the landlord is entitled to enter to do repairs: *Mint* v. *Good* [1951] 1 K.B. 517 (C.A.).

they and their possessions are reasonably safe from injury or damage caused by such defects. Furthermore, this duty is owed not merely where the council knows of the defect (through notification by the tenant or otherwise), but also where it ought to have known of it[19] (which contrasts with the narrower "knowledge" element normally required in order to succeed in a contractual claim for breach of a repairing covenant[20]). The landlord cannot exclude this liability in the tenancy agreement.[21] A similar duty may be owed by licensors.[22]

A separate provision in the Defective Premises Act 1972[23] deals **12.41** with the position where the landlord has been responsible for the building of the dwelling and the work was begun after January 1, 1974[24]: such a landlord owes a duty to every person acquiring an interest in the dwelling to see that the work is properly done, with proper materials, and that the dwelling will, as regards that work, be fit for human habitation. This duty will often be owed by council landlords, since it extends[25] to those who "in the course of a business which consists of or includes providing or arranging for the provision of dwellings," or "in the exercise of a power of making such provision or arrangements conferred by or by virtue of any enactment," arrange for another to do the relevant work. This liability also cannot be excluded by the tenancy agreement.[26]

(ii) The dwelling itself: common law liability. A landlord who **12.42** designs a dwelling, or who does other work in relation thereto (whether by way of the construction or the subsequent repair or maintenance thereof), owes a duty of care at common law to all persons (not just the tenant) who might reasonably be expected to be affected by the design, construction, repair or maintenance; the duty is to take reasonable care to see that such persons do not suffer personal injury or damage to their property as a result of the relevant

[19] D.P.A. 1972, s.4(2); see, *e.g. Clarke* v. *Taff Ely B.C.* (1983) 10 H.L.R. 44, where the council was liable for the defect because it had failed to maintain a proper system of inspection of dwellings, when it was foreseeable that the relevant defect would occur because of the age, situation and type of those dwellings.

[20] See above, paras. 12.16–12.19.

[21] D.P.A. 1972, s.6(3).

[22] *Ibid.* s.4(6).

[23] *Ibid.* s.1.

[24] *Alexander* v. *Mercouris* [1979] 1 W.L.R. 1270 (C.A.).

[25] D.P.A. 1972, s.1(4).

[26] *Ibid.* s.6(3).

work.[27] This cause of action may prove useful to a tenant who has no contractual claim.[28] However, the cost of repairing a defect which has been discovered before the defect has caused either personal injury or physical damage to other property is not normally recoverable in tort, because this cost represents purely economic loss.[29] Furthermore, no common law duty is owed by a "bare" landlord who does no work in relation to the property[30]; and, even in the case of an "active" landlord, there may on the facts be no breach of the duty of care even though injury or damage results.[31] This common law liability can be excluded by the tenancy agreement, to the extent permitted by the Unfair Contract Terms Act 1977.

12.43 Quite separately, the landlord may be liable at common law for the tort of deceit, where the tenant has been induced to enter into the lease by the landlord's fraudulent behaviour; this can include the active concealment of defects by cosmetic work[32] (as opposed merely to keeping quiet about them in the hope that the tenant will not notice!)

12.44 The council may also be liable to its tenants in negligence where trespassing vandals have damaged a neighbouring vacant property of the council in such a way that the tenant's dwelling is adversely affected (for example, by flooding caused by removal of water pipes from the vacant property)[33]; but no such duty of care will be owed if,

[27] See, *e.g. Dutton* v. *Bognor Regis United Building Co.* [1972] 1 Q.B. 373 (C.A.); *Rimmer* v. *Liverpool C.C.* [1985] Q.B. 1 (C.A.); for limitation periods, see Latent Damage Act 1986.

[28] As in *Rimmer* v. *Liverpool C.C.*, see above, n. 27., where the plaintiff tenant was injured by falling through a dangerous interior panel of thin breakable glass, which was not, however, (before the injury) in a state of disrepair; see also *Sharpe* v. *Manchester M.D.C.* (1977) 5 H.L.R. 71 (C.A.): negligence (and nuisance) established through use by the council of an incorrect treatment in attempting to remove cockroaches which gained access to the flat in question via the common parts.

[29] *D. & F. Estates* v. *Church Commissioners* [1988] 2 All E.R. 992 (H.L.); but in the case of a "complex structure" (such as a block of flats), it seems that one part of the structure can be treated as separate from another part, so that damage to one part caused by defects in another part may satisfy the "other property" test, thus allowing recovery of the repair costs (*per* Lord Bridge at pp. 1006–1007). See also *D.O.E.* v. *Thomas Bates & Son Ltd.* (1989) 139 N.L.J. 39 (C.A.), suggesting that liability might arise once the defects pose an immediate *risk* of physical injury to the building's inhabitants, even though no relevant injury or damage has yet been caused.

[30] *Rimmer* v. *Liverpool C.C.*, see above, n. 27; see also *McNerny* v. *Lambeth L.B.C.*, *The Times*, December 10, 1988 (C.A.).

[31] See, *e.g. Ryan* v. *L.B. of Camden* (1983) 8 H.L.R. 75 (C.A.: no liability for injury to tenant's child caused by contact with uninsulated central heating pipes.

[32] *Gordon* v. *Selico Co.* (1986) 18 H.L.R. 219 (C.A.).

[33] *King* v. *Liverpool C.C.* [1986] 1 W.L.R. 890 (C.A.).

on the facts, it was not possible for the council to take effective steps to prevent the trespassers from causing the damage.[34]

(iii) The common parts: the Occupiers' Liability Act 1957. A council may be liable in tort as regards the safety of the common parts under the Occupiers' Liability Act 1957: as "occupier" of the common parts (by virtue of its physical control or possession of them) a landlord or licensor owes[35] a "common duty of care" to take reasonable care to see that "visitors" lawfully on the common parts, and their belongings,[36] will be "reasonably safe." This provision is concerned only with safety, not with convenience or comfort. The council can exclude liability in the lease or licence agreement as against the tenant or licensee, but only to the extent permitted by the Unfair Contract Terms Act 1977, and not in any event as against the tenant's or licensee's own visitors.[37] **12.45**

(iv) The common parts: common law liability. A council may be liable in negligence at common law where premises which are retained in its control or possession are in disrepair, as a result of which injury or damage is suffered by the tenant or a member of his family, whether the plaintiff is on the property let or the common parts.[38] **12.46**

(d) *The council's liability for statutory nuisance*

The occupier of defective premises may have a quasi-public law remedy where the premises let or licensed to him, or the common parts, are a "statutory nuisance" under the Public Health Act 1936.[39] This remedy is considered in detail below.[40] **12.47**

(e) *The tenant's implied obligations*

A tenant holding under a weekly periodic tenancy (which is the typical form of council tenancy) is normally under no implied repairing or maintenance obligations. But he is liable in tort for **12.48**

[34] *King* v. *Liverpool C.C.* [1986] 1 W.L.R. 890 (C.A.).
[35] O.L.A. 1957, s.2; see, *e.g. Jordan* v. *Achara* (1988) 20 H.L.R. 607 (C.A.).
[36] O.L.A. 1957, s.1(3).
[37] *Ibid.* s.3.
[38] *Cunard* v. *Antifyre* [1932] All E.R. Rep. 558 (defective guttering retained in landlord's possession); *Taylor* v. *Liverpool Corpn.* [1939] 3 All E.R. 329 (defective chimney stack retained in landlord's possession).
[39] P.H.A. 1936, ss.92(1)(*a*), 99, 343(1).
[40] Paras. 12.55–12.64.

"voluntary waste" (*i.e.* for positive acts of injury to the property: "doing that which ought not to be done"), though *not* for "permissive waste" (*i.e.* neglect or omission: "failure to do that which ought to be done").[41] This liability extends at common law to the acts of the tenant himself, his family, his guests,[42] and other third parties such as trespassers.[43]

12.49 Quite separately, the tenant must use the property in a "tenant-like manner," *i.e.* he must take proper care of it; this would require the performance of such jobs as cleaning the chimney and windows when necessary, mending fuses, unstopping sinks, and taking frost precautions (such as turning off the water supply) when going away during the winter at a time when severe cold may reasonably be anticipated.[44] It also extends, in an appropriate case, to maintaining proper levels of heating in order to combat condensation and consequential damage to the fabric of the property.[45] The tenant's "tenant-like manner" obligation extends to damage caused by his family and guests,[46] though not to damage caused by trespassers.

12.50 The landlord's repairing obligations in section 11 of the Landlord and Tenant Act 1985 are expressly qualified as regards damage for which the tenant is liable at common law under his contractual duty to use the property in a "tenant-like manner"[47] (under which there is no liability for damage caused by trespassers), but are *not* so qualified regarding damage for which the tenant may otherwise have been liable in tort at common law under the doctrine of waste (which normally extends to damage caused by trespassers[48]); it therefore appears that section 11 of the 1985 Act imposes liability on the *landlord* in respect of relevant damage caused by trespassers

[41] See, *e.g.* R. E. Megarry and H. W. R. Wade, *The Law of Real Property* (5th ed., 1984), pp. 96–97, 702; *Warren* v. *Keen* [1954] 1 Q.B. 15 (C.A.); *Mint* v. *Good* [1951] 1 K.B. 517, 522 (C.A.).

[42] *Warren* v. *Keen* [1954] 1 Q.B. 15, 20 (C.A.).

[43] *Attersoll* v. *Stevens* (1808) 1 Taun. 183.

[44] *Warren* v. *Keen*, see above, n. 42; *Wycombe A.H.A.* v. *Barnett* (1982) 5 H.L.R. 84 (C.A.).

[45] *Mitchell* v. *L.B. of Brent* [1984] Legal Action 53 (Cty. Ct.); however, it appears that if the tenant's lifestyle is within the spectrum of lifestyles which the council could reasonably expect its tenants to follow, then where it is prima facie in breach of its repairing obligations it cannot allege that if the tenant could have afforded to spend more on heating there would have been no (or less) disrepair: *Quick* v. *Taff Ely B.C.* [1985] 3 All E.R. 321, 327 (C.A.).

[46] *Warren* v. *Keen*, see above, n. 42.

[47] L. & T.A. 1985, s.11(2): see above, para. 12.25.

[48] *Attersoll* v. *Stevens*, see above, n. 43.

(such as vandals),[49] unless the tenant has facilitated the damage by failing adequately to secure the property against the trespassers, in which case the tenant will probably be in breach of his "tenant-like manner" obligation.

3. *Legal Remedies Open to the Tenant*

(a) *Civil court proceedings*

(i) Breach of the contractual repairing obligations

Damages. The tenant can proceed against the council in a civil court to enforce its express or implied repairing and maintenance obligations. Appropriate heads of damages for breach of contract include: the reasonable cost of alternative accommodation and storage of furniture where the tenant has been forced by the disrepair to move out temporarily, and he moves back into possession following completion of the necessary works[50]; the cost of any relevant landlord's repairs paid for by the tenant[51]; compensation for personal injury, ill-health, and damage to property (including decorations)[52]; and compensation for inconvenience, loss of enjoyment and discomfort endured while the property was deteriorating.[53] The courts are increasingly prepared to award realistic amounts of damages, which **12.51**

[49] *Hastie* v. *City of Edinburgh D.C.* 1981 S.L.T. 61 (Sh.Ct.); D. Hoath, [1986] February Legal Action 22.

[50] *Calabar Properties* v. *Stitcher* [1984] 1 W.L.R. 287 (C.A.); see, as to storage costs, *McGreal* v. *Wake* (1984) 128 S.J. 116 (C.A.).

[51] *Calabar Properties* v. *Stitcher*, see above, n. 50.

[52] *Ibid.*; see, as to consequential damage to decorations caused by relevant disrepair, *McGreal* v. *Wake*, see above, n. 50; *Bradley* v. *Chorley B.C.* (1985) 83 L.G.R. 623 (C.A.); *Little* v. *City of Glasgow D.C.* [1988] S.C.O.L.A.G. 158.

[53] *Calabar Properties* v. *Stitcher*, see above, n. 50; the tenant's rejection of the landlord's offer of alternative accommodation will not reduce the tenant's damages unless the offer was refused capriciously (*Lubren* v. *L.B. of Lambeth* (1988) 20 H.L.R. 165 (C.A.)), but the tenant's failure to mitigate his loss by giving prompt notice of the disrepair to the landlord could reduce the damages (*Minchburn* v. *Peck* (1987) 20 H.L.R. 392 (C.A.)). There are *obiter dicta* in *L.B. of Newham* v. *Patel* [1979] J.P.L. 303 (C.A.) suggesting that in deciding whether a tenant has suffered loss arising from a breach of his landlord's repairing covenants, it is relevant that the disrepair had been taken into account in fixing a low rent; however, in *Personal Representatives of Chiodi* v. *De Marney* (1988) 21 H.L.R. 6 (C.A.) it was accepted that a low rent cannot of itself limit the damages for disrepair to which the tenant would otherwise be entitled.

can now easily reach four figures.[54] Although diminution in the market value of the premises to the tenant may theoretically be recovered in appropriate circumstances,[55] this head of damages will normally have no relevance to council tenants, since secure tenancies are not "marketable" (due to the effects of the Housing Act 1985,[56] whereby secure tenancy status is normally not assignable, and is normally lost following the sub-letting of the whole property).

12.52 *Specific performance.* In addition to damages, the tenant can seek an order for specific performance of a repairing covenant, whether the breach relates to the property let or to the common parts.[57] The order can initially be made on an interim basis where necessary.[58] This remedy is discretionary,[59] and will not be granted where it would inflict great hardship on the landlord; however, the mere fact that the landlord claims not to be able to afford to pay for the work will not necessarily stop the court granting the order.[60] Failure to comply with the order means that the defendant can be proceeded against for contempt of court.

12.53 *Appointment of receiver.* The court has a general power, in cases of serious disrepair, to appoint a receiver to receive the rents, exercise all the landlord's powers, and discharge all the landlord's obligations (including repairing obligations).[61] However, this wide-ranging remedy cannot be exercised against a council landlord, because under the Housing Act 1985[62] Parliament has provided that

[54] See, *e.g. Personal Representatives of Chiodi* v. *DeMarney*, *ibid.* (£5,460 for general inconvenience and distress endured for three and a half years); see also N. Madge, [1988] L.S. Gaz., July 20, p. 7.

[55] *Calabar Properties* v. *Stitcher*, see above, n. 50.

[56] H.A. 1985, ss.91, 93(2), see above, paras. 9.11–9.26.

[57] L. & T.A. 1985, s.17.

[58] See, *e.g. Kotecha* v. *Manchester C.C.* [1983] L.A.G. Bull. 35 (Cty. Ct.); *Parker* v. *Camden L.B.C.* [1986] Ch. 162 (C.A.); *Astro Exito Navegacion S.A.* v. *Southland Enterprise Co.* [1982] Q.B. 1248 (C.A.).

[59] See, *e.g. Jeune* v. *Queens Cross Properties* [1974] Ch. 97.

[60] *Francis* v. *Cowcliff* (1976) 120 S.J. 353.

[61] S.C.A. 1981, s.37 (applicable to county courts also, under C.C.A. 1984, s.107); see, *e.g. Hart* v. *Emelkirk Ltd.* [1983] 1 W.L.R. 1289; *Daiches* v. *Bluelake Investments Ltd.* (1985) 275 E.G. 462; this general jurisdiction is excluded where the statutory power of the court to appoint a manager under L. & T.A. 1987, Pt. II (below) can be used: L. & T.A. 1987, s.21(6).

[62] H.A. 1985, s.21(1).

the general management, regulation and control of council housing is vested in and exercisable by the authority, so that it is not proper for the court to assume the relevant powers and duties itself by appointing a receiver (who would act as the agent of the court).[63] Furthermore, the provisions in Part II of the Landlord and Tenant Act 1987 which enable the tenant of a flat to apply to court for the appointment of a manager where (*inter alia*) the landlord is in breach of his repairing obligations, are expressly excluded where the landlord is a council.[64]

(ii) Tort. In so far as a cause of action may lie in tort for the disrepair, damages will normally be recoverable only for personal injury or damage to property, and not for mere disrepair and consequent inconvenience or discomfort. Where appropriate, an injunction may also be granted compelling the landlord to carry out the necessary repairs.[65] **12.54**

(b) *Criminal court proceedings*

(i) The general power of prosecution in section 99 of the Public Health Act 1936. Councils are given extensive powers and duties in order to deal with defective housing under the Housing Act 1985[66] and the Public Health Acts.[67] However, the initiation of these procedures normally depends on the council's environmental health department serving the relevant notice, so that for obvious reasons little effective action is taken by councils under these procedures in respect of their own defective council housing.[68] Indeed, it is not possible in law for one officer of a local authority to serve a Housing Act notice on another officer of the same authority in connection with a defective council property, since the procedures necessarily envisage the existence of more than one party[69]; in this respect, **12.55**

[63] *Parker* v. *Camden L.B.C.* [1985] 2 All E.R. 141 (C.A.).
[64] L. & T.A. 1987, ss. 21(3)(*a*), 58(1)(*a*).
[65] *Barrett* v. *Lounova (1982)* (1988) 20 H.L.R. 584 (C.A.), a case on the Defective Premises Act 1972, s.4.
[66] See Pts. VI–XII.
[67] See particularly P.H.A. 1936.
[68] It is also common for authorities to establish *combined* housing and environmental health departments.
[69] *R.* v. *Cardiff C.C., ex p. Cross* (1982) 6 H.L.R. 1 (C.A.).

therefore, a council tenant may be in a more disadvantageous position than a private tenant.[70]

12.56 Nevertheless, council tenants can use a special procedure relating to "statutory nuisances" contained in section 99 of the Public Health Act 1936.[71] This allows a private individual who is "aggrieved" by a property which is a statutory nuisance to instigate proceedings in the magistrates' court on his own initiative. The procedure has been used successfully against local authorities on several occasions,[72] but it can turn out to be lengthy and complicated.[73]

12.57 **(ii) The definition of "statutory nuisance."**[74] A "statutory nuisance" is defined as including "any premises in such a state as to be prejudicial to health or a nuisance."[75] The word "premises" is itself widely defined,[76] and can extend to a whole block of flats where the defects are not restricted to the individual units, but rather relate to the block as a whole.[77] "Prejudicial to health" means "injurious, or likely to cause injury, to health"[78]; and the question of prejudice to health is quite distinct from any question of unfitness for human habitation.[79] The word "nuisance" is not defined in the Public Health Act, but has been held to mean, in this context, a public or

[70] *R.* v. *Cardiff C.C., ex p. Cross* (1982) 6 H.L.R. 1, 11 (C.A.).

[71] Quite separately, the tenant can bring a private prosecution against the council for nuisance caused by noise: see Control of Pollution Act 1974, s.59; *Joyce* v. *L.B. of Hackney* [1976] L.A.G. Bull. 211 (noisy boiler in block of flats); *A. Lambert Flat Management* v. *Lomas* [1981] 1 W.L.R. 898 (D.C.) (noisy lift).

[72] See, *e.g. R.* v. *Epping (Waltham Abbey) Justices, ex p. Burlinson* [1948] 1 K.B. 79 (D.C.); *Salford C.C.* v. *McNally* [1976] A.C. 379 (H.L.); *Birmingham D.C.* v. *Kelly* (1985) 17 H.L.R. 572 (D.C.).

[73] See, *e.g.* C. Blood, *Roof*, September 1979, p. 162.

[74] For more detail, see, *e.g.* D. Ormandy and R. Burridge, *Environmental Health Standards in Housing* (1988).

[75] P.H.A. 1936, s.92(1)(*a*).

[76] *Ibid.* s.343(1).

[77] *Birmingham D.C.* v. *McMahon* (1987) 19 H.L.R. 452 (D.C.), where, however, the defects only affected some of the individual flats, and did not affect the common parts, so that the whole block could not be treated as a statutory nuisance.

[78] P.H.A. 1936, s.343(1); this can cover, *e.g.*: defective wiring, *Bennett* v. *Preston B.C.*, October 22, 1982 (Crown Ct.): *Roof*, March 1984, p. 18; lack of artificial lighting, *Day* v. *Sheffield C.C.* [1988] August Legal Action 19 (mags. ct.); dangerous barbed wire, *Day* v. *Sheffield C.C.*, *ibid.*; and condensation (see below).

[79] *Salford C.C.* v. *McNally* [1976] A.C. 379 (H.L.); thus in *McNally's* case the council could not rely on the fact that it was retaining short-life property under the deferred demolition provisions in H.A. 1957, under which such property can be used despite its unfitness: see now H.A. 1985, s.302(*c*).

private nuisance at common law, *i.e.* one which materially affects either the public in general or neighbouring residents: thus no nuisance arises where the condition of the property only affects the personal comfort of its occupiers[80]; in such a case, it is necessary to establish that the dwelling is "prejudicial to health," as defined above, before a statutory nuisance can be said to arise.

In order for the council to be liable for a statutory nuisance, the defect must either be a "structural" one[81] (in which case the council is liable as "owner" of the premises[82]), or the council must be "the person by whose act, default or sufferance the nuisance arises or continues."[83] **12.58**

Several cases have been concerned with the question whether condensation can give rise to a finding of statutory nuisance on the ground of prejudice to health, and, if so, whether the landlord is liable therefor. It is now clear that condensation can be sufficient of itself to make a dwelling "prejudicial to health," even though the structure has not yet been affected by the dampness,[84] provided the "person aggrieved" can point to the necessary "personal link" between "the danger to the health through condensation and mould" and himself as "the person exposed to the danger."[85] However, in cases where the condensation has not affected the structure,[86] it will be necessary for the "person aggrieved" to satisfy the court that the council is the person responsible for the condensation[87]; this can sometimes be shown even though the council is not in breach of any material duty or obligation (whether contractual or statutory) as landlord, and even though it is not in breach of the building regulations or any other statutory requirements (although the absence of such breach may on the particular facts mean that the **12.59**

[80] *N.C.B.* v. *Neath B.C.* [1976] 2 All E.R. 478 (D.C.); compare the situation where the common parts retained by the landlord are defective: the common parts rank as distinct "premises" from the individual dwellings affected by the defects, so that the "nuisance" limb may be satisfied.

[81] P.H.A. 1936, s.93, proviso (*a*); *Warner* v. *L.B. of Lambeth* (1984) 15 H.L.R. 42 (D.C.).

[82] P.H.A. 1936, s.343(1).

[83] *Ibid.* s.93; see, *e.g. Dover D.C.* v. *Farrar* (1982) 2 H.L.R. 32 (D.C.); *Warner* v. *L.B. of Lambeth*, see above, n. 81.

[84] See, *e.g. G.L.C.* v. *L.B. of Tower Hamlets* (1983) 15 H.L.R. 54 (D.C.); *Birmingham D.C.* v. *Kelly* (1985) 17 H.L.R. 572 (D.C.).

[85] *Birmingham D.C.* v. *McMahon* (1987) 19 H.L.R. 452, 456 (D.C.), *per* Kennedy J.

[86] *Cf.* P.H.A. 1936, s.93, proviso (*a*): see above, n. 81.

[87] P.H.A. 1936, s.93: see above, n. 83.

council is not responsible for the statutory nuisance).[88] Where the council has provided an effective heating system, then if the tenant fails to use it, *he* (rather than the council) may be responsible for the statutory nuisance caused by resulting condensation, even if the system is actually too expensive for him to run[89]; but the condensation may be the council's responsibility where the type of building makes it necessary to provide some special form of heating to combat condensation, and the council fails to provide it.[90]

12.60 **(iii) Procedure.** A "person aggrieved" by a statutory nuisance may, under section 99 of the Public Health Act 1936, apply to the magistrates' court by way of information and summons.[91] Where the council is itself acting against a private landlord under the Public Health Act, it must serve an "abatement notice" on the owner of the property, requiring him to abate the nuisance and do the necessary work.[92] No such notice is necessary where a private individual is proceeding under section 99,[93] although the information must disclose in essence the same details as would have been contained in an abatement notice had the authority been bringing the proceedings: these details include the capacity in which the defendant is being served, and the steps which it is alleged have to be taken in order to abate the nuisance.[94]

12.61 Legal aid is not available for a private prosecution, but the tenant may be eligible for advice and assistance under the Legal Aid Act 1988.[95]

12.62 Since the proceedings are criminal in nature,[96] the higher criminal burden of proof applies. In determining technical issues relating to prejudice to health, the magistrates cannot throw over informed expert evidence which is not challenged by the other party.[97] In order to secure a conviction, the prosecutor must show that the

[88] *Birmingham D.C.* v. *Kelly*, see above, n. 84.
[89] *Dover D.C.* v. *Farrar*, see above, n. 83.
[90] *G.L.C.* v. *L.B. of Tower Hamlets*, see above, n. 84.
[91] Rather than by complaint: see Magistrates' Courts Act 1980, ss.1–2; *R.* v. *Newham East Justices, ex p. Hunt* [1976] 1 W.L.R. 420 (D.C.).
[92] P.H.A. 1936, s.93.
[93] *R.* v. *Oxted Justices, ex p. Franklin* [1976] 1 All E.R. 839 (D.C.).
[94] *Warner* v. *Lambeth L.B.C.* (1984) 15 H.L.R. 42 (D.C.).
[95] L.A.A. 1988, ss.8(1)–(2), 21(1).
[96] See, *e.g. R.* v. *Inner London Crown Court, ex p. Bentham, The Times*, November 26, 1988 (D.C.).
[97] *Patel* v. *Mehtab* [1981] L.A.G. Bull. 41.

statutory nuisance exists at the date of the hearing, and not just at the date when the summons is issued.[98]

(iv) Powers of the magistrates' court. Where the tenant proceeds under section 99, the section provides that "the like proceedings shall be had, with the like incidents and consequences as to the making of orders, penalties for disobedience of orders and otherwise, as in the case of a complaint by the local authority." Thus if the tenant proves his case, the court *must* make a "nuisance order" requiring the authority to abate the nuisance within a time specified in the order, and/or prohibiting a recurrence of the nuisance[99]; there is, however, considerable discretion as to the precise terms of the order[1]: in particular, the magistrates can order works beyond those covered by the landlord's contractual repairing obligations,[2] although they must have regard to the "very heavy housing responsibilities" of local authorities.[3] Furthermore, the court may impose a fine[4]; and it may order the closure of the building if the nuisance renders it unfit for habitation.[5] **12.63**

A successful prosecution allows the tenant to ask the court to make a compensation order in relation to personal injury, loss or damage resulting from the offence.[6] An award of costs may be made under the Costs in Criminal Cases Act 1973. **12.64**

98 *Coventry C.C.* v. *Doyle* [1981] 1 W.L.R. 1325 (D.C.).

99 P.H.A. 1936, s.94(2).

1 See, *e.g. Nottingham Corpn.* v. *Newton* [1974] 1 W.L.R. 923 (D.C.); *Salford C.C.* v. *McNally* [1975] 2 All E.R. 860, 864 (H.L.).

2 *Birmingham D.C.* v. *Kelly* (1985) 17 H.L.R. 572 (D.C.); *cf.* the limitations on the obligations contained in the L. & T.A. 1985 (above, paras. 12.09–12.34), exemplified by *Quick* v. *Taff Ely B.C.* [1985] Q.B. 809 (C.A.: above, para. 12.24).

3 *Birmingham D.C.* v. *Kelly* (1985) 17 H.L.R. 572, 581 (D.C.).

4 Up to level 4 on the standard scale, P.H.A. 1936, s.94(2); additional fines may be imposed for non-compliance with a nuisance order: *ibid.* s.95(1).

5 P.H.A. 1936, s.94(2); thus the tenant runs the risk of eviction where the defects are serious (see P.H.A. 1936, ss.287–289), and the only rehousing obligation on the authority would be under H.A. 1985, Pt. III (assuming priority need, see above, paras. 4.01–4.15); the rehousing duty in L.C.A. 1973 does not apply here (see ss.29(7), 39(1)(*b*), and 39(9) thereof).

6 Powers of Criminal Courts Act 1973, ss.35–38; S. Singh, [1987] December Legal Action 11; the maximum compensation is £2,000 for each offence (Magistrates' Courts Act 1980, s.40), and many magistrates in the London area are making substantial compensation orders in cases brought under P.H.A. 1936, s.99 (see N. Madge and J. Luba, [1988] December Legal Action 16, 21). If the court declines to make a compensation order, it must give its reasons: Powers of Criminal Courts Act 1973, s.35(1).

(c) *Common law and equitable rights to set off repair costs against the rent*[7]

12.65 **(i) No general right to withhold rent on account of disrepair.** It is clear that a tenant cannot simply cease paying rent where the landlord has failed to repair, since the covenant to pay rent is independent of the covenant to repair.[8] Indeed, the organisation of "rent strikes" may involve the commission of the torts of inducing breach of contract[9] and/or conspiracy.[10]

12.66 **(ii) The common law right of set off.** Although a tenant cannot withhold his rent merely in order to "teach his landlord a lesson," nevertheless, if he actually pays for the carrying out of repairs for which the landlord is contractually liable, he has an "ancient common law right" to deduct the "proper cost" from future rent[11]; he will then have an absolute defence to any possession action launched on the ground of non-payment of the relevant rent, since the remedy operates by way of set off rather than as a mere counter-claim. The effect is that the tenant has been properly paying his rent by way of discharging the landlord's own repairing obligations.

12.67 It was originally thought that this remedy was confined to deductions by the tenant from *future* rent to pay for repairs *previously executed* at his expense, but it now appears that rent already accrued in arrears can be used in discharge of the landlord's obligations, so that the tenant can in effect "save up" the rent to pay for the repairs where he cannot otherwise afford to do them.[12] A council tenant in receipt of housing benefit will frequently not be able to "save up" the rent because his rent account will automatically be credited with the amount of the benefit; however, in paying benefit the council must have regard to "the reasonable needs and convenience of the [claimant],"[13] which arguably means that such a tenant can demand payment of the benefit in cash so that he can exercise his common law rent-deduction right.

[7] See, *e.g.* A. Waite, [1981] Conv. 199, [1983] Conv. 373; R.C.A. White, [1981] L.A.G. Bull. 182.
[8] See, *e.g. Hart* v. *Rogers* [1916] 1 K.B. 646; *Camden Nominees* v. *Forcey* [1940] Ch. 352.
[9] *Camden Nominees* v. *Forcey, ibid.*
[10] *R.* v. *Parnell* (1881) 14 Cox C.C. 508.
[11] *Lee-Parker* v. *Izzet* [1971] 1 W.L.R. 1688; the tenant does not of course acquire any beneficial interest in the freehold itself by virtue of such expenditure unless he can establish a clear case of proprietary estoppel: *Brinnand* v. *Ewens* (1987) 19 H.L.R. 415 (C.A.).
[12] *Asco Developments & Newman* v. *Lower, Lewis & Gordon* (1978) 248 E.G. 683.
[13] Housing Benefit (General) Regulations 1987 (S.I. 1987 No. 1971), reg. 88(1).

(iii) The equitable right of set off. The common law right of set off appears to be available only in respect of quantified sums needed for repairs, and not for general unliquidated damages arising out of the landlord's default, such as damages for inconvenience, personal injury, etc. However, there is a separate equitable right to set off unliquidated damages where it would be manifestly inequitable to allow the landlord to recover the full rent, and there is a sufficiently close connection between the two claims: thus if the tenant claims unliquidated damages and claims bona fide that they would exceed the amount of the landlord's claim, he may have a complete defence in equity to the claim for rent.[14] **12.68**

(d) *The statutory "right to repair"*

(i) The nature of the right. The Housing Act 1985[15] confers a special self-help repairing right on secure tenants.[16] It is *not* a right to deduct from the rent the repair costs paid out by the tenant, but rather a right to recover stipulated repair costs from the council on application, following completion of the work by the tenant or his contractor. **12.69**

(ii) The relevant repairing obligations of the landlord. The relevant repairing obligations are those owed by the council under its express or implied repairing covenants to keep in repair the dwelling let to the tenant or any part thereof.[17] The scheme is therefore concerned with obligations which are contractual as opposed to tortious, and which relate to the tenant's dwelling itself rather than the common parts. Furthermore, repairs to the structure or exterior of a flat are not covered.[18] **12.70**

(iii) Procedure. The procedure is basically as follows.[19] The secure tenant must first serve a prescribed notice claiming the right to repair (called the "tenant's repair claim"); this notice must state *inter alia* whether the tenant wishes to carry out the work himself or **12.71**

[14] *British Anzani (Felixstowe)* v. *International Marine Management (U.K.) Ltd.* [1980] Q.B. 637; *Melville* v. *Grapelodge Developments* (1980) 39 P. & C.R. 179.

[15] H.A. 1985, s.96; Secure Tenancies (Right to Repair Scheme) Regulations 1985 (S.I. 1985 No. 1493), hereafter referred to as the "1985 Regs."

[16] And, in so far as they may have the benefit of repairing obligations, secure licensees: H.A. 1985, s.79(3).

[17] H.A. 1985, s.96(5); 1985 Regs., Sched., para. 1(2).

[18] 1985 Regs., *ibid.*

[19] 1985 Regs., Sched., paras. 3–11.

to have it carried out by a person named by him. Within 21 days of service of the tenant's notice, the council must either serve notice refusing the claim on prescribed grounds,[20] or it must accept the tenant's repair claim (subject if necessary to prescribed conditions). If the council fails to serve any response notice (accepting or refusing the tenant's repair claim), then if the tenant's estimate of the cost to him of doing the work is not more than £200, he can serve a default notice on the council; within seven days of the service of the default notice, the council must either accept the tenant's repair claim or refuse the claim and the default notice (on prescribed grounds). The tenant may carry out the repair work where the council either accepts the tenant's repair claim, or does not respond to the tenant's default notice.

12.72 **(iv) Payment.**[21] Once the repair work has been completed, the tenant can claim payment. Within 21 days of service on the council of the tenant's claim for payment, it must serve on the tenant a notice either accepting the claim, or refusing it on prescribed grounds.[22] The amount of the payment is normally at least 75 per cent., but not more than 100 per cent. (as decided by the council), of *the council's costs;* these are the costs, including administration costs, which in the council's opinion it would incur if it were to carry out the work. However, in a default case where the council has failed to respond to the tenant's default notice, the amount of the payment is the amount of the costs *incurred by the tenant* in carrying out the repair work, or £200, whichever is the less. Thus the council has an interest in responding to the default notice, in order to keep the costs down.

12.73 Once the council has accepted the tenant's claim for payment, it must make the payment within 14 days of such acceptance. Payment can be made in any manner the council thinks fit, save that the tenant's rent account can only be credited if the tenant is in arrears, and then only to the extent of those arrears.

[20] The mandatory grounds for refusal include situations where the works specified are not qualifying repairs or would not satisfactorily remedy the lack of repair if carried out with the specified materials. The discretionary grounds for refusal include situations where: the landlord's costs would exceed £200; the landlord intends to carry out the work within 28 days of the tenant's repair claim; the landlord intends to carry out the work within one year of the tenant's repair claim, as part of a planned programme of repair or maintenance, the work not being reasonably necessary for the occupiers' personal comfort or safety.

[21] 1985 Regs., Sched., paras. 12–23.

[22] *e.g.*, that the work has not been properly carried out or completed (a mandatory ground), or the authorised materials have not been used (a discretionary ground).

(v) Suspension of repairing obligations.[23] Where the tenant's repair claim has been accepted, the council's obligation to the tenant under its repairing covenant in relation to the lack of repair to which the repair works relate will cease to apply from the service of the council's notice accepting the tenant's claim (or, in a default case, from the date on which the tenant may carry out the repair work). The suspension normally lasts until service on the council of the tenant's claim for payment. **12.74**

(vi) Disputes. Any question arising under the scheme may be referred by either party to the county court.[24] **12.75**

(vii) Comparison of the statutory scheme with the common law and equitable rights of set off. The statutory scheme co-exists with the common law and equitable rights of set off.[25] From the tenant's viewpoint, these common law and equitable rights have several advantages over the statutory scheme: for example, the common law and equitable rights have no arbitrary cost limits, can cover extensive work, and permit the use of rent money for repairing purposes; in addition, equitable set off makes provision for unliquidated sums. However, while the council must provide the tenant with information "in simple terms"[26] concerning the statutory right to repair, there is no such information duty regarding common law and equitable set off. The statutory scheme has not been much used by tenants.[27] **12.76**

(e) *Complaint to a justice of the peace*

If the disrepair results in the property being unfit for habitation,[28] then although normally the unfitness provisions in the Housing Act 1985 do not avail council tenants,[29] the tenant can take advantage of a special procedure in the 1985 Act[30] allowing him to complain of the unfitness to a local justice of the peace (or parish or community council), and these bodies will then have power to complain to the **12.77**

23 H.A. 1985, s.96(2)(*b*); 1985 Regs., Sched., para. 25.
24 H.A. 1985, s.96(2)(*a*); 1985 Regs., Sched., para. 26.
25 See above, paras. 12.65–12.68.
26 H.A. 1985, s.104; see above, paras. 7.58–7.59.
27 See, *e.g.* H.C. Deb, December 1, 1986, cols. 520–521 (written answer).
28 H.A. 1985, s.604(1); see above, para. 12.31.
29 See above, para. 12.55.
30 H.A. 1985, s.606(2).

authority's "proper officer"[31] in writing that the property is unfit, whereupon that officer must inspect it forthwith and report on it to the local authority giving his opinion as to unfitness. While this procedure does not of itself ensure that the work is done, it does ensure that the condition of the property is officially brought to the council's attention.[32]

(f) *Complaint to a local councillor*

12.78 The tenant may ask a local councillor to put pressure on the housing department in order to get repairs done (quite apart from the councillor's role as intermediary for a complaint to a Local Commissioner[33]).

(g) *Complaint to a local commissioner*

12.79 Unjustifiable delay in carrying out repairs can amount to "maladministration" justifying a reference to a Local Commissioner ("ombudsman").[34] The reference can initially proceed via a local councillor, or it can be made direct to the local ombudsman.

(h) *Reduction in rates*

12.80 In cases of serious disrepair, the tenant may apply for a reduction in rateable value.[35]

4. *The Tenant's Right to Improve the Property*

(a) *The distinction between a "repair" and an "improvement"*

12.81 The (sometimes difficult) distinction between a "repair" and an "improvement" has been explained thus:

"If the work which is done is the provision of something new for

[31] Appointed under L.G.A. 1972, s.112.

[32] See J. Luba, [1982] L.A.G. Bull. 135, 139: "Complaints received by local authorities under [s.606(2)] usually prompt an immediate inspection and officer's report, and find their way onto Housing Committee agendas."

[33] See below, para. 12.79.

[34] See above, paras. 2.44–2.45; in Complaint No. 315/L/85 the ombudsman himself commissioned a surveyor to report on the state of the dwelling.

[35] See, *e.g. Black* v. *Oliver (V.O.)* [1978] Q.B. 870 (C.A.); *Howard* v. *Taylor (Valuation Officer)* LVC/321/1985 (Lands Trib.); *Kind* v. *Cox* [1986] L.S. Gaz. 2914 (Lands Trib.); N. Martyn, *Roof*, January 1984, p. 15; D. Forbes, [1987] January Legal Action 21, 22.

the benefit of the occupier, that is . . . an improvement; but if it is only the replacement of something already there, which has become dilapidated or worn out, then, albeit that it is a replacement by its modern equivalent, it comes within the category of repairs and not improvements."[36]

At common law, the doing of improvements by the tenant is normally regarded as an act of "ameliorating waste" (a branch of the law of tort), so that if the tenant is not expressly permitted to do the work, the landlord can in theory seek damages or an injunction. In practice, however, damages will not be recoverable where the landlord has suffered no loss, while the discretionary remedy of an injunction will usually be refused where the value of the property has been enhanced, unless the tenant has broken an express covenant against improving or otherwise altering the property.[37] **12.82**

(b) *Improvements by secure tenants*

(i) The limited statutory right to improve. Under the Housing Act 1985[38] it is an implied term of every secure council tenancy[39] that the tenant will not make an "improvement"[40] without the authority's written consent; thus it is not possible for the tenancy agreement effectively to impose an "absolute" prohibition on improvements (*i.e.* a prohibition making no provision for the council's consent). **12.83**

Such consent (which may be retrospective) must not be unreasonably withheld; if it is, it shall be treated as given.[41] The burden lies with the authority to show that the consent was reasonably withheld,[42] and the county court can decide this issue by bare declaration.[43] The court must have regard (*inter alia*) to the extent to which the improvement would be likely to affect the safety of the property, or reduce its "saleability" or "lettability," or cause expense to the **12.84**

[36] *Per* Denning L.J. in *Morcom* v. *Campbell-Johnson* [1955] 3 All E.R. 265, 266 (C.A.).
[37] *Doherty* v. *Allman* (1878) 3 App. Cas. 709 (H.L.).
[38] H.A. 1985, s.97(1).
[39] Including a secure licence: H.A. 1985, s.79(3).
[40] The definition is discussed in para. 12.87 below.
[41] H.A. 1985, s.97(3).
[42] *Ibid.* s.98(1).
[43] *Ibid.* s.110(2)(*b*).

authority which it would otherwise be unlikely to incur.[44] As regards this "expense" factor, it must be borne in mind that the subject-matter of a tenant's improvement may often become the landlord's repairing or maintenance responsibility under the Landlord and Tenant Act 1985,[45] and presumably it is not intended that an authority could give a "blanket" refusal merely on this ground: possible expense in the long term would surely not be a factor, although if the proposed work would be likely to cause expense to the authority in the short term, this may be a ground for refusing consent.

12.85 The consent may be given subject to conditions,[46] so that (for example) the authority can monitor the quality of the workmanship and materials; but the burden of showing the reasonableness of such conditions lies on the authority.[47]

12.86 The tenant must be given written reasons for any refusal of consent, and if the authority fails to respond to the tenant's request for consent within a reasonable time, the consent is taken to have been withheld.[48]

12.87 An "improvement" is specially and widely defined[49] for this purpose to cover: any alteration in or addition to the property,[50] the landlord's fixtures and fittings therein, or the provision of services; the erection of wireless or television aerials; and the carrying out of external decoration.[51] In order to amount to an improvement, the work need not necessarily enhance the market value of the property[52]: the test is not an objective one, and must in essence be viewed from the tenant's point of view rather than the landlord's.[53]

12.88 Under these provisions the tenant may therefore improve the property without any legal liability and notwithstanding the auth-

[44] H.A. 1985, s.98(2).
[45] L. & T.A. 1985, s.11: see above, paras. 12.09–12.27.
[46] H.A. 1985, s.99(1).
[47] *Ibid.* s.99(3).
[48] *Ibid.* s.98(4).
[49] *Ibid.* s.97(2)
[50] Strictly speaking, even such minor work as the insertion of a picture hook in a wall falls within this very wide definition; see J. E. Adams, [1981] Conv. 95.
[51] Such decoration may in any event be the council's legal responsibility under L. & T.A. 1985, s.11: see above, para. 12.12.
[52] *Cf.* H.A. 1985, s.100(1), see below, para. 12.89.
[53] See, *e.g. Woolworth & Co.* v. *Lambert* [1936] 2 All E.R. 1523 (C.A.); *Lambert* v. *Woolworth & Co (No. 2)* [1938] 2 All E.R. 664 (C.A.); nevertheless, the factors in s.98(2) (see above, para. 12.84) show that the council's interests are relevant to the consent issue.

ority's opposition, if such opposition is unreasonable; he naturally remains subject to the usual planning and building regulation requirements. If the tenant carries out improvements without first asking permission or in the face of a reasonable refusal, or if he fails to satisfy any reasonable condition attached to a consent,[54] then this will give the authority a "reasonableness" ground for possession.[55]

(ii) Reimbursement of the cost of tenant's improvements. The authority has a power[56] to reimburse the cost of a tenant's improvements where it has given its written consent to the improvement (or is treated as having done so[57]), work on the improvement was begun on or after October 3, 1980, and the improvement has materially added to the property's "saleability" or "lettability." Where these conditions are met, the authority may, at or after the end of the tenancy, make such payment to the tenant (or his personal representatives) as it considers appropriate in respect of the improvement, but not exceeding the (historic) cost thereof after deducting the amount of any house renovation grant.[58] There is no duty on the authority to make such reimbursement, and even if payment is made it cannot include any percentage of the increase in the property's value due to the improvement. **12.89**

In practice, however, a tenant may not need to rely on the exercise by the authority of this statutory power, since under the general law of fixtures he may be entitled as of right to remove (during or within a reasonable time after the termination of the tenancy) those articles which he attached to the property as domestic or ornamental fixtures, and which are capable of severance without unduly damaging the rest of the property.[59] **12.90**

(iii) Prohibition of rent increases on account of tenant's improvements. Where a secure tenant has lawfully made an improvement and has borne the whole or part of the cost (or would have done so but for a house renovation grant), then the authority cannot normally increase the rent on account of the improvement to **12.91**

[54] H.A. 1985, s.99(4).
[55] *Ibid.* Sched. 2, Pt. I, gd. 1 (see above, para. 8.31).
[56] *Ibid.* s.100.
[57] *Ibid.* s.97(3), see above, para. 12.84.
[58] *Ibid.* s.100(1)–(2).
[59] See, *e.g.* R. E. Megarry and H. W. R. Wade, *op. cit.* pp. 735–736.

the extent that the tenant has so borne (or might without a grant have so borne) the whole or part of the cost.[60]

12.92 This prohibition only applies while the person who did the improvement, or his "qualifying successor," is a secure tenant.[61] A "qualifying successor" of an improving tenant is defined[62] as: a person in whom the periodic tenancy vested under the statutory succession provisions on the tenant's death[63]; a person to whom the tenancy was assigned by the tenant and who would have been qualified to succeed him if he had died immediately before the assignment; a person to whom the tenancy was assigned by the tenant in pursuance of an order made under the property adjustment provisions of the Matrimonial Causes Act 1973[64]; or a spouse or former spouse of the tenant to whom the tenancy has been transferred by an order under the Matrimonial Homes Act 1983.[65]

12.93 Where the tenancy is no longer "secure," for example because the current tenant has sub-let the whole property,[66] or is a second "successor" on death,[67] then the authority can reflect the improvements in the rent charged; thus authorities should eventually be able to recoup any reimbursement payments[68] by way of future rent increases.

12.94 Furthermore, the prohibition against increasing rent on account of tenant's improvements does not prevent increases in the rent attributable to rates[69] (*i.e.* where the tenant is paying an inclusive rent).

12.95 **(iv) Tenant's right to apply for house renovation grants.** A secure tenant has a right to apply for a house renovation grant[70]; when doing so, he does not have to supply any certificate as to his future occupation.[71]

[60] H.A. 1985, s.101(1)–(2); certain tenant's improvements are similarly disregarded in determining the price on a "right to buy" purchase: *ibid.* s.127(1)(*b*), see below, para. 14.26.
[61] *Ibid.* s.101(2).
[62] *Ibid.* s.101(3).
[63] *Ibid.* s.89, see above, paras. 9.29–9.40.
[64] M.C.A. 1973, s.24, see above, paras. 11.32–11.40.
[65] M.H.A. 1983, Sched. 1, para. 2, see above, paras. 11.29–11.31.
[66] H.A. 1985, s.93(2), see above, paras. 9.25–9.26.
[67] *Ibid.* ss.87–88, see above, paras. 9.35–9.36.
[68] *Ibid.* s.100, see above, paras. 12.89–12.90.
[69] *Ibid.* s.101(4).
[70] *Ibid.* s.463(1)(*b*), (3)(*b*).
[71] *Ibid.* s.464(1)–(2).

(c) *Improvements by non-secure tenants*

Where the tenancy is not secure, the tenancy agreement may expressly prohibit the tenant from improving the property, either in "absolute" form (*i.e.* making no provision for the council's consent), or in "qualified" form (*i.e.* only prohibiting improvements done without the council's consent). In the case of a "qualified" prohibition, the Landlord and Tenant Act 1927[72] provides that, notwithstanding any express stipulation to the contrary, the prohibition is deemed to be subject to a proviso that the consent will not be unreasonably withheld. **12.96**

In the case of non-secure tenancies there are no statutory provisions allowing reimbursement of the cost of the improvement, prohibiting rent increases on account of the improvement, or permitting the tenant to apply for house renovation grants.[73] **12.97**

[72] L. & T.A. 1927, s.19(2) (inapplicable to secure tenancies: H.A. 1985, s.97(4)).

[73] Save that a tenant whose lease has at least five years left to run can apply for a grant: H.A. 1985, s.463(1)(*a*), (2)(*b*); most council tenancies are granted on a short periodic basis.

13 Tenant Involvement and Housing Co-operatives

1. *Degrees of Tenant Involvement*

(a) *General*

13.01 The Housing Act 1985 confers several *individual* rights on secure tenants, which are considered in detail elsewhere in this book. However, the Act achieved little in relation to the *collective* rights of secure tenants, and this has been seen by some as a major omission.[1] Although the Housing and Planning Act 1986 produced amendments which did increase the collective rights of tenants to a small degree, it also sought to make the "right to buy" in relation to individual council dwellings even more attractive, and it contained provisions facilitating the privatisation of council estates; these last two objectives, as we shall see,[2] were carried further in the Housing Act 1988. The collective rights of secure tenants therefore remain rather eclipsed by the other policy objectives of the legislation.

(b) *The distinction between tenant participation schemes and tenant co-operative schemes*

13.02 Collective tenant involvement can take many forms, but there is a broad division between tenant *participation* schemes, enabling tenants to *share* decision-making with the council, and tenant *co-operative*

[1] Thus the Labour party, "tak[ing] an analogy from another field," pointed out (in relation to H.A. 1980): "We do not see the individual rights of workers under employment protection legislation as any substitute for industrial democracy, or as lessening the need for collective organisation through trade unions" (*A Future for Public Housing* (1981), p. 30).
[2] See Chaps. 14 and 15.

schemes, which enable tenants actually to *control* certain areas of decision-making themselves. Both such schemes of *collective* involvement must be distinguished from the *individual* shared ownership leasing schemes discussed in Chapter 14.[3]

In practice, a more sophisticated four-fold division of schemes for collective tenant involvement has emerged.[4] First, at the lowest level, tenants may simply have the right to be consulted before the council makes certain management decisions. Secondly, there may be a "co-operative management" scheme under which the tenants, although they do not collectively hold any interest in the property, are given collective responsibility under a "management agreement" for some (or all) of the management decisions. Thirdly, the tenants may in effect collectively acquire ownership of the properties themselves from the council, through the medium of a "non-equity co-operative"[5]: here the tenants as a body will collectively hold the group of houses or flats which they individually occupy, but they will not have any personal stake in the equity, save that they may be given a stake limited to a share repayable on leaving at its original "par" value. Fourthly, there may be a "co-ownership society," which is similar to the third scheme in that the residents collectively hold and manage the property, but differs from it in that each tenant in effect shares in the equity through an entitlement to a payment on leaving (representing, for example, his contribution to paying off the group mortgage, or his share of the gain in the value of his dwelling), which exceeds the "par" value of his share. **13.03**

We shall now examine in more detail the main ways in which council tenants can become collectively involved with the running of their estates. **13.04**

[3] See paras. 14.94–14.117.

[4] See, *e.g.* D.O.E. Circ. 8/76, para. 5, and the *Final Report of the Working Party on Housing Co-operatives* (1975), p. 4 (this working party, chaired by Mr. Harold Campbell, is hereafter referred to as the "Campbell Report"); for a discussion of "non-equity co-operatives" and "co-ownership societies" from the housing association perspective, see J. Alder, [1988] Conv. 187, 254.

[5] Co-operative enterprises do, of course, extend beyond housing to many other activities, such as food retailing: for some of the early history of general co-operative ventures in Britain, see H. Campbell, *Roof*, May 1979, p. 104; co-operative developments in the housing field have tended to be more popular overseas, particularly in Scandinavia: see, *e.g.* C. Ward, *Tenants Take Over* (1974), Chap. 7.

2. *The Rights of Secure Tenants to be Consulted by the Council*

(a) *General*

13.05 At its most basic level, tenant involvement can take the form of the right to be consulted before the council reaches its decisions. A 1977 D.O.E. handbook[6] gave general advice to authorities concerning systems whereby tenants could share housing management decisions with council members and officers, including[7] the co-option of tenants (if necessary with full voting rights) onto council committees and sub-committees pursuant to the Local Government Act 1972,[8] and the involvement of tenants in special ad hoc consultative committees or in regular discussion meetings.[9]

13.06 Although there were detailed provisions in the Labour government's 1979 Housing Bill[10] for imposing uniform schemes of tenant consultation, we shall see that the various consultation provisions in the Housing Act 1985 are lukewarm by comparison.

(b) *The meaning of "consultation"*

13.07 It has been held that where Parliament imposes a duty on a particular person or body to "consult," the duty can only be discharged by the communication to those affected of a genuine invitation to give advice, followed by a genuine consideration by the decision-maker of that advice; this in turn depends on sufficient information and time being given to those consulted to enable them to tender helpful advice to the decision-maker, *i.e.* advice which is sufficiently informed and formulated to be of help to the decision-maker, and which can be communicated in time to be properly considered before a decision is reached.[11]

[6] Entitled *Getting tenants involved.*
[7] *Op. cit.* pp. 10–13.
[8] L.G.A. 1972, s.102.
[9] *Op. cit.* pp. 13–14; see also D.O.E., *Tenant participation in council housing management,* H.D.D. Occasional Paper 2/77 (1977).
[10] See cll. 20–22 and Sched. 3.
[11] *R.* v. *Secretary of State for Social Services, ex p. Association of Metropolitan Authorities* [1986] 1 All E.R. 164, 167 (D.C.) (a case concerning the duty of the Minister to consult local authority associations before issuing housing benefit regulations, in which the court granted a declaration that on the facts the Minister had not carried out a proper consultation).

(c) *Consultation duties regarding "matters of housing management"*

A general consultation duty is imposed by the Housing Act 1985[12] before the authority reaches a decision on a matter of "housing management." **13.08**

A "housing management" matter is defined[13] as one which, *in the opinion of the council,*[14] satisfies all of the following conditions: **13.09**

(i) it relates to the management,[15] maintenance, improvement or demolition of dwellings let on secure tenancies, or relates to the provision of services or amenities in connection with such dwellings (being services or amenities provided by the authority in its capacity as landlord, rather than those provided by it for the local inhabitants generally); and

(ii) it represents a "*new programme* of maintenance, improvement or demolition," or a "*change in the practice or policy* of the authority"[16]; and

(iii) it is likely (if the council implements a decision on the matter[17]) substantially to affect its secure tenants as a whole or a "group"[18] of them.

However, a matter is expressly stated not to be one of "housing management" if it relates to the rent payable under any secure tenancy or to any charge for services or facilities provided by the authority[19]—a very significant exception. Furthermore, the courts

[12] H.A. 1985, s.105.

[13] *Ibid.* s.105(2)–(4).

[14] The opinion must be properly formed in accordance with the administrative law principles (discussed in Chap. 6): see *Short* v. *L.B. of Tower Hamlets* (1985) 18 H.L.R. 171, 186 (C.A.).

[15] "Management" includes such matters as allocations, the keeping of pets, and the playing of ball games: *H.C. Standing Committee F on the Housing Bill,* March 6, 1980, col. 898.

[16] The matter in question can only represent a "new programme" or a "change in practice or policy" if there was a relevant pre-existing programme, practice or policy: *Short* v. *L.B. of Tower Hamlets,* see above, n. 14 (holding, *inter alia,* that the matter of a council not itself pursuing a policy of repair or rehabilitation in relation to a run-down estate could only represent a "new programme" or a "change in . . . policy" if there was an *existing* programme or policy for carrying out such work, and on the facts there was no such existing programme or policy).

[17] See *Short* v. *L.B. of Tower Hamlets* (1985) 18 H.L.R. 171, 185 (C.A.).

[18] A "group" of secure tenants is somewhat obscurely defined in H.A. 1985, s.105(3), by reference to the tenants forming a "distinct social group" or occupying a "distinct class" of dwellings.

[19] H.A. 1985, s.105(2).

have held that there is no duty to consult where the council has merely reached an "in principle" decision on a matter of housing management.[20]

13.10 With regard to "matters of housing management," every council must maintain such arrangements *as it considers appropriate* to enable those of its secure tenants who are likely to be substantially affected by these matters to be informed of the proposals and to comment on them within a specified period.[21] Before coming to its decision on such matters, the council must consider any representations made to it in accordance with these arrangements.[22] Furthermore, every council must publish details of its consultation arrangements; a copy of the relevant information must be available for free inspection, and must be supplied to any member of the public requesting it on payment of a reasonable fee.[23]

13.11 However, these general consultation duties do not apply to councils[24] undertaking certain specific statutory consultation processes. First, they do not apply to the consultation which must precede an application by the council to the Minister for approval of a redevelopment scheme enabling it to gain possession of a dwelling on the "privatisation" ground from a secure tenant[25]; special consultation duties apply instead to such a "privatisation with vacant possession" case.[26] Secondly, the general consultation duties do not apply to the consultation which a council must undertake before a voluntary disposal by it of a secure tenant's dwelling, with Minister-

[20] *Short* v. *L.B. of Tower Hamlets*, see above, n. 17 (where an agreement "in principle" by the council to embark on an exploratory marketing exercise with a view to privatisation of a council estate was held not to require consultation, as it would not substantially affect the secure tenants, although it was recognised that if privatisation was subsequently found viable after the marketing exercise, then the consultation duty would arise in relation to that new "matter"; *N.B.* "privatisation" consultations by councils under voluntary schemes are now governed, not by H.A. 1985, s.105, but by s.106A and Sched. 3A: see below, paras. 15.11–15.13); *cf.* with *Short*'s case, *R.* v. *Hammersmith and Fulham L.B.C., ex p. Beddowes* [1987] 1 All E.R. 369, 381–382 (C.A.), where the deliberations in question had proceeded beyond the "in principle" stage, so that the consultation duty was triggered, but on the facts it had been complied with.

[21] H.A. 1985, s.105(1).

[22] *Ibid.*

[23] *Ibid.* s.105(5).

[24] For exceptions to the general consultation duties in relation to other public sector landlords, see: H.A. 1985, s.109 (co-operative housing associations); H.A. 1988, s.84(8) (housing action trusts).

[25] H.A. 1985, s.84(2)(*b*) and Sched. 2, Pt. II, gd. 10A, Pt. V; see above, para. 8.48.

[26] *Ibid.* Sched. 2, Pt. V, para. 2; see below, para. 15.09.

ial consent, to a private sector landlord[27]; in such "privatisation with sitting tenant" cases, special consultation duties are again substituted by the 1985 Act.[28] Thirdly, the general consultation duties do not apply to the consultation which a council must undertake before entering into a "management agreement" whereby certain of its "management functions" are transferred to another person or body[29]; yet again, the Act substitutes a "tailor-made" consultation process in such a case.[30]

The general consultation duties concerning "housing management" matters are hardly onerous, and there is not even a duty to consult a tenants' association[31] as such, but merely to consult such body as the council itself may form or approve.[32] **13.12**

Where the consultation duties do apply, and have been broken, this may constitute maladministration justifying a reference to a local ombudsman.[33] Furthermore, the consultation duties are enforceable by way of injunction for breach of statutory duty in the county court, whereby the authority can be restrained from proceeding further with the proposed matter until consultation takes place.[34] Presumably an action in the High Court[35] would also lie. **13.13**

(d) *Other consultation duties*

Quite apart from (and sometimes as an alternative to[36]) the general "housing management" consultation duty just discussed, the 1985 Act contains specific consultation duties in relation to cer- **13.14**

[27] H.A. 1985, s.106A(2).

[28] *Ibid.* s.106A(1) and Sched. 3A; see below, paras. 15.11–15.13.

[29] H.A. 1985, ss.27–27A, see below, paras. 13.15–13.16.

[30] H.A. 1985, s.27A(8), see below, para. 13.16.

[31] However, tenants' associations are not necessarily very representative bodies. The National Consumer Council estimated in 1979 that only about five to eight per cent. of council tenants belonged to tenants' associations (*Soonest mended,* pp. 42–43).

[32] H.A. 1985, s.105(1); *cf.* the specific consultation provisions relating to "recognised tenants' associations" (as regards the assessment of service charges under leases of dwellings) contained in L. & T.A 1985, ss.20 and 29 (as amended by L. & T.A. 1987), which do not cover secure council tenancies (L. & T.A. 1985, s.26).

[33] See, *e.g.* Complaint No. 78/Y/84; see, as regards the local ombudsmen, paras. 2.44–2.45 above.

[34] See H.A. 1985, s.110(1); *Short* v. *L.B. of Tower Hamlets* (1985) 18 H.L.R. 171, 187–188 (C.A.); a representative action may lie under C.C.R. 1981, Ord. 5, r. 5 (see, *e.g.* A. Arden, [1981] L.A.G. Bull. 38), but there may be difficulties in obtaining legal aid (see [1987] March Legal Action 19).

[35] Via judicial review under R.S.C., Ord. 53: see Chap. 6.

[36] See above, para. 13.11.

tain particular courses of action contemplated by the council.[37] These specific duties (the details of which are considered in the appropriate places in this book) arise in the following cases: where the authority wishes to alter the terms of a secure tenancy by the prescribed notice of variation procedure[38]; where the council is claiming possession from a secure tenant on the special "privatisation" ground[39]; where the council is seeking voluntarily to "privatise" the secure tenant's dwelling by disposing of it to a private sector landlord with the tenant remaining in occupation[40]; and where the council is proposing to enter into a "management agreement" transferring its "management functions" to another person or body.[41]

3. *Management Agreements and Co-operative Management Schemes*

(a) *Management agreements*

13.15 The 1985 Act contains a general power for an authority, with the consent of the Minister, to agree that "another person" shall exercise as agent of the authority such of the authority's "management functions" as are specified in the agreement, in relation to such of the authority's dwellings (and related land) as are so specified.[42] The Minister's consent is required for both the terms of the agreement and the identity of the "manager."[43] "Management functions" are widely defined[44] as including functions conferred by any enactment, and the powers and duties of the authority as the holder of an estate or interest in the relevant dwellings or land; this definition thus covers such functions as maintenance and repair,

[37] In addition, a secure council tenant may sometimes have the right to be consulted on specific issues by other bodies than the council; see, *e.g.* H.A. 1988, s.102(1) (consultation by predatory potential landlord under the "change of landlord" privatisation scheme: see below, paras. 15.42–15.45).
[38] H.A. 1985, s.103(2) (not applying to variation of the rent or of payments in respect of services, facilities or rates: s.103(3)); see above, para. 7.66.
[39] See above, nn. 25–26.
[40] See above, nn. 27–28.
[41] H.A. 1985, ss.27–27A, see below, para. 13.16.
[42] *Ibid.* s.27.
[43] *Ibid.* s.27(5).
[44] *Ibid.* s.27(6).

allocations, and rent collection. The "persons" to whom the management functions may be transferred include bodies such as tenants' co-operatives,[45] housing associations, or management trusts. Where such a body is appointed as manager, the management agreement can provide that the manager's functions may be performed by a committee, sub-committee or officer of that body.[46]

However, before such a proposed management agreement can be referred for Ministerial approval, the authority must comply with the prescribed consultation requirements.[47] It must first serve notice on each affected tenant informing him of the appropriate details, including the identity of the proposed manager, the likely consequences of the agreement for the tenant, and the effect of the statutory consultation machinery[48]; the notice must also give him the right to make representations to the authority within a specified reasonable period.[49] The authority must then consider any such representations, following which it must serve another notice on the tenant informing him of any significant changes to its proposal, and telling him (*inter alia*) of his right to communicate his objections to the Minister.[50] **13.16**

The Minister has a wide discretion in considering the proposed management agreement, but he cannot approve it if he believes that a majority of the affected tenants do not wish the proposal to proceed.[51] Once Ministerial approval has been given, the management agreement is not invalidated by any non-compliance with the above requirements on the part of the Minister or the authority.[52] **13.17**

The fact that a council has entered into a management agreement will not of itself result in any relevant housing subsidy being reduced, discontinued or recouped.[53] **13.18**

[45] See below, para. 13.19.

[46] H.A. 1985, s.27(4).

[47] *Ibid.* s.27A; in the case of secure tenants affected by the proposed management agreement, these provisions replace the "housing management" consultation provisions in *ibid.* s.105 (see above, paras. 13.08–13.13): *ibid.* s.27A(8).

[48] *Ibid.* s.27A(1).

[49] *Ibid.*

[50] *Ibid.* s.27A(2).

[51] *Ibid.* s.27A(5).

[52] *Ibid.* s.27A(7).

[53] *Ibid.* s.427A (which also preserves subsidy where the authority has let land in connection with a management agreement: see below, para. 13.25).

(b) *Co-operative management schemes*[54]

13.19 By way of further development of the management agreement principle, the 1985 Act permits the establishing of tenants' co-operative management schemes.[55] Under these schemes, control (but not ownership, which remains in the council[56]) is vested in the co-operative (which is an association corporately representing the tenants); the co-operative acts as agent for the authority, and will normally receive funds from it, to be spent at the discretion of the co-operative on specified management activities. Between 1976 and 1986, about 40 tenants' co-operative management schemes were set up, principally in London and Glasgow.[57]

13.20 Moreover, a "qualifying tenants' association" may take the initiative by serving a notice on the authority proposing that the authority should enter into a co-operative management agreement with the association.[58] A tenants' association is a "qualifying association" for these purposes if[59]:

(i) it is a housing association[60] of which at least half the members are tenants of dwellings specified in the notice; and

(ii) it has at least 50 such members, or is registered under the Industrial and Provident Societies Act 1965[61]; and

[54] See G. Baugh, *Roof*, May 1988, p. 38.

[55] H.A. 1985, ss.27(1), (4), 27C(1)(*a*), (3); special transitional provisions (in *ibid.* s.27B) govern housing co-operative agreements entered into under superseded enactments: in particular, any term of the agreement providing for the letting of land to the co-operative is generally no longer effective (*ibid.* s.27B(2)).

[56] Thus the council can later transfer the ownership (subject to the necessary conditions and consents) to some other body, for example, under the "change of landlord" scheme in H.A. 1988, Pt. IV; *cf.* "non-equity co-operatives": see below, para. 13.25.

[57] G. Baugh, *loc. cit.*

[58] H.A. 1985, s.27C; the general formalities governing management agreements specified in *ibid.* ss.27–27A (above, paras. 13.15–13.17) will have to be complied with before the co-operative management scheme can take effect.

[59] *Ibid.* s.27C(3); it is a ground for the refusal by the authority of consent to an "exchange" assignment by a secure tenant (see above, paras. 9.20–9.23) that the dwelling is the subject of (*inter alia*) a co-operative management scheme but the proposed assignee is not, and is unwilling to become, a member of the tenants' association: *ibid.* s.92 and Sched. 3, gd. 10.

[60] Defined in *ibid.* s.5(1)(*b*) as a society, body of trustees or company which (*inter alia*) does not trade for profit, or whose constitution or rules prohibit the issuing of capital with interest or dividend exceeding the prescribed Treasury rate; see J. Alder and C. Handy, *Housing Association Law* (1987).

[61] For more detail concerning registration with the registrar of friendly societies under the 1965 Act, see, *e.g.* J. Alder and C. Handy, *op. cit.* pp. 15–18.

(iii) at least half the tenants of the specified dwellings are members of the association.

Where such a proposal is served on the authority, the authority must take it into account,[62] but it is not obliged to accept it. If the authority has not accepted the proposal in principle by the end of six months after service of the association's notice, the authority must give the association a written statement explaining why it has not accepted it.[63] **13.21**

Tenants affected by co-operative management schemes will remain secure tenants, because their immediate landlord will still be the council itself[64]; and the normal rules regarding council rent-fixing will in general continue to apply.[65] **13.22**

(c) *Financial assistance*

In order to encourage wider participation in housing management, the Minister can (with Treasury consent) provide financial assistance to persons involved in managing public sector or former public sector housing, including persons involved in setting up and running co-operatives[66]; financial assistance can also be given to the providers of educational or training courses in housing management.[67] **13.23**

4. *Non-Equity Co-operatives*

In a "non-equity co-operative," both control *and* ownership are vested in the co-operative, although each member can receive (at the most) the par value of his shareholding (which may be as little as £1), the rest of the equity in effect remaining in the hands of the co-operative. A "qualifying tenants' association"[68] may make a proposal to the council that the council should enter into a co-operative **13.24**

[62] H.A. 1985, s.27C(1).
[63] *Ibid.* s.27C(2).
[64] *Ibid.* s.80(1), see above, para. 7.07.
[65] See D.O.E. Circ. 8/76, Annex B, para. 6; the details of council rent-fixing are discussed in Chap. 10.
[66] H.A. 1985, s.429A.
[67] *Ibid.* s.429A(3).
[68] Defined *ibid.* s.27C(3): see above, para. 13.20.

ownership agreement with the association, whereby the association, as a non-equity co-operative, will acquire from the authority dwellings and other land as specified in the notice, at a specified price[69]; the proposal must then be considered by the authority.[70]

13.25 If the authority enters into such a co-operative ownership agreement, under which it lets property to the co-operative, then the council's entitlement to subsidy (if any) cannot be affected by the agreement.[71] However, the co-operative ownership agreement will prevent any other transfer of ownership by the council, under for example the "change of landlord" scheme[72]; such an agreement can therefore be very much in the interests of the tenants if they fear that their dwellings might otherwise be acquired from the council by a predatory private landlord or housing association.

13.26 Where the non-equity co-operative has acquired property from the council under these provisions prior to January 15, 1989, pre-existing tenancies of the individual occupiers will remain "secure" where the co-operative is *either* a housing association which is registered with the Housing Corporation under the Housing Associations Act 1985[73] but is not a "co-operative housing association," *or* it is a housing association which is not registered under the Housing Associations Act 1985, but which is a "co-operative housing association"[74]; a "co-operative housing association" for these purposes is a "fully mutual"[75] housing association which is registered with the registrar of friendly societies under the Industrial and Provident Societies Act 1965.[76] Most non-equity co-operatives tend to be registered under both the Housing Associations Act and the Industrial and Provident Societies Act, so that their tenants will not in any event be "secure." Where the tenants of a co-operative are not "secure" under these provisions, their right to buy will nevertheless

[69] H.A. 1985, s.27C(1)(*b*).
[70] *Ibid.* s.27C(1)–(2): the procedure is the same as that discussed above (paras. 13.20–13.21) in relation to proposals for management agreements.
[71] H.A. 1985, s.427A (see above, para. 13.18 and n. 53).
[72] H.A. 1988, Pt. IV; see below, paras. 15.14–15.60.
[73] H.A.A. 1985, ss. 3–7; H.A. 1985, s.5(4); see J. Alder and C. Handy, *op. cit.* pp. 155–161, 303–312.
[74] H.A. 1985, ss.5(2), (4), 79–80(1)–(2); H.A. 1988, Sched. 18, n. 4.
[75] For an association to be "fully mutual," its rules must restrict membership to tenants or prospective tenants of the association, and preclude the granting or assignment of tenancies to non-members: *ibid.* s.5(2).
[76] *Ibid.*; a "co-operative housing association" is thus more narrowly defined than a "qualifying tenants' association": see above, para. 13.20.

normally be preserved,[77] and they will generally either be "housing association tenants" (though not normally "protected" tenants) under the Rent Act 1977,[78] or "assured" tenants under the Housing Act 1988.[79]

Non-equity co-operatives can be formed not only on existing council estates, but also on newly-built estates specifically designed for co-operatives, and even in relation to private housing which has been bought by the authority under a municipalisation programme or at the request of the private sector tenants.[80] The D.O.E. has pointed out that although co-operatives "could be established successfully in either flats or houses," they "may work better where the property is contiguous (*e.g.* a block of flats, a whole street, or a whole estate)."[81] **13.27**

Councils cannot normally exercise direct control over the rent levels determined by non-equity co-operatives[82]; such rents will generally be "market" rents, pitched at a higher level than the former council rents. **13.28**

Despite the statutory infrastructure considered above, housing co-operatives have not proved popular, largely because of the excessive bureaucracy and legal complications with which they remain bedevilled, together with the unwillingness of many tenants to devote the necessary time to the running of the schemes; in addition, it has been pointed out that "the unusual strength of the local authority tradition in this country and the scale of provision of municipal housing" have been major obstacles to the spread of co-operatives.[83] **13.29**

[77] H.A. 1985, ss.171A–171C: see below, para. 14.07.

[78] *I.e.* where the tenancy was entered into, and the disposal by the authority to the co-operative took place, *before* January 15, 1989: see R.A. 1977, ss.15–16, 86; H.A. 1988, ss.1, 38(1)(*b*), and Sched. 1, Pt. I, para. 1; such "housing association tenants" have the benefit of the Rent Act's rent-fixing machinery, though not of its security regime.

[79] *I.e.* where *either* the tenancy was entered into *before,* but the authority disposes of the property to the co-operative *after,* January 15, 1989, *or* the tenancy from the co-operative was entered into *after* January 15, 1989: H.A. 1988, ss.1, 35, 38; but see *ibid.* Sched. 1, Pt. I, para. 12(1)(*h*) (fully mutual housing association tenancy cannot be assured).

[80] See Campbell Report, *op. cit.* p. 8; this Report also suggested that council housing co-operatives should initially be based on new developments, or at least on carefully selected estates of up to 100 units (*op. cit.* p. 12).

[81] Circ. 8/76, Annex A, para. 1.

[82] *Ibid.* Annex B, para. 7.

[83] Campbell Report, *op. cit.* p. 7.

5. *Co-ownership Societies*

13.30 We have noted[84] that a "co-ownership society" is similar to a non-equity co-operative in that the residents collectively hold and manage the property; however, it differs from a non-equity co-operative in that, although the society is "fully mutual," each member has (in effect) a substantial individual share in the equity, realisable on him ceasing to be a member of the society.[85] Where dwellings were transferred by the council to a co-ownership society prior to January 15, 1989, the sitting tenants at the time of transfer will no longer be "secure" if the co-ownership society is registered with the Housing Corporation,[86] nor will they normally have any protection under the Rent Act 1977[87] (although their individual right to buy will normally be preserved[88]). Where *either* the tenancies were entered into before January 15, 1989 but the council disposes of the properties to the co-ownership society after January 15, 1989, *or* the individual tenancies were granted by the co-ownership society after January 15, 1989, then (although the sitting tenants' individual right to buy will normally be preserved[89]) the tenants will not be "secure" under the Housing Act 1985,[90] they will not have any protection under the Rent Act 1977,[91] and they will not be "assured' tenants under the Housing Act 1988.[92]

13.31 Despite some initial enthusiasm for the idea of introducing co-ownership schemes in the local authority sector,[93] they have not proved popular, largely because many lower-paid tenants would not be able to meet the higher rents which could well result, while higher-paid council tenants are likely to be more attracted by the individual "right to buy" (discussed in Chapter 14) than by proposals for establishing co-ownership schemes.

[84] See above, para. 13.03.
[85] See definition in R.A. 1977, s.86(3A); it is also necessary to distinguish the "co-ownership" concept from the concept of the individual "shared ownership lease": see below, paras. 14.94–14.117.
[86] H.A. 1985, ss.5(4), 80(2); see above, para. 13.26.
[87] *I.e.* both the rent-fixing and (normally) the security provisions are excluded, even though the tenancies were granted before January 15, 1989: R.A. 1977, ss.15, 86(1)–(3A).
[88] H.A. 1985, ss.171A–171C: see below, para. 14.07.
[89] H.A. 1985, ss.171A–171C.
[90] H.A. 1985, s.80; H.A. 1988, ss.35, 38.
[91] H.A. 1988, ss.34–35, 38.
[92] H.A. 1988, s.1 and Sched. 1, Pt. I, paras. 1, 12(1)(*h*).
[93] See Campbell Report, *op. cit.* pp. 44, 50–51.

Part IV: The Privatisation of Council Housing

14 The Sale of Council Dwellings to Individual Purchasers

1. *General*

The sale of council housing falls into three broad categories: first, a sale of an individual dwelling can be compelled by the sitting tenant (subject to conditions and exceptions) under the "right to buy" scheme in Part V of the Housing Act 1985 (this has proved very popular, though the rate of sales has slowed recently following the "creaming off" of the better properties[1]); secondly, a sale of an individual dwelling may be effected at the discretion of the council, even where the "right to buy" does not apply, under the general power in section 32 of the 1985 Act (subject to certain conditions); and thirdly, there may be a sale of an entire council estate under powers contained in the Housing Acts of 1985 and 1988 (again subject to certain conditions). This chapter is concerned with sales in the first two categories (*i.e.* sales of individual dwellings); the sale of entire estates is dealt with in the next chapter. **14.01**

2. *Sales Under the "Right to Buy"*

(a) *The nature of the "right to buy"*

The right to buy is conferred by Part V of the Housing Act 1985 on certain secure sitting council (and other public sector) tenants. It is a right to purchase the freehold of the tenant's house, if the council **14.02**

[1] By 1987, around 800,000 dwellings had been sold under the "right to buy" scheme: D.O.E., *Tenants' Choice: The Government's Proposals for Legislation* (1987), para. 3.

owns the freehold[2]; but if the council does not own the freehold, or if the property in question is a flat (whether or not the council owns the freehold), then the tenant has a right to be granted a lease[3]: where the council holds the freehold or a lease for a term of which more than 125 years and five days are unexpired, then the tenant normally gets a term for not less than 125 years, otherwise he normally gets a term expiring five days before the term date of the council's own lease.[4]

14.03 The right to buy can be altered by Ministerial order (for example, by extension) where a prescribed public body has an interest in a dwelling let on a secure tenancy, which interest is immediately superior to the interest of the council landlord or of another prescribed body[5]; in pursuance of this power, the Minister has by order[6] enabled a secure council tenant of a house (not a flat) to buy the freehold where the council itself has a lease of the house and the freeholder and each intermediate landlord (if any) is an authority or body which would be subject to the right to buy if it were the secure tenant's immediate landlord.

14.04 There is also the right (subject to conditions) to a mortgage from the council covering the whole or part of the price,[7] and the right (again subject to conditions) to a "shared ownership lease" enabling the secure tenant to buy a lease for a premium representing a share of the market value and also to pay rent on the remaining share.[8]

14.05 Although there is no general provision in Part V of the 1985 Act stating that the tenant cannot contract out of these statutory rights,[9] such contracting out would undoubtedly be held contrary to public policy.[10]

[2] H.A. 1985, s.118(1)(*a*).

[3] *Ibid.* s.118(1)(*b*); where the council does not own the freehold, any provisions in a lease held by the council or a superior landlord (or in any agreement) are void in so far as they restrict the grant or subsequent disposal of a "right to buy" lease or a "shared ownership" lease: *ibid.* s.179(1).

[4] *Ibid.* Sched. 6, Pt. III, paras. 11–12.

[5] *Ibid.* s.171.

[6] Housing (Extension of Right to Buy) Order 1987 (S.I. 1987 No. 1732); where this extension applies, it is normally the *freeholder* (and not the council) which is required to grant the secure tenant a mortgage, and the secure tenant does not have the right to a "shared ownership" lease: 1987 Order, Sched., paras. 14,25.

[7] H.A. 1985, s.132; see below, paras. 14.78–14.91.

[8] H.A. 1985, s.143; see below, paras. 14.94–14.117.

[9] *Cf. e.g.* Leasehold Reform Act 1967, s.23(1), which prohibits contracting-out of the enfranchisement and leasehold extension rights of certain long-leaseholders.

[10] See, by analogy, *Barton* v. *Fincham* [1921] 2 K.B. 291 (C.A.), *Brown* v. *Draper* [1944] K.B. 309 (C.A.) (Rent Acts); *Johnson* v. *Moreton* [1978] A.C. 37 (H.L.) (Agricultural Holdings Act 1948).

The definition of "house"[11] for the purposes of Part V of the 1985 Act covers detached, semi-detached and terraced dwellings, but excludes both a dwelling formed by horizontal division of a building, and a dwelling of which a material part lies above or below the remainder of the structure to which it is attached.[12] Any dwelling which is not a "house" within this definition is treated as a "flat."[13] Land let together with a dwelling is to be treated as part of the dwelling, unless that land is agricultural and exceeds two acres.[14] Quite separately, land is to be included as part of the dwelling if: **14.06**

(i) the land is or has been used for the purpose of the dwelling;
(ii) the tenant, prior to exercising the right to buy or the right to a shared ownership lease, requires such land to be included; and
(iii) it is reasonable so to include it.[15]

(b) *Qualifying for the "right to buy"*

(i) The general conditions

The relevance of the secure tenancy. The right to buy and the right to a mortgage can normally only be enjoyed by a *secure tenant*.[16] However, the right to buy can generally be preserved following disposal by the council of the secure sitting tenant's dwelling to a private sector landlord,[17] even though the tenant is thus no longer a secure tenant,[18] provided (as regards subsequent dealings with the reversion) the right has been appropriately protected by registration.[19] In order successfully to complete[20] the right to buy transaction, the secure tenant must normally remain such right up until the time of **14.07**

[11] H.A. 1985, s.183(2).
[12] For example, council maisonettes built over a parade of shops would not be "houses" for this purpose.
[13] H.A. 1985, s.183(3).
[14] *Ibid.* s.184(1); for example, garages which are some distance from the dwelling, but which are let (or licensed, s.79(3)) to the tenant, may be included in the "right to buy."
[15] *Ibid.* s.184(2).
[16] *Ibid.* ss.118(1), 132(1); for the definition of a secure tenancy, see Chap. 7.
[17] *Ibid.* ss.171A–171H and Sched. 9A; see below, paras. 15.12, 15.57; see also, as regards disposals by the residuary bodies set up under L.G.A. 1985, the Local Government Reorganisation (Preservation of Right to Buy) Order 1986 (S.I. 1986 No. 2092).
[18] Because the private landlord will not satisfy the "landlord condition" for a secure tenancy: H.A. 1985, s.80 (see above, para. 7.07).
[19] *Ibid.* s.171G and Sched. 9A.
[20] See below, paras. 14.49–14.50.

completion[21]; in the case of a "preserved right to buy," however, it is merely necessary for the former secure tenant to occupy the dwelling as his only or principal home until the time of completion.[22]

14.08 *The two-years' residence requirement.* The right to buy and the right to a mortgage can normally only arise after the secure tenant has been a "public sector tenant" for not less than two years, or for periods totalling not less than two years[23]; the requirements for a "public sector tenancy" are similar to, though more widely drafted[24] than, those stipulated for a "secure" tenancy.[25] Periods spent as a "public sector tenant" of a different public landlord (not necessarily another council), or in a different public sector dwelling, are normally to be counted,[26] as is qualifying occupation which preceded the introduction of the statutory security and right to buy provisions.[27] In addition, periods of occupation of armed forces accommodation, and periods of qualifying occupation pursuant to the "preserved right to buy," are to be counted.[28] In the case of joint tenants, the residence requirements need only be satisfied by one of them.[29]

14.09 Periods also count for this purpose during which the secure tenant was the spouse of a relevant tenant or during which the secure tenant's spouse or deceased spouse was a relevant tenant or the spouse of a relevant tenant (subject to certain occupation requirements).[30]

14.10 Yet further periods can count for this purpose where a "public sector tenant" has died or otherwise ceased to be a "public sector tenant," and thereupon a child of his who occupied the dwelling as his only or principal home became the "public sector tenant" of the

[21] *L.B. of Sutton* v. *Swann* (1986) 18 H.L.R. 140 (C.A.), where the tenant ceased to occupy the dwelling in between exercising the right to buy and the time when he claimed to complete, and accordingly the right to buy was lost.

[22] H.A. 1985, s.171B.

[23] *Ibid.* s.119(1) and Sched. 4.

[24] There are far fewer exemptions from the definition of "public sector tenancy" than there are from the definition of a "secure tenancy": *ibid.* Sched. 4, para. 6(2); note also *ibid.* Sched. 4, para. 8(1), enabling the Minister to prescribe further landlords for the purpose of the definition of "public sector tenancy" (see Housing (Right to Buy) (Prescribed Persons) Order 1984 (S.I. 1984 No. 1173); this order, and the other pre-H.A. 1985 orders referred to in this chapter, remain in force under Housing (Consequential Provisions) Act 1985, s.2).

[25] See above, paras. 7.01–7.48.

[26] H.A. 1985, Sched. 4, paras. 2, 7.

[27] *Ibid.* Sched. 4, para. 6(2).

[28] *Ibid.* Sched. 4, paras. 5–5A.

[29] *Ibid.* s.119(2); Sched. 4, para. 3.

[30] *Ibid.* Sched. 4, paras. 2, 5–5A.

dwelling (whether under the same or under another "public sector tenancy"): in such cases a period will normally qualify during which the child, since reaching 16, occupied as his only or principal home a dwelling of which a parent of his was the "public sector tenant."[31]

(ii) Cases where the statutory rights do not arise. There are certain exceptional cases where the statutory rights do not arise even where the tenant is a secure tenant who has "clocked up" the two years' residence requirement. The following exceptions[32] are relevant to council landlords. **14.11**

Council has insufficient interest in the property. The right to buy cannot arise where the council does not own the freehold and does not have an interest sufficient to grant a right to buy lease for a term exceeding 21 years (where the dwelling is a house), or for a term of not less than 50 years (where the dwelling is a flat)[33]; the relevant terms run from the date of the tenant's initial right to buy notice.[34] The requirements in the 1985 Act for Ministerial consent to disposals of council property[35] prevent authorities from attracting this exemption by simply disposing of their stock on a "sale and short leaseback" basis. **14.12**

Tenants within certain council management co-operatives[36] can enjoy the right to buy, since the landlord will be the council, which will retain the relevant freehold or leasehold interest. **14.13**

Dwellings let in connection with employment. The right to buy cannot arise where: **14.14**

(i) the dwelling forms part of, or is within the curtilage of, a building which is held mainly for purposes other than housing purposes[37] and consists mainly of accommodation other than housing accommodation, or the dwelling is situated in a cemetery; and
(ii) the tenant or his predecessor in title was employed by the council or another prescribed public body; and

31 H.A. 1985, Sched. 4, para. 4.
32 Principally contained in *ibid.* s.120 and Sched. 5.
33 *Ibid.* Sched. 5, para. 4.
34 *Ibid.*
35 *Ibid.* ss.32, 43–44; see below, paras. 14.129–14.133.
36 See above, paras. 13.19–13.22.
37 "Housing purposes" means the purposes for which dwellings are held by councils under H.A. 1985, Pt. II: *ibid.* Sched. 5, para. 5(2).

(iii) the dwelling was let to the tenant or his predecessor in consequence of that employment.[38]

14.15 "Curtilage" for these purposes means a small area which is connected with a relevant building: thus a schoolhouse situated within extensive school grounds, and some distance from any other school buildings, did not come within the exception (so that the tenant had the right to buy).[39]

14.16 *Physically disabled persons' dwellings.* The right to buy cannot arise where the dwelling has features which are substantially different from those of ordinary dwellings and are designed to make it suitable for the physically disabled, and the dwelling is one of a group[40] usually let to the physically disabled, and a social service or special facilities [*sic*] are provided nearby for the occupants.[41]

14.17 When deciding whether the features in question are substantially different from those of ordinary dwellings, it is not proper to restrict consideration to the immediate locality of the subject dwelling[42]; and the reference to the features being "designed" to make the dwelling suitable for the physically disabled means that they should be specially adapted, rather than merely intended, for that purpose.[43]

14.18 *Mentally disabled persons' dwellings.* The right to buy cannot arise where the dwelling is one of a group which the council normally lets for occupation by the mentally disordered, and a social service or special facilities [*sic*] are provided wholly or partly for the purpose of assisting such persons.[44]

[38] H.A. 1985, Sched. 5, para. 5.

[39] *Dyer* v. *Dorset C.C.* [1988] 3 W.L.R. 213 (C. A.); see also *Barron* v. *Borders Regional Council* 1987 S.L.T. 36 (Lands Trib.) (exception not satisfied where schoolhouse, though adjacent to the school, was not part of its enclosure and did not share common features with the school, such as common access); *Burns* v. *Central Regional Council* 1988 S.L.T. 46 (Lands Trib.) (exception not satisfied where former schoolhouse was no longer used in connection with the school, and the applicant himself had no connection with the school either).

[40] Two adjoining houses adapted for the disabled do not form a "group" for these purposes: *Crilly* v. *Motherwell D.C.* 1988 S.L.T. 7 (Lands Trib.).

[41] H.A. 1985, Sched. 5, para. 7.

[42] *Freeman* v. *Wansbeck D.C.* (1983) 127 S.J. 550 (C.A.), provision of third lavatory for disabled occupier held not to fall within the exception, although a third lavatory was very unusual in the immediate locality.

[43] *Freeman* v. *Wansbeck D.C.*, *ibid.*

[44] H.A. 1985, Sched. 5, para. 9.

Pensioners' dwellings. The right to buy cannot arise where: **14.19**

(i) the dwelling is one of a group of dwellings which are particularly suitable (having regard *inter alia* to location, size, design and heating systems) for occupation by pensioners; and

(ii) the council normally lets the dwellings for occupation by pensioners or by pensioners and physically disabled persons; and

(iii) special facilities are provided wholly or mainly for the purpose of assisting such persons which consist of or include *either* the services of a resident warden *or* the services of a non-resident warden where there is a system for calling him and the use of a common-room near to the group of dwellings.[45]

A separate exemption from the right to buy in relation to pensioners' dwellings applies where the dwelling in question was let to the tenant or his predecessor in title for occupation by a pensioner or a physically disabled person, and the dwelling is particularly suitable for occupation by pensioners (having regard to its location, size, design, heating system, accessibility and other major features, and to whether it has no more than two bedrooms).[46] **14.20**

Crown tenancies. The right to buy normally cannot arise where the dwelling is held by the council on a tenancy from the Crown.[47] **14.21**

Dwellings within the Green Belt. The Minister retains jurisdiction under the Green Belt (London and Home Counties) Act 1938 to refuse consent to a sale under the right to buy of a council property on Green Belt land[48]: this jurisdiction has not been impliedly repealed by the introduction of the right to buy provisions.[49] **14.22**

(iii) Cases where the statutory rights cannot be exercised. Even though the right to buy has arisen, it cannot be exercised if a court order for possession has been made under which the tenant is obliged to give up possession (as opposed to an order suspended on conditions), or if the potential purchaser or one of them is (in effect) **14.23**

[45] H.A. 1985, Sched. 5, para. 10.
[46] *Ibid.* Sched. 5, para. 11.
[47] *Ibid.* Sched. 5, para. 12.
[48] 1938 Act, s.5.
[49] *R. v. Secretary of State for the Environment, ex p. Enfield L.B.C., The Times,* April 5, 1988 (D.C.).

bankrupt.[50] For these purposes the right to buy is "exercised" by way of a continuous process of prescribed steps[51]: it is not exercised once and for all when the tenant serves his initial claim to buy[52]; thus, if at any time during that process there is a relevant possession order or bankruptcy, the right to buy ceases to be exercisable.[53]

14.24 **(iv) Cases where the council is not bound to complete the transaction.** Even where the right to buy has arisen and has been initially exercised, the council is not bound to complete the transaction if the tenant has incurred arrears of rent (or of other payments due from him as tenant, for example service charges) for a period of four weeks, and these have not been fully paid off.[54]

(c) *The price*

14.25 **(i) The valuation criteria.** The purchase price is normally the market value of the dwelling at the time when the tenant serves his initial notice,[55] less the relevant discount[56]; the price may be further reduced where the tenant activates the "notice of delay" procedure.[57] The valuation is on a vacant possession basis[58] (thus ignoring the fact that *ex hypothesi* there is a sitting tenant, which would normally depress the price).

14.26 Whether the fee simple or a lease is being granted,[59] it is necessary to disregard for price-fixing purposes improvements made by, or failure to repair internally by, the tenant and certain other specified persons.[60] It must further be assumed:

(i) that any service charges or improvement contributions payable[61] will not be less than the amounts estimated in the council's second response notice[62];

(ii) that neither the tenant nor a member of his family[63] resid-

[50] H.A. 1985, s.121.
[51] See below, paras. 14.37–14.50.
[52] *Enfield L.B.C.* v. *McKeon* [1986] 1 W.L.R. 1007 (C.A.).
[53] *Ibid.*
[54] H.A. 1985, s.138(2).
[55] *Ibid.* s.122(1), see below, para. 14.37.
[56] *Ibid.* ss.122(2), 126–127.
[57] See below, paras. 14.120–14.122.
[58] H.A. 1985, s.127(2)(*a*), (3)(*a*).
[59] See above, para. 14.02.
[60] H.A. 1985, s.127(1)(*b*), (4).
[61] See below, paras. 14.62, 14.65.
[62] H.A. 1985, s.127(1)(*c*); see below, para. 14.44.
[63] H.A. 1985, s.186; see above, paras. 9.31–9.33.

ing with him wants to buy[64] (the occupier's willingness to buy would otherwise tend to increase the price); and

(iii) that the conveyance or lease will include the rights and obligations prescribed by the 1985 Act.[65]

Where a lease is to be granted, it is also to be assumed that the ground rent will not exceed £10 per annum.[66]

(ii) Calculating the discount entitlement. The discount to be allowed depends on whether the dwelling is a house or a flat, and increases with the period of residence. In the case of a house, the discount is currently 32 per cent. of the value where the relevant occupation periods (prior to the service of the tenant's initial notice[67]) total less than three years, but it rises by 1 per cent. for each "clocking-up" year thereafter, to a maximum of 60 per cent. (*i.e.* after 30 years' occupation).[68] In the case of a flat, the discount is currently 44 per cent. of the value where the relevant occupation periods are less than three years, plus 2 per cent. for each "clocking- up" year thereafter, to a maximum of 70 per cent. (*i.e.* after fifteen years' occupation).[69] The Minister has power to fix higher discount percentages.[70] **14.27**

However, the discount must not exceed £50,000.[71] Furthermore, the discount must not normally reduce the price below the amount determined by the Minister as representing (in effect) the costs of the dwelling (relating to building, improving, etc.) incurred within eight years preceding the date of service of the tenant's initial right to buy claim form[72]; thus properties built in recent years and at a high cost may attract little or no discount. If the market value is already below the amount of these costs, there is no discount.[73] In **14.28**

[64] H.A. 1985, s.127(2)(*b*), (3)(*b*).
[65] *Ibid.* s.127(2)(*c*), (3)(*d*).
[66] *Ibid.* s.127(3)(*c*).
[67] See below, para. 14.37.
[68] H.A. 1985, s.129(2)(*a*).
[69] *Ibid.* s.129(2)(*b*).
[70] *Ibid.* s.129(2A)–(2B).
[71] *Ibid.* s.131(2); Housing (Right to Buy) (Maximum Discount) Order 1989 (S.I. 1989 No. 513).
[72] H.A. 1985, s.131(1)–(1A); a council's offer to sell at a figure which ignores this "cost floor" limitation is void and unenforceable by the tenant: *McGroarty* v. *Stirling D.C.* 1987 S.L.T. 85 (Ct. of Session, O.H.).
[73] H.A. 1985, s.131(1).

addition, the discount has to be reduced to take account of any previous discount given in connection with a relevant previous purchase by the current tenant, his spouse or deceased spouse.[74]

14.29 The relevant "clocking-up" periods for discount purposes are the same as the eligible periods for basic right to buy purposes.[75] Where joint tenants exercise the right to buy, the discount is based on the *longest* of their respective periods of tenancy[76]; thus the respective periods cannot be aggregated in order to push up the discount.

14.30 Where a discount is given, stamp duty will be assessed by reference to the discounted price rather than the market value[77]; thus where the discounted price does not exceed £30,000, no duty is payable.[78]

14.31 **(iii) Repayment of discount on premature disposal.** If, following a right to buy purchase with a discount, there is a further "relevant disposal" (which is not an "exempted disposal") within three years of the original conveyance or lease to the right to buy purchaser, then, pursuant to a covenant which the council has to include in the original conveyance or lease, the former secure tenant and his successors in title must normally repay on demand[79] the discount or part thereof, on a sliding scale reducing by one third per annum for each complete year since the original conveyance or lease.[80]

14.32 A "relevant disposal" for these purposes means a disposal of the dwelling, whether as a whole or in part, by way of conveyance,[81] assignment, or the grant of a lease or sublease exceeding 21 years

[74] H.A. 1985, s.130; Housing (Right to Buy) (Prescribed Persons) Order 1984 (S.I. 1984 No.1173).

[75] H.A. 1985, s.129(1) and Sched 4; see above, paras. 14.08–14.10.

[76] *Ibid.* s.129(3).

[77] Finance Act 1981, ss.107–108.

[78] F.A. 1984, s.109(1).

[79] Although the obligation is only to repay the appropriate portion of the discount *on demand*, the government contemplated that authorities should require repayment on any relevant disposal within the three-year period: *H.C. Standing Committee F on the Housing Bill*, February 12, 1980, cols. 273–276.

[80] H.A. 1985, s.155; special rules apply where the tenant has served a "notice of delay": *ibid.* s.155(3A); "notices of delay" are discussed below, paras. 14.120–14.122.

[81] *Sic*; subsequent disposals of the freehold will in fact be by way of *transfer* rather than conveyance, since the title will have been registered (see below, para. 14.47); see also J.T. Farrand, *Contract and Conveyance* (4th ed., 1983), pp.224–225.

other than at a rack rent[82]; and the grant of an option to call for a "relevant disposal" is treated as if it were the disposal itself.[83]

However, the following "relevant disposals" are "exempted disposals"[84] (which thus do not attract discount repayment): **14.33**

(i) a disposal of the whole of the dwelling by way of conveyance of the freehold or assignment of the lease which is made to someone who is the person or one of the persons by whom it is made, or who is the spouse or former spouse of such person, or who is a member of the family of such person who has resided with him throughout the period of 12 months ending with the disposal;

(ii) a vesting of the whole of the dwelling in a person taking under a will or on an intestacy[85];

(iii) a disposal of the whole of the dwelling in pursuance of an order under section 24[86] (*not* section 24A[87]) of the Matrimonial Causes Act 1973 or under section 2 of the Inheritance (Provision for Family and Dependants) Act 1975;

(iv) a disposal where the property disposed of is acquired compulsorily; and

(v) a disposal where the property disposed of is land included in the dwelling under section 184 of the Housing Act 1985.[88]

This discount–repayment obligation constitutes a positive covenant which can normally bind successors in title, contrary to common **14.34**

[82] H.A. 1985, s.159(1).

[83] *Ibid.* s.163(1).

[84] *Ibid.* ss.160–161.

[85] Thus it may sometimes be preferable for the relevant beneficiary under the deceased's estate to take the dwelling *in specie* and pay the deceased's debts or legacies himself where appropriate, rather than for the personal representatives to sell the dwelling within the relevant three years' period in order to pay those debts or legacies: see T.M. Aldridge, *The Housing Act 1980* (1980), p. 37.

[86] This deals with *transfer* of property orders made by the *court* in matrimonial proceedings: see above, paras. 11.32–11.40; a disposal in pursuance merely of a separation agreement would therefore *not* be "exempted."

[87] This deals with *sales* of matrimonial property ordered by the court to liquidate funds for matrimonial relief; sales under s.24A orders are not exempted disposals, since the s.24A jurisdiction is different from that in s.24: *R.* v. *Rushmoor B.C., ex p. Barrett* [1988] 2 W.L.R. 1271 (C.A.).

[88] Which deals with land let with or used for the purposes of the dwelling: see above, para. 14.06.

law principles[89]; even an "exempted disposal" does not normally[90] wipe off the liability to repay discount as such, which continues to bind successors in title for the remainder of the three-year period.

14.35 **(iv) Enforcement of the discount–repayment charge.** The liability to repay discount on a premature disposal only arises on the first relevant (*i.e.* non-exempted) transaction.[91] The liability is however treated as a charge by deed by way of legal mortgage, having priority immediately after any prescribed[92] mortgage granted to enable the tenant to exercise his right to buy.[93] Further advances by a prescribed body which provided the initial right to buy mortgage similarly have automatic priority over the council's own discount-repayment charge[94]; and even as regards amounts subsequently advanced by certain prescribed bodies which have not given the tenant the mortgage which enabled him to exercise the right to buy, the council may at any time serve notice on the prescribed body postponing the council's own discount–repayment charge to any legal charge securing any amount advanced to the tenant by that body.[95]

14.36 The obligation to repay discount is a land charge[96] for the purposes of the Land Registration Act 1925[97]: thus, registration will be by notice or caution, and there is no need for separate registration as a charge or for the issue of a separate charge certificate; we shall see[98] that the title must always be registered following a right to buy transaction, even if it was not previously registered.

[89] *Cf.*, *e.g. Austerberry* v. *Oldham Corpn.* (1885) 29 Ch.D. 750 (C.A.); where appropriate, therefore, a purchaser must ensure prior to completion that his vendor will discharge the liability.

[90] Save for "exempted disposals" within categories (iv) and (v) above, where the repayment covenant is not binding on the transferee or any successor in title of his: H.A. 1985, s.162.

[91] H.A. 1985, s.155(2)–(3).

[92] *Ibid.* s.156(4)–(6); see, *e.g.* Housing (Right to Buy) (Priority of Charges) (No. 1) Order 1988 (S.I. 1988 No.85).

[93] H.A. 1985, s.156(1)–(2)(*a*)–(*b*), (3A).

[94] *Ibid.* s.156(2)(*c*), (3A).

[95] *Ibid.* s.156(2); if a right to buy purchaser with a council mortgage subsequently decides to remortgage the property to a building society, the society will almost certainly require a deed of postponement of the discount-repayment charge from the council under these provisions.

[96] But see above, n.90.

[97] L.R.A. 1925, s.59; H.A. 1985, s.156(3).

[98] See below, para. 14.47.

(d) *The purchase procedure*

(i) The initial right to buy claim. The secure tenant must first serve[99] on the council a written notice, in a prescribed form, claiming the right to buy.[1] The form must be provided by the council to the tenant, on request.[2] **14.37**

The notice cannot be invalidated by errors in or omissions from any of the prescribed particulars,[3] and it can be withdrawn by the tenant at any time.[4] **14.38**

If, after the notice has been given, a new tenant takes over the secure tenancy,[5] then he will normally be in the same position as if *he* had given the notice himself and had been the secure tenant at the time it was given[6]: this has been interpreted as meaning that the new tenant must be treated for right to buy purposes as being in exactly the same position as the former tenant, and he can thus take over the former tenant's eligibility to buy and discount entitlement[6a]; however, the right to a mortgage is separately conferred on the new tenant,[7] and the amount of the mortgage will depend on his individual circumstances. Separate provision is made for preservation of the right to buy, after it has been claimed by the tenant, where the council disposes of its interest to another public landlord[8]; and the right to buy may also be preserved where the council's interest is taken over by a private sector landlord.[9] **14.39**

In the case of joint tenants, the right to buy and the right to a mortgage prima facie belong to all of them jointly, but one or more can exercise the rights alone with the agreement of the others.[10] Thus one joint tenant cannot force the other joint tenant(s) to buy, and where only one (or some) of the joint tenants does (or do) purchase by agreement, then although the secure tenancy will end on **14.40**

[99] For the methods of service, see H. A. 1985, s.176(3), and L.G.A. 1972, s.231(1).
[1] H.A. 1985, ss.122(1), 176(1); Housing (Right to Buy) (Prescribed Forms) Regulations 1986 (S.I. 1986 No. 2194); the form is "RTB1."
[2] H.A. 1985, s.176(2).
[3] *Ibid.* s.177.
[4] *Ibid.* s.122(3).
[5] *Ibid.* ss.87–92, see above, paras. 9.11–9.24, 9.27–9.42.
[6] H.A. 1985, s.136 (not applying to "exchange" assignments: *ibid.* s.136(1)(*a*); see above, paras. 9.20–9.23).
[6a] *McIntyre* v. *Merthyr Tydfil B.C.*, *The Independent*, February 9, 1989 (C.A.).
[7] H.A. 1985, s.136(2)–(3).
[8] *Ibid.* s.137.
[9] *Ibid.* s.171H.
[10] *Ibid.* ss.118(2), 132(2).

completion of the purchase,[11] he (or they) will normally hold the purchased legal estate on trust for himself (or themselves) *and the other erstwhile joint secure tenants*, in accordance with general equitable principles.[12]

14.41 Furthermore, the secure tenant can require in his right to buy claim notice that not more than three "members of his family"[13] who are not joint tenants but who occupy the dwelling should share the right to buy and the right to a mortgage with him, in which case they are thereafter treated as joint tenants[14]; but in order for non-spouse family members to qualify for inclusion, they must satisfy a 12 months' residence requirement unless the council consents to dispense with this.[15] Even an infant family member can apparently be included, which might be useful if he is already a high earner, thus swelling the mortgage entitlement[16]; in such a case, the legal estate must be vested in the adult(s) alone, who will hold it on trust for sale for himself (or themselves) and the infant.[17]

14.42 A person who contributes financially to the purchase but is not added as a joint tenant under this provision may nevertheless acquire an equitable entitlement by virtue of his contribution (even if he is not a family member), which, if supported by occupation, may rank as an "overriding interest" under the Land Registration Act 1925,[18] and may have priority even over the council's mortgage.[19]

14.43 **(ii) The council's first response notice.** Following service of the initial right to buy claim by the tenant, the council has four weeks to serve on him a prescribed notice admitting or denying (with

[11] H.A. 1985, s.139(2).
[12] *Keech* v. *Sandford* (1726) 2 Eq. Cas. Abr. 741; *Protheroe* v. *Protheroe* [1968] 1 W.L.R. 519 (C.A.); L.P.A. 1925, s.36(1).
[13] Defined in H.A. 1985, s.186; see above, paras. 9.31–9.33.
[14] H.A. 1985, s.123.
[15] *Ibid.* s.123(2).
[16] See below, paras. 14.79–14.81.
[17] L.P.A. 1925, s.19(2).
[18] L.R.A. 1925, s.70(1)(g).
[19] *Williams and Glyn's Bank* v. *Boland* [1981] A.C. 487 (H.L.); the overriding interest must be established by actual occupation at the date of the execution of the mortgage: *Lloyds Bank plc* v. *Rosset* [1988] 3 W.L.R. 1301 (C.A.); but *cf.* the situation where the beneficiary *authorises* the mortgaging of the property by the purchaser: here the beneficiary's rights will be postponed to those of the mortgagee: *Bristol and West B.S.* v. *Henning* [1985] 1 W.L.R. 778 (C.A.); *Paddington B.S.* v. *Mendelsohn* (1985) 50 P. & C.R. 244 (C.A.).

reasons) the tenant's right[20]; the response period is extended to eight weeks where for part of the qualifying period the landlord was not the council on which the tenant's notice is served.[21] We shall hereafter call this notice from the council the "first response notice."

(iii) The council's second response notice. Once the tenant's right has been established, whether by the council's acceptance or as a result of a county court's decision,[22] the council must serve within eight weeks (or 12 weeks where the tenant is to be granted a lease[23]) a second notice on the tenant.[24] This must state the price,[25] and the terms[26] of the conveyance or lease; it must also contain prescribed information regarding the likely amounts of any service charges[27] or improvement contributions[28] where appropriate, and must inform the tenant of any structural defect known to the council which affects the dwelling or the building in which it is situated or any other building over which the tenant will have rights under the conveyance or lease.[29] In addition, the notice must tell the tenant of his right to a mortgage (a form must be included for claiming this),[30] his right to defer completion,[31] his right to be granted a shared ownership lease,[32] and his right to a valuation from the district valuer.[33] **14.44**

[20] H.A. 1985, ss.124(1)–(2), 176; Housing (Right to Buy) (Prescribed Forms) Regulations 1986 (S.I. 1986 No. 2194).

[21] H.A. 1985, s.124(2); in such a case the council may need extra time to check the alleged prior tenancies, but it may instead simply accept the tenant's statutory declaration as "sufficient evidence" of those tenancies: *ibid.* s.180.

[22] *Ibid.* s.181, see below, para. 14.54.

[23] See above, para. 14.02.

[24] H.A. 1985, s.125.

[25] *Ibid.* s.125(2); the council may use the officials of the district valuer's office to fix valuations on its behalf for s.125 purposes, since this does not conflict with the separate right which the tenant has under s.128 (see below) to appeal to the district valuer concerning the valuation: *Norwich C.C.* v. *Secretary of State for the Environment* [1982] 1 All E.R. 737 (C.A.).

[26] H.A. 1985, s.125(3); see below, paras. 14.55–14.77.

[27] *Ibid.* ss.125(4), 125A, 125C; see below, paras. 14.61–14.64; see also *Heinemann* v. *Cooper* (1987) 19 H.L.R. 262 (C.A.), a private sector case where the purchaser of a long lease recovered damages for misrepresentation where the vendor's solicitor, prior to exchange of contracts, had misstated the amount of the service charge.

[28] H.A. 1985, ss.125(4), 125B–125C; see below, para. 14.65.

[29] H.A. 1985, s.125(4A); see below, para. 14.62.

[30] H.A. 1985, s.125(5); see below, paras. 14.78–14.91.

[31] H.A. 1985, s.125(5) see below, paras. 14.84–14.85.

[32] H.A. 1985, s.125(5); see below, paras. 14.94–14.113.

[33] H.A. 1985, s.125(5); see below, para. 14.46.

We shall hereafter describe this notice as the "second response notice."

14.45 If the tenant ignores the second response notice and takes no further part in the transaction, then the tenant's claim to buy will lapse after the expiry of a reasonable time.[34]

14.46 **(iv) The role of the district valuer.** Within (normally) three months of service of the council's second response notice, the tenant can elect to have the value decided by the district valuer (an officer appointed by the Commissioners of Inland Revenue[35]), whose decision is final.[36]

14.47 **(v) The conveyancing machinery.** Where the council's title to the land has not already been registered at H.M. Land Registry, the 1985 Act provides[37] a much more streamlined conveyancing procedure than that normally applicable to unregistered titles: under this special procedure, first registration of the title must be effected even if the dwelling is outside an area within which registration has been prescribed as compulsory under the Land Registration Act 1925 (and, in the case of the grant of a lease, whether or not the lease is for a term of more than 21 years).[38] In such a case, the council must give the tenant a prescribed certificate as to the title, which the Chief Land Registrar must accept as sufficient evidence for registration purposes[39]; the council will however be liable to indemnify the Registrar against subsequent claims.[40]

[34] *L.B. of Sutton* v. *Swann* (1986) 18 H.L.R. 140 (C.A.); although the court referred to the council's "offer" lapsing, the right to buy does not depend on the formation of any contract as such.

[35] H.A. 1985, s.622.

[36] *Ibid.* ss.128, 181(1).

[37] *Ibid.* s.154.

[38] *Ibid.* s.154(1); *cf.* L.R.A. 1925, ss.120, 123. Solicitors acting either for the "right to buy" purchaser or his successors in title where the property is not within an area of compulsory registration must be alive to this point, since failure to register renders the transaction void as regards the legal estate after two months from the date of the deed (under L.R.A. 1925, s.123); however, if the right to buy is being exercised with the aid of a council mortgage, the council may be expected to ensure registration of the title; and even if the council is not the mortgagee, the first purchaser's solicitor should realise the need for registration from the special certificate whereby title is deduced (see below): T. M. Aldridge, *op. cit.* pp. 126–127.

[39] H.A. 1985, s.154(2)–(5).

[40] *Ibid.* s.154(5); *cf.* L.R.A. 1925, s.83(9)–(10).

Where the council's title is already registered, the "right to buy" lease is capable of substantive registration at the Land Registry even though it may be granted for a term not exceeding 21 years.[41] **14.48**

(vi) Completion

The effect of completion. As soon as all relevant matters[42] have been decided, the council must normally make the necessary grant (of the freehold or the lease) to the tenant (unless the tenant has incurred rent arrears of four weeks or more, of which any part remains outstanding).[43] **14.49**

On the conveyance of the freehold or the grant of the lease, the secure tenancy ends, but the rights and liabilities of any sub-tenants are expressly preserved.[44] The secure tenant can enforce the council's repairing obligations in relation to the secure tenancy until completion[45]; but the right under Part XVI of the Housing Act 1985 to apply for mandatory financial assistance relating to certain prescribed structural defects[46] only arises on completion.[47] **14.50**

Failure to complete. The council's obligation to complete is enforceable by injunction in the county court.[48] **14.51**

If it is the tenant who fails to complete, then the council may normally serve a notice requiring him either to complete within not less than 56 days if all relevant matters have been determined, or to notify it within not less than 56 days of any relevant outstanding matters.[49] This initial notice can only be served on the expiration of the relevant time limit,[50] which depends on whether the tenant has claimed the right to a mortgage, and if so whether he is entitled to defer completion. If no claim to a mortgage has been made, the completion notice can be served, in effect, 12 months after service of the council's second response notice[51]; the position concerning com- **14.52**

[41] H.A. 1985, s.154(6); *cf.* L.R.A. 1925, ss.8, 22.
[42] H.A. 1985, s.138(1) (mortgage matters are included).
[43] *Ibid.* s.138(1)–(2).
[44] *Ibid.* s.139(2).
[45] See ombudsmen decisions No.828/C/84 and 842/A/85, reported in [1986] Legal Action 33, 165.
[46] See below, paras. 14.151–14.154.
[47] *McSweeney* v. *Dumbarton D.C.* 1987 S.L.T. 129 (Sh. Ct.).
[48] H.A. 1985, ss.138(3), 181.
[49] *Ibid.* s.140(1)–(2), (4)–(5).
[50] *Ibid.* s.140(3).
[51] *Ibid.* s.140(3)(*a*).

pletion notices where the right to a mortgage is claimed, and where completion is deferred, is dealt with later.[52]

14.53 If the tenant fails to comply with the initial completion notice then the council may serve on him a second completion notice requiring him to complete within a further period of not less than 56 days (which can be extended by the council)[53]; if the tenant does not comply with this second completion notice (and outstanding rent arrears are deemed to constitute non-compliance), then his right to buy claim notice is deemed to be withdrawn at the end of the period stated in the second completion notice (as extended, where appropriate).[54] However, the tenant is under no further liability, since the transaction is not contractual in nature[55]: thus there is no question of either an equitable claim against him for specific performance, or a common law action for damages for failure to complete.[56] Indeed, there is nothing to prevent the tenant from serving another right to buy claim form immediately after his original one has been deemed to be withdrawn.

14.54 **(vii) Jurisdiction of the county court.** The county court has jurisdiction over any question concerning the right to buy (other than the price), even if no other relief is sought than a bare declaration.[57]

(e) *The terms of the purchase other than the price*

14.55 **(i) General.** The 1985 Act contains very detailed provisions concerning the terms of the conveyance or long lease, designed principally to preserve certain rights for (respectively) the council, the former secure tenant, and neighbouring occupiers.[58] What follows is an attempt to draw attention to some of the more important terms governing right to buy transactions.[59]

52 See paras. 14.86–14.88.

53 H.A. 1985, s.141(1)–(3).

54 *Ibid.* s.141(4)–(5).

55 *Ibid.* s.122(3).

56 *Cf., e.g. Raineri* v. *Miles* [1981] A.C. 1050 (H.L.), and the Leasehold Reform Act 1967, s.5(3) of which expressly confers "the like rights and remedies as in the case of a contract freely entered into."

57 H.A. 1985, s.181(1)–(2).

58 *Ibid.* s.139(1) and Sched. 6; for precedents of standard conveyances and leases pursuant to the right to buy, see *e.g.* The Conveyancer and Property Lawyer, *Precedents for the Conveyancer*, Forms 16–38 and 5–73.

59 For more comprehensive treatment, see, *e.g.* J. E. Adams, [1981] Conv. 92, 197; A. Arden, *Housing Act 1985*, Current Law Statutes Annotated; M. Grant and C. Hunter, *Housing and Planning Act 1986*, Current Law Statutes Annotated.

Any provision of the conveyance or lease is void insofar as it purports to enable the council to charge the purchaser or tenant a sum for or in connection with the giving of a consent or approval.[60] Furthermore, the Minister has a wide power to "outlaw" (if necessary with retrospective effect) covenants and conditions inconsistent with the 1985 Act.[61] **14.56**

(ii) Leases[62]

Ground rent. As regards the lease of a house or flat, the ground rent cannot exceed £10 per annum[63]; thus it seems not to be possible for service charges to be reserved in the form of *rent*, as opposed to a mere covenant to pay the charges. **14.57**

Repairing obligations. There are important provisions governing liability for the condition of a flat.[64] Unless the county court otherwise orders with the consent of the parties, the council normally[65] retains liability for: repairing the structure and exterior of the flat and the building in which it is situated[66]; making good any defect affecting that structure[67]; repairing any other property in respect of which the tenant has rights[68]; maintaining so far as practicable those services[69] to which the tenant is entitled (whether alone or with others); repairing installations connected with the provision of **14.58**

60 H.A. 1985, Sched. 6, Pt. I, para. 6.

61 *Ibid.* ss.167–168; a Ministerial example of a suitable clause for "outlawing" is one requiring that the dwelling should be occupied only as a single private house for the exclusive use of the purchaser and his family, a restriction which is narrower than the tenants' charter provisions governing secure tenancies (see above, paras. 9.01–9.10): H.C. Deb., March 23, 1983, col. 881.

62 For the length of the lease, see above, para. 14.02.

63 H.A. 1985, Sched. 6, Pt. III, para. 11.

64 *Ibid.* para. 14.

65 These covenants do not impose on the council any obligations which it is not entitled to discharge under the provisions of its own lease or a superior lease, where the council's own interest is leasehold; but in such a case the council must use its best endeavours to ensure that any other person who has covenanted to do the work, duly does it: *ibid.* para. 15(3)–(4).

66 This avoids the problems presented by *Campden Hill Towers* v. *Gardner* [1977] Q.B. 823 (C.A.) (see above, para. 12.14).

67 Thus clearly imposing liability for inherent defects: *cf. Ravenseft Properties* v. *Davstone (Holdings)* [1980] Q.B. 12 (see above, para. 12.21).

68 Subject to contrary agreement, where the tenant enjoyed the use, during the secure tenancy, of any premises, facilities or services in common with others, the lease of a flat must include such rights: H.A. 1985, Sched. 6, Pt. III, para. 13.

69 Such as lifts: *cf. Liverpool C.C.* v. *Irwin* [1977] A.C. 239 (H.L.) (see above, para. 12.38); see also n.68 above.

those services; and rebuilding or reinstating the flat and the building in which it is situated in case of destruction or damage by fire, tempest, flood, or any other cause against which it is normal to insure.

14.59 The tenant impliedly covenants to keep in repair (including decorative repair) the interior of a flat, and the interior and exterior of a house (subject in either case to contrary agreement).[70]

14.60 Where the council's own interest in the dwelling (whether a house or a flat) is leasehold, then the council impliedly covenants to discharge its own obligations under the covenants contained in that lease (except in so far as they fall to be discharged by the "right to buy" tenant).[71]

14.61 *Recovery of the council's expenditure on repairs etc.* There are complicated provisions[72] relating to the extent to which the council can pass on to the "right to buy" purchaser the costs which it has incurred in relation to the dwelling and (in respect of a flat) the surrounding building. Broadly speaking, where the dwelling is a *flat*, the lease may require the tenant to pay a "reasonable part"[73] of the costs of discharging or insuring against[74] the council's implied obligations set out above.[75] However, as regards the council's implied covenant to rebuild or reinstate in case of destruction or damage,[76] only a "reasonable part" of the *insurance costs* (rather than of the costs incurred in doing the actual rebuilding or reinstatement work) can be passed on to the tenant.[77]

[70] H.A. 1985, Sched. 6, Pt. III, para. 16.

[71] *Ibid.* para. 15(1)–(2).

[72] *Ibid.* paras. 16A–16D, 18.

[73] Bearing in mind that the council's obligations relate to the surrounding building as well as to the individual flat, it may be reasonable for it to pass on to the tenants the entire cost of the relevant works incurred in relation to the whole building, provided that each tenant is charged no more than a reasonable part of the entire cost: *Sutton (Hastoe) Housing Association* v. *Williams* (1988) 20 H.L.R. 321 (C.A.).

[74] The 1985 Act imposes no obligation on the council actually to take out or maintain insurance on the block of flats of which the tenant's dwelling forms part (see, *e.g. ibid.* Sched. 6, Pt. III, para. 16A(3)); the tenant could well be refused a private sector mortgage in such a case, so that he could try to secure the insertion of an insuring obligation in the lease by complaining to the Minister (*ibid.* s.170, see below, para. 14.126), and/or requesting a county court judge to declare that the insertion of the insuring obligation is "reasonable" (*ibid.* s.181 and Sched. 6, Pt. I, para. 5, see below, para. 14.77); see also an editorial note in [1984] Conv. 337.

[75] Para. 14.58; see H.A. 1985, Sched. 6, Pt. III, para. 16A(1).

[76] See above, para. 14.58.

[77] H.A. 1985, Sched. 6, Pt. III, paras. 16A(1), 18.

Where the dwelling is a *flat*, further restrictions are imposed on the tenant's liability in respect of the cost of repairs (including structural repairs) carried out by the council within (normally) the first five years from the grant of the lease[78]: in respect of works which are itemised in the estimates contained in the council's "second response notice,"[79] the tenant is not required to pay more than his estimated contribution (as shown in the notice) in respect of those items, together with an inflation allowance; while in respect of works which are not itemised in the "second response notice," he is not normally required to pay more than, in effect, the estimated annual average amounts shown in the "second response notice," together with an inflation allowance. It is not possible to contract out of these service charge restrictions.[80] **14.62**

In certain prescribed circumstances, the tenant is entitled to a loan from the council to assist him in meeting service charges in relation to repairs (including structural repairs) incurred during the first ten years of the lease in relation to a *flat*[81]; the loan is effected by way of leaving the whole or part of the service charge outstanding.[82] **14.63**

Where the tenant of a *flat* or a *house* is required to pay a "service charge" in respect of services, repairs, management or insurance, then the general service charge provisions in the Landlord and Tenant Act 1985[83] will be relevant, whereby (*inter alia*) the county court can pronounce on the reasonableness of the charges.[84] However, these provisions in the Landlord and Tenant Act do not restrict the amounts recoverable in respect of works of pure improvement (as opposed to repair).[85] **14.64**

Separate provisions in the Housing Act 1985 govern the recovery of "improvement contributions" in relation to a *flat*, *i.e.* sums payable under the lease by the tenant in respect of improvements which do not fall within the above-mentioned obligations concerning **14.65**

[78] H.A. 1985, Sched. 6, Pt. III, paras. 16A(5), 16B, 16D; Housing (Right to Buy) (Service Charges) Order 1986 (S.I. 1986 No. 2195).

[79] See above, para. 14.44.

[80] H.A. 1985, Sched. 6, Pt. III, para. 18.

[81] *Ibid.* s.450A.

[82] *Ibid.* s.450A(4)(*b*).

[83] L. & T.A. 1985, ss.18–30 (as amended by L. & T.A. 1987); see particularly L. & T.A. 1985, s.26(1), (2)(*c*); L. & T.A. 1987, s.41(2); see also, as regards service charges imposed on the *conveyance of the freehold* (as opposed to the lease) of a *house*, H.A. 1985, ss.45, 47–51, 621A.

[84] L. & T.A. 1985, s.19.

[85] *Sutton (Hastoe) Housing Association* v. *Williams* (1988) 20 H.L.R. 321 (C.A.); but the "improvement contributions" provisions in H.A. 1985 may now apply: see below.

repair and reinstatement.[86] Although the lease can lawfully include a provision requiring the tenant to pay towards the costs of improvement work carried out by the council,[87] the tenant cannot be required to pay improvement contributions for works unless an estimate for them has been given in the council's "second response notice," and for the first five years of the lease he normally cannot be required to pay any more than the amount shown in the notice as his estimated contribution in relation to the relevant improvement work, together with an inflation allowance.[88] Again, it is not possible to contract out of this restriction.[89]

14.66 *Assignment and subletting*. The imposition in a "right to buy" lease of a restriction on the tenant prohibiting assignment or sub-letting is normally void.[90]

14.67 **(iii) Defects in title.** Turning to liabilities which already affect the title, the purchasing secure tenant (whether he is acquiring the freehold or a lease) will of course be bound according to the normal rules by pre-existing *non-financial interests* of third parties, such as easements and restrictive covenants.[91] However, he will automatically take free of all pre-existing *financial charges* on the council's title (such as mortgages, liens, etc.), save for rentcharges where he is acquiring the freehold[92]; the council's personal liability regarding the obligations which the charges were designed to secure is of course preserved.[93]

14.68 **(iv) Discount-repayment clauses.** Where a discount from the price has been given, we have seen that the conveyance or lease must contain a covenant binding the tenant and his successors to repay the discount or part thereof on certain premature disposals.[94]

[86] H.A. 1985, s.187 and Sched. 6, Pt. III, paras. 16C–16D; Housing (Right to Buy) (Service Charges) Order 1986 (S.I. 1986 No. 2195).
[87] See *Sutton (Hastoe) Housing Association* v. *Williams*, above, n. 85.
[88] See above, n. 86.
[89] H.A. 1985, Sched. 6, Pt. III, para. 18.
[90] *Ibid.* para. 17(1).
[91] *Ibid.* Sched. 6, Pt. I, paras. 2–4.
[92] *Ibid.* Sched. 6, Pt. IV, paras. 20–21.
[93] *Ibid.* para. 21(2).
[94] *Ibid.* ss.155–156, see above, paras. 14.31–14.34.

(v) Disposals in special areas: restrictive covenants and pre-emption clauses. In the case of properties in certain special areas, the conveyance or lease *may* contain additional stipulations designed to avoid the disappearance of low-priced housing for rent. **14.69**

Restrictive covenants. The 1985 Act provides[95] that where the dwelling is in a National Park, or an area designated as one of outstanding natural beauty,[96] or an area designated by the Minister as a rural area,[97] then the conveyance or lease *may* contain a restrictive covenant[98] to the effect that, until such time as may be specified by the council, the council's written consent is required before there can be any further "relevant disposal" (which is not an "exempted disposal"),[99] or any disposal by way of tenancy or licence[1] (which does not constitute an "exempted disposal" or a disposal by a person who retains his only or principal home in the dwelling), by the purchaser, his successors in title or any person deriving title under him or any such successor.[2] However, if the disposal is to someone who for the previous three years lived or worked in a region designated by the Minister,[3] which region or part of which region is comprised in the National Park or designated area concerned, then if it is a "relevant disposal," consent must not be withheld, and if it is a disposal by way of tenancy or licence, it is permitted without the need for consent.[4] **14.70**

95 H.A. 1985, s.157(1)–(3), (6A).

96 National Parks and Access to the Countryside Act 1949, s.87: H.A. 1985, s.157(1).

97 H.A. 1985, s.157(1), (8); see the following Housing (Right to Buy) (Designated Rural Areas and Designated Regions) Orders: S.I. 1980 No. 1375; S.I. 1981 Nos. 397, 940; S.I 1982 Nos. 21, 91, 187; S.I. 1986 No. 1695; S.I. 1988 No. 2057.

98 The burden of the restrictive covenant runs against successors by force of the statute, so that it is not necessary to satisfy the normal equitable rules: see *Governors of the Peabody Donation Fund* v. *London Residuary Body, The Times,* July 25, 1987.

99 As defined in H.A. 1985, ss.159–162; the same definition, with its exemptions and qualifications, applies in relation to the discount-repayment provisions in *ibid.* s.155, and has therefore been discussed above, paras. 14.32–14.33.

1 This refers to tenancies or licences which are not already covered by the expression "relevant disposal": H.A. 1985, s.157(6A).

2 This is designed to ensure that *mortgagees* who want to sell are bound by the restrictive covenant: a purchaser buying from a mortgagee exercising a power of sale derives title from the mortgagee, not from the mortgagor.

3 H.A. 1985, s.157(3), (8); see the following Housing (Right to Buy) (Designated Rural Areas and Designated Regions) Orders: S.I. 1980 Nos. 1345, 1375; S.I. 1981 Nos. 397, 940; S.I. 1982 Nos. 21, 187; S.I. 1986 No. 1695; S.I. 1988 No. 2057.

4 H.A. 1985, s.157(2)–(3).

14.71 *Pre-emption clauses.* With the Minister's consent[5] (which has been given in general terms[6]) then as an alternative to the restrictive covenant just discussed, the council may (in the case of the special areas mentioned above) insert[7] a pre-emption clause; this is to the effect that for the next ten years there will be no further "relevant disposal" (which is not an "exempted disposal")[8] unless (in relation to that or a previous such disposal) the purchaser or his successor or the person deriving title under him or his successor[9] has first offered to reconvey the dwelling or surrender the lease to the council, and the council has either refused the offer or has failed to accept it within one month.

14.72 The consideration for the offer must be an amount representing[10] the price which, at the time of the offer, the interest to be reconveyed or surrendered would realise if sold on the open market by a willing vendor, on the assumption that any liability to repay discount[11] or to pay for an outstanding share on disposal of a dwelling held under a "shared ownership lease"[12] would be discharged by the vendor. If the council accepts the offer, the price must normally be reduced by such amount (if any) as would be due by way of discount repayment or payment of the outstanding "shared ownership" share if a relevant (non-exempted) disposal had been made at the time of the offer.[13]

14.73 Only in this very limited situation, therefore, can a pre-emption clause be inserted.

14.74 *Breach of the restrictions.* Any disposal in breach of the restrictive covenant or the right of pre-emption is void.[14]

14.75 *Registration of the restrictions.* The restrictive covenant is treated as a local land charge,[15] but the Chief Land Registrar must enter the appropriate registered land "restriction" on the register of title.[16] It

[5] H.A. 1985, s.157(4)–(5).
[6] See Ministerial Letter dated September 22, 1980, para. 28.
[7] Pursuant to H.A. 1985, s.157(4).
[8] See above, n. 99.
[9] This ensures that mortgagees who want to sell are bound by the pre-emption clause: see above, n. 2.
[10] H.A. 1985, s.158(1)–(2).
[11] *Ibid.* s.155, see above, paras. 14.31–14.35.
[12] *Ibid.* Sched. 8, para. 6 (see below, para. 14.112).
[13] *Ibid.* s.158(3)–(4).
[14] *Ibid.* s.157(6).
[15] *Ibid.* s.157(7).
[16] *Ibid.*; thus the covenant cannot constitute an overriding interest under L.R.A. 1925, s.70(1)(*i*).

is not so clear how the right of pre-emption may be protected.[17] Although under the general law a right of pre-emption does not as such create an interest in land,[18] this does not apparently affect the enforceability and registrability of this statutory right of pre-emption in the 1985 Act,[19] since the Act[20] expressly makes this right binding on successors in title.

(vi) Conveyancing costs. Any agreement between the council and the secure tenant is normally void in so far as it purports to oblige the tenant to pay the council's costs in connection with the tenant's exercise of the right to buy, the right to a mortgage, or the right to a shared ownership lease[21]; but he can be required to pay the council's costs of providing the mortgage, on the execution of the mortgage deed, so long as those costs do not exceed £50.[22] **14.76**

(vii) Settling "reasonable" terms. Finally, as regards the terms of the purchase, the 1985 Act provides that, subject to the detailed provisions of Schedule 6, the conveyance or lease may include "such covenants and conditions as are reasonable in the circumstances."[23] In cases of dispute, the county court has a general jurisdiction.[24] **14.77**

(f) *The right to a mortgage*

We have seen that a secure council tenant who has the right to buy also has the right to a mortgage from the council,[25] which does not depend on him first having unsuccessfully sought finance from private sector institutions. Where the right to buy has been "pre- **14.78**

[17] H.A. 1985, s.157(7), refers back to s.157(2) and not expressly to s.157(4) (which deals with the right of pre-emption); but arguably, since s.157(2) is expressly made subject to s.157(4), the protection by way of restriction in s.157(7) is available.
[18] *Pritchard* v. *Briggs* [1980] Ch. 338 (C.A.).
[19] H.C. Deb, April 3, 1980, col. 338; see also: *First National Securities* v. *Chiltern D.C.* (1975) 119 S.J. 461; *Governors of Peabody Donation Fund* v. *London Residuary Body*, *The Times*, July 25, 1987.
[20] H.A. 1985, s.157(1), (4).
[21] *Ibid.* s.178(1).
[22] *Ibid.* s.178(2)–(3); Housing (Right to Buy) (Mortgage Costs) Order 1980 (S.I. 1980 No. 1390).
[23] H.A. 1985, Sched. 6, Pt. I, para. 5.
[24] *Ibid.* s.181.
[25] *Ibid.* s.132(1).

served" following disposal by the council of the secure sitting tenant's dwelling to a private sector landlord,[26] the right to a mortgage is still exercisable against the council itself.[27]

14.79 **(i) The amount.** The amount of the mortgage will basically be the purchase price, plus the council's costs of providing the mortgage up to a maximum of £50, together with such of the secure tenant's costs as the council agrees to pay for him, if any.[28] But there is *no obligation* on the council to provide a mortgage exceeding a specified multiple of the secure tenant's "available annual income" (or of the combined "available" incomes of joint purchasers[29]), as prescribed by the Minister.[30]

14.80 The relevant regulations[31] include within the term "annual income" not merely income from employment or business, but also long-term State benefits (such as retirement benefits, invalidity benefits, widow's benefits, and disability benefits), although short-term State benefits are excluded (such as unemployment or sickness benefits, income support, and family credit). From the "annual income," certain prescribed deductions have to be made for long-term commitments (in the form of maintenance payments and payments under credit agreements or court orders), so as to arrive at the "*available* annual income."

14.81 Having ascertained this figure, the prescribed multiple for the "principal earner" depends on his age when the initial right to buy claim notice[32] was served: the multiple is 2.5 if he was then under 60, 2.0 if he was then between 60 and 64, and 1.0 if he was then 65 or over; for the other purchasers who are the non-principal earners (assuming a joint purchase), the multiple for their "available annual incomes" is 1.0.[33] In the case of purchasers approaching or above retiring age, the prescribed multiples are thus much more generous

[26] H.A. 1985, ss.171A–171H and Sched. 9A; see above, para. 14.07.
[27] H.A. 1985, s.171C(2)(*b*).
[28] *Ibid.* ss.133(1), (5), 178(2)–(3); Housing (Right to Buy) (Mortgage Costs) Order 1980 (S.I. 1980 No. 1390).
[29] H.A. 1985, ss.132(2), 133(2).
[30] *Ibid.* s.133(2)–(3), (6).
[31] Housing (Right to Buy) (Mortgage Limits) Regulations 1980 (S.I. 1980 No. 1423).
[32] H.A. 1985, s.122(1) (see above, para. 14.37).
[33] See above, n. 31.

than those which the private sector lending institutions would normally contemplate.[34]

(ii) The mortgage procedure

The initial mortgage claim. The secure tenant must claim the right to a mortgage by serving written notice on the council in a prescribed form, normally not later than three months from the date of service on him of the council's "second response notice"[35]; but the council must, on reasonable grounds being shown, extend this period, failing which the county court can do so.[36] **14.82**

The council's response notice relating to the mortgage. "As soon as practicable" after service of this mortgage claim notice by the tenant, the council must give him notice of the amount of the mortgage, how this figure has been arrived at, and the terms of the mortgage.[37] The council must further include with this notice a form whereby the tenant can claim to defer completion, and must inform him of his right, on deferring completion, to serve a new notice claiming a mortgage.[38] In addition, where in the council's opinion the tenant is not entitled to a full mortgage,[39] the notice must inform the tenant of his right to be granted a shared ownership lease, and include the appropriate form.[40] **14.83**

The right to defer completion. Where the tenant claims a mortgage but he is entitled to less than the full mortgage,[41] he may defer completion if within three months (extendible by the council or the county court) of service of the council's notice giving details of the mortgage,[42] he serves notice on the council claiming to defer completion and deposits £150.[43] He may then, at any time before service of a first notice to complete on him,[44] serve a further notice[45] claim- **14.84**

[34] *Cf.* the Minister's promise in 1980 that the multiples would be based on "normal commercial practice": H.C. Deb, January 15, 1980, col. 1447.

[35] H.A. 1985, ss.125, 134(1)–(2), 176; Housing (Right to Buy) (Prescribed Forms) (No. 2) Regulations 1980 (S.I. 1980 No. 1465).

[36] H.A. 1985, s.134(3)–(4).

[37] *Ibid.* s.135(1).

[38] *Ibid.* s.135(2); see further below, paras. 14.84–14.85.

[39] H.A. 1985, s.133(1), (5); see above, para. 14.79.

[40] *Ibid.* s.135(3).

[41] See above, para. 14.79.

[42] See above, para. 14.83.

[43] H.A 1985, s.142(1)–(3).

[44] See below, para. 14.87.

[45] H.A. 1985, s.134(1): above, para. 14.82.

ing a mortgage[46]; this could result in a higher mortgage being offered, for example where he has since changed to a better-paid job. The "mortgage information" provisions[47] will then apply again, although apparently he cannot defer completion a second time.[48]

14.85 If the deferred transaction is duly completed, then the £150 deposit is treated as having been paid towards the price.[49]

14.86 *Service of completion notice where tenant has no right to defer completion.* If the tenant, having claimed a mortgage, is not entitled to defer completion,[50] the council can serve a first completion notice[51] after nine months have passed since service of its notice giving details of the mortgage.[52]

14.87 *Service of completion notice where tenant has the right to defer completion.* Where completion is deferred, the council can only serve a first notice to complete on the tenant once three years have elapsed following the tenant's initial notice[53] claiming the right to buy, or, if later, nine months after service of the notice from the council giving details of the mortgage.[54] Furthermore, it is important to appreciate that the price remains frozen throughout at the valuation figure as at service of the tenant's original right to buy claim notice,[55] which can constitute a real bargain for the tenant if house prices are rising.

14.88 *Effect of tenant's non-compliance with first notice to complete.* Failure by the tenant to comply with the first notice to complete means that a second notice to complete can be served, and if the tenant fails to comply with this second notice, his right to buy notice is deemed to be withdrawn.[56] However, where the tenant had originally deferred completion, the £150 "deposit" must now be returned to him.[57]

[46] H.A. 1985, s.142(4).
[47] *Ibid.* s.135(1): see above, para. 14.83.
[48] *Ibid.* s.142(4); it seems that s.135(2) (see above) does not on this occasion apply.
[49] *Ibid.* s.142(5)(*a*).
[50] See above, para. 14.84.
[51] See above, para. 14.52.
[52] H.A. 1985, ss.135, 140(3)(*b*).
[53] *Ibid.* s.122.
[54] *Ibid.* ss.135, 152(3).
[55] *Ibid.* ss.122(2), 126(1).
[56] *Ibid.* s.141 (1)–(4); see above, para. 14.53.
[57] H.A. 1985, s.142(5)(*b*).

(iii) The terms of the mortgage other than the amount. The length of the mortgage term must normally be 25 years, or at the mortgagor's option a shorter period, although it may subsequently be extended by the council.[58] However, where the mortgagor's interest is leasehold and the term of the lease is less than 25 years, the mortgage term shall be the term of the lease, or, again, a shorter period at the mortgagor's option.[59] **14.89**

Repayment must be made by way of instalments of capital and interest combined.[60] The rate of interest must be (in effect) the *higher* of the cost of the council's own borrowing plus 0·25 per cent, or of the "standard national rate" declared from time to time by the Minister after taking into account building society interest rates.[61] Since council mortgagors could thus well be paying more than mortgagors with private sector mortgages, this provides some incentive for a secure tenant to seek a mortgage from a source other than the council, in preference to exercising his "right to a mortgage." There are detailed provisions for adjusting the rate of interest[62]: note particularly that the authority must in effect reduce the periodic payments where the interest rate itself is reduced, but if the interest rate is increased, the authority can extend the mortgage term instead of varying the periodic payments.[63] **14.90**

Although the Act does not provide expressly for the imposition by council mortgagees of restrictions on the letting of the property by the mortgagor, such as are common in private sector mortgages,[64] the parties are nevertheless permitted to agree upon the inclusion of such a term, failing which the county court can require its insertion.[65] **14.91**

(iv) Mortgage default. Once the tenant has acquired his dwelling under the right to buy, there are no provisions enabling him as of right to resell to the council if he should wish to revert to being a **14.92**

[58] H.A. 1985, s.139(3) and Sched. 7, para. 2.
[59] *Ibid.*
[60] *Ibid.* Sched. 7, para. 1.
[61] *Ibid.* s.438 and Sched. 16, paras. 1–4.
[62] *Ibid.* Sched. 16, paras. 5–6.
[63] *Ibid.* s.139(3) and Sched. 7, para. 2(2), Sched. 16, para. 6.
[64] See also L.P.A. 1925, s.99(13).
[65] H.A. 1985, s.139(3) and Sched. 7, para. 4; *cf.* the embargo on impediments to subletting contained in *ibid.* Sched. 6, Pt. III, para. 17 (1), which only relates to a lease granted under the right to buy and not to any mortgage needed for its acquisition.

secure tenant because he finds he cannot afford the mortgage instalments.[66]

14.93 However, in cases of mortgage default the council has the normal remedies of a mortgagee.[67] In addition, the council is given a special remedy as mortgagee in cases where a pre-emption clause has been inserted in the conveyance or lease[68]; in this situation, if the council has become entitled to exercise the mortgagee's power of sale,[69] and the pre-emption period has not expired, then the council may, with the leave of the county court, vest the dwelling in itself by deed: where this is done, a fund has to be appropriated representing the price which the interest thereby vested in the council would realise at the time of vesting if sold on the open market, which is used for discharging prior incumbrances, legal costs, outstanding sums due on the mortgage, discount repayment, and payment for any outstanding share under a shared ownership lease, with any balance being paid to the mortgagor.[70]

(g) *The right to a shared ownership lease*

14.94 **(i) Definition.** A shared ownership lease allows the purchaser to reduce his mortgage commitments by paying a mixture of mortgage instalments and rent; in effect,[71] he buys a lease for a premium representing a share of the market value of the property, and also pays rent on the remaining share. He has the additional right to buy up further shares at any time (popularly called "staircasing"), paying the appropriate portion of the then current market value, although he cannot normally enfranchise or extend the lease under the Leasehold Reform Act 1967.[72] When he has bought up the full

[66] See *R.* v. *L.B. of Hillingdon, ex p. Tinn* (1988) 20 H.L.R. 305, 311 (D.C.); for the homelessness implications of mortgage default, see above, para. 4.61.

[67] See, *e.g.* Sir Robert Megarry and H.W.R. Wade, *The Law of Real Property* (5th ed., 1984), pp.931–960.

[68] H.A. 1985, s.157(4): see above, paras. 14.71–14.73.

[69] L.P.A. 1925, ss.101, 103.

[70] H.A. 1985, s.452 and Sched. 17 (which also apply to sales outside the right to buy); this reverses the effect of *Williams* v. *Wellingborough B.C.* [1975] 1 W.L.R. 1327 (C.A.), which had held that the right of pre-emption did not give the council, as mortgagee, the right to sell to itself, because it was restricted by the normal power of sale provisions in L.P.A. 1925, s.101 (which include an obligation to obtain the true market value: *Cuckmere Brick Co. Ltd.* v. *Mutual Finance* [1971] Ch. 949 (C.A.)), and the right of pre-emption would reduce the sale price.

[71] H.A. 1985, s.622.

[72] H.A. 1980, s.140 (which has not been repealed); H.A. 1985, s.173.

100 per cent., and the property is a house of which the council owns the freehold, then the tenant will be entitled to a conveyance of that freehold.

A shared ownership lease granted under the right to buy must conform with the detailed terms in Schedule 8 to the 1985 Act, together with the general provisions in Schedule 6 relating to the terms of right to buy leases[73] (as suitably modified).[74] Many of the other right to buy provisions are also extended to cover shared ownership leases, such as the provisions relating to registration of title, payment of costs, notices, Ministerial powers of intervention, general definitions, and the jurisdiction of the county court. **14.95**

(ii) Qualifying for the right to a shared ownership lease. A secure tenant has the additional right to be granted a shared ownership lease of the dwelling (whether house or flat), where *all* of the following conditions are satisfied[75]: he has claimed to exercise the right to buy; the right to buy has been established; his right to buy claim notice remains in force; he has claimed the right to a mortgage, but is entitled to less than a full mortgage[76]; and he is entitled to defer completion.[77] **14.96**

(iii) The purchase procedure. The purchase procedure is in effect a truncated version of the "normal" right to buy procedure, discussed earlier.[78] **14.97**

Assuming the above conditions are satisfied, then the secure tenant can serve a notice on the council claiming to exercise the right to be granted a shared ownership lease, and stating the initial share[79] which he proposes to acquire.[80] On service of this notice, any completion notice[81] from the council is blocked while the tenant's shared ownership claim notice remains in force.[82] **14.98**

[73] See above, paras. 14.02, 14.58–14.67; note in particular that the normal rules apply in relation to the length of the lease (see above, para. 14.02).
[74] H.A. 1985, s.151(1).
[75] *Ibid.* s.143(1).
[76] *Ibid.* s.133(1), (5): see above, para. 14.79.
[77] See above, paras. 14.84–14.85.
[78] See above, paras. 14.37–14.53.
[79] See below, para. 14.105.
[80] H.A. 1985, s.144(1).
[81] *Ibid.* ss.140–141; see above, paras. 14.52–14.53.
[82] H.A. 1985, s.144(3).

14.99 After service of the tenant's shared ownership claim notice, the council then has four weeks to serve on him a notice admitting or denying (with reasons) the tenant's right.[83]

14.100 Once the tenant's right to a shared ownership lease has been established, whether by the council's acceptance or as a result of a county court's decision,[84] the council must serve within eight weeks thereafter a second notice on the tenant stating the price and the terms of the shared ownership lease, and any variation in the mortgage terms.[85]

14.101 As soon as all relevant matters have been decided, the council must grant the shared ownership lease (unless the tenant has built up rent arrears of four weeks or more of which any are still outstanding), and this duty is enforceable by injunction in the county court.[86]

14.102 On the grant of the shared ownership lease, the secure tenancy ends, but the rights and liabilities of any sub-tenants are expressly preserved.[87] The sum of £150 which the tenant deposited with the council is treated on completion as having been paid towards the tenant's initial contribution.[88]

14.103 If the tenant fails to complete, the council may, after all relevant matters have been determined, serve a first notice to complete, requiring him to complete the transaction within not less than 56 days,[89] provided that at least three years have elapsed from service of the tenant's initial notice[90] claiming the right to buy, or, if later, nine months have elapsed after service of the notice from the council giving the mortgage terms.[91]

14.104 If the tenant fails to comply with this first completion notice (and he is deemed not to comply while relevant rent arrears are outstanding[92]), then the council may serve on him a second notice to complete, requiring him to complete within a further period of not less than 56 days (which is extendible by the council)[93]; and if the tenant does not comply with this second notice to complete, then his notice

[83] H.A. 1985, s.146.
[84] *Ibid.* s.181(1).
[85] *Ibid.* s.147(1)–(4).
[86] *Ibid.* ss.150, 181(1).
[87] *Ibid.* s.151(2).
[88] *Ibid.* s.151(3); this deposit is explained above, para. 14.84; the initial contribution is discussed below, para. 14.106.
[89] H.A. 1985, s.152(1)(*a*), (2), (5).
[90] *Ibid.* s.122.
[91] *Ibid.* ss.135, 152(3); see above, para. 14.83.
[92] *Ibid.* s.153(5).
[93] *Ibid.* s.153(1)–(3).

claiming to exercise the right to a shared ownership lease and his initial right to buy claim notice are both deemed to be withdrawn at the end of the period stated in the second completion notice (as extended, where appropriate).[94]

(iv) The terms of the shared ownership lease

The tenant's initial share. The tenant's initial share must be stated in the shared ownership lease itself[95] (and must also be stated in the tenant's notice claiming the shared ownership lease[96]); this share must not be less than 50 per cent., and it must be a multiple of 12·5 per cent.[97] **14.105**

The tenant's initial contribution. The initial contribution is the consideration for the grant of the lease. It is determined by a prescribed formula,[98] which takes account of any discount received[99]; the initial contribution may be further reduced where the tenant activates the "notice of delay" procedure.[1] **14.106**

The tenant's additional shares. The shared ownership lease must enable the tenant to acquire additional shares at any time by serving notice on the council, but each share must be 12·5 per cent. or a multiple thereof.[2] **14.107**

Where the dwelling is a house and the council owns the freehold, the lease must provide that the tenant is entitled, on acquiring the full 100 per cent. of the shares, to a conveyance of the freehold.[3] **14.108**

The tenant's additional contributions. These represent the consideration for the additional shares; the contributions are determined by a prescribed formula which takes account of any discount received.[4] **14.109**

The rent. The shared ownership lease must provide that for any period for which the tenant's total share is less than 100 per cent., the rent payable under the lease shall be determined by the pre- **14.110**

[94] H.A. 1985, s.153(4).
[95] *Ibid.* Sched. 8, para. 1(1).
[96] *Ibid.* s.144(1); see above, para. 14.98.
[97] *Ibid.* s.145.
[98] *Ibid.* s.148.
[99] *Ibid.* s.129; see above, paras. 14.27–14.28.
[1] See below, paras. 14.120–14.122.
[2] H.A. 1985, Sched. 8, para. 1(1)–(2).
[3] *Ibid.* para. 2.
[4] *Ibid.* para. 3.

scribed formula (which has regard *inter alia* to "normal" council house rents in the locality); and the lease must also provide that for any period for which the tenant's total share is 100 per cent., the rent payable shall be £10 per annum.[5] The Minister can by order prescribe, for any period for which the tenant's total share is less than 100 per cent., appropriate adjustments to the rent or to any amount payable by the tenant under the lease for repairs, maintenance or insurance, having regard to the differing responsibilities as between a tenant under a shared ownership lease and a secure tenant.[6]

14.111 *Repayment of discount on premature "disposal."* The shared ownership lease must contain a covenant binding the tenant and his successors in title to repay the discount (or part thereof) on certain premature "disposals."[7]

14.112 *Payment for outstanding share on "disposal."* The shared ownership lease must contain a covenant binding the tenant and his successors in title to pay to the council on demand a prescribed amount for the outstanding share if there are certain "disposals" (in respect, normally, of the whole of the dwelling[8]) at a time when the tenant's total share is less than 100 per cent.[9] In such a case, where the dwelling is a house and the council owns the freehold, the lease must also provide that following payment for the outstanding share the tenant for the time being is entitled to a conveyance of the freehold.[10]

14.113 *No "disposals" of part of dwelling while share outstanding.* The shared ownership lease must contain a covenant binding on the tenant and his successors in title prohibiting any relevant "disposal" of *part* of the dwelling (other than a compulsory disposal) at any time when the tenant's total share is less than 100 per cent.[11] Any such disposal in breach of this covenant is void.[12]

[5] H.A. 1985, Sched. 8, paras. 4–5.
[6] *Ibid.* para. 4(3)–(5); see the Housing (Right to a Shared Ownership Lease) (Repairs Etc. Adjustment) Order 1984 (S.I. 1984 No. 1280).
[7] H.A. 1985, s.155(1), (3); for the relevant "disposals," see above, paras. 14.32–14.33.
[8] See below, para. 14.113.
[9] H.A. 1985, Sched. 8, paras. 6–8; for the relevant "disposals," see above, paras. 14.32–14.33.
[10] H.A. 1985, Sched. 8, para. 8.
[11] *Ibid.* para. 9(1); for the relevant "disposals," see above, paras. 14.32–14. 33.
[12] *Ibid.* para. 9(2).

(v) The terms of a shared ownership mortgage. Where the right to a mortgage is exercised by a secure tenant who also exercises the right to be granted a shared ownership lease, the mortgage deed must normally enable the tenant to require further sums to be advanced to him.[13] This right is exerciseable by the tenant serving written notice on the council within three months of the tenant claiming to exercise the right to acquire an additional share.[14] **14.114**

The amount which a tenant exercising the right to a further advance is entitled to have advanced to him is usually the amount of his additional contribution,[15] subject to prescribed available income limits.[16] **14.115**

As soon as practicable after receiving a notice requiring a further advance, the council must serve on the tenant a response notice giving details of (*inter alia*) the amount to which the tenant is entitled.[17] **14.116**

The remaining terms of the mortgage deed are governed by the normal "right to a mortgage" provisions[18]; the ordinary mortgage claim procedure must, of course, have been initiated before the right to a shared ownership lease can have arisen.[19] **14.117**

(h) *Enforcing the right to buy, the right to a mortgage, and the right to a shared ownership lease*

(i) Individual enforcement by the tenant

Court action. The Minister has stated that he normally expects authorities to be in a position to complete within three to four months of the right to buy being admitted.[20] Nevertheless, delays on the part of authorities in completing right to buy sales are quite common.[21] The 1985 Act specifically provides that the duty of the council to complete the relevant transaction (after the appropriate right has been established) is enforceable by injunction[22]; indeed, the county court has a general jurisdiction (other than as regards the **14.118**

[13] H.A. 1985, s.151(4) and Sched. 9, para. 1(1).
[14] *Ibid.* Sched. 9, para. 1(2).
[15] *Ibid.* para. 2; see above, para. 14.109.
[16] *Ibid.* Sched. 9, paras. 3–4; Housing (Right to a Shared Ownership Lease) (Further Advances Limit) Regulations 1985 (S.I. 1985 No. 758).
[17] H.A. 1985, Sched. 9, para. 5.
[18] *Ibid.* s.151(4)(*a*) and Sched 7; see above, paras. 14.89–14.91.
[19] *Ibid.* s.143(1); see above, para. 14.96.
[20] D.O.E. Circ. 21/84, para. 5.
[21] For example, the D.O.E. stated in 1988 that 12 councils were taking a year to process applications, which was twice the average period: *The Times*, March 2, 1988.
[22] H A. 1985, ss.138(3), 150(3).

price[23]), which includes the power to make a bare declaration.[24] We have seen that the tenant's rights stem from the statute and not from any contract as such (although a change of public landlord after the tenant has exercised the relevant rights cannot in general adversely affect him[25]). Nevertheless, the tenant should be able to enforce the relevant rights (which spring from duties owed by the council to him by virtue of his private law status as an individual tenant[26]) by way of a tortious action for breach of statutory duty, and thereby obtain damages in an appropriate case; although Part V of the 1985 Act specifically provides for Ministerial intervention,[27] this would not exclude remedies by way of county court action,[28] since the Act also expressly contemplates their availability.[29]

14.119 It seems, however, that the aggrieved tenant does not have the alternative remedy of claiming judicial review in the High Court under Order 53 of the Rules of the Supreme Court[30]; this is because (as will be seen below) the 1985 Act has provided the specific remedy of intervention by the Minister, so that "[n]othing [can] be done effectively by mandamus."[31]

14.120 *Self-help: the "notice of delay" procedure.* Quite apart from seeking the intervention of the court, the tenant also has a self-help remedy for enforcing the right to buy (and the right to a shared ownership lease) under section 153A of the 1985 Act. This procedure allows the tenant to serve on the council an "initial notice of delay" where the council has failed to serve a first response notice or a second response notice within the prescribed period,[32] or where the tenant considers that the council's delay is preventing him from exercising his rights "expeditiously."[33] The "initial notice of delay" must

[23] H.A. 1985, s.128.
[24] *Ibid.* s.181(1)–(2).
[25] *Ibid.* ss.137, 149; see also *ibid.* ss.171A–171H, concerning the "preserved right to buy" (see above, para. 14.07).
[26] *Wandsworth L.B.C.* v. *Winder* [1985] A.C. 461 (H.L.), see above, para. 6.32.
[27] See below, paras. 14.123–14.126.
[28] Contrary to the normal rule: see, *e.g. L.B. of Southwark* v. *Williams* [1971] 2 All E.R. 175 (C.A.), discussed above, para. 2.10.
[29] H.A. 1985, s.181; *cf. ibid.* Pt. III (see above, para. 6.01).
[30] See above, paras. 6.22–6.30.
[31] *Norwich C.C.* v. *Secretary of State for the Environment* [1982] 1 All E.R. 737, 747 (C.A.), *per* Lord Denning M.R.
[32] See above, paras. 14.43–14.45, 14.99–14.100.
[33] H.A. 1985, s.153A(1).

specify the "most recent action" taken by the council, and also specify a "response period" which allows the council at least a month to serve a counter-notice.[34]

Within the specified "response period," *or at any time thereafter*, the council can serve a counter-notice specifying *either* that it has served (or is now serving with the counter-notice) the relevant first or second response notice,[35] *or* that no action is required in order to permit expeditious exercise of the tenant's rights (as appropriate)[36]; service of such a counter-notice within the "response period" cancels the "initial notice of delay."[37] Once the "response period" expires, then at any time before service of a counter-notice[38] the tenant can serve on the council an "operative notice of delay."[39] **14.121**

Once an "operative notice of delay" is served, then rent payments can generally be deducted from the purchase price provided they are made *on or after either* the "default date" (*i.e.* the end of the period for service by the council of the first or second response notice, if appropriate) *or* the date of service of (*semble*) the "*operative* notice of delay" (where the tenant alleges delay preventing expeditious exercise of his rights), and provided the rent payments are made *before either* service of a counter-notice by the council *or* subsequent completion of the purchase.[40] As regards relevant rent within this period (excluding payments for rates or service charges), this is treated not just as rent but also as a *payment on account of the purchase price*, so that the **14.122**

[34] H.A. 1985, s.153A(2); forms for the "initial notice of delay" and the other notices under this procedure are prescribed by the Housing (Right to Buy Delay Procedure) (Prescribed Forms) Regulations 1989 (S.I. 1989 No. 240).

[35] See above, n. 32.

[36] H.A. 1985, s.153A(3)–(4).

[37] *Ibid.* s.153A(2); service of a counter-notice outside this period will (depending on the time of service) either prevent the tenant serving an "operative notice of delay" or prevent the relevant "deduction from purchase price" period from running: see below.

[38] Where a counter-notice is served, the tenant can then serve (where the facts are appropriate) a *further* "initial notice of delay," whereupon the whole procedure begins again: *ibid.* s.153A(6).

[39] *Ibid.* 153A(5).

[40] *Ibid.* ss.153A(1), (5), 153B(1); however, the right to have rent payments deducted from the price ceases to apply after any of the following events: (i) service by the tenant of a notice claiming to defer completion (see above, para. 14.84); (ii) withdrawal or deemed withdrawal of the tenant's notice claiming to exercise the right to buy or the right to a shared ownership lease (see above, paras. 14.38, 14.53); (iii) cessation of the tenant's entitlement to exercise the right to buy (see above, para. 14.23): *ibid.* s.153B(1)(*c*)-(*e*), (2).

price is reduced by the relevant rent payments, and if the relevant period exceeds 12 months, then an additional 50 per cent. "bonus" is notionally added to the relevant rent payments for the purposes of deduction from the price.[41]

14.123 **(ii) Intervention by the Minister.** Quite apart from any individual remedies which may be open to the secure tenant, the Minister has very wide powers of intervention where it appears to him that "tenants generally, a tenant or tenants of a particular landlord, or tenants of a description of landlords, have or may have difficulty in exercising effectively and expeditiously the right to buy or the right to be granted a shared ownership lease."[42] These powers (which relate also to the right to a mortgage[43]) can culminate in the Minister's execution of a "vesting order" conveying the freehold or granting the lease to the tenant, and the conveyance or lease has effect as if it had been duly executed by the council.[44]

14.124 The Minister can recover all his costs from the council, if necessary by withholding money otherwise due to it, for example, by way of subsidy.[45] Furthermore, the Minister can order the council to produce documents or supply information, and can even order individual officers of the council to do so "without instructions from the [council]"[46]; failure by the officer to carry out such an order would give the Minister the right to obtain an order for mandamus from the High Court against that officer personally, and could ultimately lead to his imprisonment for contempt of court.

14.125 The Minister's decision to intervene against a council under these powers can only be challenged on judicial review if he has acted in bad faith, or taken into account extraneous considerations, or otherwise misdirected himself.[47] However, the Minister stated in 1980 that he regarded his powers of intervention as "reserve" powers, which he would only use against councils guilty of "illegal behaviour or deliberate delaying tactics."[48]

14.126 An individual tenant can ask the Minister to intervene by initially contacting the appropriate regional office of the Department of the

[41] H.A. 1985, s.153B(2)–(4).
[42] *Ibid.* s.164(1).
[43] *Ibid.* ss.164(5), 166(6).
[44] *Ibid.* s.165.
[45] *Ibid.* s.166(3)–(5).
[46] *Ibid.* s.169(1)–(2).
[47] *Norwich C.C.* v. *Secretary of State for the Environment* [1982] 1 All E.R. 737 (C.A.).
[48] H.C. Deb., January 15, 1980, col. 1447.

Environment, and the Minister can give assistance to the tenant in connection with relevant proceedings against the council, including legal assistance and arranging legal representation,[49] even though the tenant is not eligible for legal aid.

(iii) Intervention by the auditor. Where individual councillors or officers have deliberately obstructed the right to buy, then in respect of any "loss . . . or deficiency" suffered by the authority due to their "wilful misconduct" the auditor (who is appointed by the Audit Commission) may recover the amount of that "loss . . . or deficiency" from them.[50] The tenant in his capacity as local government elector can make the initial objection to the auditor.[51] However, it may well prove controversial as to whether the suppression of council house sales in fact involves an authority in a "loss . . . or deficiency." **14.127**

(iv) Intervention by the local ombudsmen. Where the council's default amounts to "maladministration," complaint may be made to a local ombudsman.[52] **14.128**

3. *Sales Outside the "Right to Buy"*

(a) *The permitted sales*

Council tenants who are excluded from the right to buy (either because they are not secure tenants[53] or because they fall within one of the categories which are specifically excluded from the right to buy[54]), and those who are not council tenants but who wish to buy council dwellings, may be able to do so through the exercise by councils of their general powers of disposal in the 1985 Act.[55] **14.129**

[49] H.A. 1985, s.170 (not applying to valuation proceedings before the district valuer: ss.128, 170(1)).
[50] Pursuant to L.G.F.A. 1982, s.20; see *Asher* v. *Lacey* [1973] 1 W.L.R. 1412 (D.C.).
[51] L.G.F.A. 1982, s.17(3)–(4).
[52] See above, paras. 2.44–2.45.
[53] See above, paras. 7.01–7.48.
[54] See above, paras. 14.11–14.22.
[55] H.A. 1985, ss.32–33.

14.130 However, Ministerial consent is required for all disposals,[56] save for (*inter alia*) sales under the right to buy, and lettings on secure tenancies or on what would be secure tenancies if they did not fall within one of the statutory exemptions (other than the "long tenancy" exemption).[57] General consents have been given by way of a Ministerial Letter,[58] permitting councils to sell *vacant* houses and flats at discounts of up to 30 per cent. to specified priority groups of buyers, including homeless persons, first-time buyers, and job movers.[59] This Ministerial Letter also permits councils to sell dwellings to most *sitting council tenants* (even though they are excluded from the right to buy), with similar discounts to those available under the right to buy.[60] Furthermore, consent is given to sales, other than through the right to buy procedure, to tenants with the right to buy, provided that the terms offered are at least as good as those which the tenant would get if he exercised the right to buy[61]; and, with the *consent* of a secure tenant who has the right to buy, the authority may even transfer his entitlement to discount from a flat or prefab of which he is the secure tenant to a vacant dwelling which he prefers to buy instead, though he is, of course, entitled to insist on purchasing his present dwelling if he wishes.[62]

14.131 Disposals for which consent has been obtained "may be effected in any manner,"[63] so that the council may, in disposing of land to a purchaser, validly bind itself as to the particular housing use which it makes of land which it retains.[64]

[56] H.A. 1985, s.32(2).

[57] *Ibid.* s.32(1), (3) and Sched. 1 (for these exemptions, see above, paras. 7.25–7.47); in addition, disposals under the "change of landlord" scheme in H.A. 1988, Pt. IV (discussed in Chap. 15 below) do not require Ministerial consent: H.A. 1985, s.32(1).

[58] *Sales of Council Houses and Flats and Disposal of Housing Land,* June 2, 1981, as amended by the *Amendment of the General Consents for the Disposal of Houses 1984,* contained in D.O.E. Circ. 21/84, Annex C; see also, as regards Wales, the Ministerial Letter dated June 4, 1981.

[59] Ministerial Letter of June 2, 1981, *loc. cit.* Annex A, General Consent B(2), (5) and App. 2.

[60] *Loc. cit.* Annex A, General Consent B(1), (4), and App. 1.

[61] *Loc. cit.* Annex A, General Consents A and C.

[62] *Loc. cit.* Annex A, General Consent B(6).

[63] H.A. 1985, s.32(2).

[64] *Estmanco (Kilner House)* v. *G.L.C.* [1982] 1 All E.R. 437, 448 (sale of flats on long leases: agreement by council with flat management company to endeavour to sell remaining flats on long leases, rather than on secure tenancies); *R.* v. *Hammersmith & Fulham L.B.C., ex p. Beddowes* [1987] Q.B. 1050 (C.A.) (sale of housing estate:

Provisions for repayment of discount[65] (where appropriate) *must* be inserted in the deed.[66] Restrictive covenants or pre-emption clauses relating to further disposals *may* be inserted where the dwelling is in a National Park, designated area of outstanding natural beauty, or designated rural area[67]; and pre-emption clauses *may* also be inserted where certain dwellings designed for the elderly or the disabled are sold.[68] **14.132**

A disposal by an authority without the requisite consent is void, unless it was made to an individual (or to two or more individuals), as opposed to a body corporate, and did not extend to any other dwelling.[69] **14.133**

(b) *Special sale schemes*

(i) "Build for sale" schemes. The 1985 Act makes it clear that the power of councils to acquire land for the provision of housing accommodation "includes power to acquire land for the purpose of disposing of [dwellings] provided, or to be provided, on the land or of disposing of the land to a person who intends to provide housing accommodation on it."[70] Thus authorities can (finance permitting) themselves "acquire and build for sale."[71] **14.134**

These provisions[72] also permit authorities to sell their land to private developers for the erection of "starter homes," on which council tenants and those on the general waiting list could perhaps be given the first option.[73] Furthermore, authorities can enter into "partnership" arrangements with builders under which the builders are **14.135**

restrictive covenants imposed affecting council's retained land whereby no new lettings would be made other than by way of long leases at a premium, rather than on secure tenancies).

65 Similar to those required in right to buy cases: see above, paras. 14.31–14.34.

66 H.A. 1985, ss.35, 41; Ministerial Letter, *loc. cit.* Annex A, General Consent B(4)–(5).

67 H.A. 1985, ss.33(2), 37, 41; Ministerial Letter, *loc. cit.* Annex A, General Consent B(12); the provisions are similar to those applying to right to buy cases: see above, paras. 14.69–14.75.

68 H.A. 1985, s.33(2)–(3); Ministerial Letter, *loc. cit.* Annex A, General Consent B(13).

69 H.A. 1985, s.44.

70 *Ibid.* ss.9(3), 17(1)–(2).

71 For a discussion of possible "build for sale" schemes, see D.O.E. Handbook, *Local Authorities and Building for Sale* (1977).

72 H.A. 1985, ss.9(3), 17(1)–(2).

73 1981 Ministerial Letter, *loc cit.* Annex A, General Consent F(1).

given licences[74] to erect "starter homes" on council land, the freehold of which can later be transferred by the councils to the individual purchasers; the 1981 Ministerial Letter was anxious to encourage such schemes, with a view to subsequent sales to purchasers at the maximum allowable discounts.[75]

14.136 **(ii) "Improvement and sale" schemes.** The 1985 Act also allows councils to acquire land for the purpose of disposing of dwellings already erected on it[76]; and vacant council dwellings in need of repair, improvement or conversion may be sold to private individuals or builders who undertake to repair, improve or convert them for sale into owner-occupation.[77] In addition, where land with dwellings already on it is acquired by a council with a view to repairing, improving or converting the dwellings and thereafter selling them (*i.e.* pursuant to an "AIMS" scheme–Acquisition for Improvement and Sale), or where land with dwellings on it is already owned by a council which now wishes to repair, improve or convert the dwellings for sale (*i.e.* pursuant to an "IFS" scheme–Improvement for Sale), then the Minister has power to make contributions to the council's net cost of operating the scheme (*i.e.* after deducting the resale price received).[78]

14.137 **(iii) "Shared ownership" schemes.** We have seen that a "shared ownership lease" scheme has now been incorporated into the "right to buy" provisions in Part V of the 1985 Act.[79] Such schemes may also be used (with Ministerial consent) for voluntary sales,[80] where they are sometimes still referred to, misleadingly, as

[74] The grant of such a licence does not constitute a "disposal" for the purposes of H.A. 1985, ss.9(3), 17(1)–(2) and 32–34 (discussed above): see Ministerial Letter dated September 2, 1980, para. 12, and the 1981 Ministerial Letter, *loc. cit.* Annex A, General Consent B(8), (16).

[75] *Loc. cit.* Annex B, para. 7(iv).

[76] H.A. 1985, ss.9(3), 17(2).

[77] 1981 Ministerial Letter, *loc. cit.* Annex A, General Consent B(3).

[78] H.A. 1985, s.429; see further D.O.E. Circ. 20/80, paras. 3–24 and Annex A, as amended by D.O.E. Circ. 18/81.

[79] See above, paras. 14.94–14.113.

[80] The granting of the necessary option to purchase and the making of further mortgage advances are permitted by H.A. 1985, ss.32(4), 453; shared ownership leaseholders cannot be "secure" tenants (*ibid.* Sched. 1, para. 1: see above, para. 7.26), nor can they normally enfranchise or extend their leaseholds under Leasehold Reform Act 1967: see H.A. 1980, s.140 (which remains in force).

"equity-sharing" schemes. Specific consent for voluntary "shared ownership" sales is included in the 1981 Ministerial Letter.[81]

(c) *Special mortgage schemes*

Quite apart from the schemes for the sale of council properties just considered, councils possess specific statutory powers to grant mortgages in very flexible ways (in addition to the general statutory power to allow the price or part thereof to be secured by mortgage[82]). Thus councils may, for a period of up to five years from the date of the mortgage, charge a lower rate of interest than normal,[83] or waive payments of interest entirely, or dispense with repayments of capital, provided that the mortgagor has acquired a house "in need of repair or improvement," that the scheme is approved by the Minister, and that the mortgagor has agreed to carry out specified works of repair or improvement within a stipulated period.[84] Such arrangements are popularly called "homesteading" schemes.[85] **14.138**

Authorities have a separate and rather more general power (without the need for Ministerial approval) to grant a "low-start" mortgage allowing repayments of the *capital* (not the interest) to begin at a later date than the beginning of the advance, or at the end of a fixed period, or on the happening of a specified event before the end of that period.[86] **14.139**

In addition, there is a general scheme for assisting first-time buyers who take mortgages from "recognised lending institutions" (which comprise not just councils, but also building societies, banks, etc.): subject to certain conditions, a proportion of the loan may be made free of interest, and of any obligation to repay capital, for up to **14.140**

81 *Loc. cit.* Annex A, General Consent D.

82 H.A. 1985, s.437.

83 For the "normal" interest rate, see *ibid.* s.438 and Sched. 16; these provisions cover voluntary as well as "right to buy" mortgages, and are discussed above, para. 14.90.

84 *Ibid.* ss.438(2), 441.

85 See D.O.E. Circ. 20/80, paras. 25–27 and Annex C.

86 H.A. 1985, s.436(5); such provisions may be particularly helpful for young first-time buyers, or for older purchasers who do not intend to move again and who wish to take out a "maturity loan" whereby interest only is payable during the life of the loan and the capital is repaid in a lump sum on termination: see D.O.E. Circ. 67/74, para. 7.

five years from the date of the purchase, and the mortgagee can provide the borrower with a tax-free bonus towards the purchase.[87]

(d) *Conveyancing machinery*

14.141 The legal formalities for a non-right to buy purchase do not generally differ from those of a normal conveyancing transaction, but certain special features merit brief discussion.

14.142 **(i) The contract.** The normal conveyancing practice is, of course, for the early negotiations between the parties to be conducted "subject to contract," so that neither party will be bound to proceed until formal contracts are exchanged. However, this "no liability without exchange" principle is not a universal legal rule; on the facts, a binding contract between council and tenant may have been concluded at an earlier stage.[88] We have seen[89] that, by contrast, where the right to buy is involved there is no contractual element at all.

14.143 A contract for sale to a sitting tenant will not normally operate to end the tenancy, whether by surrender or otherwise, so that he will remain liable for rent until the date when the sale is completed, or such other date as may be specified in the contract.[90]

14.144 **(ii) Investigation of title.** It is quite common, where a council house with an unregistered title is being sold, for the authority to insist on a clause in the contract stating that there shall be no abstract or investigation of title.[91] Such clauses (which are comparatively rare in private sales) will not, however, absolve the authority

[87] H.A. 1985, ss.436(5), 438(2), 445–449; however, cl. 132 of L.G. & H.B. 1989 permits the Minister to wind up the home purchase assistance scheme for first-time buyers contained in H.A. 1985, ss.445–450.

[88] As in *Storer* v. *Manchester C.C.* [1974] 1 W.L.R. 1403 (C.A.), where the contract was held to have been concluded once the tenant had accepted the council's "offer" by signing and returning the form of agreement, despite the absence of any traditional "exchange"; *cf. Gibson* v. *Manchester C.C.* [1979] 1 W.L.R. 294 (H.L.), where the negotiations were not so far advanced, and the council was held not to have proceeded beyond the "invitation to treat" stage.

[89] See above, paras. 14.38, 14.53.

[90] *Doe d. Gray* v. *Stanion* (1836) 1 M. & W. 695; *Nightingale* v. *Courtney* [1954] 1 Q.B. 399 (C.A.); for the position in right to buy cases, see H.A. 1985, s.139(2) (above, para. 14.50).

[91] See, *e.g.* the contract in *Storer* v. *Manchester C.C.*, above, n. 88.

from the duty to convey free from undisclosed incumbrances of which it either knows or ought to know.[92]

Where the title to the property is unregistered but the property is in an area of compulsory registration of title,[93] then the council may be prepared to offer a certificate as to the title containing a statement of all incumbrances affecting it, in a form agreed with the Land Registry, thus easing the task of the purchaser's solicitor in applying for first registration.[94] **14.145**

(iii) The purchase deed. The contract will usually provide that the deed of conveyance, transfer or lease (and mortgage where appropriate) must be drawn up in the standard form favoured by the particular vendor-authority.[95] **14.146**

Where a discount from the price has been given, a covenant governing repayment of all or part of the discount on certain premature disposals will have to be inserted in the deed.[96] **14.147**

(e) *Assistance with purchase costs*

Where a council tenant moves to another[97] dwelling (whether in the public or private sector), the council may pay his removal expenses[98]; it may also pay any other expenses (for example, conveyancing fees) incurred in connection with the purchase of the other dwelling (with the exception of the price![99]), save that if the dwelling being bought is owned by the authority of which he is already a tenant, these other expenses can only be paid by the authority if the dwelling being bought has never been let and was built expressly for sale or letting.[1] **14.148**

[92] See, *e.g.* *Goold* v. *Birmingham, Dudley and District Bank* (1888) 58 L. T. 560; *Becker* v. *Partridge* [1966] 2 Q.B. 155 (C.A.); *Rignall Developments Ltd.* v. *Halil* [1987] 3 W.L.R. 394.

[93] L.R.A. 1925, ss.120, 123.

[94] Land Registry Practice Note, *First Registration of Title—Purchasers from Local Authorities* (1974); *cf.* the special provisions in H.A. 1985, s.154, relating to the right to buy: see above, para. 14.47.

[95] *Cf.* H.A. 1985, Sched. 6, which contains standard terms for right to buy conveyances and leases: see above, paras. 14.55–14.67.

[96] H.A. 1985, ss.35, 38–41.

[97] *I.e.* these provisions do not apply to sales to sitting tenants of the dwellings occupied by them.

[98] H.A. 1985, s.26(1)(*a*).

[99] But see below, para. 14.150.

[1] H.A. 1985, s.26(1)(*b*), (2); the conveyancing costs of right to buy transactions are dealt with by *ibid.* ss.133(1)(*c*), 178, see above, paras. 14.79, 14.76.

14.149 As a separate incentive for a council house purchaser to seek private sector mortgage finance, the 1985 Act allows the council to contribute up to £200 towards the borrower's mortgage costs (such as legal expenses and survey fees), provided the mortgagee is a building society or other "recognised body."[2]

14.150 The Housing Act 1988 contains a significant provision which is designed principally to encourage council tenants to move into the private sector; it has been popularly described as facilitating "portable discounts." Although this provision relates exclusively to the obtaining by council tenants of accommodation which is *not* owned by their council, and therefore does not concern the sale of council housing as such, it deserves a brief mention here. Section 129 of the 1988 Act permits an authority to create a scheme, with the Minister's approval, whereby the authority can make grants enabling the authority's tenants and licensees to be assisted to obtain accommodation "otherwise than as a tenant or licensee of the authority"; where such a scheme has been approved, the authority must take appropriate steps to bring it to the attention of such of its tenants and licensees as are "likely to be able to benefit from it."[3]

4. *Purchases of Dwellings which Prove to be Defective*

14.151 There is a special system in Part XVI of the 1985 Act under which authorities must give grants and other financial relief in relation to certain defective dwellings acquired from the public sector (whether or not under the right to buy). In order for the purchaser to claim assistance, the dwelling must be of a designated type[4] built with pre-

[2] H.A. 1985, ss.443–444; Housing (Local Authority Contributions towards Mortgage Costs) Order 1984 (S.I. 1984 No. 1174); for "recognised bodies," see *e.g.* Mortgage Indemnities (Recognised Bodies) (No. 1) Order 1988 (S.I. 1988 No. 87); see also H.A. 1985, s.442, permitting authorities, with the consent of the Minister, to enter into mortgage indemnity agreements with building societies and other "recognised bodies."

[3] H.A. 1988, s.129(3).

[4] Designation can be by the Minister (see H.A. 1985, s.528; D.O.E. Circ. 28/84, para. 3; Housing Defects (Prefabricated Concrete Dwellings) (England and Wales) Designations 1984; Housing Defects (Smith (BSC) Prefabricated Dwellings (England and Wales) Designation 1986); or it can be by an individual housing authority (*ibid.* s.559); the designation must specify the "cut-off date" by which the existence of the defect became generally known; normally, the purchaser must have bought before the cut-off date, or within 12 months thereof and in ignorance of the defect (*ibid.* ss.528(2)–(3), 531). Designation will not automatically entitle the purchaser to a reduction in rateable value: *Thomas* v. *Dyer (Valuation Officer)* LVC/215/1986 (Land Trib.).

fabricated reinforced concrete, and, subsequent to the purchase, it must have been found to be defective by reason of its construction or design.

If the defective dwelling is a house (not a flat), and after reasonable expenditure on reinstatement would have a further life of at least 30 years and would be mortgageable with a private sector lending institution, then the owner is normally entitled to a "reinstatement grant" representing 90 per cent. of the reinstatement costs.[5] **14.152**

If any of these conditions is not met (*i.e.* in effect, the dwelling is a flat or the remedying of the defects is not economically viable), then the authority must offer to repurchase the dwelling at 95 per cent. of its defect-free value; if the purchase goes ahead, the authority must also pay the owner's reasonable legal expenses, and must on being requested to do so grant him a secure tenancy of the house or flat in question or of other suitable accommodation.[6] **14.153**

Central government may meet, in effect, 90 per cent. of the authority's loan charges relating to the repair costs paid by the authority under a reinstatement grant, or, in cases of repurchase of a dwelling with a defect designated by the Minister,[7] 75 per cent. of the authority's loan charges relating to the difference between the price paid to the owner of the defective dwelling and its defective value.[8] **14.154**

[5] H.A. 1985, ss.538, 541–545; see D.O.E. Circ. 14/86; there is a maximum level of eligible costs, currently ranging from £14,000 to £31,000 depending on the various categories of defective dwelling: Housing Defects (Expenditure Limits) (No. 2) Order 1988 (S.I. 1988 No. 923).

[6] H.A. 1985, ss.537, 547–558 and Sched. 20; the authority must determine promptly which form the assistance will take (*i.e.* reinstatement grant or repurchase): *R.* v. *Thamesdown B.C., ex p. Pritchard, The Times*, December 30, 1988 (C.A.); see, as regards the conveyancing aspects of repurchase, M. Turnbull, [1987] L.S. Gaz. 2754.

[7] See above, n. 4.

[8] H.A. 1985, s.569.

15 The Privatisation of Council Estates

1. *The Changing Role of Local Housing Authorities*

15.01 The government envisaged in 1987 a "change in emphasis . . . for the housing role of local authorities, from acting as landlords towards acting as enablers and facilitators of housing provision by others"[1]; by the summer of 1988, it was estimated that some 130 out of 401 local housing authorities were thinking of disposing of their estates, spurred on by a variety of motives.[2]

15.02 While individual council tenants have been encouraged to exercise their "right to buy" under the scheme in Part V of the Housing Act 1985,[3] there will always be some tenants who prefer not to buy. The government considers that, even as regards such tenants, a change of landlord may be desirable. There are basically three methods whereby tenanted council properties may be "privatised": voluntarily, at the instigation of the council itself; compulsorily, at the instigation of the tenants or a potential private landlord under the "change of landlord" scheme; and compulsorily, at the instigation of the Minister under the "Housing Action Trust" scheme.

2. *"Voluntary" Privatisation at the Instigation of the Local Authority*

(a) *The need for ministerial consent*

15.03 Under the 1985 Act,[4] Ministerial consent is normally required for a disposal of land which an authority holds for housing purposes. A local authority may therefore seek Ministerial approval for a dis-

[1] D.O.E., *Housing Action Trusts: A Consultation Document*, para. 24; see also *Housing: The Government's Proposals* (1987), Cm. 214, para. 5.1.

[2] D. Coleman, *The Times*, July 26, 1988.

[3] See Chap. 14.

[4] H.A. 1985, ss.32, 43: see above, paras. 14.130–14.133; ss.32 and 43 do not affect disposals under the "change of landlord" scheme in H.A. 1988, Pt. IV (see below).

posal by it of all its housing stock, or part thereof, to some other person or body. Where the authority takes the initiative in this way, it can either seek to transfer the relevant property after gaining vacant possession from the sitting tenants, or it can seek to transfer the relevant property with the tenants remaining *in situ*.

In deciding whether to give his consent to such "voluntary" transfers, the Minister may consider (*inter alia*) the extent to which the proposed purchaser is or is likely to be independent of the local authority[5]: the D.O.E. has recommended that any council membership or shareholding in the purchasing body should not exceed 20 per cent., and that the council should not normally retain nomination rights over the transferred dwellings, save that contracts may be entered into with the purchaser regarding the provision of accommodation for those for whom the council retains statutory obligations (such as the homeless).[6] The Minister expects councils to extract undertakings from purchasers that re-lets of vacant dwellings will be at rents within the reach of persons in lower-paid employment.[7] **15.04**

In order to avoid the emergence of "large private housing monopolies," the Minister may also have regard, when deciding whether to give consent, to the extent to which the proposed purchaser would become a substantial owner of rented housing in the area if the disposal were to take place.[8] Council stock should therefore preferably be disposed of to more than one purchaser: Ministerial consent is unlikely where a proposed disposal is to a single purchaser and involves more than 5,000 to 10,000 properties.[9] **15.05**

Sales should take place on a "market value subject to tenancy" basis.[10] **15.06**

(b) *Privatisation after securing vacant possession*

If the council proposes to dispose of the relevant dwellings with vacant possession, then, as we have seen,[11] it can take advantage of a mandatory ground for possession against the relevant secure tenants, provided it obtains the Minister's approval to a "redevelopment scheme" (under which, normally, work will be carried out by **15.07**

[5] H.A. 1985, ss.34(4A)(*a*), 43(4A)(*a*).
[6] D.O.E., *Large Scale Voluntary Transfers of Local Authority Housing to Private Bodies* (1988), paras. 3–4, 10–11.
[7] *Ibid.* para. 5.
[8] H.A. 1985, ss.34(4A)(*b*), 43(4A)(*b*).
[9] *Large Scale Voluntary Transfers, op. cit.* paras. 6–7.
[10] *Ibid.* para. 13.
[11] See above, para. 8.48.

the purchaser rather than the council itself), and provided it can satisfy the court both that suitable accommodation will be available for the relevant tenants when the possession orders take effect and that it intends within a reasonable time of obtaining possession to dispose of the dwellings in accordance with the "redevelopment scheme."[12]

15.08 For these purposes, "redevelopment" means the demolition or reconstruction of buildings or the carrying out of other works to buildings or land (though it is immaterial whether the redevelopment precedes or follows the disposal).[13] The "redevelopment scheme" can relate to an area as small as part of a single dwelling.[14]

15.09 Where the authority proposes to apply to the Minister for approval of a "redevelopment scheme," it must serve a notice giving full details of the scheme and its effects on each affected tenant, and give him the right to make representations to the authority within a period of not less than 28 days from service of the notice.[15] Before applying to the Minister, the authority must consider any such representations.[16] The general consultation procedure regarding "matters of housing management" does not apply in relation to these "redevelopment schemes."[17]

15.10 Among the matters which the Minister must take into account in considering the authority's proposal are any representations made to him or to the authority, and the extent to which housing provided under the scheme may be sold or let to the existing tenants or to persons nominated by the authority.[18]

(c) *Privatisation with the tenants remaining in situ*

15.11 If the council proposes to dispose of the relevant dwellings to a "private sector landlord"[19] with the existing tenants remaining *in situ*, then special consultation duties are imposed on the council (in place of the general consultation procedure regarding "matters of housing management"[20]) before Ministerial consent can be given[21];

[12] H.A. 1985, s.84(2)(*b*) and Sched. 2, Pt. II, gd. 10A, Pts. IV–V.
[13] *Ibid.* Sched. 2, Pt. V, para. 1(2).
[14] *Ibid.* para. 1(1).
[15] *Ibid.* para. 2(1).
[16] *Ibid.* para. 2(2).
[17] *Ibid.* para. 2(3); *cf. ibid.* s.105, see above, paras. 13.08–13.13.
[18] *Ibid.* Sched. 2, Pt. V, para. 3(1).
[19] *I.e.* a person or body who will not satisfy the "landlord condition" for secure tenancies: *ibid.* Sched. 3A, para. 1(4); *ibid.* s.80, see above, para. 7.07.
[20] *Ibid.* s. 106A(2); *cf. ibid.* s.105, see above, paras. 13.08–13.13.
[21] *Ibid.* s.106A and Sched. 3A; see also D.O.E. Circ. 6/88.

the idea is that the secure tenants, who would lose that status following the disposal, should "have their say" on the matter. Under this "voluntary" privatisation scheme, the new landlord takes over *all* the tenancies: there is no right for dissenting tenants to insist on remaining with the council.[22]

The Minister cannot entertain the authority's application unless the authority certifies that it has complied with the special consultation requirements.[23] These requirements oblige the authority to give each affected secure tenant information concerning (*inter alia*) the identity of the proposed purchaser, the consequences of the disposal for the tenant, and the effects of the "preserved right to buy" provisions in the 1985 Act[24]; he must also be told of his right to make representations to the authority within a reasonable period, and the authority must consider any such representations.[25] The authority must then inform him of (*inter alia*) any significant changes in its proposal, and of his right to communicate his objections to the Minister.[26] **15.12**

The Minister has a broad discretion to give or withhold his consent, but he cannot consent if it appears to him that a majority of the tenants are opposed to the proposed disposition.[27] However, if Ministerial consent is obtained, it is not invalidated by any failure by the Minister or by the authority to comply with the above requirements (so that the purchaser is protected).[28] **15.13**

3. *Privatisation Under the "Change of Landlord" Scheme*

(a) *Conditions for the exercise of the right to acquire the freehold reversions to council dwellings*

(i) General. Part IV of the Housing Act 1988 introduces a scheme whereby any person or body approved by the Housing Corporation or "Housing for Wales"[29] may acquire (subject to the provisions **15.14**

[22] *Cf.* the "change of landlord" scheme in H.A. 1988, Pt. IV, see below, paras. 15.22–15.23.
[23] H.A. 1985, Sched. 3A, para. 2.
[24] *Ibid.* para. 3(2); for the preserved right to buy, see *ibid.* ss.171A–171H (discussed above, para. 14.07.
[25] *Ibid.* Sched. 3A, paras. 3(2)–(3).
[26] *Ibid.* para. 3(3).
[27] *Ibid.* para. 5.
[28] *Ibid.* para. 6.
[29] H.A. 1988, s.114(1); in the remainder of this chapter, the expression "the Corporation" is used to denote both the Housing Corporation and "Housing for Wales."

and exceptions in Part IV) the fee simple estates in any dwellings owned by a council or other "public sector landlord" and occupied by "qualifying tenants."[30] The tenants can themselves take the initiative in approaching suitable potential landlords, and in the consultation paper introducing the scheme the government referred to it as a "tenants' choice" measure[31]; the scheme was in consequence popularly referred to as the "pick-a-landlord" scheme. However, the emphasis of the legislation itself has proved somewhat different, so that the scheme which has emerged confers something resembling a "predatory private landlord's choice."

15.15 The government believed that the reasons for tenants agreeing to such a scheme might include a wish for improved standards of repair or maintenance, or for a faster response rate to day-to-day maintenance needs.[32]

15.16 **(ii) Eligible properties.** Subject to the exclusions mentioned below, the eligible properties are *buildings* the fee simples[33] of which are owned by the council, and each of which comprises or contains one or more dwellings which, at the date of the application to buy, are occupied by "qualifying tenants,"[34] together with any other *property* the fee simple of which is owned by the council and which is reasonably required for occupation with such buildings.[35] The relevant dwellings may thus be flats or maisonettes, each forming part of a whole block or of several blocks, or they may be houses grouped together or separately on estates; the scheme can operate even in relation to one single, isolated dwelling. In the case of a block of dwellings, it is not necessary that *all* the dwellings in the block

[30] H.A. 1988, s.93; "public sector landlords" include not only local housing authorities, but also new town corporations, housing action trusts (see below, paras. 15.61–15.113) and the Development Board for Rural Wales: *ibid.* s.93(2); in the remainder of this chapter it will be assumed that the relevant landlord is the council. The public sector landlords whose properties are *excluded* from the scheme include county councils, the residuary bodies in Greater London and the former metropolitan counties, housing associations or charities, and housing co-operatives (co-operatives are discussed in Chap. 13). The definition of "qualifying tenant" is discussed below, para. 15.24.

[31] D.O.E., *Tenants' Choice: the Government's Proposals for Legislation* (1987).

[32] *Ibid.* para. 7.

[33] H.A. 1988, s.93(1), (3); thus the scheme does not apply where the council only owns a leasehold interest in the relevant dwellings, although such cases are likely to be rare: D.O.E., *Tenants' Choice, op. cit.* para. 12.

[34] See below, para. 15.24.

[35] H.A. 1988, s.93(1), (5).

should be occupied by "qualifying tenants" before a purchaser can acquire the block.[36]

(iii) Excluded properties. Even where the council owns the relevant freehold interests, various categories of property are excluded from the statutory scheme. The following are the more important exclusions. **15.17**

First, a *building* is excluded if (at the date of the application to purchase) any part (or parts) thereof is (or are) occupied or intended to be occupied otherwise than for residential purposes, and the internal floor area of that part (or of those parts, taken together) exceeds 50 per cent.[37] of the internal floor area of the building (taken as a whole, but excluding the internal floor area of any common parts or common facilities).[38] This exclusion is intended to cover dwellings provided purely for incidental purposes, such as a caretaker's flat situated in school or office premises.[39] **15.18**

Secondly, a *building* is excluded if it contains two or more dwellings which (at the date of the application to purchase) are occupied by secure tenants who are not "qualifying tenants,"[40] and the number of dwellings which (at that date) are occupied by such non-qualifying tenants exceeds 50 per cent. of the total number of dwellings in the building.[41] **15.19**

Thirdly, a *house*[42] is excluded if it is occupied (at the date of the application to purchase) either by a secure tenant who is not a "qualifying tenant" because the circumstances fall within one of the prescribed exceptions to the tenant's individual "right to buy" in Part V of the Housing Act 1985, or by a tenant who is not secure.[43] **15.20**

[36] H.A. 1988, s.93(1)(*a*); but see below, paras. 15.19–15.20, 15.22–15.23.

[37] The Minister can specify some other percentage: *ibid.* s.95(7).

[38] *Ibid.* s.95(1); there are modifications to these conditions where the property is reasonably required for occupation with relevant dwellings: *ibid.* s.95(2).

[39] D.O.E., *Tenants' Choice, op. cit.* para. 13.

[40] See below, para. 15.24.

[41] H.A. 1988, s.95(3).

[42] As defined in H.A. 1985, s.183(2), see above, para. 14.06: H.A. 1988, s.114(2); a dwelling which is not a "house" is treated as a "flat" for these purposes, even if it is, *e.g.* a maisonette: H.A. 1985, s.183(3).

[43] H.A. 1988, s.95(4); for the relevant "right to buy" exemptions which operate as an exclusion from the definition of "qualifying tenant," see below, para. 15.24; for the exemptions from the definition of a "secure tenant," see above, paras. 7.25–7.48. The Part IV rights can apply under s.93(1) (see above) in relation to a *block* of terraced or semi-detached houses even though only some of the tenants are "qualifying tenants."

15.21 Fourthly, a *building* or other *property* is excluded if it was specified in some other "change of landlord" application made before the date of the subject application, and the earlier application has not yet been disposed of.[44] Thus the scheme incorporates an element of "first come, first served," preventing competing bids (even from the sitting tenants themselves if, for example, they wish to form a co-operative to take over their housing).

15.22 Fifthly, a *house*[45] is excluded if it is occupied by a "qualifying tenant" whose tenancy commenced before the date of the application to purchase and who notifies the applicant of his wish to continue as a tenant of the council.[46] This exclusion must be activated by Ministerial regulations.[47] If a pre-application qualifying tenant of a *flat*[48] notifies the applicant of his wish to remain a tenant of the council, then, although the flat will not be excluded from the acquisition (if it goes ahead[49]) of the freehold of the block in question, the applicant must (pursuant to Ministerial regulations) grant the council a lease of the flat immediately after the freehold is transferred.[50] These provisions ensure that any "qualifying tenant" (whether of a house or flat) whose tenancy pre-dates the Part IV application can refuse to have a new landlord under the "change of landlord" scheme (*i.e.* he can insist on remaining a secure tenant of the council).

15.23 Sixthly, a *house*[51] is excluded if it is occupied by a tenant of any description prescribed by the Minister and who notifies the applicant of his wish to continue as tenant of the council.[52] Where a *flat*[53] is occupied by such a tenant falling within such a prescribed description, or by a tenant of some other prescribed description, then, although the flat will be included in the acquisition (if it proceeds), the applicant must grant to the council (pursuant to Ministerial regulations) a lease of the flat immediately after the freehold is transferred.[54]

[44] H.A. 1988, s.95(5).
[45] See above, n. 42.
[46] H.A. 1988, s.100(1)(*a*), (2)(*a*).
[47] *Ibid.* s.100(1).
[48] A maisonette is included in the definition of a flat for these purposes; see above, n. 42.
[49] The acquisition of the block cannot go ahead if a majority of the affected tenants object: see below, para. 15.45.
[50] H.A. 1988, s.100(1)(*b*), (2)(*a*); see below, para. 15.51.
[51] See above, n. 42.
[52] H.A. 1988, ss.100(1)(*a*), (2)(*b*), 111–112.
[53] See above, n. 48.
[54] H.A. 1988, s.100(1)(*b*), (2)(*b*); see below, para. 15.51.

(iv) Definition of "qualifying tenant." We have seen that Part IV of the 1988 Act imposes a requirement that the relevant buildings must normally be occupied (in whole or in part, as appropriate) by "qualifying tenants."[55] A "qualifying tenant" means a secure tenant whose tenancy is held directly from the council as fee simple owner, but *excluding* both a secure tenant who is obliged to give up possession of the dwelling in pursuance of a court order (or who will be obliged to do so at a date specified in such an order), and a secure tenant who is prevented from exercising the individual "right to buy" because one of the relevant statutory exclusions applies.[56] **15.24**

(v) Approval of the applicant by the Corporation. An applicant can only claim to buy under Part IV of the 1988 Act if he (or it) is approved by the Corporation.[57] Approval can be given by the Corporation to a particular person or body, or to persons or bodies of a particular description[58]; the approval may also be made applicable either generally, or in relation to particular acquisitions, or acquisitions made in a particular area or within a particular period.[59] **15.25**

However, the Corporation cannot approve any of the following bodies for these purposes: a local housing authority; a county council; a housing action trust[60]; a new town corporation; the Development Board for Rural Wales; or any other body which the Corporation has reason to believe may not be independent of any of the above prescribed bodies (and a body is not to be treated as independent if it appears to be under the control of or subject to influence from one of the above prescribed bodies).[61] **15.26**

The approval process "will aim to ensure that new landlords are financially stable and capable of managing their homes to a high standard while giving value for money."[62] Suitable landlords might **15.27**

[55] H.A. 1988, s.93(1); see above, paras. 15.14, 15.16.

[56] *Ibid.* s.93(3)–(4); for the definition of "secure tenant" and the exemptions therefrom, see above, Chap. 7; for a discussion of possession orders, see Chap. 8; with regard to the statutory exclusions from the individual "right to buy," the relevant exclusions for present purposes are those contained in H.A. 1985, Sched. 5, paras. 5–11 (see above, paras. 14.14–14.20).

[57] H.A. 1988, ss.93(1), 94.

[58] *Ibid.* s.94(4).

[59] *Ibid.*

[60] HATs are discussed below, paras. 15.61–15.113.

[61] H.A. 1988, ss.93(2), 94(1)–(2).

[62] D.O.E., *Tenants' Choice: the Government's Proposals for Legislation* (1987), para. 16.

include[63] registered housing associations, tenants' co-operatives,[64] and private firms.

15.28 The Corporation has established criteria, pursuant to the duty in the Housing Act 1988,[65] for the approval of landlords under this scheme.[66] The relevant criteria include requirements that the new landlord must comply with the Corporation's guidance on housing management practice,[67] and must retain the acquired dwellings for letting at rents affordable by those in low-paid employment.[68]

15.29 The Corporation can charge for entertaining applications for approval, and can make approval conditional on the applicant entering into undertakings.[69]

15.30 Once approval of a landlord has been given, the Corporation can subsequently revoke that approval,[70] for example on the ground of serious breach of (or continued non-compliance with) the Corporation's guidance on housing management practice.[71]

15.31 The Corporation must keep a public register of approved applicants.[72]

(b) *Initial procedure*

15.32 **(i) Application to the council.** The application to purchase must be made to the council in the prescribed form, specifying the buildings and other property which the applicant proposes to acquire.[73]

15.33 **(ii) Council's first response notice.** Within four weeks of the making of the application, the council must serve on the applicant a notice specifying the name and address of every affected tenant or licensee, and the general nature of each such tenancy or licence.[74]

63 D.O.E., *Tenant's Choice: the Government's Proposals for Legislation* (1987), para. 16.
64 Tenants' co-operatives are discussed in Chap. 13.
65 H.A. 1988, s.94(3).
66 *Tenants' Choice Landlords: criteria for approval and grounds for revoking approval* (1988) (see also, as regards procedure, the Corporation's guidance on *Approval, post-approval and revocation procedures* (1988)).
67 *Tenants' Choice Landlords, op. cit.* para. 1G 3; see, as regards the Corporation's guidance on housing management practice, below, para. 15.58.
68 *Ibid.* para. 1G 2.
69 H.A. 1988, s.94(4).
70 *Ibid.* s.94(5).
71 *Tenants' Choice Landlords, op. cit.* para. 2F.
72 H.A. 1988, s.94(7).
73 *Ibid.* s.96.
74 *Ibid.* s.97(1).

The applicant will need this information for the purpose (*inter alia*) of consulting affected tenants.[75]

(iii) Applicant's inspection and information rights. After the expiry of four weeks from the making of the application, the applicant has a right of reasonable access to any untenanted property covered by the application, together with rights to receive a list of relevant documents, and to inspect and be provided with copies of such documents.[76] The relevant documents are those in the council's possession, the sight of which is reasonably required for the purpose of pursuing the application, and which the council, on a sale as a willing vendor to a willing purchaser, would be expected as vendor to make available to that purchaser.[77] These rights will assist the applicant in negotiating the price.[78] **15.34**

(iv) Council's second response notice. Within 12 weeks of the making of the application, the council must serve on the applicant a notice which contains (*inter alia*) the following information[79]: which (if any) of the buildings or property proposed to be acquired should be excluded because they fall outside the scope of Part IV[80]; which property (if any) the council desires to have included in the acquisition on the ground that it cannot otherwise be reasonably managed or maintained; which rights (if any) the council desires to retain over property included in the acquisition on the ground that they are necessary for the proper management or maintenance of land to be retained by the council; the other proposed terms of the conveyance; and such other particulars as the Minister prescribes. **15.35**

(v) Applicant's challenge to the contents of the second response notice. Within four weeks of the service of the council's second response notice, the applicant must notify the council of any matters stated in that notice which are not accepted.[81] **15.36**

(vi) Resolution of disputes regarding matters stated in the second response notice. A dispute regarding any matter stated in the second response notice is to be determined by the person agreed **15.37**

[75] See below, paras. 15.42–15.45.
[76] H.A. 1988, s.97(2).
[77] *Ibid.* s.97(3).
[78] See below, paras. 15.38–15.41.
[79] H.A. 1988, s.98(1).
[80] *Ibid.* ss.93(1), 95; see above, paras. 15.16–15.21.
[81] *Ibid.* s.98(4).

upon by the parties or (in default of such agreement) by the person appointed by the Minister, in accordance with prescribed provisions.[82]

15.38 **(vii) Determination of the price.** Within eight weeks of service of the second response notice (or, in the case of a dispute regarding any matter stated in the notice, within eight weeks of the determination of that dispute), the council must serve on the applicant a notice specifying the price which it considers to be payable for the property to be acquired, or the "disposal cost" attributable to the property to be acquired, and showing how this figure was arrived at.[83] A "disposal cost" will normally be attributable if,[84] having regard to the cost of the reasonably necessary repair works,[85] the property would not realise any price by reference to the statutory assumptions[86]; the amount of the "disposal cost" will be the amount by which the expense likely to be so incurred exceeds what would be determined as the price, on the statutory assumptions, if those works had already been carried out.[87]

15.39 The price payable (if any) must normally reflect the open market value as at the date of the original application,[88] based on the following assumptions[89]: that there is a willing vendor; that the property is sold subject to tenancies subsisting at the date of the original application but otherwise with vacant possession; that the property will be conveyed with the rights and burdens appropriate to the transfer under the right of acquisition; that the only bidders in the market are the persons who at the date of the original application were either approved by the Corporation for Part IV purposes or fulfilled the established criteria for approval[90]; that the applicant will, within a reasonable period, carry out such works as are reasonably necessary to put the buildings acquired into the state of repair required by the landlord's repairing obligations[91]; and finally, that the applicant

[82] H.A. 1988, s.98(5).
[83] *Ibid.* s.99(1), (4).
[84] *Ibid.* s.99(3).
[85] See below, para. 15.39.
[86] Set out below, para. 15.39.
[87] H.A. 1988, s.99(3).
[88] *Ibid.* s.99(2).
[89] *Ibid.*
[90] *Ibid.* s.94; see above, paras. 15.25–15.28.
[91] For the relevant obligations, see above, paras. 12.05–12.39.

will not be required to lease back to the council any flats occupied by non-consenting tenants or other prescribed tenants.[92]

The application of these assumptions in the case of severely run-down dwellings could well result in a negative value, and therefore in a "disposal cost" having to be paid by the council *to* the applicant (rather than vice versa).[93] **15.40**

The applicant has four weeks, running from the service of this notice stating the price, within which to notify the council of any matters stated in the notice which are not accepted.[94] Any dispute relating to such matters is to be determined by the district valuer, in accordance with prescribed provisions.[95] **15.41**

(c) *Final procedure*

(i) Consultation by applicant with affected tenants. During such period as the Minister prescribes, the applicant must consult any "qualifying tenants," or tenants under "long tenancies," who occupied an affected dwelling at the date of the initial application and continued to occupy the dwelling during the whole of the prescribed period.[96] The Minister may prescribe further categories of tenants who must be consulted.[97] **15.42**

The period within which such consultation must take place normally runs from the service of the council's notice stating the price, but if there has been a determination by the district valuer, then the period runs from the notification of his decision to the applicant.[98] **15.43**

The consultation procedure must comply with the provisions prescribed by the Minister.[99] In essence,[1] the applicant will serve a notice on the relevant tenants which sets out proposals for the terms **15.44**

[92] *Cf.* H.A. 1988, s.100; see above, paras. 15.22–15.23.

[93] See above, para. 15.38; D.O.E., *Tenants' Choice, op. cit.* para. 24.

[94] H.A. 1988, s.99(5).

[95] *Ibid.* s.99(6).

[96] *Ibid.* s.102(1)–(2); tenants of a description prescribed under s.100(2) (see above, para. 15.23) must also be consulted: s.102(2)(*b*); "qualifying tenants" are discussed above, para. 15.24; "long tenancies" are normally tenancies for a term certain exceeding 21 years: H.A. 1985, ss.115, 187; H.A. 1988, s.114(2); the holders of such "long tenancies" in the present context will normally be former secure tenants of flats who have bought long leases, under, *e.g.* the individual "right to buy": see above, para. 14.02.

[97] H.A. 1988, s.102(2)(*c*).

[98] *Ibid.* s.102(1).

[99] *Ibid.*

[1] The following account of the consultation process is taken from D.O.E., *Tenants' Choice, op. cit.* paras. 25–28.

of the new tenancies if the acquisition goes ahead. The applicant and the secure tenants will eventually need to settle terms if the tenants do not opt out of the acquisition, since those tenants will cease to be "secure" and will become "assured,"[2] although their individual "right to buy" will be preserved by the Housing Act 1985.[3] The applicant's notice will tell the relevant tenants about such matters as rent levels, rent reviews, and any initial renovation or improvement work to be undertaken, and it will explain the consultation procedure itself.

15.45 If only one tenant is eligible to be consulted, he will be asked whether he agrees to the acquisition going ahead; if he disagrees, the application will fail. Where more than one tenant is eligible to be consulted, then they will be able to vote on the acquisition. Under the 1988 Act, if *either* less than 50 per cent. of the tenants eligible to be consulted have responded to the consultation, *or* the number of tenants eligible to be consulted who have indicated their *opposition* to the acquisition going ahead exceeds 50 per cent. of the total number of tenants eligible to be consulted, then the application will fail[4]; otherwise, the applicant will be able to continue with the acquisition of the freehold (although, as we have seen, the individual objecting tenants will remain tenants of the council[5]). Thus, where at least 50 per cent. of the eligible tenants respond to the consultation, any tenant who has failed to respond, or whose response is to the effect that he has no strong feelings either way regarding the proposed acquisition, will be deemed to be registering an "inertia" vote in *favour* of the proposed acquisition. Furthermore, where the acquisition goes ahead, the consulted tenants who did not express opposition to the acquisition are taken to have accepted any terms relating to their future occupation which were proposed by the applicant during the consultation period.[6]

15.46 **(ii) Notice by applicant of intention to proceed.** Once the prescribed consultation period has expired, the applicant normally has the right within two weeks thereafter to serve on the council a notice of intention to proceed with the acquisition.[7] However, no such

[2] H.A. 1988, ss.1, 38; see below, paras. 15.45, 15.56–15.57.
[3] H.A. 1985, ss.171A–171H; see above, para. 14.07.
[4] H.A. 1988, s.103(2); joint tenants are treated as a sole tenant for this purpose: *ibid.* s.103(3).
[5] *Ibid.* s.100: see above, paras. 15.22–15.23.
[6] *Ibid.* s.103(6); see below, para. 15.57.
[7] *Ibid.* s.103(1).

notice can be served where (as noted above) either less than 50 per cent. of the tenants eligible to be consulted have responded to the consultation, or the number of eligible tenants who have indicated their opposition to the acquisition exceeds 50 per cent. of the total number of eligible tenants.[8]

Where the applicant is entitled to serve a notice of intention to proceed, the notice must contain[9]: a list of the names and addresses of relevant tenants who were eligible to be consulted and who have notified the applicant of their opposition to the acquisition[10]; a list of any *houses* which are to be excluded from the acquisition[11]; a list of any *flats* which the applicant is required to lease back to the council,[12] together with a statement of the proposed terms of such leases; such information as may be necessary to show how these lists were prepared; and a statement of the price payable, or the attributable "disposal costs," in relation to the property to be acquired. **15.47**

(iii) Council's challenge to the notice of intention to proceed. Within two weeks of service of the applicant's notice of intention to proceed, the council must notify the applicant of any matters stated in the notice which it does not accept.[13] **15.48**

(iv) Withdrawal of application. We have seen that the applicant has to take action within prescribed time limits by way of consultation with affected tenants and service on the authority of notice of intention to proceed. Before the expiry of the relevant time limit, the council may extend (or further extend) that time limit.[14] However, if the relevant time limit (as extended, where applicable) has expired without the applicant having taken the necessary action, then the application to exercise the Part IV acquisition rights is deemed to be withdrawn (although a further application can subsequently be made).[15] **15.49**

[8] H.A. 1988, s.103(2).
[9] *Ibid.* s.103(4).
[10] *Ibid.* s.103(2).
[11] *Ibid.* s.100; see above, paras. 15.22–15.23.
[12] *Ibid.*
[13] *Ibid.* s.103(5).
[14] *Ibid.* s.110(1)–(2); conversely, the applicant may extend any relevant time limit which governs the council's actions: *ibid.*
[15] *Ibid.* s.110(4).

15.50 **(v) Council's duty to complete.** Where the applicant has correctly and timeously operated the above procedures, including service of a proper notice of intention to proceed, then as soon as any dispute regarding a matter stated in that notice has been determined[16] the council must convey or transfer to the applicant the fee simple estate in the property included in the acquisition, subject to any rights to be retained by the council.[17] The terms of the conveyance or transfer must comply with the requirements prescribed by the Minister.[18]

15.51 The applicant must then immediately grant to the council any leases of flats which are required to be made under the lease-back provisions[19]; again, the terms of such leases must comply with the requirements prescribed by the Minister.[20] The sitting tenants to whose flats these lease-back provisions relate will thus normally remain secure tenants of the council.

15.52 The duty imposed on the council to execute the conveyance or transfer to the applicant, and the duty imposed on the applicant to execute any relevant leases back to the council, are both enforceable by injunction.[21]

15.53 Any rent or other sum which arises under a tenancy of any property included in the acquisition and which falls due before the date of the grant of the fee simple to the applicant, continues to be recoverable by the council to the exclusion of the applicant.[22]

(d) *Jurisdiction of the county court*

15.54 Save for disputes concerning the property to be included in the acquisition or the terms thereof,[23] and disputes concerning the price,[24] the county court has a general jurisdiction regarding pro-

[16] The county court has jurisdiction over any such dispute: *ibid.* s.113; see below, para. 15.54.
[17] *Ibid.* s.104(1)(*a*).
[18] *Ibid.* s.104(2).
[19] *Ibid.* ss.100(1)(*b*) (see above, paras. 15.22–15.23), 104(1)(*b*).
[20] *Ibid.* s.104(2).
[21] *Ibid.* s.104(3).
[22] *Ibid.* s.104(4) (which applies notwithstanding L.P.A. 1925, s.141, whereby the benefit of the tenant's covenants normally runs with the reversion).
[23] H.A. 1988, s.98(5); see above, para. 15.37.
[24] *Ibid.* s.99(6); see above, para. 15.41.

ceedings and questions arising in relation to Part IV of the 1988 Act, including jurisdiction to make a bare declaration.[25]

(e) *Provisions governing the grant by the council of tenancies and licences after the date of the application*

Where a tenancy or licence of any part of the property included in the acquisition commences *after* the making of the initial Part IV application, then (subject to any regulations to the contrary) that tenancy or licence cannot be "secure" (under the Housing Act 1985) or "assured" (under Part I of the Housing Act 1988), and the council may determine it by giving not less than four weeks' notice to quit (even if it is for a fixed term).[26] The Minister can make consequential regulations, regarding for example the giving of vacant possession to the applicant of the affected dwellings on completion of the acquisition, and the disapplication of these provisions where the acquisition proves abortive.[27] **15.55**

(f) *Effect of the acquisition on the existing tenants*

We have seen that those sitting tenants who opt out of the acquisition will not normally be affected by it, since they will remain council tenants.[28] **15.56**

Sitting tenants who do not opt out will become, on the completion of the purchase, "assured tenants" under Part I of the Housing Act 1988, although their "right to buy" will normally be preserved.[29] The terms of these new assured tenancies will largely be those agreed, or deemed to have been agreed, between the tenants and the purchaser of the reversion. Although assured tenants have statutory security of tenure under Part I of the 1988 Act, this is less comprehensive than the scheme protecting secure tenants under the Housing Act 1985; furthermore, the rents will be capable of being pitched at market levels. **15.57**

The Housing Corporation has produced, in accordance with section 36A of the Housing Associations Act 1985, guidance as to the contractual rights which it expects landlords acquiring council stock **15.58**

[25] H.A. 1988, s.113.

[26] *Ibid.* s.101; thus even the common law rights of such occupiers may be sacrificed on the altar of privatisation!

[27] *Ibid.* s.101(4).

[28] See above, paras. 15.22–15.23.

[29] H.A. 1988, ss.1, 38; for the "preserved right to buy," see above, para. 14.07.

to offer their tenants.[30] These rights go beyond the basic statutory protection in Part I of the 1988 Act: for example, the guidelines recommend that rents should be maintained at levels within the reach of persons in low-paid employment, which will normally entail setting rents below the market level.[31]

(g) *Subsequent disposals by the applicant-purchaser*

15.59 Following a Part IV acquisition, the purchaser (and the purchaser's mortgagee or chargee) cannot dispose (whether by way of letting or by way of sale into owner-occupation) of any of the property acquired from the council, unless either the consent of the Minister is obtained,[32] or the disposal is a prescribed "exempt disposal."[33] The purpose of this restriction is both to safeguard the interests of the tenants who have been affected by a Part IV acquisition, and to attempt to ensure a continuing stock of rented accommodation in the area after the council has disposed of its housing.[34]

(h) *Powers of the Corporation to provide information, advice and assistance*

15.60 The Corporation may provide a service of information, advice and assistance relating to the "change of landlord" scheme for applicants, potential applicants, and tenants of "public sector landlords."[35] The Corporation also has powers to provide legal assistance to tenants involved in disputes before, during and after an acquisition under the "change of landlord" procedure[36]; these powers are similar to those possessed by the Minister in "right to buy" cases.[37]

30 *"The Tenants' Guarantee": Guidance on Housing Management Practice for Registered Housing Associations letting Accommodation under 1988 Act Assured Tenancies* (1988); *Tenants' Choice Landlords: Guidance on Housing Management Practice* (1988) (this latter guidance extends to include assured landlords who are not registered housing associations).

31 *"The Tenants' Guarantee", op. cit.* para. D2; *Tenants' Choice Landlords, op. cit.* para. D1.

32 H.A. 1988, s.105(1)–(2), (8); where Ministerial consent is thus required for the disposal of property which a housing association has acquired under Part IV, and *prima facie* the consent of the Corporation would also be required under H.A.A. 1985, s.9, then the Minister must consult the Corporation before giving his consent, but where such consent is given by the Minister, the consent of the Corporation is not in fact required: H.A. 1988, s.105(5)–(6).

33 H.A. 1988, s.105(7).

34 D.O.E., *Large Scale Voluntary Transfers, op. cit.* para. 16.

35 H.A. 1988, s.106.

36 *Ibid.* s.107.

37 H.A. 1985, s.170; see above, para. 14.126.

4. *Privatisation by way of Disposal to a Housing Action Trust*

(a) *General*

Part III of the Housing Act 1988 introduces the concept of the Housing Action Trust (hereafter referred to as a "HAT"); this is a temporary vehicle for achieving the eventual privatisation of council housing, although the machinery adopted is very different from that of the "change of landlord" scheme in Part IV, discussed above. The government has recognised that some council estates are so run-down that it is unlikely that the "change of landlord" scheme could be operated; such estates need "more direct action–involving both public and private sectors" in order to achieve "major improvements . . . in the fabric and general environment,"[38] and for this purpose the concept of the HAT was created. **15.61**

Under the HAT scheme, the Minister can designate an area of council housing for which a HAT is then established. The HAT will take over the ownership of that council housing; it will also have wide-ranging powers, including the power to renovate the dwellings. However, the HAT will only have a limited life, since its primary role will be to transfer the dwellings, after refurbishment, into other ownership; the new owner will normally be found from the private sector: transfers back to the council will be possible, but unusual. **15.62**

A discussion of the detailed operation of HATs would not be appropriate in this book, which is primarily concerned with local authority housing. What follows is therefore an outline account of HATs, with particular emphasis on their significance for local authorities and their tenants. **15.63**

(b) *Designation of a HAT area*

(i) HAT areas. The Minister can designate, by order, an area for which "it is expedient" that a corporation known as a HAT should be established.[39] The Minister is given a wide discretion in deciding whether to make a designation order,[40] but he may have specific regard to the following matters[41]: the extent to which the housing accommodation in the area is occupied by tenants or owner-occupiers, and the extent to which it is local authority housing; the **15.64**

[38] *Housing: the Government's Proposals*, *op. cit.* para. 6.1.
[39] H.A. 1988, s.60(1).
[40] *Ibid.* s.60(4).
[41] *Ibid.* s.60(5).

physical state and design of the housing accommodation in the area and any need to repair or improve it; the way in which the local authority housing in the area is being managed; and the living conditions and general environment of the area.

15.65 The designated area can comprise two or more parcels of land which need not be contiguous, and which need not all be in the district of the same local authority.[42] The D.O.E. has stated that HATs are designed to "bring . . . both private and public sector resources to bear on some of the worst areas of public sector housing."[43] Such areas "[t]ypically . . . comprise large concentrations–running to several thousand dwellings–of poor quality public sector housing which have associated with them a combination of social, economic and environmental problems: a high level of crime and vandalism; high unemployment; a concentration of families with severe disadvantages and heavily dependent on income support; a low level of commercial and economic activity; badly designed estates and dwellings; a poor environment and an atmosphere of general decay and decline."[44] The D.O.E. further envisaged that HATs should be broadly modelled on urban development corporations, although it recognised that "[t]he problems with which HATs will be dealing will . . . be rather different from the problems of derelict [industrial] land and buildings which UDCs normally tackle."[45]

15.66 HAT areas are therefore likely to consist predominantly of large, run-down council estates, but they might also include some privately-owned dwellings if they "naturally form part of the local community."[46] It is open to the council itself to propose a HAT area.[47]

15.67 **(ii) Consultation and publicity.** Before designating a HAT area, the Minister must consult every local housing authority in the area.[48] The Minister must also endeavour to secure that notice of the proposal is given to all tenants of dwellings in the area who are either secure tenants or other prescribed tenants.[49] The Minister must then either himself arrange a "ballot or poll" of the notified tenants, or arrange for appropriate independent persons to do so, in

[42] H.A. 1988, s.60(2).
[43] D.O.E., *Housing Action Trusts: A Consultation Document* (1987), para. 1.
[44] *Op. cit.* para. 3.
[45] *Op. cit.* para. 5.
[46] *Op. cit.* para. 8.
[47] *Op. cit.* para. 10.
[48] H.A. 1988, s.61(1).
[49] *Ibid.* s.61(2).

order to discover the tenants' opinions on the proposal.[50] Following such ballot or poll, if the majority of the tenants *responding to the ballot or poll* are *opposed* to the proposal, the Minister cannot make the proposed designation order.[51]

(c) *Effects of designation of a HAT area*

(i) Establishing the HAT. Where the Minister designates a HAT area, he must (either in that designation order or by a separate order) establish a HAT for that area.[52] HATs are bodies corporate,[53] but are not servants or agents of the Crown[54]; they do not enjoy any status, immunity or privilege of the Crown, and their property is not treated as Crown property.[55] **15.68**

Detailed provisions govern the constitution of the HAT.[56] Basically, the membership must consist of a chairman together with between five and eleven other persons appointed by the Minister, all of whom may be remunerated by the HAT. The Minister must have regard to the desirability of appointing members with special local knowledge, and must consult the relevant local authorities before appointing such members. Members must not have interests likely to conflict with their HAT functions, but tenants and potential tenants of HATs may be appointed as members.[57] The staff consists of a chief officer and such number of other employees as the Minister may approve; while local authority housing staff will have appropriate skills, they have no preferential right to employment with the HAT.[58] **15.69**

The 1988 Act also regulates the finances of the HAT.[59] The Minister may pay to the HAT such sums as he determines, and he may require the HAT to pay any of its surplus funds to him. The HAT will derive its income from several sources, including not only **15.70**

[50] H.A. 1988, s.61(3).

[51] *Ibid.* s.61(4); thus if a tenant abstains from voting he is *not* treated as voting in favour of the HAT area.

[52] *Ibid.* s.62(1)–(2).

[53] *Ibid.* s.62(3).

[54] *Ibid.* s.62(6).

[55] *Ibid.*; thus the HAT is not immune from the statutory repairing responsibilities in L. & T.A. 1985, s.11: *cf. Department of Transport* v. *Egoroff*, *The Times*, May 6, 1986 (C.A.).

[56] H.A. 1988, s.62(5) and Sched. 7.

[57] See also, as regards the role of tenants as members, D.O.E., *Housing Action Trusts*, *op. cit.* para. 29.

[58] D.O.E., *ibid.*

[59] H.A. 1988, s.62(5) and Sched. 8.

borrowing and grants from central government, but also rent income, and support from the private sector.[60]

15.71 **(ii) Primary objects and powers of the HAT.** The Housing Act 1988 states that the primary *objects* of the HAT are as follows[61]: securing the repair or improvement of housing accommodation held by the HAT; securing the proper and effective management and use of that housing accommodation; encouraging diversity in the interests by virtue of which accommodation in the area is occupied (and, as regards tenanted properties, diversity in the identity of the landlords); and generally securing or facilitating the improvement of living conditions in the area and the social conditions and general environment of the area.

15.72 The *powers* of the HAT include the following[62]: providing and maintaining housing accommodation; facilitating the provision of shops, advice centres, and other amenities for the benefit of the community; acquiring, holding, managing, reclaiming and disposing of land and other property; carrying out building and other operations; seeking to ensure the provision of water, electricity, gas, sewerage and other services; carrying on any business or undertaking; and generally doing anything necessary or expedient in relation to the above objects and powers.

15.73 These powers relate only to the capacity of the HAT as a statutory corporation, and do not authorise it to disregard any enactment or rule of law[63]; however, a transaction between any person and the HAT shall not be invalidated because of failure by the HAT to observe the above objects or to exercise the above powers for the purposes for which they are conferred.[64]

15.74 In exercising its functions, the HAT must comply with any directions from the Minister, which must be published[65]; but a transaction between any person and the HAT is not void merely because any such Ministerial direction has been contravened, and persons dealing with the HAT are not concerned with whether such a direction has been given or complied with.[66]

[60] D.O.E., *Housing Action Trusts, op. cit.* para. 30.
[61] H.A. 1988, s.63(1).
[62] *Ibid.* s.63(2)–(3).
[63] *Ibid.* s.63(4).
[64] *Ibid.* s.63(6).
[65] *Ibid.* s.72(1)–(3).
[66] *Ibid.* s.72(4).

(iii) Preparation of the HAT's proposals, and publicity therefor. As soon as practicable after the HAT has been established, it must prepare a statement of its proposals.[67] The HAT must consult the relevant local authorities on the proposals,[68] and secure that adequate publicity is given to the proposals in the area.[69] The inhabitants themselves must also be given an adequate opportunity to make representations concerning the proposals, and must be made aware of this opportunity.[70] The HAT must then consider such representations.[71] Thus, as well as having a say in whether a HAT area should be designated by the Minister, the inhabitants also have consultation rights regarding the plan of action of any HAT which is eventually established. 15.75

Once the HAT has complied with these requirements, it must send the Minister a copy of the statement of its proposals, together with a report of the steps taken to consult the local authorities and inhabitants, and of the consideration it has given to the points raised in the course of consultation and to the representations received.[72] 15.76

In addition, at such times as the HAT considers appropriate, or as directed by the Minister, the HAT must prepare a further statement of its proposals, whereupon the publicity and consultation duties will again apply.[73] 15.77

(iv) Transfer to the HAT of local authority functions. The Minister may by order provide for the transfer to the HAT of local authority functions concerning (*inter alia*) housing,[74] planning,[75] and public health.[76] As regards local authority housing functions, the 15.78

[67] H.A. 1988, s.64(1).
[68] *Ibid.* s.64(2).
[69] *Ibid.* s.64(3).
[70] *Ibid.*
[71] *Ibid.*
[72] *Ibid.* s.64(4).
[73] *Ibid.* s.64(5).
[74] *Ibid.* s.65; the housing functions may be conferred on the HAT to the exclusion of, or concurrently with, the local authority: *ibid.* s.65(3).
[75] *I.e.* the HAT can become the local planning authority: *ibid.* s.67; quite separately, the Minister can grant the HAT planning permission for the development of the land, after consulting with the local planning authority: *ibid.* s.66.
[76] *Ibid.* s.68; the relevant public health functions can be conferred on the HAT to the exclusion of, or concurrently with, the local authority (s.68(2)); these functions include those in P.H.A. 1936 concerning "statutory nuisances" (see above, paras. 12.55–12.64).

HAT may be given (*inter alia*[77]) the functions conferred on councils by Parts II, VI, VII, IX to XII, and XVI of the Housing Act 1985 (*i.e.* dealing with the provision of housing accommodation, the service of repair notices and improvement notices, slum clearance, overcrowding, houses in multiple occupation, common lodging houses, and defective housing).[78] Moreover, the Minister may modify Parts XVII and XVIII of the 1985 Act (relating to compulsory purchase, land acquisition, and general provisions) in relation to the HAT.[79]

15.79 The HAT cannot however be given the homelessness functions conferred on councils by Part III of the 1985 Act,[80] apparently because the imposition of such duties would "distract [the HAT] from its regeneration function."[81] Nevertheless, HATs will be "well-placed to assist local authorities in finding homes for homeless people," and "should be able to enter into local agreements giving authorities access to their accommodation."[82] Furthermore, where a local housing authority requests a HAT to assist it in discharging the authority's homelessness functions, the HAT must render "such assistance . . . as is reasonable in the circumstances."[83]

15.80 **(v) Powers of the HAT to give financial assistance.** For the purpose of achieving its objects, a HAT may, with Ministerial consent, give financial assistance to any person, by way of (for example) grants, loans, guarantees, incurring expenditure for the benefit of the assisted person, or purchasing loan or share capital in a company.[84]

15.81 **(vi) Power of the HAT to enter into agency agreements.** With Ministerial consent, a HAT may enter into an agreement with another person or body whereby, in relation to any of the HAT's housing accommodation or other land, that other person or body shall exercise specified functions as its agent.[85]

[77] Also included are local authority housing functions under H.A.A. 1985, Pt. II, and L.C.A. 1973, ss.39–41: H.A. 1988, s.65(2)(*b*)–(*c*).
[78] H.A. 1988, s.65(1)–(4), (7).
[79] *Ibid.* s.65(6).
[80] See Chaps. 4–6.
[81] D.O.E., *Housing Action Trusts*, *op. cit.* para. 26.
[82] *Ibid.*
[83] H.A. 1985, s.72; see above, paras. 5.61–5.64.
[84] H.A. 1988, s.71.
[85] *Ibid.* s.87.

(d) *Acquisition and disposal of land by a HAT*

(i) Transfer of property from a local authority to a HAT. A HAT will normally take over the ownership of all local authority housing in the relevant area, and will thus become the landlord of dwellings already occupied by council tenants. Accordingly, the Minister may by order provide for the transfer from a relevant local housing authority to a HAT of all or any of the authority's housing, and of any other land which is held or provided in connection with that housing or is otherwise owned by the local authority.[86] Similar powers apply to a local authority's chattels, rights and liabilities.[87] 15.82

The terms of the transfer, including the financial terms, are to be decided by the Minister, and he may stipulate for payments *by* the local authority, as well as or instead of payments *to* it[88]; furthermore, no transfer of local authority property under these provisions can give the authority any right to compensation.[89] The government has envisaged that the price will normally be geared to the current market values of the properties, subject to tenancies (if any), and that the HAT would not inherit any outstanding loan debt incurred by the authority.[90] 15.83

Before making any transfer order, the Minister must consult the transferor-authority.[91] In the case of local authority housing or other land, he must also bring the proposed transfer to the attention of any secure tenant or other person with an interest in the relevant property, whether as lessor, lessee, mortgagor or mortgagee[92]; this duty involves merely the conveying of information, as opposed to consultation. 15.84

There is a general duty imposed on the local authority and its officers to co-operate with the Minister and provide information,[93] which will be particularly relevant regarding these transfer orders.[94] 15.85

[86] H.A. 1988, s.74(1)–(2); the order may provide that rent and other sums under a tenancy which fall due *before* the date of the transfer shall continue to be recoverable by the authority, to the exclusion of the HAT (notwithstanding L.P.A. 1925, s.141, whereby the benefit of the tenant's covenants normally runs with the reversion): H.A. 1988, s.74(4).

[87] H.A. 1988, s.74(3).

[88] *Ibid.* s.74(4)–(5).

[89] *Ibid.* s.74(5).

[90] D.O.E., *Housing Action Trusts*, *op. cit.* para. 12.

[91] H.A. 1988, s.75(1)–(2).

[92] *Ibid.* s.75(3).

[93] *Ibid.* s.90.

[94] *Ibid.* s.90(3)(*b*), (4).

15.86 The Minister has a wide discretion as to the terms of the transfer order, including a power to "modify the operation of any provision made by or under any enactment."[95]

15.87 **(ii) Transfer of land from other public bodies to a HAT.** The Minister may also make an order providing that relevant land vested in statutory undertakers or other public bodies or their subsidiaries shall vest in a HAT, subject to the payment of compensation[96]; however, such an order cannot include land vested in statutory undertakers which is used or held for the purpose of carrying out their undertakings.[97]

15.88 **(iii) Acquisition of land by a HAT itself.** Quite apart from being the recipient of property formerly held by public bodies, and transferred to it by the Minister under the above powers, a HAT may take an active role by way of itself acquiring land. The 1988 Act gives the HAT a general power to acquire land within, adjacent to or outside its designated area, either by agreement or (with Ministerial consent) compulsorily[98]; the Minister may also authorise a HAT to acquire by compulsory purchase order *new* rights over land (*i.e.* rights not in existence when the compulsory purchase order is made), being rights over land which the HAT could be authorised to acquire compulsorily under the above powers.[99] Detailed supplementary provisions govern the processes of vesting, acquisition and compensation.[1]

15.89 The government envisaged that HATs would only need to acquire privately-owned properties under these provisions in "the occasional instance" where this is necessary "in order to achieve its objectives."[2]

15.90 **(iv) Disposal of land by a HAT.** A HAT may, with the Minister's consent, dispose of its land as it considers expedient, subject to restrictions (discussed below) in relation to dwellings held on secure tenancies.[3] The Minister's consent may be given in general or specific terms, and may impose conditions which can, for example, affect

[95] H.A. 1988, s.75(4).
[96] *Ibid.* s.76 and Sched. 9.
[97] *Ibid.* s.76(2).
[98] *Ibid.* s.77(1)–(2).
[99] *Ibid.* s.77(5)–(6).
[1] *Ibid.* s.78 and Sched. 10.
[2] D.O.E., *Housing Action Trusts*, *op. cit.* para. 13.
[3] H.A. 1988, s.79(1)–(3).

the price, premium or rent which the HAT can receive.[4] Disposals of *dwellings* by HATs without Ministerial consent are void, save for a disposal to one or more individuals which does not extend to any other dwelling[5]; but the absence of such consent does not invalidate a disposal by the HAT of any *other* land, and purchasers of such land are not concerned to inquire whether consent has been obtained.[6]

However, a HAT cannot dispose of a dwelling which is subject to a *secure tenancy*, except[7]: **15.91**

(a) to a person or body approved by the Corporation (which cannot approve certain prescribed landlords, such as local housing authorities and bodies likely to be influenced by local housing authorities); or
(b) to a local authority, with Ministerial consent[8]; or
(c) where the disposal is pursuant to the "right to buy."

A HAT is treated as a relevant vendor or landlord for the purposes of the statutory restrictions on service charges.[9] **15.92**

Separate provisions govern a disposal by a HAT which allows the purchaser a discount[10]: these provisions deal with covenants for repayment of the discount on premature disposal by the purchaser, provide for the obligation to repay the discount to be a charge on the dwelling, and define relevant disposals and exempted disposals for discount repayment purposes. **15.93**

Where housing has been refurbished by the HAT, potential transferees would include housing associations, tenants' co-operatives,[11] private sector landlords, and owner-occupiers[12]; furthermore, the "change of landlord" scheme could be operated,[13] since a HAT is a "public sector landlord" for the purposes of Part IV of the 1988 Act.[14] However, the government would regard it as "exceptional" for such refurbished properties to be transferred to *local authorities*, **15.94**

[4] H.A. 1988, s.79(4)–(5).
[5] *Ibid.* ss.80(1), 92(1)(*b*).
[6] *Ibid.* s.80(2).
[7] *Ibid.* s.79(2), (6)–(7).
[8] *Ibid.* s.84; see below, paras. 15.102–15.106.
[9] *Ibid.* s.79(11)–(12); H.A. 1985, ss.45–51; L. & T.A. 1985, ss.18–30 (see above, para. 14.64 and n. 83).
[10] H.A. 1988, s.79(13) and Sched. 11; the provisions are similar to those affecting the individual "right to buy," which are discussed above, paras. 14.31–14.36.
[11] See Chap. 13.
[12] D.O.E., *Housing Action Trusts, op cit.* paras. 15, 23.
[13] *Ibid.* para. 23.
[14] H.A. 1988, s.93(2)(*c*); see above, para. 15.14 and n. 30.

since the emphasis of their housing role is thought to be moving away from landlordism[15]; nevertheless, HATs could enter into agreements giving local authorities the right to nominate tenants of vacant property remaining in HAT ownership.[16]

15.95 With regard to unimproved properties, the HAT could sell the properties to developers or other bodies who could refurbish them before selling or letting them.[17]

15.96 As will be seen,[18] before disposing of properties occupied by secure tenants, the HAT must consult the tenants.

(e) *Effects of the creation of a HAT on the occupiers*

15.97 **(i) Owner-occupiers and private sector tenants.** As we have noted, a HAT will not normally acquire any privately-owned dwellings. Owner-occupiers and private sector tenants will therefore not normally be affected by the creation of a HAT, save that they may have to deal with the HAT, rather than the local authority, in relation to council functions transferred to the HAT under Part III of the 1988 Act, such as the granting of planning permission and action relating to unfit property or statutory nuisances.[19]

15.98 **(ii) Former council tenants.** Where a HAT acquires the ownership of tenanted council dwellings, tenants who were previously secure will continue to enjoy that status while the reversion remains in the ownership of the HAT, since a HAT satisfies the "landlord condition" for a secure tenancy.[20] Such tenants therefore retain all the "tenants' charter" rights in the Housing Act 1985 (including the individual "right to buy" and the right to be consulted on matters of housing management).[21] However, there is no power for the tenants to opt out of the HAT and choose to remain with the council.[22]

15.99 **(iii) Tenancies granted by a HAT.** For the reasons given in the previous paragraph, tenancies granted by a HAT remain secure while the HAT retains the freehold, and the tenancies attract all the

[15] D.O.E., *Housing Action Trusts*, *op. cit.* para. 24; but see below, paras. 15.102–15.106.
[16] D.O.E., *Housing Action Trusts*, *ibid.*
[17] D.O.E., *Housing Action Trusts*, *op. cit.* para. 15.
[18] See below, paras. 15.102–15.106.
[19] H.A. 1988, ss.65–69; see above, para. 15.78.
[20] H.A. 1985, s.80(1), see above, para. 7.07; H.A. 1988, ss.38(1), (5)(*b*), 83.
[21] See the various amendments made to H.A. 1985 by H.A. 1988, s.83.
[22] *Cf.* the "change of landlord" scheme: see above, paras. 15.22–15.23.

"tenants' charter" rights, assuming that the general conditions for secure tenancy status are met.[23]

(iv) Rents of properties of which a HAT is the landlord. Where a HAT acquires property occupied by council tenants, the government does not expect that rent levels will normally change by virtue of the transfer of the reversion to the HAT, *until* refurbishment has taken place.[24] However, HATs have a general power, both as regards "inherited" tenancies and tenancies which they have themselves granted, to make such reasonable charges as they may determine.[25] HATs must review the rents from time to time, and make such changes as the circumstances may require.[26] When the properties have been refurbished, "[r]ents may have to rise to allow the improvements to be maintained."[27] **15.100**

In the case of non-secure periodic tenancies, HATs may increase the rents by serving at least four weeks' written notice on the tenants, without the need to terminate the tenancies.[28] **15.101**

(v) Need for a HAT to consult councils and secure tenants before relevant disposals. Where a HAT proposes to dispose of a dwelling, and the disposal will result in a secure tenant of the HAT becoming the tenant of another person or body, then, before applying to the Minister for the necessary consent[29] or serving the necessary notice (discussed below) on the secure tenant, the HAT must notify every relevant local authority, requiring it within not less than 28 days to inform the HAT, in the case of each relevant dwelling, whether or not it wishes to acquire it[30]; if the authority does wish to acquire any dwelling, it must inform the HAT of the likely consequences for the tenant.[31] **15.102**

Furthermore, before applying to the Minister for consent but after the expiry of the period for the provision by the authority of the requisite information to the HAT (above), the HAT must inform each affected secure tenant of the proposed disposal, and of the iden- **15.103**

[23] See Chap. 7.
[24] D.O.E., *Housing Action Trusts, op. cit.* para. 20.
[25] H.A. 1988, s.85(1); the power is basically the same as that given to councils by H.A. 1985, s.24, discussed in detail in Chap. 10.
[26] H.A. 1988, s.85(2); see by analogy, H.A. 1985, s.24(2), above, para. 10.03.
[27] D.O.E., *Housing Action Trusts, op. cit.* para. 21.
[28] H.A. 1988, s.86; see by analogy, H.A. 1985, s.25, above, para. 10.19.
[29] H.A. 1988, s.79; see above, para. 15.90.
[30] *Ibid.* s.84(1)–(3).
[31] *Ibid.* s.84(3).

tity of the proposed transferee[32]; he must also be informed of the likely consequences of the disposal on his tenancy status, and (if appropriate) of the effects of the preserved right to buy.[33] Each tenant must, in addition, be informed of the wishes of the local authority, of the likely consequences for him if the authority acquires the dwelling, and of his right to make representations to the HAT (within not less than 28 days) concerning the proposed disposal.[34] Although a HAT tenancy is a secure tenancy, a proposed disposal by a HAT to another landlord under these provisions does not constitute a "matter of housing management" within the general consultation provisions applicable to secure tenancies under the Housing Act 1985.[35]

15.104 The HAT must next consider the tenants' representations, if any[36]; and if it considers it appropriate, having regard to those representations and to any further information provided by a relevant local authority, the HAT may amend its proposals (in which case it must serve a further notice on the affected secure tenants).[37]

15.105 When applying for consent to the disposal, the HAT must furnish the Minister with copies of the relevant notices served by it or on it, a copy of any representations received, and a statement of the consideration given by the HAT to those representations.[38]

15.106 Following the application to the Minister for his consent, he may require the HAT to carry out further consultation, and to inform him of the result thereof.[39]

(f) *Disposals by purchasers from HATs: the need for ministerial consent*

15.107 **(i) When purchaser needs Ministerial consent for disposal.** In the case of a disposal by a HAT of a dwelling subject to a secure tenancy to a person approved by the Corporation,[40] that approved

[32] H.A. 1988, s.84(4)(*a*).

[33] *Ibid.* s.84(4)(*c*); for the tenant's "preserved right to buy" following disposal of the reversion to a private landlord, see H.A. 1985, ss.171A–171H (discussed above, para. 14.07).

[34] H.A. 1988, s.84(4)(*d*)–(*f*).

[35] *Ibid.* s.84(8); the general consultation provisions are contained in H.A. 1985, s.105, and are discussed above, paras. 13.08–13.13.

[36] H.A. 1988, s.84(5).

[37] *Ibid.*

[38] *Ibid.* s.84(6).

[39] *Ibid.* s.84(7).

[40] *Ibid.* s.79(2)(*a*); see above, para. 15.91.

purchaser in turn cannot dispose of the dwelling (other than by specified "exempt disposals") without the consent of the Minister.[41]

(ii) Consultation with affected tenants. Before giving his consent, the Minister must ensure that the relevant tenants have been consulted by the approved purchaser, and that their wishes have been considered.[42] **15.108**

(g) *Dissolution of HATs*

The Minister may order the dissolution of a HAT with a view to the transfer of its functions, property, rights and liabilities to another HAT[43]; before ordering such a dissolution and transfer, the Minister must consult with the HATs concerned.[44] **15.109**

The Minister also has a more general power to order the dissolution of any HAT, and the disposal or transfer (on such terms as he thinks fit) of its remaining property, rights, liabilities or functions.[45] **15.110**

The normal way in which the dissolution of a HAT will come about, however, is through the HAT itself taking the initiative. Every HAT must use its best endeavours to secure that its objects are achieved as soon as practicable.[46] When it appears to the HAT that its objects have been substantially achieved, it must dispose or arrange to dispose of any remaining property, rights or liabilities in accordance with Part III of the 1988 Act, and must submit proposals to the Minister for: the dissolution of the HAT; the disposal to any person or body of any remaining property, rights or liabilities of the HAT which it has not been able to deal with; and the transfer of its functions to another person or body (including, where appropriate, a person or body with whom the HAT has entered into an agency agreement).[47] The Minister may then order the winding up of the HAT under his general powers.[48] **15.111**

When the HAT transfers its tenanted properties to new landlords, the tenants will normally become "assured tenants" under Part I of the Housing Act 1988: they will thus become subject to a regime of **15.112**

[41] H.A. 1988, s.81.
[42] *Ibid.* s.81(5).
[43] *Ibid.* s.73.
[44] *Ibid.* s.73(3).
[45] *Ibid.* s.88(3).
[46] *Ibid.* s.88(1).
[47] *Ibid.* s.88(2); agency agreements are dealt with by *ibid.* s.87 (see above, para. 15.81).
[48] *Ibid.* s.88(3); see above, para. 15.110.

market rents,[49] reduced succession rights[50] and reduced security of tenure[51] as compared with the rights which they enjoyed as secure tenants.

(h) *Power of the Corporation to provide legal assistance to tenants after disposal by HAT*

15.113 Where a dwelling subject to a secure tenancy has been disposed of by a HAT to a person approved by the Corporation,[52] or to a local authority,[53] then the Corporation has wide powers[54] (similar to those possessed by the Minister in "right to buy" cases[55]) to provide legal assistance to the sitting tenant in relation to a dispute between himself and the purchaser from the HAT.

[49] H.A. 1988, ss.13–14.
[50] *Ibid.* s.17.
[51] *Ibid.* ss.5, 7–9 and Sched. 2 (see particularly Sched. 2, Pt. I, gd. 8: mandatory ground applicable where there are substantial rent arrears).
[52] *Ibid.* ss.79(2)(*a*), 94; see above, paras. 15.91, 15.25.
[53] *Ibid.* s.84; see above, paras. 15.102–15.106.
[54] *Ibid.* s.82.
[55] H.A. 1985, s.170; see above, para. 14.126.

Index